ENLIGHTENING ENCOUNTERS

Photography in Italian Literature

Enlightening Encounters

Photography in Italian Literature

EDITED BY GIORGIA ALÙ AND NANCY PEDRI

UNIVERSITY OF TORONTO PRESS
Toronto Buffalo London

Toronto Buffalo London
www.utppublishing.com

ISBN 978-1-4426-4807-4

Toronto Italian Studies

Library and Archives Canada Cataloguing in Publication

Enlightening encounters : photography in Italian literature / Giorgia Alù, Nancy Pedri.

(Toronto Italian studies)
Includes bibliographical references and index.
ISBN 978-1-4426-4807-4 (bound)

1. Italian literature—History and criticism. 2. Literature and photography—Italy—History. 3. Photography in literature. I. Alù, Giorgia, editor II. Pedri, Nancy, 1970–, editor III. Series: Toronto Italian studies

PQ4053.P46E55 2014 850.9'357 C2014-905229-4

University of Toronto Press acknowledges the financial assistance to its publishing program of the Canada Council for the Arts and the Ontario Arts Council, an agency of the Government of Canada.

Canada Council for the Arts
Conseil des Arts du Canada

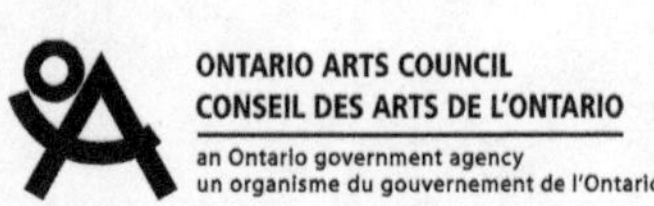

University of Toronto Press acknowledges the financial support of the Government of Canada through the Canada Book Fund for its publishing activities.

Contents

List of Figures vii
Acknowledgments ix

Photo-Literary Encounters in Italy 3
GIORGIA ALÙ AND NANCY PEDRI

Part One: The Lure of Photography

1 Spectres of Photography: Photography, Literature, and the Social Sciences in Fin-de-Siècle Italy 27
MARIA GRAZIA LOLLA

2 Authoring Images: Italo Calvino, Gianni Celati, and Photography as Literary Art 51
PASQUALE VERDICCHIO

3 Fossati's and Messori's Vision of Landscape in *Viaggio in un paesaggio terrestre* 70
MARINA SPUNTA

Part Two: Photography Structuring Narrative

4 The Fiction of Photography: Vittorio Imbriani's *Merope IV – Sogni e fantasie di Quattr'Asterischi* (1867) 101
SARAH A. CAREY

5 Narrated Photographs and the Collapse of Time and Space in Erri De Luca's *Non ora, non qui* 122
NANCY PEDRI

Part Three: Narrated Photographs and Photographs Narrating

6 Photo-Poems: Visual Impact Strategies and Photo-Story in the Work of Mario Giacomelli and Luigi Crocenzi 141
MARCO ANDREANI

7 What the Writer Saw (and the Camera Didn't): Antonio Tabucchi's *Notturno indiano* and Daniele Del Giudice's *Lo stadio di Wimbledon* 169
DONATA PANIZZA

8 Photographs Illustrating and Photographs Telling: Exercises in Reading Lalla Romano and Elio Vittorini 191
EPIFANIO AJELLO

Part Four: Through the Lens

9 Narrative Scopophilia as Seen through the Lens of a Photographic Camera: Intersemiotic Translation and Voyeurism in Alberto Moravia's *L'uomo che guarda* (1985) 217
MARIARITA MARTINO

10 Photography into the Limelight: Andrea De Carlo's *Treno di panna* 233
SARAH PATRICIA HILL

11 Looking through Coloured Shards: Words and Images in Ornela Vorpsi's Works 254
GIORGIA ALÙ

Writing with Light: Concluding Remarks 279
GIORGIA ALÙ AND NANCY PEDRI

Bibliography 285

Contributors 309

Index 313

Figures

3.1 Vittore Fossati, *Dintorni di Ornans*, 1999. 82
3.2 Vittore Fossati, *Montagna Sainte Victoire*, 1999. 85
3.3 Vittore Fossati, *Isola di Capri*, 2002. 92
6.1 Luigi Crocenzi, *Un seminarista*, 1955. 149
6.2 Luigi Crocenzi, *Un seminarista*, 1955. 150
6.3 Mario Giacomelli, *Io non ho mani che mi accarezzino il volto*, "Surrealist Seminarians." *Jubilee* (March 1965). 152
6.4 Mario Giacomelli, *Io non ho mani che mi accarezzino il volto*, "Surrealist Seminarians." *Jubilee* (March 1965). 153
6.5 Mario Giacomelli, *Io non ho mani che mi accarezzino il volto*, "Surrealist Seminarians." *Jubilee* (March 1965). 154
6.6 Mario Giacomelli, *Le prospettive dell'uomo d'oggi*, 1963. 155
8.1 Photograph by Roberto Romano. In Lalla Romano, *Nuovo romanzo di figure*. 201
8.2 Photograph by Luigi Crocenzi. In Elio Vittorini, *Conversazione in Sicilia*. 210
11.1 Ornela Vorpsi. "Pomeriggi." In *Vetri rosa*. 269
11.2 Ornela Vorpsi. In *Nothing Obvious*. 271
11.3 Ornela Vorpsi. In *Nothing Obvious*. 273
11.4 Ornela Vorpsi. In *Nothing Obvious*. 274

Acknowledgments

We are very grateful to the anonymous readers who provided smart, constructive, and helpful comments. Their critical responses were crucial to ensuring the quality of this work.

We would like to thank our contributors for having worked hard and patiently with us throughout the long publication process.

We also extend our thanks to the Italian Department at the University of Warwick (UK), especially Jennifer Burns, Simon Gilson, and Loredana Polezzi, for having supported our initial discussion on Italian literature and photography in March 2009. Since that occasion, other people have contributed with constructive suggestions, helpful material, and encouragements, among them Cesare Colombo, Sarah Hill, Linda Hutcheon, Millicent Marcus, and Marina Spunta.

We are thankful to all the people who have helped with the translation and proofreading of some of the articles, in particular Matthew Kudelka, Colin Campbell, Lucy Davey, Meg Greenberg, Barbara McGilvray, Nerida Newbigin, and Diana Modesto.

At Memorial University of Newfoundland, we would like to thank the various offices that provided financial support, and the wonderful ladies in Financial and Administrative Services, who, with smiles on their faces, tackled formatting issues and other such seemingly impossible matters.

We were fortunate to work with professional, enthusiastic, and devoted project editors at University of Toronto Press. A special thank you goes to Ron Schoeffel, who supported our project from the very beginning and willingly offered direction until he passed away in July 2013. Our gratitude goes also to Siobhan McMenemy and Anne Laughlin, who skilfully guided the enterprise to completion. Without the devotion and expertise of UTP's editorial department, this would have been a very different book.

For permission to reproduce images and texts, we would like to thank the following individuals and institutions: Vittore Fossati, Simone Giacomelli, Antonio Ria, Demetrio Vittorini, Ornela Vorpsi, CRAF-Centro di Ricerca e Archiviazione della Fotografia, Einaudi, and Agenzia Letteraria Internazionale, Bompiani-RCS.

Funding for this project has been kindly provided by the Department of Italian Studies and the School of Languages and Cultures, University of Sydney, and by Memorial University of Newfoundland's SSHRC Publication Subvention Grant.

Lastly, we extend our gratitude to the many colleagues, friends, and family members who offered words of encouragement at various stages of this project, who have shown interest in its growth, and who never lost faith.

ENLIGHTENING ENCOUNTERS

Photography in Italian Literature

Photo-Literary Encounters in Italy

GIORGIA ALÙ AND NANCY PEDRI

Ella riesce a compiere il veloce prodigio serrando uno spirito di sole nella piccola nera prigione di metallo e di cristallo. La macchina che prima non era adatta se non alla rappresentazione brutale della realtà è oggi divenuta nelle Sue mani uno strumento di infinita delicatezza poetica. In uno di questi volti, specialmente, sembra ch'Ella abbia tratto alla superficie la grazia stessa dell'anima e ve l'abbia resa visibile.

Gabriele D'Annunzio, November 1906, qtd in Andreoli 103

You manage to work this rapid miracle by shutting a spirit from the sun in the small, black prison made of metal and crystal. That machine, which before was only suitable for a brutal representation of reality, now, in your hands, has become an instrument of infinite poetic delicacy. Especially in one of these portraits, it seems that you have brought the true grace of the soul to the surface and have made it visible.[1]

The Italian poet, novelist, dramatist, and journalist Gabriele D'Annunzio wrote this to his friend the photographer Mario Nunes Vais at the beginning of the twentieth century. The epistolary note tells of an encounter between a writer and a photographer, as well as of the relationship between literature and photography, product and practice. D'Annunzio himself produced works inspired by photographic images. His writing inspired photographs, and he used the camera as a powerful instrument for aesthetically representing the Self. The lines above also serve as a defence of the camera's ability to catch and frame nuances and emotions against the more popular view of photography at the time – almost seventy years after its birth – as detached, scientific recorder of life. Photography, too, like words and poetic writing (to which D'Annunzio seems to compare it), can fix – both intimately and objectively – emotions, people, events, and objects. Unlike words, however, it conveys its subject visually.[2]

This book explores the relationship between literature and photography in Italy, focusing on the encounter between language and narrative literary forms with photographic images. While the relationship between literature and photography has been widely studied in the field of North American literature, as well as in Latin American, English, French, and German Studies,[3] in Italian Studies (both in Italy and abroad) the strength of the relationship between literature and the photographic image has been surprisingly underestimated.[4]

This book fills this gap by bringing together critical essays that explore the reciprocal relationship between photography and literature in an Italian context from the nineteenth century up to today. Divided into four parts that introduce various relationships between photography and literature, it presents case studies of both canonical and lesser known works, both fictional and non-fictional, ranging from photo-texts to travel accounts and migration literature.

Filling a Gap

From its inception in 1839, photography has been in constant dialogue with literature. "Literature and photography," Marsha Bryant comments, "have been crossing each other's representational borders ever since Edgar Allan Poe acclaimed the invention of the daguerreotype in his essays of 1840" (11). At times, this crossing of disciplinary borders is overtly aesthetic – for example, when photographs are physically reproduced in literary texts; when verbal text is added to photographs, as with captions; or when words and photographs are combined more seamlessly, as in photo-texts or iconotexts.[5] At other times, the interaction between photography and literature is implicitly aesthetic, as in the subtle but significant narratological changes in literary realism influenced by photography.[6] However their interaction is manifested, there is no doubt that photography has had a massive impact on literature, just as literature has had and continues to have a massive impact on photography. Literary practice, Bryant explains, "continues to negotiate with photography practice" (11).[7] And photographers too have engaged in "literary imaginations and aspiration," as François Brunet remarks (145).

Although "a wide and diverse group of writers of fiction have made photography, photographs, and photographers important points of reference in their stories" (Horstkotte and Pedri 8) since the first days of photography, it was not until the late 1970s and 1980s that critics, especially literary critics, began to systematically examine the intersection between photography and literature (Montier 7). The incentive for pursuing this interdisciplinary field of study arose in part from the work of a handful of critics, many of whom were critically interested in both literature and photography. For instance, during this time, Roland Barthes was caught up in the phenomenology of viewing photographs and the nature of photographic meaning;[8] Allan Sekula challenged notions of photographic truthfulness and objectivity as well as the singularity of photographic meaning;[9] and Susan Sontag examined photography's role in media, pushing for a more socially oriented understanding of how photography impacts knowledge.[10] The photographic theory of these authors remains highly influential to this day, and as the essays in this collection affirm, the issues they raised some decades ago continue to inform the study of photography as it intersects with literature. These authors – and others like Neil Walsh Allen, André Bazin, John Berger, Hubert Damisch, W.J.T. Mitchell, and Joel Snyder, to mention but some – have informed the work of academics from a variety of disciplines who have taken a growing interest in the interaction between literature and photography. Recently, scholars as diverse as Timothy Dow Adams, Nancy Armstrong, Jan Baetens and Mireille Ribière, François Brunet, Marsha Bryant, Marta Caraion, Marianne Hirsch, Erwin Koppen, and Linda Haverty Rugg have published monographs on the subject. The relationship between literature and photography has also been the focus of a number of edited volumes and journal special issues.[11] Given the sustained interest in this field of inquiry, it is difficult to find a clear explanation for the lack of critical studies on literature and photography in Italy, especially given that there is no lack of literary material.

Since the invention of photography, photographic practices and products have inspired and occupied pages and pages of Italian writing and literature. Since the Renaissance, Italian art and culture (in its broadest sense) have expressed a sociopolitically conscious desire to visually assert perceptions, beliefs, and events as a means to ensure their survival.[12] The invention of the photographic camera in the nineteenth century – preceded by the magic lanterns, panoramas, and *mondi nuovi* of the eighteenth century – reinforced an already entrenched visual approach to things and events, an approach that has always extended to literature. Hence, the influence of photography on Italian authors has been felt from Verga to Pirandello, from Calvino to Romano, from Sanguineti to Eco.

The lack of critical inquiry into the relationship between photography and literature in Italy may be attributed to the historical identification of culture with high art within Italian academia and to the prestige and durability of a classical humanist tradition there. Indeed, the relations among culture, intellectuals, and book learning have long generated diffidence towards interdisciplinary fields of study in general and towards the links between literature and the visual arts (such as cinema) in particular.[13] The development of interdisciplinary academic modules and degree programs abroad has encouraged critical explorations between cultural, visual, and literary studies, but even so, little attention has been devoted to the interface between Italian writing and photography.

An international conference held at the University of Warwick (UK) in March 2009 was the first attempt to gather scholars from around the world – together with historians of photography and professional photographers – who were interested in the relationship between photography and Italian literature. The event attested to a growing conviction among Italian Studies scholars that it was important to address systematically and critically the dialogue between these two media. It also drew attention to the urgent need to fill in this gap in scholarship. Taking heed of this call, the main aim of *Enlightening Encounters* is to continue the work of thinking through the relationship between photography and Italian literary practice.

A Wealth of Material

The contributors to this book begin to trace photography's influence on Italian literature from its invention in 1839 to the present day. With their critical examinations of the attraction that photography held for a wide range of Italian writers, they open up a dialogue that begins to probe how Italian narrative has been responding to photographic practices and aesthetics. Taken together, the essays thus invite readers to continue investigating the ways in which photography has impacted Italian literature. Before we discuss the key theoretical issues that emerge in the following essays, however, it is important to provide a brief account of the reception of the photographic medium in Italy over the years in order to contextualize the photo-literary experiences this book examines. In addition, a brief historical overview of the interaction that has developed between photography and literature in Italy will provide readers with some avenues for further reflection so that they can join our contributors in promoting further research in this field of study.

In the Italian cultural and literary landscape, very specific sociohistorical factors have influenced the interchange between the photographic and the literary.[14] The factors that set Italy apart from other Western countries have included a late Italian Unification (1848–70) and slow economic development in the second half of the nineteenth century; the popularity of positivist realism – in particular, the literary phenomenon of *verismo* – at the beginning of the twentieth century; post–Second World War ethical neorealism; and a traditional devotion to classical literature and "pure arts" together with an Italian attitude towards vision and attention to aesthetics (also in terms of style, fashion, and appearance). These and other sociohistorical factors have informed the evolving encounter between writing and photography in Italy and have made that encounter particularly exciting and complex.

In Italy between 1840 and 1870, photography was essentially perceived as a technical means for faithfully reproducing the objects framed by the lens; in part, this was because it was thought to lack the intervention of a creative hand.[15] Moreover, although the camera was introduced to the Italian public quite soon after Daguerre and Talbot invented it, an awareness of photography as a vehicle for collective and/or personal expression developed slightly more slowly than in other parts of Europe. Italy began to industrialize in a major way later than France and England, only after its unification at the end of the nineteenth century. The lack of a strong economic and political bourgeoisie in pre-Unification times, the slow circulation of ideas due to censorship, and poor infrastructure have often been identified as the principal reasons for the slow cultural – and literary – attention paid by Italians to the photographic camera (Miraglia, "Note per una storia" 427–9). Nevertheless, professional and amateur photographers sprang up around the country quite quickly, and photographic manuals and related publications were soon being published.

The first intermodal literary texts to be published in Italy involved reproductions of daguerrotypes and calotypes of places and monuments in photographic books and illustrated travel guides. For instance, in 1842 and 1843, in Milan, Artaria published *Vues d'Italie d'après le daguerréotype* (*Views of Italy after the Daguerreotype*); and a series of Italian views, *Excursions daguerriennes, vues et monuments les plus remarquables du Globe* (*Daguerreotype Excursions, the Most Remarkable Views and Monuments on Earth*), were published in Paris in 1842.[16] It is not difficult to understand the appeal of the photographic image as illustration: it is in line with the writing's realist aesthetics and indeed accentuates them. From a sociohistorical perspective, these two early and very popular attempts to turn daguerreotype plates into plates for engraving were central to the first creative stage that joined photographic images to written words.[17]

Towards the end of the nineteenth century, photography entered into dialogue not only with writing inspired by naturalism and realism but also with anthropology, ethnology, and folklore, as well as hard sciences such as medicine and physics.[18] At the time, these disciplines viewed the products of the photographic camera as true and faithful representations of the actual world. Indeed, the extraordinary discovery of photography appeared to embody the ideal model of that objective relationship to reality longed for by positivism. During Italy's transition from a pre-industrial age to an industrial one, the multifaceted relationship between photography and writing offered new strategies – activated by the imaginary – for the interaction between the arts and positive science (Abruzzese and Grassi 1185). Leone Carpi, for example, adopted a photographic visual style in his *L'Italia vivente* (*Living Italy*) (1878) so to "ritrarre in azione la società vivente, come il fotografo sorprende la natura e la costringe a riflettersi nei suoi apparati" ("portray a living society in action, as the photographer catches nature and forces it to mirror itself in photography's medium"; 50). A similar style informed Antonio Stoppani's *Il bel paese: Conversazioni sulle bellezze naturali, la geologia e la geografia fisica d'Italia* (*The Beautiful Country: Conversations on the Natural Beauties, the Geology and the Physical Geography of Italy*) (1876), a sort of "visual guide" (Bollati 29–33) to Italy's natural beauties.

Also during this period, claims that photography was objective came into question and a critical reaction developed against positivism and the emerging literary trend of realism. For instance, Vittorio Imbriani's novel *Merope IV* (1867) and the poem "L'Amica di nonna Speranza" ("Grandmother Speranza's Friend") (1907) by Guido Gozzano offered similar critiques of photographic objectivity as well as sustained celebrations of the photograph's textuality. Both writers, who constructed their critique of photography around an imaginary photographic portrait of a woman, exploited the photograph as fictional construct, promoting and celebrating its textuality as well as its ability to contain an imagined story.[19]

By contrast, the camera's potential power to record the "truth" about people and things enchanted the Sicilian *veristi* Luigi Capuana and Giovanni Verga and, later, Federico De Roberto. Naturalists and realists alike attempted to balance photography and literature by incorporating photography and its principles into their writing. In the growing magazine culture of the time, we see evidence of an acute awareness of photography's power to authenticate (Abruzzese and Grassi 1187–8). Periodicals like *L'Illustrazione italiana* (*Italian Illustration*), *Emporium*, and *La Lettura* (*The Reading*) often featured texts by writers and poets – among them Carducci, Pascoli, De Amicis, and Fogazzaro, as well as Deledda, Rosso di San Secondo, and Pirandello – accompanied by photographic images. Photography also complemented the new writing genre of investigative journalism and supported its project of representing the real present-day Italy (Abruzzese and Grassi 1188). From framing classical ruins and magnificent architecture, photography had moved on to representing the urban poor in large Italian cities.[20]

Generally, however, throughout the nineteenth century, photographs and words occupied distinct cultural domains – they did not blend easily. Even *veristi* like Verga and De Roberto did not illustrate their books with photographs. But while photographic images may have been absent from their books, writers often turned to photography as inspiration for the drawings that illustrated them. D'Annunzio, for example, turned to the picturesque and aesthetically composed photographs of his friend Francesco Paolo Michetti for inspiration when illustrating a number of his works. And his faith in photography as an aid to literary creation led him to commission Count Giuseppe Primoli to produce photographic *tableaux vivants* as an inspiration for his novel *Vergini delle rocce* (*Virgins of the Cliffs*).[21] Sicilian novelist and playwright Luigi Pirandello, a Nobel Prize recipient, introduced photographs and the camera as thematic subjects in his experimental novel of 1925, *Quaderni di Serafino Gubbio operatore* (*Notebooks of Serafino Gubbio Operator*). Although he was drawn to photography, Pirandello also explored and demonstrated the bleak consequences arising from intense instrumental mediations of reality.[22]

Questions about the artistic status of photography have largely abated, and creative writers throughout the twentieth century and well into the twenty-first have continued to find new and exciting ways to incorporate photography into their work.[23] By the end of the First World

War, new visual technologies were influencing all arts and threatening the strict boundaries that had long separated verbal from visual media. Both literature and photography responded to the rapid changing reality, often coming together to produce new forms of communication and representation that were more in line with the advances of the new technological revolution. In Italy, this was the time of Futurism, of the photodynamic images of the Bragaglia brothers (Antonio Bragaglia's *Fotodinamismo futurista* [*Futuristic Photodynamism*]; 1913), and of Carlo Carrà's visual poetry. During this period of visual and multimedia experiments, so evident in the work of the European avant-garde writers, intellectuals and artists alike pondered more critically the effects of photography on literature (and on society in general).

The increased contact between photographers and writers, partly due to artists' international mobility, revolutionized the relationship between literature and the photographic image. Indeed, new collaborations between writers and photographers proliferated in Italy, spurring various forms of multimodal creative work. In 1940, writer and film director Mario Soldati and photographer Federico Patellani co-produced a movie based on Antonio Fogazzaro's novel *Piccolo mondo antico* (*The Little World of the Past*). In 1941, novelist Elio Vittorini, influenced by Walker Evans's *American Photographs* (1939), edited the illustrated anthology *Americana*, a pastiche of American short stories accompanied by photographs. Also during this time, photography began to adopt literary compositional strategies more openly and pervasively than before, thus answering Clement Greenberg's call to "let photography be literary" (63). Neorealist photography, like neorealist literature and cinema, relied on mechanisms associated with oral narration to couple its accurate representations of postwar Italy with an ethical point of view. Writing and photography came together in order to respond to the urgent need for accuracy as well as for human solidarity and social commitment.[24] Some noteworthy examples of this trend towards collaboration are Carlo Levi and photographer Mario Carbone's photo-book *In Lucania* (1960); Elio Vittorini's return to Sicily in 1950 to complete his new edition of *Conversazione in Sicilia* (*Conversations in Sicily*), illustrated with photographs by Luigi Crocenzi; and Franco Pinna's collaboration with ethno-anthropologist Ernesto de Martino in Lucania.[25] The 1950s also witnessed an amplification of earlier patterns of fictional investigations involving the process and product of photography, as with Italo Calvino's essay "La follia del mirino" ("The Madness of the Viewfinder"), published in *Il contemporaneo* (*The Contemporary*) in 1955 and reworked in 1970 into a fictional short story, "L'avventura di un fotografo" ("The Adventure of a Photographer").[26]

By the 1960s, Italy had witnessed an explosion of literary, photographic, photo-literary, and conceptual experiments, which continue to this day.[27] Collaborations between photographers and writers during this period often focused on projects in which showing and telling teamed up in representations of the Italian landscape – often with a clear regional tendency. Two examples are *Sardegna, una civiltà di pietra* (*Sardegna, a Civilization of Stone*), published in 1961 and edited by writer Giuseppe Dessì with Franco Pinna and Antonio Pigliaru; and *16 fotografie siciliane dall'archivio Enzo Sellerio* (*16 Sicilian Photographs from Enzo Sellerio's Archive*), a 1969 collaboration between Leonardo Sciascia and Enzo Sellerio. Later, in 1984, a highly sophisticated collective project would bring together landscape photography and literary narration in *Viaggio in Italia* (*Journey in Italy*), carried out largely by the photographer Luigi Ghirri, with an accompanying text by Gianni Celati.[28] A work with a more social and political intention than these is *Morire di classe* (*To Die of Class*) (1969), a photo-book produced by photographers Carla Cerati (also a writer) and Gianni Berengo Gardin about the conditions in Italian psychiatric hospitals of the time. By the 1970s, literature had joined theory more closely to investigate the tenets of photography, its social and political impact, and its historical and artistic significance. An extended fictional examination of photography and the photographic can be found in Emanuele Martino's *Cara fotografia* (*Dear Photograph*) (2008), a collection of sixteen multimodal short stories about the photographic image, its "complex relation to other photographic images and to photography, as well as its role within the photographic act" (Pedri, "Disenchanted with the Referent," 204). Diego Mormorio's recent theatrical monologue, *Io, la fotografia ovvero l'attimo quotidiano* (*I, the Photograph or rather the Quotidian Moment*) (2008), offers a similar extended reflection on photography, but with an eye towards the sociohistorical impact of photography and the theories that have informed it. Tellingly, these writers are often also photographers and thus have a practical and not just theoretical interest in photography.

Indeed, in literary works, photography is often assigned an essential narrative role, often related to memory and family relations. Lalla Romano's photographic works, which span several decades, are perhaps the best-known explorations into the narrative function of photographic images in the Italian canon. In her experimental photo-texts, she puts into practice her understanding of the photographic image as *text* to be *read*. A similar approach to the photographic image is elaborated in Giorgio Messori's collaboration with photographers Luigi Ghirri and Vittore Fossati.

The late twentieth century also witnessed the playful coupling of the photograph's capacity to offer precise details of the real with its simultaneous ability to provoke significant referential uncertainty. Indeed, the photograph's duality has been foregrounded and celebrated by a number of postmodern writers. In Italy, the borders between fact, fiction, and imagination in both literature and photography continue to blur in the work of authors such as Andrea De Carlo, Erri De Luca, Daniele Del Giudice, Antonio Tabucchi, and Melania Mazzucco.[29]

Considering how many Italian writers have engaged with photography through their writing, the time is ripe to critically examine the interaction between word and photographic image in the Italian context. Scholars of Italian literature have not altogether overlooked this interdisciplinary field of inquiry; indeed, the number of scholarly articles on the topic has increased significantly over the past ten years. We do, though, suggest that much more critical work is needed, given the quality, quantity, and diversity of Italian literature that intersects with photography in exciting and innovative ways.

Studying the Encounter: Issues and Structure

The approach adopted by the following essays is not, however, strictly historical. Rather, *Enlightening Encounters* seeks to trace how the relationship between literature and photography in Italy is conceived through a determinately theoretical approach. This heralds a rigorous critical perspective on a field within Italian Studies that is already manifesting signs of growth. Furthermore, bringing together essays that draw on theory to inform literary analysis will shed light on the stylistic and thematic particulars of the intersection of writing and photography in Italy's unique literary production. This book thus complements the many studies that have focused on the relationship between writing and photography in other national literatures.

Looking specifically at the Italian case, two main questions intersect throughout the collection: How does photography evoke, comment on, and develop within Italian literary texts? And how do Italian literary texts respond to a photographic aesthetic? To engage with these questions, this book begins with reflections on the attraction that photography has held for Italian writers and intellectuals and then examines the associations between photographic images, literature, and language that accentuate the narrative potential of photographs. The book ends with an examination of the camera's power as expressed through language.

Some of the contributors focus on one Italian writer or text; others conduct a comparative analysis of two or more texts. The contributors draw from the work of established theorists of photography and other fields (such as feminism, philosophy, psychoanalysis, and translation studies) to enrich their close readings of photography's role in Italian literature. The book thus brings together various models and practices of literary analysis. It does so in the hope that a diverse collection of critical investigations of Italian literary texts that intersect with photography will shed light on how rich this field of study is and thereby encourage further inquiry and reflection.

The link between literature and photography is already present in the Greek etymology of the word "photography," which connects *photo* (light) to *graphos* (writing and drawing). The reproductive power of photography was once believed to be so strong that, as Jay Prosser writes, "the first names for photography suggest the marvelling in a form of creation almost beyond human capacity, that required limited human intervention: *heliographs*, or 'sun-drawings.' It was as if light alone produced the image. The name eventually chosen, *photography,* means 'light-writing'" (2, emphasis in original). What the etymology of "photography" seems to overlook is the role of human agency throughout the photographic process. Not surprisingly, when photography and literature have intersected, such a role has rarely been pushed into the background, much less forgotten. Instead, the two have come together to initiate significant changes in creative practices.

As argued above, since its inception, photography (and all that is tied up with it) has inspired a multitude of creative writers in Italy, shaping – stylistically, linguistically, aesthetically – fictional and nonfictional writing alike. But this interaction is far from the tidiness suggested by the word's etymology. Many of the contributors to this book are aware of this complexity and draw from the work of Barthes, who in many of his writings grappled with the representational status of photography. For over two decades, Barthes returned again and again to the question of photography's relationship to language. On the one hand, photographs are messages without codes (they are free of language); on the other, they are comprised of connotative codes (they are *of* language). With photography, there is no relay between the object and its image; there is instead a direct, physical connection between the sign and its object.[30] Elaborating on the observations first offered by Walter Benjamin about the guiding role of the written text that accompanies a photograph, Barthes asserts that one way to anchor the floating chain of signifieds is to root it with a linguistic message. Unlike Benjamin, who argues that a verbal text can rescue photography from contingency and approximation and photographic meaning from surface meaninglessness,[31] Barthes considers the text repressive insofar as it helps the viewer select one meaning instead of others.[32]

More recently, W.J.T. Mitchell has also examined the relationship between photography and language. Ultimately, he contends that "photography is and is not a language; language also is and is not a photography" (281). Extending this observation into the realm of literature, he concludes that there is no definite boundary dividing literature and photography. "All arts," he insists, "are 'composite' arts (both text and image); all media are mixed media" (94–5). Mitchell, like Barthes before him, grapples with and unveils the complex exchange between photography and writing. Both representational systems possess narrative and textual elements, and both engage in a process of framing. In other words, photography and literature tell a story, and they do so through a point of view.[33] Both can influence how events, things, and people are perceived, understood, and remembered.[34]

The first section of this book, "The Lure of Photography," addresses the complexity of the relationship between photography and writing, tracing photography's stylistic, aesthetic, and thematic impact on literature. It examines literary responses to photography and its social influence, tracing how photography gave rise to very real changes in imaginative rendering. Technology, then, led to adjustments in the eye's intuitive and recording capabilities. It follows that theme and style in a number of Italian writers can be examined as literary responses to photography and its ability to affect society.

The first contribution, by Maria Grazia Lolla, begins to chart a photographic history as it is manifested in a number of Italian literary texts spanning the fifty years that followed the invention of photography. She provides a provocative examination of early literary conceptions of photography, which – surprisingly – contrasted general perceptions of photography as a detached observer of reality. After discussing Paul Valéry's promotion of photography as a recording technology that could free literature from any obligation towards realist representation, Lolla emphasizes how the nineteenth-century Italian intelligentsia (writers, photographers, journalists, social scientists) turned to photography not to provide a solid, verifiable description of their world, but rather to evoke what could have been or what might still be. Counter-intuitively, writers in nineteenth-century Italy did not facilely associate photography with positivism. Instead, as Lolla proves with examples from De Amicis, Valera, Serao, Verga, Capuana, and others, their focus often fell on photography's lack: they introduced photography into their work to secure not a "reality effect" but an effect of the unreal. She reaches the surprising conclusion that the culture of positivism actually rendered photography and the documentary work it supposedly carried out absent, invisible, and immaterial.

Pasquale Verdicchio's contribution to this section also delves into the sociocultural status of photography. It does so by examining the shift from a painterly to a photographic representational style in writers from Manzoni and Verga to Calvino and Celati. In his analysis of photography as both literary and pictorial, Verdicchio presents an overview of a visual modality in Italian literature that is powerfully dependent on the mandates of photography. He traces the impact of photography as a literary medium on visibility and visuality to propose a way towards configuring what a photographic/visual language might look like. Through a close reading of photo-literary tropes in a number of classic Italian literary texts, Verdicchio strongly suggests that such a language resembles that of cognitive science and is characterized by the exploratory interstices of literary language.

The sociocultural impact of photography through literature can also be approached by examining how the intermingling of word and photographic image practised by a number of Italian writers has helped organize and shape specific personal visions of the world. A focus on the power of photography and writing to reconnect with, represent, and aestheticize the exterior directs Marina Spunta's examination of the notion of landscape in *Viaggio in un paesaggio terrestre* (*Journey on an Earthly Landscape*), a collaborative work by photographer Vittore Fossati and writer Giorgio Messori. Spunta engages critically with Benjamin's photography theory and with his notions of "experience" and "aura" to demonstrate how strongly his thought influenced the work of Fossati and in particular that of Messori and how they appropriated it in their photo-book. Benjamin theorized that the beautiful and the auratic no longer have a place in photography due to its technological apparatus, which allows it to reproduce endless copies of documents but prevents it from creating original artworks, whereas Fossati and

Messori posit photography as a means of re-creating the aura, of reconnecting with a notion of experience (*Erfahrung*) as a long practice, and of rediscovering the beauty and artistic value of both artistic and everyday landscapes. Benjamin maintained that photographs could no longer return the viewer's gaze and thus were no longer artworks; by contrast, Fossati and Messori posit photography as an artwork and as a means of aestheticizing the exterior, and they use both photographs and writing to re-establish a relation between subject and landscape. Thus, photography and literature can interact to establish a close dialogue with landscape and place, and they reproduce an auratic effect that is consonant with the postmodern age with regard to its serious undermining of any claims to objectivity.

Indeed, as is suggested at various points throughout the essays in this collection, the encounter between literature and photography has repeatedly put into play the highly contested issue of the objectivity of photographic images and, by extension, realism in fiction. As Liliane Louvel so clearly states: "photography lends itself to the 'revelation' of a truth at the same time that it easily verges on the fantastic that it paradoxically seems to authenticate, playing on the presence of an absence" (*Poetics of the Iconotext* 115). According to Barthes, a photographic image does not describe reality; rather, it reproduces reality mechanically and so is characterized by "immediacy." It is, as he puts it, "literally an emanation of the referent" (*Camera Lucida* 80).[35] So, for him, a photograph signifies first and foremost by denotation. However, the question is not so simple. Barthes also argues that a photograph is not purely "objective" and that in every photographic image there are connotated meanings, second order meanings within a particular culture and society.[36] Paradoxically, the photograph's meaning is governed simultaneously by its privileged relation to the referent and by the systems of connotation and signification in which it partakes.

For Bazin, too, an important aspect of photography's ontology is its objective access to the real: "No matter how fuzzy, distorted or discoloured, no matter how lacking in documentary value the image be, it shares, by virtue of the very process of its becoming, the being of the model of which it is the reproduction; it *is* the model" ("The Ontology of Photography" 241). At the same time, Bazin points out that photography delivers hallucinations even while it delivers facts offering the viewer an image of the real (an image we can hold, frame as in a photographic novel, or paste as in a family album or memoir), but of a real that does not physically exist in our time and space. Barthes also insists on the hallucinatory mystery of photography despite its mechanical and chemical nature. In *Camera Lucida*, Barthes reminds us how photography provides viewers with traces of things and places that have been, arguing that it is, among other things, a spectre of death and that it announces an absence.

Writers have relied on and experimented with the duality of the photographic image – which is both an evidential document and a symbolic object – to support, contrast, and challenge the ins and outs of narration. This is discussed, in particular, in the second section of this book, "Photography Structuring Narrative." The two chapters that comprise this section look at two fictional works – Vittorio Imbriani's *Merope IV* (1867) and Erri De Luca's *Non ora, non qui* (*Not Now, Not Here*) (1989) – in which the photographic image, although never reproduced, serves as a structuring agent for the narrative while at the same time reflecting the text's narrative structure.

Sarah Carey, in her analysis of Vittorio Imbriani's *Merope IV*, argues that the photographic image's potential for storytelling depends heavily on its duality, that is to say, on its somewhat uneasy (but nonetheless exciting) blending of objectivity and imagination, fact and fiction, the real and the invented. In his novel, Imbriani highlights the fictional aspect of photography and uses it to create a visual metaphor for writing. The photograph thus structures the narrative as it breaks away from any claims to objectivity. Similarly, Nancy Pedri examines the way in which the photograph's meaning in Erri De Luca's *Non ora, non qui* lies not in what is seen on its surface but rather in what the reader brings to it. The act of looking or subjective viewing is, therefore, what secures the photograph's claim to the real. As Pedri demonstrates, this leads to the collapsing or fusion of a past, present, and future time and place in the book. It also grants the photograph the possibility to push the narrative forward.

The third section, "Narrated Photographs and Photographs Narrating," reflects further on the photograph's narrative potential, relating it specifically to its capacity to operate as an indexical sign of the world-out-there.[37] Theories that address how the photograph functions as an indexical sign draw largely on the work of the American semiotician Charles Sanders Peirce, to whom some of the authors here are also indebted, as in the case of Marco Andreani's discussion of Giacomelli's and Crocenzi's works. For Peirce, "photographs, especially instantaneous photographs, are very instructive, because we know that they are in certain respects exactly like the objects they represent. But this resemblance is due to the photographs having been produced under such circumstances that they were physically forced to correspond point by point to nature" (*Collected Papers* 2: 159).

This indexicality (the Barthesian that-has-been) seems to guarantee photography's truth to reality. It is this easy association between the indexical and the documentary – a collision that enforces what Georges Didi-Huberman calls the "fantasy of referentiality" ("The Index of the Absent Wound" 74) – that the essays in the third section problematize. In particular, the documentary nature of the photographic image as contiguous with that which it represents is put into discussion in the cultural perception of photography of postwar Italy and during the so-called neorealist period. Torn between a claim for truth and scientific objectivity on one hand and "a quest for underlying patterns of significance" (Marcus 14) on the other, photography, together with cinema and literature, contains the duality of realism and illusion, documentary reality and referential ambiguity or allegory.[38] The contributions to this section come to this conclusion even while strongly suggesting that photography, as manifested in literature, proposed a new way of seeing the world anew and representing it in different terms.

Marco Andreani, in his analysis of Luigi Crocenzi's photographic novel *Un seminarista* (*A Seminarian*) (1954–5) and Mario Giacomelli's photographic series *Io non ho mani che mi accarezzino il volto* (*No Hands Are there to Caress my Face*) (1961–3), emphasizes the photograph's narrative potential as opposed to its indexicality. Andreani argues that whereas Crocenzi suggests that literary, photographic, and cinematic discourses are equivalent, Giacomelli concentrates on the photographic so as to bring its ambiguity to narrative fruition. By pairing these two approaches to photography, Andreani brings forward the photograph's duality for explicit consideration.

In her study of Antonio Tabucchi's *Notturno indiano* (*Indian Nocturne*) (1984) and Daniele Del Giudice's *Lo stadio di Wimbledon* (*Wimbledon Stadium*) (1983), Donata Panizza examines photography's structural and thematic role. Beginning with Peirce's notion of photographic indexicality, she draws on the work of Henri Van Lier and Jean-Marie Schaeffer, who argue provocatively that because of their very indexicality, photographs elude stable readings and are independent of both the represented scene and the photographer who tried to fix it. From this starting point, she asks how photography gains meaning in Tabucchi's and Del Giudice's literary texts. Here, she pays particular attention to the complex way in which photography enters the literary text, relates to both the fictional world and the real one, and is juxtaposed with the act of fiction writing. Throughout, Panizza strongly suggests that literature reaches its full potential through photography.

Similarly, Epifanio Ajello examines the photograph's narrative power in two books: Lalla Romano's *Nuovo romanzo di figure* (*New Novel of Images*) (1997) and Elio Vittorini's *Conversazione in Sicilia*, whose illustrated edition was published in 1950. He notes that in Romano, words and images are interdependent, giving rise to a narrative that is "born from the images and develops with them," whereas in Vittorini, the writing actually inspired Crocenzi's photographs. These books, then, take different approaches to the photographic image, but neither subordinates photography to the written word. Indeed, in both Romano and Vittorini, the photograph carries out its own narrative function.

From the neorealist socially and politically committed photo-novels and photographic series of Giacomelli and Crocenzi and the illustrated novel of Vittorini to the autobiographical writing of Romano and the purely fictional writings of Tabucchi and Del Giudice, one can see how the narrative comes to its full potential through the photograph – indeed, how the narrative itself gives rise to the photographic image. In this regard, an additional question that most of the essays in this book seek to answer is, how does Italian narrative respond to and inform the cultural representations of memory and time posited by photography?

To illustrate photography's social role, several contributors refer to Sontag's point that photographs serve as a means for limiting our experience of the world. For Sontag, photography makes things and people safe by transferring them into a photogenic image or a souvenir. While the photographer's preying eye may assert itself without the "victim's" awareness, photography – as will be discussed in the third section of this book – violates people: it sees them as they cannot see themselves and turns them into objects that can be "symbolically possessed" (14). This offers photographers privileged knowledge of their subjects that the subjects themselves do not and cannot have.

The camera has often been perceived as a means of social control, and throughout the history of the photographic medium, its capacity to document and surveille has been vital to efforts to regulate society. Building on Foucault, John Tagg has consistently regarded photography as an instrument for controlling and imposing knowledge on relatively powerless subjects. In *The Burden of Representation*, Tagg argues for a history of photography predicated on the conviction that "the photograph is not a magical 'emanation' but a material product of a material apparatus set to work in specific contexts, by specific forces, for more or less defined purposes" (3).[39]

"Through the Lens," the final section of this book, reflects mainly on how words and photographic practices and products can become powerful means to control and make sense of the world around us. The final three contributions deal with visual strategies developed by a (fictional) observer to frame people, places, and things deemed exotic, distressing, or even inconceivable. Once "captured" through the camera lens or by way of a photographic gaze, these photographic subjects are rendered visible (and thus knowable). The final three essays examine texts that are characterized by a visual style that (especially in two cases) is also a strategy for the narrator (often also a photographer) to maintain his or her distance from the reality represented. Yet there is no documentary intention in these texts; rather, the photographic perception of the world expresses subjectivity and the narrating agent's unique personal vision of facts and people.

Mariarita Martino takes a psychoanalytically informed approach to Alberto Moravia's *L'uomo che guarda* (*The Voyeur*) (1985). In her contribution, she considers the photographic practice narrated in this novel as a translative process of scopophilia, a "twofold tendency indicating voyeurism and exhibitionism." She examines the intersemiotic translation of an erotic poem by Mallarmé into a fictive photograph inspired by Manet's *Olympia* (1863). Through a reading of these four texts – novel, poem, painting, and photograph – Martino demonstrates how the poem's translation into a photograph involves not the poem's content but rather its scopophilic mechanism, which is facilitated by the very nature of the photographic medium.

In her essay, Sarah Patricia Hill analyses how Andrea De Carlo's work as a photographer influenced his use of photography in *Treno di panna* (*Cream Train*) (1981). Focusing on what it means for a literary text to represent via photographic effects (something for which various critics praised the novel), Hill asks what these effects are, how they are achieved, and what function they serve within the novel. She concludes that the desire for photographic visibility – a visibility that extends no further than surface details – actually exposes knowledge and experience as contingent.

The act of looking and the function of photographs and literary images as agents of empowerment and corporality are examined by Giorgia Alù. The perspective, however, moves from a male, voyeuristic gaze on a female body (as in Moravia's novel) to a woman's photographic perception of things and people and her use of photography as a way to assert femininity and body against the control of others. Alù examines a number of alternative strategies of photographic representation in the Italian literary works by Albanian writer and photographer Ornela Vorpsi. She argues that Vorspi's literary scenes overlap with – or, better, are portraits of – the author's self. Her photographs, in particular, become acts of self-extension and, together with her fragmentary visual writing, are sites for cognition and memory as well as resistance against a totalitarian politics of spectatorship and control.

The texts and issues analysed in this book reflect the diverse interfaces and exchanges between the art of writing and that of photography in Italy. Inevitably, there are omissions, and we make no claims to have included discussions about all the theoretical issues that arise from the interactions of these two media or the methodologies that can be used to study them. Nor do we suggest that this book is an exhaustive overview of Italian literature that has used, referenced, or reproduced photographic images. With *Enlightening Encounters*, we have set out to raise awareness of the interaction between writing and photography in Italian literature and to encourage discussion within genres and across areas and themes where further exploration is needed. We hope this book will spark interest in photo-textual relations among both emerging and established scholars.

NOTES

1 Unless otherwise stated, translations from the Italian are the authors'.
2 For a detailed history of the theory of photography, see Kriebel.
3 See, for instance, Bogardus; Duttlinger, *Kafka and Photography*; Entin; Gidley; Henninger; Hunter; Patt, Dillbohner, and Sebald; Schwartz and Tierney-Tello; Schloss; and Vogl.
4 There are abundant books on the cultural and social history of Italian photography published in Italy, yet theoretical works and poetics of photographic narration are quite rare. Mormorio published an edited anthology in 1988 titled *Gli scrittori e la fotografia* (*Writers and Photography*). Recent volumes published in Italy have examined the relationship between literature and photography, looking, however, at various authors and artists both foreign and Italian. Examples of these include Albertazzi and Amigoni;

Dolfi, *Letteratura & fotografia;* Marzocchini; and Mercenaro. A recent, rare text that focuses essentially on Italian literature and photography is Ajello's *Il racconto delle immagini.* Abroad, monographs or edited volumes devoted entirely to the interaction of photography and Italian narrative have not been published at the time of writing.

5 Talbot's *The Pencil of Nature*, published in 1844 (less than ten years after photography was invented), was the first book to reproduce photographs (more precisely, calotypes) on its pages. For a poetics of the iconotext, see Louvel, *Poetics of the Iconotext.*

6 See N. Armstrong. See also Ortel for a discussion of how photography changed the face of literature.

7 For an extended analysis of photography's influence on twentieth-century American black writers, see Blair. For a critical discussion of how literature shaped our understanding of photography, see Baetens.

8 See Barthes's *Camera Lucida,* "The Photographic Message," and "Rhetoric of the Image." For a discussion of Barthes's legacy in the study of images, including the photographic image, see Rabaté.

9 See Sekula's "The Invention of Photographic Meaning" and *Photography Against the Grain.*

10 See Sontag's *On Photography.*

11 See, for instance, McCance, special issue of *Mosaic: A Journal for the Interdisciplinary Study of Literature* (2004); Jacobs, *Photography and Literature,* special issue of *English Language Notes* (2006); and Horstkotte and Pedri, special issue of *Poetics Today* (2008). Recent collections of essays include those edited by Cunningham, Fisher, and Mays (2005); Dolfi (2005); and Montier, Louvel, Méaux, and Ortel (2008).

12 See, for instance, White 28–58.

13 See Brunetta; see also Rak. Nevertheless, especially in the past few years, the relationship between cinema and Italian literature is gaining currency both within Italy and abroad. See Abruzzese for an overview of this development.

14 See Pelizzari, *Photography and Italy.* This is actually the first study on the history of photography in Italy to be published in English.

15 See Maffioli for a critical history of the daguerrotype in Italy. For a general history of photography, see Henisch and Henisch.

16 See Henisch and Henisch ch. 14; see also Bollati 29–33.

17 On the assimilation of the image into the printed page in the nineteenth century (particularly in Britain), see C. Armstrong.

18 By translating into images *tòpoi* from a variety of sources and producing others, photography collaborated in the creation of a "visual dictionary" of Italians, a didactic and celebratory national rhetoric (Bollati 31).

19 See Ajello, "Guido Gozzano."

20 Here, reference is made to the various essays – often characterized by sensationalism – that aimed to reveal the problems of the proletariat and sub-proletariat in big Italian cities. But unlike the neorealist versions of postwar Italy, such representations usually took a far from straight "documentary" approach to representing the poor. Such essays included Serao's "Il ventre di Napoli" ("The Belly of Naples") (1884) and Valera's *Milano sconosciuta* (*Unknown Milan*) (1879).

21 See Miraglia, "D'Annunzio e la fotografia"; and Woodhouse. On the relationship between D'Annunzio and Michetti, see Di Tizio. D'Annunzio also approached photography as a means to record fragile cultures eroded by industrialization.

22 For discussions on the lure that new visual technologies – including photography – held for Pirandello, see Ceserani 245–64; Gieri 30–81; and Moses.

23 Roy DeCarava, the first black artist to win a Guggenheim Fellowship, wrote a letter to Minor White in 1953 arguing that photography needed to accept its place among the arts. See Rabb, *Literature and Photography* 390.

24 See Taramelli.

25 Levi's *Cristo si è fermato a Eboli* (*Christ Stopped at Eboli*) (1945) was a source of inspiration for postwar humanist photographers. For an overview of collaborative efforts between photographers and writers in Italy during this time, see Morello 55–64.

26 On Calvino and visual culture, see Ricci. The photographer and the act of taking photographs appear in a significant number of Italian literary texts throughout the twentieth century. In Stefano D'Arrigo's *Horcynus Orca* (1975), Mr Monanin, a frenzied photographer of dolphins, shoots pictures, an act that seems to echo that of shooting a gun. In 1996, Gesualdo Bufalino published *Tommaso e il fotografo cieco* (*Thomas and the Blind Photographer*), which deals with the relationship between a writer and a photographer, who have taken on the mission to freeze time. The figure of the photographer is also prominent in Alberto Moravia's *L'uomo che guarda* (*The Voyeur*) (1985) and in many novels by Andrea De Carlo (as will be discussed in this volume), as well as in Paolo Maurensig's *L'ombra e la meridiana* (*The Shadow and the Sundial*) (1998).

27 See, for instance, Giulia Niccolai's 1966 novel, *Il grande angolo* (*Wide Angle*), which was inspired by her ten years as a photographer.

28 On Ghirri and Celati, see in particular Spunta, "The New Italian Landscape"; and West 91–137.

29 A similar blurring of the factual and the fictional in photography is characteristic of the photographic portraits of writers that have been reproduced

on book jackets or in the pages of their books. Photographer Giovanni Giovannetti's ongoing project *Un archivio italiano* (*An Italian Archive*), devoted to fixing and framing popular Italian literati and intellectuals, attests to the value – historical, cultural, and social – these somewhat innocuous photographic portraits hold.

30 See Barthes, "The Photographic Message."
31 See Benjamin, "A Short History of Photography."
32 See Barthes, "The Photographic Message."
33 See Entin 26–9.
34 The relationship between photography and memory, in particular, is treated in great detail in Barthes's *Camera Lucida*, as well as in Kracauer's reflections. For Kracauer, photography's records overtook memory's fragmentariness.
35 For similar readings of the photographic image, see Sontag 154; and Krauss, "The Photographic Conditions."
36 See Barthes, "The Photographic Message."
37 For an overview of the photograph as index, see Dubois, *L'Acte photographique* 19–53. For an analysis of the photograph as index, see Doane; see also Lefebvre. See also Krauss's *The Originality of the Avant-Garde*, in which she postulates the photograph as index. For a sustained argument against the photographic image's indexicality, see Creekmur.
38 See Taramelli.
39 Tagg also addresses the politics of photographic representation throughout *The Disciplinary Frame*. See also Solomon-Godeau as well as Ryan.

PART ONE

The Lure of Photography

1 Spectres of Photography: Photography, Literature, and the Social Sciences in Fin-de-Siècle Italy

MARIA GRAZIA LOLLA

On 7 January 1939, on the hundredth anniversary of photography's momentous declaration into public existence, Paul Valéry delivered a speech designed to shock the literary world into thinking about photography in a new key. He addressed an academic audience at the Sorbonne, speaking on behalf of the literary Academie Française, and issuing a resounding and unconditional thank you for the services rendered by that "marvellous invention" to the wider "Empire of Letters." Picking up the conversation that François Arago had opened in front of the French Parliament a hundred years earlier, he began by displaying the same patriotic credentials that had inspired his predecessor: "The Academy, invited to take part in the ceremony marking the centenary of a truly French invention, indeed one of the most admirable to emerge in the course of the nineteenth century, could not fail to pay its own respects to our great compatriots" (192). Valéry's photography, however, hardly matched that of Arago, which was, after all, the invention of a painter – and a painter of the lowbrow art of the diorama at that. It had been patronized by a scientist whose interlocutors were fellow scientists, artists, archaeologists, and politicians; and once it exited the lofty halls of the parliament, it began a life as a circus attraction, exhibited – as was the case at the Italian National Exposition of 1861 – "in the equatorial regions of the gallery," far from books or paintings and close to "mineral waters, drugs and anatomical pieces" (Zannier, *Segni di luce* 2: 58). As to literature, the poet who picked up the pen to acknowledge photography's existence used the opportunity to issue a resounding and unconditional malediction. For fellow French poet Charles Baudelaire, writing in 1859, photography was "an industry" fit for "those deplorable times"; it was "the refuge of all failed painters with too little talent, or too lazy to complete their studies." Its habitat was "the traveller's album," "the library of the naturalist," "the hypotheses of the astronomer." And it must not touch the world of art and literature: "If once it be allowed to impinge on the sphere of the intangible and the imaginary, on anything that has value solely because man adds something to it from his souls, then woe betide us" (86–9).

The venue, the audience, and the tone of Valéry's centenary speech all pointed to a desire to rethink a photography that indeed, in name, technique, and social practice, was hardly what it was a hundred years before. What had been patented as the "daguerreotype" was now universally referred to as "photography." What had been conceptualized as the "pencil" that gave nature the power to reproduce herself – but only once, very slowly and quite expensively – was now susceptible to infinite, fast, and cheap reproductions. What had initially been presented as a labour-intensive discovery and as a mysterious process whose mastery required a delicate alchemy and a quasi-exoteric knowledge was now defined by the lack of skill of its practitioners. What had begun as a matter of the state had grown into the domain of the private. What had been destined for the monumental, the valuable, and the exceptional was now routinely being employed to document humanity's prosaic contractual existence: marriages, births, and criminal records. Tentative then, it was now here to stay. In one hundred years, photography had become so ubiquitous and so utterly mundane as to have grown, paradoxically, invisible; it had become so ordinary as to have compromised the possibility of being noticed or thought about at all. And could it be that in one hundred years, from being art and literature's worst enemy, photography had become their best friend?

Valéry's centenary speech set out to reconcile photography and fiction. Reflecting, prospectively and retrospectively, on the impact of the "mere idea" of photography (rather than the practice) on the "Empire of Letters," Valéry argued that despite the lack of "obvious affinity" between literature and photography, photography was having a profound impact on the world of letters, and furthermore, that it had changed literature for the better. But in his rush to promote a new idea of literature, he projected onto the past an "idea" of photography, and his narrative of how photography had affected the scholarship and literature of the time was deeply anachronistic. Building on Liborio Termine's enlightening close reading of Valéry's centenary speech, and wishing, with Robin Kelsey and Geoffrey Batchen, to contribute towards "an appropriate historical framework for photography" (Batchen, "*Camera*

Lucida" 78), I would like to engage once more Valéry's reconceptualization of photography and return to photography some of the connotations it had in the first decades of its life. I would like to draw attention to the "idea" of photography that was articulated by Daguerre himself and to the image of photography that can be discerned in the writings of journalists, novelists, photographers, and social scientists working in Italy in the fifty-odd years following the invention of photography. Where Valéry was keen to forward a view of photography as positive, tangible, and incommensurable with the "intangible and imaginary" of literature, a closer scrutiny of the culture of positivism that supposedly revered the objective and the measurable surrenders an idea of photography as surprisingly absent, invisible, immaterial, imponderable, indeed, and, most problematically, ineffectual.

Valéry and the "What Has Been" of Photography

Let us begin with Valéry's evocation of the cultural landscape before and after the birth of photography. As he sought to redirect the attention of the scholarly community to photography's impact on literature, he spent no time discussing photography's process or detailing its practical applications for archaeologists, tourists, or property owners, as his predecessor had done. Instead, he immediately addressed the fear that photography would render art and literature obsolete. First, he pointed out that one hundred years of photographic practice had brought photography to the point that it could accommodate motion, thereby equipping painters to reproduce it more accurately: "Directly the process of fixation made it possible to study, at one's leisure, beings in motion, a great many errors of observation came to light ... Thanks to photography, the eye grew accustomed to anticipate what it should see, and to see it; and it learned not to see nonexistent things which, hitherto, it had seen so clearly" (192).

Moving quickly to the world of letters – concisely, modernly, photographically, indeed – Valéry acknowledged the fear that photography might "ultimately restrict the importance of the art of writing and act as its substitute, rather than help enlarge its scope" (192); but he then offered the counter-argument that photography would ultimately advance literature. At first tentatively – "I see no harm," "I am strongly inclined to believe that it might," "could indirectly" (193) – but with increasing confidence, Valéry argued that photography had allowed literature to move towards a truer "end," a purer form of art. Deploying somewhat Taylorist language, he showed how one hundred years of photographic practice had allowed literature's true vocation to emerge:

> A literature would purify itself if it left to other modes of expression and production the tasks which they can perform far more effectively, and devoted itself to ends it alone can accomplish. It would thus protect itself and advance along its true paths, one of which leads toward the perfecting of language that constructs or expounds abstract thought, the other exploring all the variety of poetic patterns and resonances. (193)

Photography, according to Valéry, had freed literature from the obligation to reproduce the material context of our daily life and had accelerated its pursuit of the abstract, the spiritual, the intangible, and the pure.

Photography, then, was propelling literature into a better and more rarefied future. Next, turning to the literary past, Valéry noted how when it "first made its appearance," photography had rescued the world of letters from "the all-invading fashion" of the "descriptive genre": "The background and outward aspects of life figured almost disproportionately in works of verse and prose alike" (193). Daguerre's invention, according to Valéry, had exposed at once Romanticism's "cavalier treatment of people as well as objects" (193) and its fanciful and laughable constructions, especially of the Orient and the Middle Ages. In the aftermath of photography, both looked embarrassingly "cut whole cloth from the sensibility of the period, with the aid of some small erudition. And then came Daguerre" (193). Moving on in the course of literary history, Valéry noted that if the absence of photography had shaped the Romantic fictions of the historical novel, the "advent of photography" explained the demise of those fictions and (partly) the rise of "the literary system of Flaubert, of Zola, or of Maupassant" (194). In sum, for Valéry, Romanticism, realism, and naturalism, just like modernism, were all defined by their relative distance from the advent of photography.

But for Valéry, photography was doing much more for literature than shaping current literary practice and rearranging literary history. He argued that it was affecting literature the most where it was supposed to matter the least – namely, in the "vast domains of History and Philosophy": "It is here, in these vague regions of knowledge, that the coming of Photography, or the mere idea of it, acquires remarkable and specific importance, for it introduces into these venerable disciplines a new condition, perhaps a new uncertainty, a new kind of reagent whose effects have certainly not as yet been sufficiently explored" (194–5).

Valéry reminded his audience that by forcing its destabilizing power onto the practice of historiography, photography was exposing how speculative, imaginative, and indeed literary the practice of history really was. Some fifty years before Barthes was to attribute to photography's "*having-been-there*" the introduction of a "type of consciousness" that was "indeed truly unprecedented" ("Rhetoric" 278, emphasis in original), Valéry noted that "the mere notion of photography, when we introduce it into our meditation on the genesis of historical knowledge and its true value, suggests this simple question: *Could such and such a fact, as it is narrated, have been photographed?*" (195, emphasis in original). That "simple question," that "mere notion," according to him, had transformed the practice of history and literature: "Since History can apprehend only sensible things, being based on verbal testimony relayed through words, everything on which it grounds its affirmations can be broken down into things witnessed, into moments that were caught in 'quick takes' or could have been caught had a cameraman, some star news photographer, been on hand. *All the rest is literature*" (195, emphasis in original).

At the touch of Daguerre, for Valéry, the once solid domains of historiography and the historical novel had instantly melted into the thin air of literature. To the "canvas," the "cardboard," the "fancy," and the "imaginary" of literary and historical representations, photography responded with the solidity of fact. And just as photography had conquered the unphotographable to literature, it was relentlessly despoiling the literature of the photographable – something that was no small loss. Suddenly, literature's claim to the visible seemed utterly delusional, even comical: "It is a very largely illusory claim that language can convey the idea of a visual object with any degree of precision … Open a passport for proof of this: the description scrawled there does not bear comparison with the snapshot stapled alongside it" (192).

Valéry's insights into photography were novel indeed. It is striking how in Valéry's reconceptualization, photography had ceased being the "pencil of nature" and a technology for reproducing things and people in space, to become the handmaid of history, the technology with the power to capture events, "such and such a fact," and "moments" in time. Valéry's daring new taxonomy made it hopelessly old-fashioned to think about photography in relation to painting. Even more striking was his belittling of literature's ambition to deal in the visible and to produce knowledge – an approach that modernism had made normative but that was far from operative in the nineteenth century. Most striking of all was the unprecedented reification of photography. Inversely proportional to a literature becoming more and more rarefied was a photography that was weighed down – "grounded," to use Valéry's vocabulary (195) – by its materiality.

Reading such modern classics on photography as Barthes's *Camera Lucida* and Sontag's *On Photography,* we gain an even stronger sense of how dominant Valéry's key has become. Half everyman and half sophisticated historian of photography, in *Camera Lucida* Barthes writes about photography's "scandalous effect": "The photograph does not call up the past ... The effect it produces upon me is not to restore what has been abolished (by time, by distance) but to attest that what I see has indeed existed. Now, this is a strictly scandalous effect" (82).[1] Fact, rather than reverie, for Barthes, is photography's mood: "In front of a photograph, our consciousness does not necessarily take the nostalgic path of memory ... but for every photograph existing in the world, the path of certainty" (85). Like Valéry, Barthes lingers on photography's superior power to overcome any shade of historical Pyrrhonism and thus help make historians a bit more dispensable:

> I remember keeping for a long time a photograph I had cut out of a magazine – which showed a slave market: the slavemaster, in a hat, standing; the slaves, in loincloths, sitting. I repeat: a photograph, not a drawing or engraving; for my horror and my fascination as a child came from this; that there was *certainty* that such a thing had existed: not a question of exactitude, but of reality: the historian was no longer the mediator, slavery was given without mediation, the fact was established *without method.* (80, emphasis in original)

For Barthes the child and then the common adult, just as for Valéry, photography enjoyed a privileged relationship with the what-has-been that was forever closed to literature: "The photograph is literally an emanation of the referent. From a real body, which was there, proceed radiations which ultimately touch me, who am here." (80) "No writing," he specifies, "can give me this certainty" (85). Above all, photography transformed time into a thing: "henceforth the past is as certain as the present, what we see on paper is as certain as what we touch" (88).

Both acknowledging and distancing herself from photography's "scandalous effect," Sontag also highlights its power to deliver a tangible piece of the world: "What is written about a person or an event is frankly an interpretation, as are handmade visual statements, like paintings and drawings," whereas "a photograph passes for incontrovertible proof that a given thing happened" (5). "Photographed images," she writes, "do not seem to be statements about the world so much as pieces of it, miniatures of reality that anyone can make or acquire" (4).

Thinking of photography as "a radiation" from a body and "a piece" of reality and thinking of it as the obverse of immaterial literature have become so much second nature that we have lost the memory of those times when photography might have carried different and indeed opposite connotations. Without wishing to detract from Valéry's insights into the changing status of the experience of documentary evidence with the advent of photography, I would like to argue that Valéry's historical evocation of the moment "when photography first made its appearance," the (photographable?) instant when "a marked revision occurred in all standards of visual knowledge," when "Man's way of seeing began to change, and even his way of living" (193–4), should be challenged with a more nuanced and less prejudiced look at the earliest conceptualizations of photography.

The most memorable words in Valéry's speech, "And then came Daguerre," have contributed to an unproductive flattening of the historical horizon of photography. In this essay, I would like to argue that just as Valéry wished onto literature a *levitas* that Daguerre's contemporaries would not have recognized, he projected onto photography a *gravitas*, a solidity, an irrevocable and almost incriminating facticity that was not rightfully claimed by photography's first witnesses or for a long time afterwards. For photography he claimed a solidity that eluded (as I will show) both its first practitioners and the social scientists and men and women of letters who envied even while emulating photography in their endeavours. I have discussed elsewhere the extent to which social scientists partnered with novelists in producing what was understood as positive knowledge; how far from laughable was the literary exploration of the new Italy; how social scientists and novelists competed as equals for the reader's attention; and how readers themselves had a hard time suspending disbelief when faced with realistic fictions.[2] I wish to argue here that on Daguerre's arrival, the status of documentary evidence was far more uncertain; that both literature *and* photography were conceptualized differently; and, more importantly, that *both* were practised in an intellectual environment that did not allow for a clear distinction between "what has been" and what could, might, or should have been. If literature was gifted with the solidity of photography, photography came across as tainted (or blessed) with the insubstantiality of literature. Allowed to sit undefined for a long time, the domain of the taciturn practices of engineers, army generals, surveyors, archaeologists, pedlars, and charlatans, photography's first conceptualizations were barely articulate and quite evasive. Photography resembled a genie or a ghost or – better still – one of the many spectres that were known to haunt nineteenth-century Europe. It was perhaps ill-defined, yet it was defined in dialogue with some of its perceived obverses, such as literature and statistics.[3] Quite simply, I wish here to return to photography some of the disparate and sometimes contradictory connotations that it carried in the first decades of its life.

Of Genies, Goblins, Ghosts, and the Not-Being-There of Photography

Early observers were aware that photography ought not to be taken too easily as coextensive with "what has been." As Jennifer Tucker has recently argued, "although nineteenth-century faith in photography was powerful, the idea that people over a hundred years ago accepted photographs at face value is exaggerated and misleading. Indeed, nineteenth-century viewers frequently asked many of the same questions that are asked about photography today" (4). At the inaugural meeting of the newly founded Società Fotografica Italiana, established in 1889 to mark the fiftieth anniversary of the invention of photography, the journalist Pietro Ferrigni (better known to readers by the pseudonym Yorick) reminded fellow members that because of the routine practice of photomontage, photography sometimes "proves nothing": "the deceit is too easy and too ordinary" (45). Indeed, one of the earliest existing photographs was the self-portrait as a drowned man that Hyppolite Bayard exhibited on 14 July 1839 to protest the French Parliament's lack of attention to his experiments with the direct positive process.[4] But far more common, and significant, than the fraudulent or playful practice of photomontage was the cavalier deployment of photographs *in absentia*. It is remarkable how often photography was evoked as an absence rather than as a piece of the world; how often it was invoked to provide a record of what could have been rather than to memorialize what *had* been; how often it was valued for its allegorical significance rather than for its capacity to document an event; how often it was deployed for its ability to summon the average and the repeatable rather than the exceptional; how often it was used for its power to shape the future rather than to capture the past; how often it was cited to convey the irreality effect of a given situation. How often, quite simply, photography was materially not there.

The early decades of photographic practice in Italy are littered with events, people, and objects that could have been photographed but were not. Take, for instance, the reporting that the Italian writer Edmondo De Amicis offered the readers of the magazine *Vita militare* (*Military Life*) in the aftermath of the inglorious Italian conquest of Rome in September 1870:

> I bersaglieri mangiavano; due o tre frati rivolgevano tra le mani una gamella, guardandola di sopra e di sotto; altri tenevano in mano un pane di munizione; altri osservavano con molta curiosità i cappelli pennati appesi al muro. Ci fosse stato un fotografo!

> The *bersaglieri* were having lunch; some friars were turning their bowls, looking them over; others were handling a piece of bread as ammunition; others still were looking intently at the feathered hats hanging from the wall. I wish a photographer had been there! (121)

Pleasantly surprised by the exceptional sight of an army at peace and eager to dispel fears that the new Italian state would conduct itself in an anti-clerical manner, De Amicis wished for the magical power of photography to persuade Italians not that something had really happened *once* but that it happened *always*. This sort of photography was intended to show not a moment in time, not an event, but a way of being: an un-event. A photograph of soldiers and friars sitting, eating, looking at their food, and handling their utensils, fraternizing like long-lost friends minutes after the breach of Porta Pia, would reassure Italians that the "conquest of Rome" had been bloodless – indeed, profoundly harmonious – and that the soldiers were more than welcome. In fact, the non-existent photograph is quickly followed by what would have been the ideal caption. When asked by the journalist what the friars were saying, in an improbable mixture of Neapolitan and Piedmontese, a soldier replied: "so' chiu' etaliani de noautri" (the friars were more Italian than us!; De Amicis 121). Rather than being wished for as the gold standard of historical occurrence – did it really happen? – and rather than memorializing an event, this would-be photograph is invoked and evoked to capture normalcy. Its tense was definitely not the aorist of a moment in time, to use Barthes's terminology; its value and significance were not those of a souvenir of the past. It is hard to overlook the surrealistic quality of this imaginary photo, its wishfulness and its happily-ever-after connotation, and, more importantly, its allegorical and indeed deeply unphotographable undertone. What De Amicis really wished for was an emblem, not a photograph.

Like De Amicis, the journalist Paolo Valera foregrounded photography's conditional existence. In the aftermath of a far more infamous breach, General Bava Beccaris's 1898 assault of the Milanese Capuchin convent where beggars had congregated to receive their daily meal, Valera published a book that openly addressed the lack of photographic evidence of the events. His would-be reportage begins with the chapter "Il fotografo delle barricate" ("The Photographer of the Barricades"), an imaginary interview with the photographer Luca Comerio about a set of photographs that were never taken:

> Ah, se lo avessimo conosciuto prima! Con Luca Comerio avremmo potuto riprodurre Milano terrorizzata con l'esattezza della macchina fotografica. Le scene fotografate sarebbero state testimoni implacabili e avrebbero permesso al lettore di assistere allo scempio del popolo che pagava la decima del sangue senza combattere, senza insorgere, senza talvolta rivoltarsi con un'imprecazione. [...] È il Victor Hugo della riproduzione istantanea. (*Le terribili giornate* 20)

> If only we had known him then! With Luca Comerio, we could have reproduced a terrified Milan with the precision of the camera. The photographed scenes would have been implacable witnesses and would have allowed readers to assist in the carnage of the people who paid with their blood the tithe without fighting back, without revolting, without even turning with a curse ... He is the Victor Hugo of instantaneous reproduction.

Valera wished for a photographer – in this instance, however, to distance himself from the new state's lack of social cohesion. He evoked Comerio as the Victor Hugo of photography, emphasizing his reputation for conveying indignation rather than documentary evidence. Regarding the purpose of such photographs, Valera made clear that their value was to provide not a document but a monument – to shape the future so as not to repeat the past: "E noi, raccontando gli episodi raccapriccianti, ci serviremmo di alcune delle sue istantanee, non per suonare a stormo le campane degli odii, ma per impedire con gli esempii, che si rinnovi lo spettacolo degli assassinii legali" (Narrating such blood-curdling episodes we would make use of some of his photographs not to incite hatred, but to prevent the recurrence of the spectacle of legal assassinations; *Le terribili giornate* 20). Summoning up non-existent photographs – rather than having them document the existent – Valera now offered a hallucinatory description of several invisible photographs:

> Egli ha veduto e ci ha conservato in una bella e nitida fotografia – un gruppo di soldati che faceva fuoco dal bastione di Porta Venezia su due individui che passavano al largo della sottostante circonvallazione. La precisione dei proiettili è stata documentata sotto gli occhi del fotografo. L'uno è caduto a pochi passi dall'altro. Ci ha regalato la barricata di Porta Volta, che è un vero capolavoro. I combattenti sono con le mani in tasca, con le braccia incrociate, con la pipa in bocca. Hanno l'aria di posare per il fotografo. (20)

> He has seen and preserved in a beautiful and terse photograph a group of soldiers opening fire from Porta Venezia on two individuals walking along the boulevard. The precision of the bullets has been documented by the eyes of the photographer. One fell a few feet from the other. He has presented us with the barricade of Porta Volta, which is a true masterpiece. The fighters have their hands in their pockets, their arms crossed, pipe in their mouth. They look like they are posing for the photographer.

Journalists and novelists alike relied on what should have come across as an oxymoron: imagined photographs. Photographs worked just as well, if not better, when they were not there. Not unlike De Amicis and Valera, the novelist Vittorio Imbriani in *Merope IV* (1867) foregrounded five non-exhibited photographs of a woman nicknamed Merope, describing them in exhaustive detail. Fortuitously rescued from a crowded desk, these five photographs are evoked as the inspiration for the novel: "Dunque stava per buttar quello scartafaccio nella cesta dei fogli inutili che poi soglio vendere al pizzicagnolo, quando nello scuoterlo ne caddero cinque fotografiuzze" (So, I was about to throw that bunch of papers into the basket for useless papers to sell it later to the cheesemonger when on shaking it five small photographs fell out; 11–12). Five, conveniently, like the acts of a tragedy, and in those five, Merope has posed in the ways actresses like to have themselves photographed: "Si direbbe che come alcune celeberrime attrici si fanno fotografare nelle mosse più spiccate de' cinque atti di una tragedia in cui maggiormente vennero applaudite, così la mia signora nelle cinque principali scene del nostro breve dramma" (One would say that like some renowned actresses that have themselves photographed in the most effective poses of the five most applauded acts of a tragedy, thus is my lady in the five principal scenes of our brief drama; 16). The five photographs are turned into captions that serve as chapter headings. Determined to convince the reader that writer and reader are in the presence of real photographs, Imbriani evokes a witness and stages the experience of handling five individual photographs of disparately different formats taken from different angles: "Guardala qui! Svelta svelta ma bassina; in abito di seta nera [...]. Di profilo [...] nel secondo ch' è un medaglione, non abbiamo che testa e busto [...] Chi è mai codesta contadinotta [...]. Eccola qua di prospetto [...]. Ed in quest'ultima imagine [...]." (Look here! Nimble but a little too short; in a black silk dress ... In profile ... in the second, which is a medallion, we only have head and bust ... Who could be this peasant ... Here she is in a frontal view ... And, in the last image ....; 12-6). Curiously silent on the woman's somatic traits and uninterested in documenting her looks and actions, Imbriani meticulously renders Merope's jewellery, her clothing, and her hairdo, all of which are extraordinarily alive: "qualche ciocchetta rubella scherza sulla tempia e sulla fronte [...] la lunga veste increspandosi per terra fa un'ombra fortissima [...]" (some locks of red hair run loose on her temples and forehead ... rippling, the long gown casts the strongest shadow on the ground; 13). These photographs are valuable to the writer because of the guesswork they occasion: "S'indovina che è seduta [...]. Si vede che non è stata lungo tempo allo specchio [...]. Si vede che ha da fare" (You can guess that she is sitting ... You can see that she has not spent so much time in front of the mirror ... You can tell she is busy; 14–15). The moments preceding or following the snapshot are dearest to the writer:

> L'abito poi è semplicissimo [...]. Si vede che ha da fare [...] che adesso per una combinazione strana ha un momento d'ozio e si riposa e fantastica; ma che il lavoro, le cure che riprenderà subito, subitissimo le son care e gradite più che i pensieri importuni i quali l'assalgono nelle quiete. (15)
>
> Her dress is very simple ... You can tell that she is busy, that she cannot waste her time ... that now for a strange coincidence she has a moment of

> leisure and reverie; but that work, her occupations, which she'll resume soon, very soon are dear to her more than the unwelcome thoughts that assail her in the quiet moments.

It is fitting that when taking leave of the reader, Imbriani reveals that those photographs are of a woman he does not know and that they do not belong to him: "V'ho ammannito un sacco di bugie […]. I cinque ritrattini sono di una ignota e non mi appartengono. […] [M]a quel che ho narrato e non è accaduto, avrebbe potuto accadere" (I have served you a heap of lies … Those five portraits are of a woman I don't know and I don't own them … But what I have narrated and which did not happen could have happened; 285–6). It does not matter to him that those photographs do not radiate from a real being but are merely imagined. Both the photographs and the narrative have captured what might have been.

There was an expectation that Daguerre's invention would lead to the immediate dismantling of cardboard, fanciful, and imaginary representations of the past and their replacement by precise and accurate photographic counterparts. But as it turned out, more often documented was a yearning for photographs. Photography's conditional existence was invoked by both novelists and social scientists. For instance, the glaring absence of photographs was lamented by both enemies and friends of the new Italian state. Not unlike De Amicis, Valera, and Imbriani, the criminologist Cesare Lombroso expressed a wish for non-existent photographs when he regretted the sporadic presence of photography in state life. Lombroso pointed out that where other states had deployed the new invention to deter crime and subversion, "the taking of prisoners' photographs, which are then filed alphabetically with a short biography," was "yet to arrive to Italy" (136). Indeed, "yet to arrive to Italy" is the phrase that best describes the glaring absence of photography from both scholarly and more general publications of the time.

Photography in its early years seemed to thrive more as a metaphor than as a real presence. Neera's *Fotografie matrimoniali* (*Wedding Photographs*) (1883) – which I will discuss later – neither exhibited nor described wedding photographs past the title. The reader was invited to imagine the narrative "as if" it were a fleeting photograph. The same perplexing yearning for photography is apparent in the magazine *Il fotografo* (*The Photographer*), a short-lived weekly of the 1850s that, notwithstanding its title, did not include a single photograph in its pages. Again, readers were to imagine a photographer reporting from all over the world. Imagined as characteristically disconnected from the "what has been," on one occasion photography was evoked to render the surreal. In *La conquista di Roma* (*The Conquest of Rome*) (1885), to give her readers an idea of the "irreality" effect of a crowd momentarily stopped in its tracks waiting for the opening of parliament, Matilde Serao conjured up an imaginary giant camera:

> La folla delle strade, dei vicoli, dei balconi, delle finestre, sembrava travolta, come colpita da un'improvvisa immobilità, quasi un incantesimo l'avesse pietrificata, come se una immensa invisibile macchina fotografica stesse fotografandola; e si potevano discernere le facce immote, gli occhi arrossati, i bimbi tenuti in collo dalle mamme, una carrozza da nolo ferma, fra la gente, su cui erano salite venti persone, in piedi. (31)

> The crowds in the streets, the alleys, the balconies, the windows seemed at moments to have been suddenly stricken lifeless as if petrified by magic, as if a huge invisible photographic machine was photographing them and one might have observed blank faces with staring eyes, children whom their nurses held by the collar or a dozen people who had scaled a hackney coach. (30)

Serao here was invoking photography to render the surreal stillness of a crowd gathered outside the Italian Parliament. A giant invisible camera was the genie responsible for achieving the impossible task of disciplining a large body of people into complete and unnatural stillness. For inducing, that is, a state that could not have been photographed but for the presence of a photographer! Photography here does not capture an event; rather, it is introduced as the technology capable of halting events. The surrealism of the scene is compounded by the fact that Serao gives the reader the impression that she is describing a scene "as if" it were a real photograph. That photography should be invoked as the measure of the eeriness of a situation and for its magical power to halt the natural flow of events is a reminder of photography's uncertain belonging to the sphere of positive fact.

Invisible and powerful, there and not there, photography was often summoned as a genie or a goblin when not a spectre. Arnaldo Corsici, when presenting a brief history of photography to the Società Fotografica Italiana, described it as a goblin from whose pranks no one was immune:

> col progresso la fotografia ha anche moltiplicato le sue qualificazioni; prima la si diceva p. es. *fedele* nelle sue riproduzioni; oggi la si può dire

> p. es. *indiscreta*, poiché a nessuno oggi è permesso di passare in un luogo aperto, senza tema che per mezzo di un apparecchio insidioso, dissimulato in qualche parte, una persona possa prendere la immagine di un altro, a sua insaputa, malgrado la sua volontà. (14, emphasis original)
>
> The progress of photography has resulted in a multiplication of its qualifications; once it was called *faithful* in her reproductions; now we would call it for instance *indiscrete*, since nobody is allowed to pass through a public space without being afraid that through an insidious device, hidden somewhere, someone could catch the image of someone else, without them knowing, against their will.

In Yorick's testimony, photography resembled an invisible yet all-seeing and ubiquitous mythological creature:

> Questa benedetta fotografia è petulante insieme e indiscreta. Ha un senso solo – quello della vista – ma se ne serve con una audacia e con una prepotenza spaventosa. Vede tutto ... e segna tutto ... senza esitazione e senza compassione ... per tutto dove andate, inciampate in una macchina rizzata sulle sue tre zampe ... che sta lì a occhio spalancato, a lente pronta; che vi insidia, vi pedina, vi spia ... e vi piglia a volo coll'istantaneità d'una fucilata [...]. (43-4)
>
> This blessed photography is petulant and indiscreet at the same time. It has a single sense – that of sight – and it uses it with a frightening audacity and arrogance. It sees everything ... and records everything without hesitation or compassion ... Everywhere you go you stumble in a machine standing on three feet ... that is there, wide eyed, lens ready; it harasses you, it stalks you, it spies on you ... and then it kills you with the instantaneity of a gunshot.

Yorick's humorous description underscored photography's demonic powers by conjuring up an infinite number of swiftly moving cameras operated without human intervention. For Paolo Mantegazza, president of the Società Fotografica Italiana, photography had a look dangerously close to the spectre of communism as summoned in Marx and Engels's *Manifesto*. He described it as democracy's third-most-powerful ally after the railway and electric street lighting:

> La ferrovia che trasporta oggi con egual velocità il principe e il proletario e la luce elettrica brilla per le nostre vie sul capo del povero come del ricco.

Così è della fotografia, che oggi con pochi soldi permette a tutti di conservare le fisiche sembianze della persona più cara, ciò che una volta non era concesso che ai grandi signori. (7)

The railway that carries today the prince and the proletarian at the same speed and electrical light that shines on the head of the poor as well as the rich. The same we can say of photography, which with little money today gives everybody a chance to preserve the physical appearance of our dearest one that was once the privilege only of the very rich.

Be it spectral or goblinesque, photography was consistently defined by an original deficiency, a lack. It was routinely prefaced by "mere" or referred to *as if* prefaced by "mere." Even as Émile Zola propounded the newfangled *roman experimental,* he distanced himself from suspicions that he was colluding with photography. First he praised Balzac for not "*remain[ing] satisfied* with photographing the facts collected by him" (4, emphasis added). A few lines later, he defended himself from accusations that he was promoting a form of literature that too closely ressembled photography. "The desire to be *solely* photographers," he writes, is "a contemptible reproach which they heap upon us naturalistic writers" (4, emphasis added). Giovanni Verga was able to pin down with a direct quotation what Zola had reported as hearsay. In a letter to Luigi Capuana about the unfavourable reception of *Eros,* Verga wrote that according to the literary critic of *L'Opinione* (*The Opinion*), the novel's worst offence was that it had allowed photography to diminish dialogue, as if having degraded painting were not enough. He was accused of "rimpicciolimento dell'arte, per aver sostituito la fotografia alla pittura, fotografia anche nel dialogo" (belittling art, for having replaced painting with photography, photography even in the dialogue; *Carteggio Verga–Capuana* 41). Capuana attempted to frighten off the malignant spectre of photography with a booming voice. Of Verga's "La Lupa" ("The She-Wolf"), he wrote: "Era la *Lupa* dell'arte, la *Lupa* creata dal Verga che sopraffaceva quella della realtà e me la metteva sotto gli occhi più viva della viva quando era viva. Tanto è vero che l'arte non sarà mai la fotografia!" (It was the *She-Wolf* of art, the one created by Verga far superior to the real one and he placed it under my eyes more alive than the live one when she was alive; 35). The characters of *I Malavoglia* (*The House by the Medlar Tree*), Capuana insisted, had nothing to do with photography: "Quei personaggi il Verga non li ha visti, come crede il critico, né li ha fotografati" (Verga did not see those characters, nor did he photograph them, as the critic wants to believe; 58).

With less pathos and far more didacticism, in the preface to the novel *Fotografie matrimoniali*, Neera suggested that photography was fleeting, insubstantial – anything but solid:

> Come il sostantivo fotografie indica, sono macchiette prese a volo; pose ed espressioni colte nella vita solitaria sopra fisionomie comuni. Non hanno intendimenti d'arte, salvo il debito rispetto, e corrono leste per la loro via nella stessa guida di scolaretti senza pensieri, facendo un po' quello che i francesi chiamano *l'école buissonière*, raccattando cioè fiori e farfalle lungo il sentiero. Lieve bagaglio: dirà qualcuno. Sì, lieve come i bei giorni di primavera che passano per non più ritornare; come il raggio di sole che raccoglie una immagine fuggitiva e la fissa sulla carta nell'attitudine irrevocabile dell'istante. (vii–viii)

> As the word photographs indicates, these are caught in mid air; poses and expressions caught in the solitary life over common physiognomies. They have no pretensions to art; they only mean to pay their respects to art; and they run fast down the road like carefree schoolchildren, doing what the French call *l'école buissonière*, picking up, that is, flowers and butterflies along the way. Light luggage: some will say. Yes, as light as the beautiful days of spring that pass and never come back; as the sunray that captures a fugitive image and fixes it on paper in the irrevocable attitude of the instant.

For Neera, then, photography was defined not by its incriminating facticity, by the unimaginative souvenirs of the world that it offered, but by its weightlessness, artlessness, immaturity, and playfulness.

Either as diminished art or diminished reality, photography was marked by a radical insubstantiality – a ghostliness. I would like to argue here that it was precisely that insubstantiality that appealed most to the social scientists who furthered the culture of positivism and to the novelists who cultivated naturalism in their work. In photography could be found the true spirit of practices as disparate and seemingly incommensurable as Claude Bernard's experimental medicine, the new pedagogy of Maria Montessori, Clarence King's geological explorations, and the naturalistic novel. In his epoch-making *Introduction to the Study of Experimental Medicine* (1865), which Zola used as the blueprint for the experimental novel – "I intend on all points to entrench myself behind Claude Bernard" and "replace the word 'doctor' by the word 'novelist'" (1) – Bernard explicitly evoked the photographer as the scientist's alter ego: "Men of science … must be anxious only to forearm themselves against errors of observation which might make them incompletely see or poorly define a phenomenon ... Observers, then, must be photographers of phenomena ... The experimenter must now disappear or rather change himself instantly into an observer" (22). For Bernard, photography was attractive to the scientist because it made it possible to inhabit a place in spirit but not in body – to be invisible.

The same spirit can be felt in Maria Montessori's radical reconceptualization of the teacher's purpose and the nature of the learning experience. A social scientist who linked herself to Bernard's revolutionary scientific method, Montessori propounded the invisibility of the observer. Of her teachers, she expected nothing less (more accurately, nothing more). Striving to do nothing was part of the teacher's job description: "In our system, she must become a passive, much more than an active, influence" (*The Montessori Method* 87); indeed, resisting the temptation to teach was the most challenging aspect of her work (88). A *lack* of qualifications was the teacher's main asset, which perhaps explains why, as Rita Kramer notes, "Montessori chose an untrained – therefore from her point of view, unspoiled – young woman as directress" (125). When some of her power to intervene in learning was taken away, the teacher had no choice but to relinquish her authorial role, even in name: "With my method the teacher teaches little and observes much ... For this reason I have changed the name of teacher into director" (*The Montessori Method* 173). She designed a pedagogy that put a premium on self-teaching and self-correction, with the goal of creating "the impression" that both teaching and learning happened spontaneously. What Montessori offered was "culture acquired spontaneously":

> We had prepared a place for children where a diffused culture could be assimilated from the environment, without any need for direct instruction ... If visitors asked them, "Who taught you to write?," they often answered with astonishment: "Taught me? No one has taught me!" ... At that time it seemed miraculous that children of four and a half should be able to write, and that they should have learned without the feeling of having been taught. The press began to speak of "culture acquired spontaneously." (*Absorbent Mind* 7)

In the same spirit, in *Mountaineering in the Sierra Nevada* (1871), the geologist Clarence King invoked photography to render the welcome feeling of watching nature display her data without the need for tedious and laborious human mediation: "I was delighted to ride thus alone, and expose myself, as one uncovers a sensitized photographic plate, to be influenced; for this is a respite from scientific work, when through months you hold yourself accountable for seeing everything, for analyzing, for instituting perpetual comparisons, and, as it were, sharing in the administering of the physical world" (qtd in Kelsey xiii). Here, photography was a metaphor for research without the researcher: "respite from scientific work."

Although not in so many words, the numen of photography can be detected in the "spirit" of the modern novel championed by Verga and Capuana. Time and again, Verga and Capuana wrote about impersonality as "the triumph of the novel," the "artistic ideal," the "theory," the "ideal" of modern art, the "greatest achievement of the contemporary novel" (Capuana, *Scritti critici* 32, 45, 335). Almost in unison, Verga and Capuana clamoured for the author to be banished from the page, to disappear, leaving no trace of his mouth, his hand, his eye, or even his name. Here is Capuana's classic formulation of what came to be known as the "theory of the impersonality of the author":

> Un'opera d'arte, novella o romanzo, è perfetta quando l'affinità e la coesione d'ogni sua parte divien così completa che il processo della creazione rimane un mistero; quando la sincerità della sua realtà è così evidente, il suo modo e la sua ragione d'essere così necessarie, che la mano dell'artista rimane assolutamente invisibile e l'opera d'arte prende l'aria d'un avvenimento reale, quasi si fosse *fatta da sé* e avesse maturato e fosse venuta fuori spontanea, senza portar traccia nelle sue forme viventi nè della mente ove germoglio, nè dell'occhio che la intravvide, nè delle labbra che mormorano le prime parole. È la teoria dell'arte moderna; il Verga l'ha espressa quasi con le stesse parole. (32, emphasis in original)

> A work of art, short story or novel, is perfect when the affinity and the cohesion of all its parts are so thorough that the process of creation remains a mystery; when the sincerity of its reality is so evident, its way and its *raison d'être* so necessary that the hand of the artist remains absolutely invisible and the work of art starts looking like a real event, almost *as if it made itself* and had matured and come out spontaneously without showing any trace in its living forms either of the mind from where it sprouted or of the eye that saw it or the lips that whispered the first words. It is the modern theory of art; Verga articulated it almost with the same words.

Verga had indeed articulated this theory almost verbatim, down to the italicization of "essersi fatta da sè" in the preface to the short story "L'amante di Gramigna" ("Gramigna's Lover"). There, in a passage that reads like a word-for-word rebuttal of Barthes's view of photography as a transfer of matter from a real body to the viewer, Verga was keen to stress the absence of physical contact between the artefact and the author: "senza serbare alcun punto di contatto con l'autore" (without retaining any point of contact with the author; *Le novelle* 157). Verga confessed to Capuana his "fixation" with suppressing the name of the author: "Parmi che si deve arrivare a sopprimere il nome dell'artista dal piedistallo della sua opera quando questa vive da sè. Sai, la mia vecchia fissazione di una ideale opera d'arte tanto perfetta da avere in se stessa tutto il suo organismo" (I almost feel like the name of the artist should be erased from the pedestal of his work when this lives on its own. You know of my old fixation of an ideal work of art which is perfect when it has all its organism; qtd in Fava 149–50). For Verga, what made Francesco Torracca's review "the most beautiful and most important article to have been written on *I Malavoglia*" was that it recognized that novel's "perfectly objective and impersonal" nature (Melis 57). For the doctor, as for the writer, the hoped-for effect – one is tempted to quote from another context – was to give the impression that "nature reproduced herself."

In *I Malavoglia,* the novel Capuana promoted as the "highest peak" of the impersonal novel (*Scritti critici* 44), Verga was keen to describe his narrative as a (Bernardian) "study" of the irresistible impulse to social mobility that defined the capitalist transformation of the world's economy:

> Questo racconto è lo studio sincero e appassionato del come probabilmente devono nascere e svilupparsi nelle più umili condizioni le prime irrequietudini pel benessere; e quale perturbazione debba arrecare in una famigliuola, vissuta sino allora relativamente felice, la vaga bramosia dell'ignoto, l'accorgersi che non si sta bene, o che si potrebbe star meglio. (*I Malavoglia* 107)

> This story is the sincere and dispassionate study of how the first anxious desires for material well-being must probably originate and develop in the humblest social conditions, and of the perturbations caused in a family, which had until then lived in relative happiness, by the vague yearning for the unknown and by the realization that they are not so well off or that they could indeed be better off. (*The House* 3)

And if the novel is a "study," then the author is a nimble and intrepid "observer": "chi osserva questo spettacolo non ha il diritto di giudicarlo. È già tanto se riesce a trarsi un istante fuori dal campo della lotta per studiarla senza passione e rendere la scena nettamente, coi colori adatti, tale da dare la rappresentazione della realta com'è stata, o come avrebbe dovuto essere"; 110 (The one who observes this spectacle does not have the right to judge it; it is already much if he can draw aside from the field of struggle for an instant, to study it without passion, and to render the scene clearly and with appropriate colours so as to offer the picture of reality as it was, or as it should have been; *The House* 5). Unfazed by the inhospitable environs that destroyed his characters' future, the author–observer–photographer is remarkably agile: it takes him only one "instant" to gain a safe distance from danger so as to maintain the scientific equanimity so essential to the impersonal rendering of "the spectacle."

Implementing impersonality meant, first of all, doing away with a "present" author who addressed the reader and replacing him with an invisible narrator who would register all the information that entered his field of perception. In this way, the reader would be deprived of the narrative and moral guidance of a strong authorial voice yet would still be able to discern a story and draw a moral lesson. Readers would be left to infer the plot, but in the end – not unlike a class of Montessori pupils – they would learn without being taught. As Verga explained to his friend Filippo Filippi, the reader's (photographic) unawareness was key to the novel's success: "Io non giudico, non m'appassiono, non mi interesso o piuttosto non devo mostrare nulla di tutto questo […]. Questo effetto è tanto più sicuro quanto meno sei messo in guardia quanto più la simpatia è *tua*" (I do not judge, do not become passionate, do not get interested or rather I should not show any of this … This effect is all the more certain the less you are prepared for it, the more the sympathy is *yours*; Tellini 60–1, emphasis in original). The goal was to leave the reader with the impression that the narrative had been self-generated and that a moral lesson had been gained without having been taught.

Rizzoli's decision to place a vintage black-and-white Alinari photo of an unspecified large family on the cover of a recent edition of *I Malavoglia* is understandable, given that in the novel, the spirit of photography seems ubiquitous.[5] It can be detected in 'Ntoni's Orpheus-like backwards, destructive glance at a world that photography was in the habit of immortalizing on paper before destroying forever, and it can be discerned in the sepia colours of 'Ntoni's final gaze at Aci Trezza at dawn on his way out of town. Indeed, we see it in Verga's parade of modern greyness, in open polemic with the "turquoise skies" and "green pastures" punctuated by "the red and yellow of poppies and chrysanthemums" of the old-fashioned novel that Capuana mocked. And it can be discerned in the tempo of the novel – the dilated present of the time it takes for the photographic image to appear on paper – as well as in the tempo of fruition of a novel that, made to be thought of only retrospectively, "a libro chiuso" ("at the end of the book"; *Carteggio Verga–Capuana* 108), and known to be impossible to be summarized (Capuana, *Scritti critici* 44), carries some of the iconic message generally attributed to photography. But nowhere is the presence of photography stronger than in its aspiration to "give nature the power to reproduce herself" and in the creation of a novel that reads like the "spontaneous reproduction of the images of nature."

There are striking parallels to be found among Bernard's "disappearing" the scientist into the observer, Montessori's and King's demoting the teacher and the geologist respectively, Verga's and Capuana's pleas for the author to be invisible, and the way photography was first conceptualized. In a broadsheet he published in January 1839, Daguerre began and ended by promoting the new technology's same asset: the invisibility of the photographer. This broadsheet began by advertising the invention as "the spontaneous reproduction of the images of nature received in the camera obscura" and closed by reiterating that "the DAGUERREOTYPE is not merely an instrument which serves to draw Nature; on the contrary, it is a chemical and physical process which gives her the power to reproduce herself" (Gersheim and Gersheim 77–8). Wishing to offer nature the power to reproduce herself, writing novels that read as if no one had written them, patenting a pedagogy in which learning seemingly took place without being taught, imagining a science that was infinitely better because of the (momentary) absence of the scientist – all of these expressed a yearning to do away with human mediation in the study of nature and in the creative process.

Conclusion

Weighed down as we are by almost two hundred years of photographs, it is easy for us to forget that their early existence was precarious, that photography's output was fragile and sparse, and that the idea of photography conjured the elegant flimsiness of its products just as often as it did the heavy and cumbersome apparatus that produced tangible souvenirs of the past. Noticeable to early observers was the effortlessness and weightlessness of the technology and, especially, photography's capacity to grant man his wish for invisibility. Photography, that is, was a realization of the writer's *and* the scientist's strong desire for temporary respite – to use King's word (qtd in Kelsey xiii) – from human mediation and its indelible traces. Writers and natural and social scientists envied photography's super (or less than) human power not to interfere with observation and representation; they wished for "relief" – King's word again – from exerting an impact on the world they were observing.

Photography was imagined for a long time as literature's natural opposite. It is hard to recall a time when photography was profoundly conditional – indeed, hardly there at all – and was thought of as subject to the laws of the possible and the plausible, no less than literature. No less than a story, a photograph could be imagined and then put into words. And no less than a story, say, by Verga – a novelist who repeatedly and cavalierly moved between the "as it was," the "as it could have been," and the "as it should have been" – a photograph could capture "what might have been" but perhaps never was. Sometimes condemned as a malignant spectre, but far more often evoked as a genie that could inspire writers and social scientists alike to rethink their practices in the hope of achieving the same invisibility it had ushered in, photography was entitled to some of the insubstantiality that Valéry had claimed for literature after (indeed, because of) its invention. Likewise, remembering like Batchen that "unproblematized positivism" is "something that we desire more than they did" (*Burning with Desire* 138), a photography less securely ensconced in the world of stackable, tangible, ponderous facts should encourage us to rethink the very culture of positivism with which photography is customarily associated, a culture tainted by or blessed with a more nuanced understanding of the "what has been." In this regard, it is not surprising that Capuana referred to positivism and "its craze for facts" as the "spirit" of the times and as the product of an evolutionary movement that "no man in the world could resist or stop" (143). For the critic in the *Domenica letteraria* (*Literary Sunday*), positivism was the supernatural force that drove literature, "fatally, to its end" (143).[6] Positivism was irresistible, unstoppable, fatal, and beyond man's control – like the slow swelling of the spring of progress into a deadly flood evoked by Verga and like the inexorable appearance of the image on the page following the damning and casual movement of the shutter. Increasingly the social sciences that were born with photography – statistics, anthropology, and psychoanalysis come to mind – embraced the invisible. They told stories that did not need man's consent and that revealed man to be at the mercy of forces beyond his control. It is hard not to wonder whether a photography reconceptualized to highlight man's wish for invisibility and respite from affecting the observed world should not also include a preoccupation with man's own irrelevance to the representation of nature, a concern for the abdication from the hope of affecting the course of history, and, more generally, a growing anxiety over the limits of human agency that came after Daguerre. It is hard not to notice the impressive coincidence between a literature that aspired to the in-personality of photography and the representation of a world where the belief in the power of human agency is severely compromised; between a literary product that gave the impression that the author did nothing and narratives that foreground man's helplessness; between the technology that, as the later Valéry put it, "required the least of man possible" and narratives that expect the least of man.

NOTES

1 See Batchen, "*Camera Lucida*" 76–91.

2 See Lolla.

3 The complex relationship between photography and another of its perceived obverses, statistics, is the subject of my forthcoming essay "Photography, Fictional Averages, and Sociological Fictions in Fin-de-Siècle Italy."

4 See Warner 32.

5 In recent years there has been a flurry of research on Verga and photography. The consensus seems to be that photography "has" to be there. For a discussion of Verga's *I Malavoglia* and photographic practice, see Minghelli 59–86.

6 See Madrignani 92.

2 Authoring Images: Italo Calvino, Gianni Celati, and Photography as Literary Art

PASQUALE VERDICCHIO

> The art in photography is literary art before it is anything else: its triumphs and monuments are historical, anecdotal, reportorial, observational before they are purely pictorial ... The photograph has to tell a story if it is to work as art.
>
> (Clement Greenberg 183)

Art historian Clement Greenberg's declaration regarding photography is indeed provocative in its suggestion that one of this medium's most valuable traits may be something more than its obviously visual one. By seeming to represent photography as a lesser art for its literary qualities, Greenberg contradicts the medium's by now fully established cultural value. If photography were literal, the value of its images would be restricted to the hierarchal sociocultural standing of the "things" they re-present. The qualities assigned to photography by the respected art historian as a vehicle by which history, anecdote, report, and observation are indicative of its literariness, and the qualification that "the photograph has to tell a story if it is to work as art," are more relatable to our ways of seeing than to something inherent in the medium itself. Taking Greenberg's provocation as a proposal for reconsidering the status of photography leads me to suggest that it is not an either/or proposition, but simultaneously literary and pictorial. By extension, the cultural value of images depends on both sides of the argument being available and operable at the same time.

Whether as advertising or journalism, as documentation or illustration, a cave painting or the latest in digital technology, images will always project onto our psyches evidence of some presence as well as a correspondence to a seemingly material (even if non-existent) world of perception. Current photographic criticism and theory has attempted to distance itself from earlier commentators such as Benjamin for the constraints they are thought to have placed on photography via more obviously ideologically rooted discourses. Nevertheless, while a more specific and specialized vocabulary is emerging, the terms of reference used in photographic criticism have tended to remain tied to semiology and semiotics, the latter more adept at describing how signs have historically adapted and evolved into broader systems of signification. We have yet to form a clearly definable critical or theoretical language that is uniquely applicable to the visual. As digital photography and its variations evolve, what may come to define a photographic/visual language may be more akin to the language of cognitive sciences and, I would suggest, to the exploratory interstices of literary language. While I do not mean here to suggest what that language might be, the works I cite could be considered ones that provide the loose schema of a possible plan for developing such a language. In this chapter, therefore, I demonstrate that photography is a technology particularly suited to the development of visual consciousness in and through literature.

A Case of Appearances

Photography's literary possibilities have inspired writers since its invention. Italian culture seems to have been shaped by a visual proclivity that today is known as "Italian style," and Italian writers have been influenced by visual media. *Verismo* and neorealism, Renaissance and Baroque, contemporary fashion and classical design all seem to have emerged out of a sociopolitically conscious desire to state and restate a position or an event visually as a way to ensure its survival. Neorealism and *verismo*, for example, emphasize an objective reporting of reality that takes as a starting point its restatement. It may be useful to note, however, that what neorealism and *verismo* share that is illustrative of the power of images is their historical specificity. Each period's pressing historical issues make something expressible, knowable, and, in terms of this essay, visible (even in writing). Recognizing the temporal distance that separates the periods I have named from the invention of photography, I would even suggest that the passage from the painterly to the photographic, from the pigments of painting to those of inkjet printers, reflects an evolutionary continuum that represents shifts and advances in both technology and imaginative rendering. The visual apparatus that is the eye remains throughout unmodified; its intuitive and recording capabilities are merely retrained by the culture at hand.

Italo Calvino, perhaps Italy's premier novelist of the late twentieth century, stands out as an important commentator on the media. His position regarding the effectiveness of visual (including photographic) and linguistic representation in relation to our feeble attempts to fix meaning in the world is always decidedly ambiguous and, in this way, he expresses the contemporary age's struggle with visual technology's perceived promises of literalness. Calvino explicitly addresses the importance of the literary visual in the essay "Visibilità" ("Visibility"), a section of *Lezioni Americane: Sei proposte per il prossimo millennio* (*American Lessons: Six Proposals for the Next Millenium*).[1]

The author's thoughts on the origins, workings, and effects of images begin with a consideration of none other than Dante, who attempts a definition of "imagination" in six verses of "Purgatory XVII":

O imaginativa che ne rube
tal volta sí di fuor, ch'om non s'accorge
perché dintorno suonin mille tube,
chi move te, se 'l senso non ti porge?
Moveti lume che nel ciel s'informa,
per sé o per voler che giú lo scorge. (13–18)

O imagination, which sometimes steals us
So far from external things, which we do not notice
Since a thousand trumpets sound about us,
Who moves you, if the senses yield you nothing?
Light formed in heaven moves you,
Of its own or by the will that guides it down.

At this point in his journey, Dante *viator* begins to experience a differentiation in his perception of images: some he sees with his eyes, others he experiences directly as mental images. While the former are supposedly "objective" or unconditioned images of reality that one registers in viewing the world, the latter are projected or received directly onto/by one's mind without any external referent. Calvino points out that Dante the pilgrim (as opposed to Dante the writer) experiences everything in the latter form, which would seem to imply that the visual part of the imagination is either "precedente o contemporanea all'immaginazione verbale" (either precedes or is simultaneous to verbal imagination; 93).

Italian literary tradition from Dante Alighieri to Francesco Petrarca, to Alessandro Manzoni, to Giovanni Verga, to Calvino himself, and on to contemporary writers like Gianni Celati, has consistently assigned an obvious primacy to visuality or visibility. The function of the eye in Petrarch is clearly illustrated throughout his *Canzoniere* (*The Canzoniere*), and the sometimes detailed descriptions of it resemble those of the mechanical recording apparatus that will be the camera (*lucida* and *obscura*). Manzoni's "opening sequence" of *I promessi sposi* (*The Betrothed*) is an exemplary photographic zooming in on the landscape and an influential prototype of what we might call a photo-literary trope:

> Quel ramo del lago di Como, che volge a mezzogiorno, tra due catene non interrotte di monti, tutto a seni e a golfi, a seconda dello sporgere e del rientrare di quelli, vien, quasi a un tratto, a ristringersi, e a prender corso e figura di fiume, tra un promontorio a destra, e un'ampia costiera dall'altra parte; e il ponte, che ivi congiunge le due rive, par che renda ancor più sensibile all'occhio questa trasformazione, e segni il punto in cui il lago cessa, e l'Adda rincomincia, per ripigliar poi nome di lago dove le rive, allontanandosi di nuovo, lascian l'acqua distendersi e rallentarsi in nuovi golfi e in nuovi seni. (5)

> That part of the lake of Como, that winds south, between two uninterrupted chains of mountains, all fjords and gulfs, according to their exposure or seclusion, comes all of a sudden to a narrow, and continues along as if it were a river, between a hill on one side and a wide open coast on the other; and the bridge that connects the two shores, it seems to make this transformation even more sensitive to the eye, and marks the point at which the lake ceases to be and the Adda begins again, where it will once more become a lake where the shores, again distant, allow the water to stretch out and slow down in new gulfs and new fjords.

The introductory section of *I promessi sposi* is an attentive framing of geographic points of reference that lead the reader to speculate, in the visual sense, on the meaning of landscape as a patrimony both literary and cultural. "Par che renda ancor più sensibile all'occhio questa trasformazione" (It seems to make this transformation even more sensitive to the eye) expresses Manzoni's speculative visual sensibility, which he wishes to share with his readers. He taps into it through the description of a landscape – a description that, while impressively rendered, is also an effective means for garnering adherence to his "vision," given its familiarity to those who read it.

Giovanni Verga, who was also a photographer, constructed a narrative "modality" that Epifanio Ajello suggests in *Il racconto delle immagini: La fotografia nella modernità letteraria italiana* (*The Tale of Images: Photography in Italian Literary Modernity*) was akin to that of taking a photograph. Ajello takes the 1881 novel *I Malavoglia* (*The House by the Medlar Tree*) as his primary example of this Sicilian author's modality. He observes that "tutta l'introduzione del Verga a *I Malavoglia* sembra passare attraverso la metafora fotografica, a sua volta intercettata mediante altrettanti sinonimi, se il registro del *riprodurre* (scientificamente) è poi al fondo del discorso prefativo" (the whole of Verga's introduction to *The House by the Medlar Tree* seems to be filtered through a photographic metaphor, in turn interpolated through other synonyms, if the *reproductive* register in scientific terms is at the bottom of the pre-factual discourse; 35, emphasis in original).

However, this visual modality is also strongly evident in Verga's writings before *I Malavoglia*. I would, in fact, suggest that within the realist canon and that of *verismo* in particular, Verga's visual modality was his signature trait. Short stories such as "La Lupa" ("The She-Wolf") (1880) and "Fantasticheria" ("Fantasizing") (1878) offer a vivid visual landscape that handles the narrative much as one might a zoom lens. Beginning from positions of distance and remove, which suggest an observer's cultural and social distance from the characters in the stories, there is a progressive closing in towards more detailed descriptions that lead to an intimate acknowledgment of their plight.

The following excerpt from "Fantasticheria" gives a sense of the initial, distant view that first catches the eye of those foreign to the place. What is interesting about this particular passage is that it also turns the gaze back upon the privileged viewers, who, witnessing the spectacle, become themselves subjects of curiosity. This is indeed a unique representation of agency, one not easily or often made apparent in relation to marginalized classes and populations:

> Una volta, mentre il treno passava vicino ad Aci-Trezza, voi, affacciandovi allo sportello del vagone, esclamaste: – Vorrei starci un mese laggiù! – Noi vi ritornammo, e vi passammo non un mese, ma quarantott'ore; i terrazzani che spalancavano gli occhi vedendo i vostri grossi bauli avranno creduto che ci sareste rimasta un par d'anni. (67)

> Once, when the train passed by Aci Trezza, you looked out the car window and said: – I'd like to spend a month down there! – We returned, and spent not a month but forty-eight hours there; the people of the town watched with great big eyes as we unloaded our trunks. They must have thought that you had come to settle there for a few years.

The Self-Consciousness of the Image Maker

The effects of photography as a literary medium are more than evident in Verga and in others whom I have cited as examples, but I return to the work of more contemporary writers such as Italo Calvino and Gianni Celati for photo-literary examples of a more radical and incisive expression.

The use of "self-consciousness" here does not refer only to those who make visual images, mechanically or otherwise. In keeping with the Dantean "vision" cited by Calvino in his *Lezione*, I intend such a description to apply to all image manifestations, regardless of media, materiality, or temporal stability and duration. Self-consciousness is the driver of one's imagination. In Calvino's *Palomar* (*Mr Palomar*) (1983), Mr Palomar displays a curiosity that leads him (Palomar) not only to observe what is in front of him but also to visually and mentally record it and then speculate on the phenomena. This is representative of a self-consciousness whereby the world is recognized not just as comprised of images and objects but as a series of processes of which we humans are an integral part. The receptive/perceptive apparatus that is the body is brought into a state of self-recognition by this marked sense of belonging or self-consciousness. As I will show, this is certainly what happens to Antonino, the protagonist of Calvino's "L'avventura di un fotografo" ("The Adventure of a Photographer"), even as he at first attempts to use the photographic image as a shield against the undeniable conclusion.

Calvino is prominent among those literary figures who concern themselves with the influence of the visual. Indeed, in his writings he is always teasing the fabric of appearances not to find the "real" or the "true" but to question our assumptions about what is "real" or "true." "Visibilità" sheds some light on the writer's extensive relationship with the visual and the function he assigns to it as an innovative cultural element:

> Torniamo alla problematica letteraria, e chiediamoci come si forma l'immaginario di un'epoca in cui la letteratura non si richiama più a un'autorità o a una tradizione come sua origine o come suo fine, ma punta sulla novità, l'originalità, l'invenzione. Mi pare che in questa situazione il problema della priorità dell'immagine visuale o dell'espressione verbale (che è un po' come il problema dell'uovo e della gallina) inclini decisamente dalla parte dell'immagine visuale. (97)

> Returning to the literary problem, let's ask ourselves how the imaginary of an era is formed in which literature no longer looks to an authority or a tradition as its origin or end, but stakes everything on novelty, originality, and invention. I think that in such a situation the problem of the primacy of the visual image or verbal expression (which is after all a little like the chicken-and-egg problem) leans most decidedly toward the visual image.

Situating visual images as the primary generators of words makes them brilliantly and inexorably literary. The only restriction on the process of literary composition that is possible through images is that it arises from our desire to know all their potential associations. Calvino's meditation on the function of the image leads him to recognize that when an "immagine è diventata abbastanza netta nella mia mente, mi metto a svilupparla in una storia, o meglio, sono le immagini stesse che sviluppano le loro potenzialità implicite, il racconto che esse portano dentro di sè" (image has become abundantly clear in my mind, I begin to develop it into a story, or rather, the images themselves begin to develop their own implicit potential, the stories they carry within themselves; 100). Stated as such, "Visibilità" recalls Calvino's preface to his first novel, *Il sentiero dei nidi di ragno* (*The Path to the Nest of Spiders*) (1947): "I set out from that urchin character, from an element of direct observation of reality" (xv).[2]

The relations among *The Path to the Nest of Spiders*, neorealism, and *verismo* have been made rather clear by literary critics, but not the less direct line to photography. Yet it should not require much of a stretch to open up to just such a relationship. And I would even suggest that a photographic, or phototropic, sense of image making – a "photo-literary" trope, if you will – extends as far back in Italian literature as Dante and Petrarch, in whose works the play of light, and the emphasis on seeing and on the projective power of images (not to mention the photosynthetic capabilities of the vegetation that is omnipresent in their verses, often standing in lieu of their loved ones and finally crowning their achievements as laurels), become photo-literary tropes *par excellence*.

Calvino's *The Path to the Nest of Spiders* is a fantasy-laden reminiscence of the days of partisan warfare seen through the eyes of an imaginative nine-year-old boy. The result is far from the nitty-gritty realism we might anticipate. However, given that the novel carries the weight of the "neorealist" label, Calvino thought it important to return to it in successive editions by providing an explicative introduction.

In post–Second World War Italy, *The Path to the Nest of Spiders* sought to construct a collective response to past history and to propose new directions for a historicized future. Calvino declares that the novel was "born anonymously" (v): "this is what especially touches us today; the anonymous voice of that time, stronger than our still-uncertain individual reflections" (v). Even as his desire to write a book situated in "a literature of the Resistance" (xi) necessitated a rebellion against the conformism of Fascism and the residues of "right-minded respectability" (xiii), by his own declarations he seems to have intended to downplay an ideological point of view, by writing through an anonymous persona representative of a collective identity.

The collectivity idealized by Calvino and others during that period does, however, create a contrast with the very form of the work and its preface, in which Calvino uses techniques that will reappear in all his other works: reiteration and recapitulation. We find in the preface at least six new or false starts that rhetorically support the attempt "to get it right" and that, as such, illustrate the historical moment and cultural activity of his generation. Nevertheless, even as Calvino continues to stress the collective aspect of his exercise, he emphasizes that "*neorealism* was not a school" (vii, emphasis in original). He proposes that the dominant trait of neorealism may be "a contamination or constraint suffered by literature for extra-literary reasons, … a collection of voices, largely marginal, a multiple discovery of the various Italies, even – or particularly – the Italies previously unknown to literature" (vii).[3]

However, Calvino also differentiates the "realism" of his national project of the postwar period from that of Verga. The line we draw between Verga's regional realism (Sicilian) and Calvino's national realism is between *verist* detail and imaginative anonymity. By no means is this meant to diminish Verga's contribution to neorealist filmmaking, which defined national character through its diverse and decentralized sense of culture.

Calvino's episodic style could be seen as amounting to snapshot iterations of particular situations or actions that revisit and re-view the narration and its writing almost obsessively. It is as if he were taking the same photograph from different angles. This technique reveals how stories change as they are passed from person to person, thus undermining the notion of "getting it right" while further accentuating a collective participation in the telling of history. The definition of "snapshot" given in *Looking at Photographs: A Guide to Technical Terms*, a publication of the J. Paul Getty Museum, is rather simple and straightforward: "This term applies to an informal and apparently unposed and instantaneous photograph, usually made by an amateur, without artistic intention and as a keepsake of persons, places, or events" (Baldwin 76). This is paralleled in Calvino's narratives by the use of instantaneous frames that seem unrelated because of their discontinuity. The photographic snapshots composed by our author find their continuity in their viewer/narrator; thus they are snapshots not only in form but, most importantly, in the changes in perspective and detail they reveal.

Although the snapshot is generally regarded as something usually made by an amateur, it has staked its own ground in the art world as a genre. The photographs we take for ourselves are valuable more for their context than for their aesthetic qualities. Outside of that context, which has its particular code of meaning within a familial circumstance, a specific event, or a situation, the snapshot offers what may turn out to be rather little in terms of meaningful content for an external and unrelated viewer. Calvino's snapshot narratives find their context in a subjective viewer or in parameters that require effort on the part of the viewer/reader. Books such as *Le città invisibili* (*Invisible Cities*) (1974), *Se una notte d'inverno un viaggiatore* (*If on a Winter's Night a Traveller*) (1979), *Palomar* (*Mr Palomar*) (1983), and even *Il sentiero dei nidi di ragno* (*The Path to the Nest of Spiders*) (1947) challenge definitive and completely intelligible identities through a layering of representations. The people, events, and places in these works can only be the blurred images of stories in constant flux.

Aware that readers seek direction and conclusiveness in what they read, Calvino writes about the "remorse" he feels for having distorted reality. Nevertheless, his distortions are liberating in that they are meant to remove the veil of an overriding authoritative narrative. By providing a variety of possible entries into and exits from the work, Calvino's layered descriptions make each narrative that much more immediate. They also dilute any remnants of a sense of ideological partisanship:

> I will have to start this preface once more, from the beginning. I have not yet got it right. From what I have said, it would seem that, writing this book, I had the whole thing quite clear in my mind: the reasons, arguments, the adversaries to combat, the poetic to sustain ... Instead, if all this was there, it was still in a confused, shapeless stage. Actually the book came forth as if by chance; I started writing without a precise plot in mind. I set out from that urchin character, from an element of direct observation

> of reality, a way of moving, of speaking, of establishing a rapport with grownups. (*The Path* xv)

Successful as the approach was, it also underscored the impossibility of the task. Calvino's "failings" towards reality must be taken as the inherent failings of representation rather than those of the writer himself.

The blurred images of experience reside in the mnemonic device of repetition. Calvino links the visual to the written by identifying images and their repetition or progression as the basis of the written word.[4] If experiences and events were recollected within a definitive and singular narrative form, they would be doomed to be reconstructed falsely, whether in language or images:

> Memory – or rather experience, which is memory plus the wound it has left in you, plus the change it has worked in you that has made you different – experience, first nourishment also of literary work (but not only of that), true wealth for the writer (but not only for him), now, as soon as it has given shape to a literary work, declines, is destroyed. The writer finds himself once again the poorest of men. (*The Path* xxiv)

One of today's most common digital formats, the jpeg (joint photographic experts group), works much like a memory bank, serving as an illustration and metaphor for the notion that what is represented is partly destroyed through its re-membrance or reconstitution as a saved memory. Every time jpeg images are opened, viewed, and reviewed, the data are resampled and reorganized to render the pixels into a discernible image. This process slightly degrades the data, and the image is partly altered every time it is re-membered. Calvino's realism is similar to this modern-day process for storing visual memories. As an expression of realism, a statement of possible narrative effacement may constitute a sort of theory of relativity of literature and culture that has influenced much of Italian society since the immediate postwar period.

"L'avventura di un fotografo" ("The Adventure of a Photographer"), from Calvino's collection *Gli amori difficili* (*Difficult Loves*) (1970), is the story of Antonino Paraggi. An employee in a small firm, Antonino is unmarried and decidedly not a photographer, and "per atteggiamento mentale, un filosofo" (by intellectual proclivity, a philosopher; 50). Everyone around him appears to live for the photographs they have taken during their weekends, images that will give them "tangibile possesso della giornata trascorsa" (tangible possession of the day; 49).

Feeling more and more isolated, Antonino undertakes the task of analysing the situation. He concludes that the "secret" of everyone's fascination with photography must be found somewhere beyond their mere personal ability or the technical advances that yield increasingly better results (50).

Antonino also notices that as his friends marry and start families, their interest in photography grows. The association of photography with paternity suggests that the desire to photograph may somehow be a physiological response: "la passione dell'obiettivo nasce in modo naturale e quasi fisiologico come effetto secondario della paternità" (the passion for photography arises in a natural and almost physiological manner as a secondary affect to paternity; 50). What better way for photography to declare its authenticity than by "marrying" itself to physiological pro-creation?

As photography and creation come together in Antonino's perception, his rejection of the mechanical medium distracts him from the fact that he is not married and not procreating. It veils the fact that he lacks not only photographs to document the stages of his life but also the very subject matter that marks a conventional life. As the only bachelor in his circle of acquaintances, he is often asked to take a photograph of his friends' family groups – something he relishes as a way to sabotage what he considers a foolish attempt at halting reality. The action he takes in such cases is to cut off the heads of his subjects as he frames them. Antonino attempts to warn his friends that their attitude can only lead to the insane notion that "tutto ciò che non è fotografato è perduto, che è come se non fosse esistito" (all that is not photographed is lost, and it's as if it had never existed; 52), but to no avail. Calvino here is suggesting, through Antonino's actions, that it is impossible to engage photography – or at least single photographs – as a residual memory. The photographic act, the attempt to fill in every lived gap with a photographic record, itself becomes an expression of memory. As such it is continuously and constantly unsatisfying.

"The Adventure of a Photographer" refers directly to photography's function as a social or socializing practice. Besides establishing a sense of memory – one that is threatened with dilution with each passing moment – Antonino's photographing of his acquaintances serves to reentrench and solidify their participation in maintaining what has come to represent a fundamental and normative element in their society: the family. This is important, given the historical moment at which Calvino is writing – the postwar reconstruction period and the beginning of the economic boom, a period during which the basic family unit stood for the rooted certainties that had been brought into question by Fascism (although Fascism had manipulated this very same standard to its own ends). Even as the association of photography with the physiological function of reproduction leads to the acknowledged victory of convention – something that determines Antonino's failure and his friends' victory – our "hero" succeeds in the rather revolutionary act of establishing that theirs is but an ephemeral victory.

Narrare narrando: To Narrate by Narrating

Closer to us chronologically, Gianni Celati's engagement with photography is evident in his snapshot-type narratives. *Quattro novelle sulle apparenze* (*Four Stories on Appearances*) (1987) and *Narratori delle pianure* (*Voices from the Plains*) (1985) offer narratives that allow the reader to linger over landscapes and stories that have already left photo-literary traces of themselves in the writer. Not surprisingly, Celati had a longtime collaborative friendship with the photographer Luigi Ghirri, whose work could be considered a visual correlative of Celati's.

Gianni Celati is arguably the most visually interested and active contemporary Italian writer today; some consider him to be Calvino's heir.[5] Although Celati would probably be the first to deny a long-term attachment to any one place, his geographical relationship is to central Italy. Emilia-Romagna and the cities of Bologna and Reggio-Emilia (the latter through his friendship with Ghirri) have shaped Celati's visual literary horizon and vocabulary. While his writings and projects have moved him all over the world, he has had a long and close working relationship with the Po River region.

Early on, Celati's work began to play with notions of unknowing and uncertainty; this necessitated a shift from conventional realist forms and literary genres. His explorations of various forms of expression have led him to embrace the term *avventura* ("adventure") to signify what will come in the future.

Narratori delle pianure (1985) represents a close engagement with particular landscapes and their inhabitants. Celati lends his ear to geography for this book's narrative, dedicating it "a quelli che mi hanno raccontato storie, molte delle quali sono qui trascritte" (to those who have told me stories, many of which are transcribed herein; 7). We are left to consider what this rather Verghian declaration might mean in the context of the arc of time – approximately 150 years – during which photography and the written word have alternated or corresponded in their assertions to be faithfully representing facts, peoples, and events.

Landscape offers a highly effective place from which to begin an exploration of knowing and unknowing, seeing and observing, belonging and not belonging. Celati's interest in the conundrum of what it means to be *of* a place finds just the sort of unstable ground he can appreciate in the kindred work of Ghirri. Just as Celati's writing travels towards and within a narrative of what he calls "finzioni a cui credere" (believable fictions) (Sironi 175), Ghirri's photography sets out to narrate the spaces of Emilia-Romagna. Because there is so little of it, space in Italy is the expression of a contradiction and a fiction. In general terms, appearances define the cardinal points by which we orient ourselves within a place, and it is through the thread of appearances, through the suturing of appearances as narrative, that we experience and define that place.

Celati's writing hints at the presence of the border between adventure (what is to come) and familiarity (what is): a border that is not trespassed and that retains a sense of ambiguous in-betweenness rather than division. The writer/observer's task is to attempt to make apparent that which is *celato* (unapparent) in that border.

My pun on Celati's name is meant to be more than just a clever instance of fortuitous correspondence; it actually points to the writer's approach to writing as a mode of photography and thus his close relationship to Ghirri's work. The approximation of Celati to *celato* is indicative of his view of language as a place in which

> non facciamo altro che citare la nostra appartenenza a un terreno comune, quello del parlare, dei legami verbali, e del sentito dire delle parole in cui siamo immersi. È ciò che ci costituisce, l'ovvietà, che possiamo anche chiamare abitudine, habitus, terreno o tradizione. (Sironi 30)

> we do nothing more than quote our belonging to a common terrain, that of the spoken, of linguistic ties, and of the said words in which we are submerged. And that which constitutes us, the obvious, which we could also refer to as habit, habitus, terrain or tradition.

Celati made the above observation in the context of a conference on Calvino held shortly after the latter's death. Celati reads Calvino's *Palomar* as an expression of writing that has reached beyond the point of knowledge, writing that has become a point of observation and renarration rather than authoring. Mr Palomar's observations of commonplace events situate him as an observer rather than a participant or initiator. While those observed events add up to the world in which *Palomar* is situated, that world becomes apparent only when one stops to look. Celati seems to be suggesting that in the familiar we find the obvious and that the obvious appears as a novelty when we finally open our eyes and pay attention. What is hidden is right before our eyes; it only requires a direct engagement with the present moment and the present situation in order to be seen.

Calvino's "Visibility" therefore also becomes useful in reading Celati for his own emphasis on the visible as a place in which to situate a culture that is seeking to establish itself in relation to the authoritative voice of tradition. The visible may be a place where language loses its primacy, so that the visual becomes a point of reference that carries all the hidden but obvious messages that the literal might well seek to rhetorically veil. Celati and Calvino distance themselves from those cultural impositions that they see as conditioning their vision of place, language, literature, and citizenship. It may be no coincidence that both writers chose at some point in their lives to live outside of Italy while continuing to write in Italian.[6]

Celati's statements regarding place are quite interesting in how they delineate his writing. His novels, stories, commentaries, and documentaries author places only as they disappear from his perception. Having formed a temporary bond with them and then broken that bond – by either removing himself or being removed from them – words become the residue of a connection, the echo of experience, in much the same way that some words may be particularly evocative of a place (geographical or otherwise):

> Per pensare a un luogo devi poter pensare dei confini e delle differenze, e poi avere delle immagini di quello che succede entro quei confini [...]. Nel momento in cui qualcosa che vedo come un luogo sta per perdere i suoi connotati, l'essenza del luogo mi si rivela come uno spazio per certi incontri, con un'atmosfera, con certe facce, certe abitudini, che non saranno mai più quelle. [...]
>
> I rappresentanti del fanatismo territoriale vogliono sempre farci credere che qualcuno è installato nel suo posto naturale, e parla la sua lingua naturale, con radici che affondano nel suo terreno d'origine, come una specie di limbo dove niente va perso. (Celati, qtd in Sironi 226–7)

In order to think of a place you have to be able to think of its borders and its differences, and then have some images of what might happen within those borders … The moment in which something that I see as a place begins to lose its traits, the essence of it reveals itself to me as a space for encounters, with an atmosphere, with certain faces, with certain habits, that will never again be the same …

Those who are fanatically territorial would have us believe that someone is planted in his natural place, and speaks his natural language, with roots that go deep into some land of origin, like in some sort of limbo where nothing ever changes.

This last statement offers an opportunity to speculate on what constitutes and distinguishes literal from literary photography. Celati identifies the moment in which things begin "to lose [their] traits" as the opening for a more incisive and in-depth relationship with them, as a "space for encounters." This aperture, unhindered by labels and well-defined traits, is where the possibilities of meaning and being are amplified, where the literary resides. Contrast this with the literal, well-defined, and rooted expression that Celati relates to "fanatical" territoriality. This extension, even more expressive of the writer's preference for things "that will never again be the same" and are therefore unencumbered by definition, is also what brings him closer to the photographer Ghirri, whose photographs, Celati declares, "non documentano mai niente di preciso, soltanto ti *fanno vedere*" (never document anything specific; they merely *enable one to see*; 227, emphasis in original).

What do they enable one to see? Conveniently enough, Ghirri's sense of photography corresponds to Celati's sense of the function of literature. Ghirri states "che fotografare i luoghi ci dà la coscienza di trovarsi sempre al confine tra conosciuto e ignoto, questo ci indica la fine di un sentimento di appartenenza" (that to photograph a place makes one conscious of being always at the border between the known and the unknown, and this signifies the end of a sentiment of belonging; 201). Perhaps it is the instability of images that attracts these writers, whose sense of place depends both existentially and politically on the impermanence of narratives or on the open work:[7]

[Ghirri] dice che ogni foto […] in realtà rimanda ad un'altra foto già fatta o da fare, o ad altre immagini viste. La situazione è quella d'un racconto, che è composto di stati di contingenza, passaggi da un momento all'altro. Però se ogni momento è uno scarto rispetto al precedente che rinnova

> le aspettative, ogni momento rinnova la percezione di tutto il racconto. (Celati qtd in Sironi 178)
>
> [Ghirri] says that every photograph … actually recalls another photo, either existing or yet to be made, or other images one might have seen. The situation is the same as for a story, which is made up of contingencies, passages from one moment to another. However, if every moment is a choice made in relation to the preceding one which renews expectations, every moment renews how the story will be perceived.

Celati lends us the words through which we might reconsider the uses of photography when establishing national or cultural origins: "sotto o dentro ogni stabilità naturale sociale o familiare" (beneath or within every natural social or familiar stability; 50). Finding the origins, however, does not mean finding the point from which everything began but rather finding that movement that perpetuates social or familial stability.

At this point, it may be time to address an issue that is sure to have arisen: the apparent disregard for the differences between photography and cinematography and the emphasis I have placed on the photographic in the work of Calvino and Celati. To briefly address this point, I reiterate my earlier statement regarding the photo-literary in Dante and Petrarch. Recognizing the genre distinctions between painting, photography, and cinematography, the image-capturing techniques represent, in my view, the continual renewal of evolving techniques through the imaginative curiosity of cultural sophistication. It goes without saying, although I feel I must say it in order to pre-empt likely objections to the preceding statement, that each engages materials and expression differently, all the while also communicating in modes greatly different from one another. Perhaps my (mis)understanding stems from the fact that I tend to see little difference between pre-perspective painterly narratives, the photographs of Mario Giacomelli, and cinematographic narrative. Michelangelo Antonioni's film *Blow Up* (1966) collapses all of these categories in its sequencing of photo-stills as cinema within the film and is illustrative of the self-consciousness I have been outlining here.

In closing, I return to Luigi Ghirri, photographer, and Gianni Celati, writer and filmmaker, who in their individual and collaborative efforts have consistently blurred genre lines and restrictive dictates. Ghirri suggests that we might guardare alla fotografia come a un modo di relazionarsi col mondo, nel quale il segno di chi fa fotografia, quindi la sua storia personale, il suo rapporto con l'esistente, è sì molto forte, ma deve orientarsi, attraverso un lavoro sottile, quasi alchemico, all'individuazione di un punto di equilibrio tra la nostra interiorità – il mio interno fotografo-persona – e ciò che sta all'esterno, che vive al di fuori di noi, che continua a esistere senza di noi e continuerà a esistere anche quando avremo finito di fare fotografia. (21)

regard photography as a way in which to relate to the world, in which the sign of those who make photographs, in other words their personal history, their relationship with the existing world, is indeed very strong, but must be oriented, through subtle and almost alchemical work, to the identification of a point of equilibrium between our interior – my interior as photographer-person – and that which is outside, that lives outside of us, that continues to exist without us and will continue to exist even when we will have stopped making photographs.

Celati, in a description of his short story collection *Cinema naturale* (*Natural Cinema*), suggests that the shifts and alterations that take place in remembering and writing enact precisely that sort of blurring by which genre is negated and expression exalted: "scrivendo e leggendo dei racconti si vedono dei paesaggi, si vedono figure, si sentono voci: è un cinema naturale della mente" (writing and reading stories one can see landscapes, see figures, hear voices: it is a natural cinema of the mind; *Passar la vita* 154).

In *Passar la vita a Diol Kadd* (*Passing Life in Diol Kadd*), his diaries released with a DVD of the footage shot in Senegal between 2003 and 2006, Celati presents a scene that illustrates the ease with which the transition between genres, the undoing of a cinematographic sequence into its individual photographic frames, might take place:

Muran e Borsetti si sono dedicati a un lavoro di esposizione fotografica offerta al villaggio. Avevano raccolto un repertorio di foto delle signore di Diol Kadd, e ora le avevano incollate su una lunga parete di cannella palustre, lunga quanto la scuoletta di fronte. [...] è stata una serata bellissima, dove le signore potevano portarsi a casa la loro immagine ringraziando con gran sorrisi. (101)

Muran and Borsetti dedicated themselves to a photographic exhibition that they offered to the village. They had gathered a repertoire of

> photographic images of the ladies of Diol Kadd, and now had pasted them on a long wall of swamp cinnamon as long as the schoolhouse across the way ... It was a beautiful evening, where the ladies could take home their images thanking us with great smiles.

In other words, we would do well to look for the stories photography has to tell in its erratic moments, in the motion we discern within and beneath the apparently stable pictured moments, in the belated images of blurred subjects that make photography a literary art.

NOTES

1 All translations from the Italian texts in the body of this chapter are mine unless otherwise stated.

2 This quote, and all other quotes from *The Path to the Nest of Spiders,* are taken from the English translation by Colquhoun.

3 Without question, the "collective voice" of the Resistance was multifaceted with regard to its regional origins and political affiliations. This is clear in many works, fictional and not, dealing with that period. Among the best known is Roberto Rossellini's film *Rome, Open City* (1946), in which the Nazi commander Bergman tries without success to exploit the Resistance's internal differences to generate division among the ranks.

4 Calvino applies the same sense of decipherability and interpretation to reality and written narratives that he does to photography. This suggests the latter's terms of physiological function.

5 Ajello points to certain (consecutive) parallels between Calvino and Celati: "[Celati] anche lui, immerso in altre visioni [...] e nel tentativo di 'pensare con ordine': 'Si è disposti all'osservazione quando si ha voglia di mostrare ad altri quello che si vede. È il legame con gli altri che dà colori alle cose, le quali altrimenti appaiono smorte. C'è sempre il vuoto centrale dell'anima da arginare, per quello si seguono immagini viste o sognate, per raccontarle ad altri e respirare un po' meglio.'" ([Celati] too is immersed in other visions [...] and in the attempt to "think with order": "One is disposed to observation when one wants to show others what one sees. It is one's relationship with others that gives things their colour, which would otherwise seem dead. There is always the central emptiness of one's soul to overcome; that is why we follow seen or dreamed images, so as to tell others stories and breathe a little easier"; *Il racconto* 192. Celati began publishing in the 1970s, which places him in what might be considered an older generation.

Yet even among the multilayered, multimedial, omnivorous "cannibali" (cannibals) generation of writers or their younger manifestations, it is hard to find anyone who engages visuality so thoroughly.

6 To posit that language is unimportant for a writer is not to dismiss language; it is merely to comment on the notion of Italian as a language and on its history in the Italian literary tradition. This runs sharply against the many literary traditions that exist in Italy as a consequence of its various so-called dialects. In this context, Italian becomes a normative force and, possibly, an instrument of coercion.

7 See Umberto Eco's *Opera aperta* (*The Open Work*) (1968). Generally, in semiotics, an open text is one that allows multiple interpretations by the reader. For writers such as Celati and Calvino, photography's lure is precisely its multivalency – the possibility of inserting a photograph within any series of other photographs generates endless narrative and interpretative possibilities and lends photography a poetic edge.

3 Fossati's and Messori's Vision of Landscape in *Viaggio in un paesaggio terrestre*

MARINA SPUNTA

In this essay, I explore a recent phototext,[1] *Viaggio in un paesaggio terrestre* (*Journey on an Earthly Landscape*) by the photographer Vittore Fossati and the late writer Giorgio Messori, a text that successfully brings together different media, namely photography and writing, and that newly explores the ever-central and recently renewed debate on landscape and its representations. The coexistence of photography and writing in the text can be usefully inscribed within the growing and heterogeneous field of visual culture studies,[2] which includes interdisciplinary, intermedial, and intersemiotic studies, and, more specifically, within the renewed debate on writing and photography and on the different typologies of their interaction in a text.[3] As Silke Horstkotte and Nancy Pedri argue in the introduction to their special issue of *Poetics Today*, titled *Photography in Fiction*, intermedial/intersemiotic studies often differentiate between "manifest" and "hidden" intermedial references, that is, between the "actual combination of two media" and "the implicit evocation of one medium *within another*" (5, emphasis in original). It is the first modality – of the phototext or "iconotext" (Montandon 1990) – that is of interest here and that most clearly addresses the relation between photography and writing and the artists' aesthetic consonance. With their book, Messori and Fossati set out to "far dialogare fra loro immagini e parole" (engage in dialogue images and words; Fossati and Messori 10) by assigning equal importance on the page to writing and photography; in so doing, they seek to redress the clear-cut separation between image and word that has traditionally informed many photobooks.

While adding to the visual culture debate, *Viaggio in un paesaggio terrestre* makes an original contribution to the critical debate on landscape and to its artistic representations, which in the text span from the early modern period to the present day. In particular, this photo-text can be inscribed within the discussion on landscape, space, and place that since the 1970s has engaged many disciplines and arts as a preferred means of exploring the postmodern condition. This renewed debate – both within and outside Italy – is partly due to the intrinsic liminality of landscape, which can be analysed within different disciplines and from multiple critical perspectives, as Michele Di Monte convincingly argues in a recent special issue on landscape of *Rivista di estetica* (*Journal of Aesthetics*) (2005). In what follows, while drawing on other disciplines, such as geography and visual/cultural studies, I adopt a broadly aesthetic approach, one that recognizes the fundamentally aesthetic nature of landscape as "una distesa di paese abbracciato dallo sguardo di un soggetto" (a portion of a territory gazed by a subject; Jakob, *Il paesaggio* 30), and addresses notions of visuality, contemplation, and subjectivity that are key to the text and to its authors' poetics. This approach has been revitalized by recent theories of landscape, such as those of Italian philosophers Paolo D'Angelo and Luisa Bonesio, or English philosopher Emily Brady, all of whom, in different ways, take pains to emphasize the role played by imagination, memory, and affectivity in our experience of landscape, and all of whom stress the aesthetic value of any landscape, not just the "artistic" ones. This recent revival of the aesthetics of landscape draws on a long theoretical/aesthetic tradition that has explored the act of contemplating natural beauty – from Petrarch through German Romanticism to modern thinkers such as Benjamin or Joachim Ritter. In this essay, I suggest that Fossati's and Messori's work can be fruitfully inscribed within an aesthetic theory of landscape; this is both consonant with recent theories – specifically in their efforts to value any-places-whatsoever alongside "artistic" places and to highlight the intrinsically imaginative and affective nature of landscape – and also with more traditional aesthetic theories of landscape, such as those put forward by the above thinkers, all of whom are quoted in the book, and by the painters whose work is acknowledged in the text.

In particular, Messori and Fossati's approach to landscape can be fruitfully read through Benjamin's concepts of "experience" and "aura," which are key to his aesthetics (alongside the concepts of history and the *flâneur*). These seem to underpin *Viaggio in un paesaggio terrestre*, coming to the fore most prominently in the final chapter, where his thought is openly acknowledged. Benjamin's influence on Messori and Fossati is not coincidental; rather, it stems from the growing interest in his thought in Europe and in Italy since the 1970s and 1980s, when his work began to be translated and edited more systematically.[4] Messori studied Benjamin at length as part of his philosophy degree at the University of Bologna. According to one of his close friends, Pietro Bevilacqua, he attended two courses on Benjamin in 1974 and 1975: the first of these on the "artwork essay" with Luciano Anceschi, as part of his course on aesthetics, and the second on the concept of aura with Fernando Bollino, Anceschi's research assistant at the time. Both courses deeply impressed Messori, who continued to study Benjamin after completing his degree. This interest led him to Luigi Ghirri and Gianni Celati, two prominent Italian artists and intellectuals, who in those years were engaged in a close dialogue with Benjamin's aesthetics, as is evidenced in Celati's fiction from the mid-1980s, starting with his stories *Narratori delle pianure* (*Voices from the Plains*) (1985) and his project *Narratori delle riserve* (*Voices from the Reserves*) (1992), and in many of Ghirri's individual and collaborative works, such as the seminal *Viaggio in Italia* (*A Journey through Italy*) (1984). These and other projects – some of which, as we will see, involved Messori and Fossati – were informed by an effort to recover and give voice to individual everyday experiences that had been excluded from the literary/artistic canon and to preserve and pass on a sense of collective experience and cultural rootedness that was deemed to be threatened in postmodernity, that is, in an increasingly globalized and media-saturated society. Similar intentions inform Messori and Fossati's photo-text, which draws on the lessons of Celati and Ghirri and on Benjamin's aesthetics in an effort to recover a sense of "experience"[5] in the Benjaminian sense of *Erfahrung*, as the experience of privileged, "auratic" inwardness, which results from everyday life and artisanal labour and from there can migrate into aesthetic "experience" in front of the artwork. As opposed to *Erlebnis*, which Benjamin saw as the directly lived "shock" experience of modernity and of the New, *Erfahrung* links the self to the world and vice versa (Weber 236), thus allowing one to locate oneself historically in space and time. This experience is no longer possible in modernity, for modern urban life has severed a deep connection with the exterior and with tradition. Like Ghirri and Celati before them, Fossati and Messori take stock of the epochal shift of postmodernity, seeing it in the light of Benjamin's reflections on modernity – more specifically, as a loss of a shared culture acquired through practical knowledge and artisanal labour that can no longer be passed down through generations, given the present scarcity of cultural communities that are bound by the same values. Echoing

Benjamin's "self-consciously heterogeneous and anti-systematic" approach (Schmitz 160), Messori experiments with a hybrid, fragmented prose that cuts across genres and allows for contemplation, for a "rallentamento dell'esperienza" (a slowing down of experience; La Porta, n. pag.). This results in narrations that, in Belpoliti's words in a letter to Messori, "partono sempre da tue esperienze e lì ritornano [dando vita a una] modalità di scrittura [...] molto rara" (always start from your own personal experiences and return there [giving rise to] a very rare modality of writing; 204). Similarly, in his work, Fossati reflects on Benjamin's notion of experience and on the link between the individual and the landscape (as each serves to define the other) by exploring both literary landscapes and places in general, which he turns into aesthetically pleasing sites through his photographs so that they can speak to everyone. In so doing, both Fossati and Messori closely follow the example of Ghirri, whose photographs, according to Messori, "più che i luoghi stessi, [...] suggerivano l'esperienza che si può fare di un luogo" (rather than the actual places ... suggested how one can experience a place; "Il mio incontro" 103). With these words, Messori points to the ground-breaking nature of Ghirri's photography, which for the first time spoke to the viewers' personal experience of places, thus reclaiming a space for the individual in contemporary cultural practice while at the same time recognizing the value of a shared tradition that both Messori and Ghirri deemed to be vanishing in postmodernity.

Aura, like experience, is a key concept in Benjamin's aesthetics and is equally complex. According to Richard Wolin, aura in Benjamin's thought refers "to the customary historical role played by works of art in the cultural legitimization of traditional social formations" (187), a role that Benjamin saw as threatened in modernity by the loss of an unmediated sense of experience owing to the onset of mechanical modes of reproduction and of artistic practice, such as film and photography. For Benjamin, film and photography, being based on technical reproduction, do not have an aura, that is, a unique presence in space and time of the sort that grants authenticity to artworks such as paintings and that links them back to art's mythical origins. In "A Short History of Photography," Benjamin defined aura as "a strange weave of space and time: singular appearance of distance, however near it may be. Resting on a summer afternoon, following the line of a mountain on the horizon, or a twig, which casts its shadow on the viewer, until the moment or the hour takes part in its appearance – that is to breathe the aura of these mountains, of this twig" (trans. and qtd in Lesley 51).[6] Here, aura is posited in terms of distance–closeness – that is, temporal distance (of memory) and spatial closeness of a landscape view – and its ephemeral nature is rendered as an "apparition." As we will see, this is a prominent theme in Messori's description of landscape, one that emerges most clearly in the chapters on Courbet and on Cézanne (see below). According to Lesley, Benjamin defined aura "as the fruit of the experience of someone who sinks into a panorama and forgets activity, adopting a contemplative attitude to nature ... To breathe the aura means to experience perception in terms of a moment, an *Augenblick*, when subject and object seem to be indistinguishable and united" (51–2). This position is consonant with the one adopted and described by Messori, who in the book embraces a contemplative approach and emphasizes the inherently contingent nature of all perception. Benjamin endowed the auratic object or landscape with the capacity to respond to the human gaze, to look back, that is, to enter into a dialogue with a subject – in his words, "to perceive the aura of an object we look at means to invest it with the ability to look at us in return" (*Illuminations* 190). This testifies to the object's power to attract the subject's gaze and thereby trigger memories and imagination; it also suggests the key role played by landscape in the formation of human subjectivity. Similarly, Fossati and Messori in their text celebrate the connection established with the landscape and with works of art that can reproduce auratic views. However, while Benjamin believed the dialogue between subject and object to be threatened by mechanical reproduction, which he saw as a one-way process that signalled the end of an era, as presaging the decay of the aura and of a society that values artists and original artworks, Fossati and Messori do not dismiss photography. Rather, they investigate how it engages with literature and with landscape and how it can be used to create and preserve both a sense of individual, everyday experience and an auratic effect in contemporary society. It can do so by reawakening a shared imagination, which in medieval times, according to Agamben in *Infanzia e storia* (*Infancy and History*) (18), was synonymous with experience, with sharing a sense of humanity by realizing one's place in the world – a point that Messori makes cogently in the book's conclusion.[7]

As I will demonstrate, *Viaggio in un paesaggio terrestre* is consonant with Benjamin's aesthetics, particularly with the notions of experience and aura, in that it puts forward a similarly contemplative approach to the exterior (in this case, landscape) that seeks to rediscover its beauty and artistic value by re-establishing an equal dialogue between the subject – a sensitive onlooker who is deeply in tune with the history of a place and of its artistic representations – and the object, which is endowed with a special beauty as an "apparition" in a specific time and place. Drawing on Benjamin, Fossati and Messori aim for a contemplative state that allows viewers to experience and narrate the landscapes they have chosen, to capture the beauty both of the physical landscapes and of their literary and artistic representations, and to auratize these places through the photographic and literary renditions they offer. In their efforts to resurrect this auratic effect, the authors lament the passing of the pre-modern era, which was based on a deep connection with landscape and attached a high value to landscape and to art as somewhat removed from contingency. At the same time, they embrace the postmodern condition of displacement, aware that it is impossible for them to find the actual landscape they are looking for. Interestingly, instead of accusing photography of destroying the artwork's aura, the authors set out to show how photography and literature can interact to establish a closer dialogue with landscape and to reproduce an auratic effect that is consonant with the postmodern age. The text's originality is to be found in the dialogue it establishes between photography and literature on the theme of landscape, in the gap it bridges between modern and postmodern aesthetic sensibilities, and in its effort to convey the aura not just of already "canonized" landscapes but of any places whatsoever as experienced by an individual – namely, landscapes that can equally well convey the subject's struggle to find his or her own place in the world through a sense of having achieved peace with nature and of stepping outside of time into the realm of art.

Drawing on the critical approaches outlined above, I will explore how, through a variety of intertextual references, *Viaggio in un paesaggio terrestre* builds a notion of landscape on the foundation of coexisting personal and cultural memories. Carrying forward a long tradition of landscape representation, the text places great emphasis on vision, particularly on the close examination of everyday reality; on contemplation, that is, reflection built on an empathetic relation to landscape; and on imagination, which is posited as essential to real vision and as intrinsic to landscape representation. A striking feature of the book is its close engagement with places that have become renowned as a result of their literary or artistic representations, such as Giacometti's Engadina, Courbet's Jura, Petrarch's Mount Ventoux, the ideal city of Chaux, Cézanne's Sainte-Victoire, Vermeer's Delft, Friedrich's Pomerania, and Capri. Each of these places is the subject of a chapter, starting with the second chapter. The book also explores – indeed, opens with – a non-descript place: the landscape around Villa Minozzo, in the Apennines of Reggio Emilia (Messori's place of birth). In so doing, it collapses any clear-cut distinction between everyday and literary places, thus highlighting the aesthetic nature of every place. In an introductory essay on this text, I have argued that the book's novelty lies in that it both revisits the Western literary and artistic tradition of landscape representation and redresses the relationship between image and word on the page (Spunta, "Fossati's and Messori's" 104–22). I have also demonstrated that, while following the teachings of the above-mentioned masters of European painting and literature, Messori and Fossati draw on Celati's lesson and particularly that of Ghirri in order to forge their own aesthetics of affectivity and re-enchantment, an aesthetics that seeks to rediscover beauty in marginal objects and vanishing places. Building on all of this, I will analyse in greater detail four chapters that I believe are key to Messori and Fossati's book as well as three photographs that powerfully convey both the book's aesthetics and its dialogue between image and word. I will discuss the authors' vision of landscape as it emerges particularly in the juxtaposition of "real" and imagined landscapes, in the frequent intertextuality with the artistic representations of the chosen literary places, and in the consonance between the written and photographic texts.

To understand what Fossati and Messori are seeking to achieve in *Viaggio in un paesaggio terrestre*, it is necessary to explain how they came to work on this project and to situate it in the context of their aesthetics and of the renewed attention to landscape and to the dialogue between photography and literature in Italy since the 1980s. Messori and Fossati met in 1984 through Ghirri[8] when both were invited to a conference on landscape representation in Reggio Emilia. This resulted in the collaborative work *Esplorazioni sulla via Emilia* (*Explorations on the Via Emilia*), an ambitious project co-edited by Giorgio Bizzarri and Eleonora Bronzoni that involved photographers and writers, as well as geographers and economists, in a close observation and narration of the *Via Emilia* and of the traces of its past.[9] The encounter with Ghirri and the growing attention on landscape had a deep impact on both authors' aesthetics, which emerged as they started working together in the late 1990s on *Viaggio in un paesaggio terrestre*. All of this is testified by Fossati, who, in his presentation at the photographic exhibition in Castelnovo ne' Monti (Reggio Emilia) in March 2008, stated that this book originated in their desire to "riprendere dei ragionamenti interrotti con la morte di Ghirri" (continue a dialogue that was interrupted by Ghirri's death). Besides this seminal work, Fossati and Messori collaborated on other projects led by Ghirri. In particular, Fossati contributed to the influential work *Viaggio in Italia* (1984), which redirected contemporary Italian photography towards nondescript, everyday places and which had a clear impact on *Viaggio in un paesaggio terrestre,* starting with the title itself. Messori worked with Ghirri in Giorgio Morandi's studio on *Atelier Morandi* (1992), for which he wrote an insightful essay titled "Le mattine del mondo: L'incontro di Luigi Ghirri con l'opera di Giorgio Morandi" ("The Mornings of the World: Luigi Ghirri's Encounter with Giorgio Morandi's Work").

Having been influenced by Ghirri, Fossati and Messori came to share a keen interest in place and landscape as well as in visuality and contemplation. As the closest follower of Ghirri's "school" (Guerrieri 21), Fossati investigated various places, both urban and rural, in an effort to convey their beauty and to express a sense of displacement through his ironical rewriting of the tradition of landscape painting, in the sense that he simultaneously quoted and played with this tradition. His style is in many ways similar to that of Ghirri – strikingly harmonious, geometrical, precisely composed in all its parts, both classical and deeply self-aware and self-reflexive (Fossati, "Vedi alla lettera 'C'" 156–7). Like Fossati with his photographs, Messori with his prose expresses the present condition of displacement, combining a deep nostalgia for belonging to a "home" and a tradition with a profound sense of "exile" and isolation, which, somewhat paradoxically, is seen as necessary to achieve empathy with exterior reality. Perhaps the best description of Messori is provided by his close friend and colleague, the poet Carlo Bordini, who, in a recent seminar on Messori at the Università La Sapienza, held in Rome on 23 and 24 February 2010, presented him as an isolated writer who believed in writing as practice for living, who favoured silence and contemplation, and who sought a sense of place. Messori's style is based on subtraction, on an effort to "ridurre il linguaggio al minimo" (reduce language to a minimum; Ruozzi 10), and his prose is distinguished by its hybrid nature, which seamlessly combines fiction, autobiography, travel writing, and reflection and thereby narrates the complexity and fragmentation of our time.[10]

Messori's and Fossati's aesthetic consonance emerges in their contemplative attitude, in their many shared literary and artistic influences, in their focus on the minimal and the fragmented, and in their openness to each other's outlook. It is interesting that in the book, Messori posits photography, like writing, as "notes," thus as a fragmented narrative that the reader is meant to assemble. In this regard, we could argue that the written text shares the preliminary, incomplete nature of the visual text, as "appunti presi in viaggio" (notes taken while travelling; Fossati and Messori 10). That text was developed, edited, and rearranged at different stages throughout their ten-year collaboration (since Messori's death in 2006, it has mostly been edited by Fossati). The emphasis on fragmentation (and ephemerality) can be seen as a metaphor for human mortality in relation to nature's "immortality" – a key theme in the book. The centrality of fragmentation in the photo-text confirms its consonance with the aesthetics of Benjamin, who posited writing as inherently "interrupted," as "discrete moments punctuated by pauses" (Ferris 5), like tiles in a mosaic. For Benjamin, it is the fragmented, digressive nature of writing – which reflects the very nature of thought – that allows the necessary pausing for breath and enables contemplation both in the writer and in the reader. I believe that Messori seeks to reproduce a similar effect by adopting a fragmented style, which in turn is consonant with the intrinsically fragmented nature of photography as "the art of interruption" (Roberts, *The Art of Interruption*). If, as David Ferris suggests, "to read Benjamin is to face the form, the style of his writing as much as it is to register what he says about a given subject" (8), then similarly, to read Messori and Fossati's *Viaggio in un paesaggio terrestre* is to understand its style as much as its content – the two are deeply interconnected – while also seeking to bridge two different media. Through their collaboration, Messori gained a greater sensitivity to visuality and the ability to be inspired by an image; for his part, Fossati learned to appreciate the importance of narrative sequence and broadened his focus beyond mere technical aspects of photography and the purely aesthetic value of the image. Both approaches assume "l'idea che immagini e parole possano in qualche modo combinarsi fra loro, anche per aiutarsi a cercare un senso più nascosto, che non sia immediatamente visibile" (the idea that words and images could somehow combine and help each other in their search for a hidden meaning, that is not immediately visible; Fossati and Messori 10). This further meaning can be found in the contemplation of nature and of works of art that attune themselves with it, particularly with a "paesaggio terrestre" (earthly landscape).[11]

The adjective *terrestre* (earthly), which appears in the book's title, is not redundant; instead, it encapsulates the very essence of the authors' aesthetics, understood as an effort to look anew at everyday places through a reversal or imaginative perspective that makes the old and obvious appear new and interesting (and this is in line with Ghirri's teaching). The emphasis on vision and imagination points to a key aspect of landscape: the coexistence of real landscapes and their mental images or artistic representations, of a natural *and* a human dimension. This is poetically voiced by Messori, who in the first chapter defines a "paesaggio terrestre" as a merging of earth with sky, that is, of the realm of materiality with that of the imagination:

> fin dall'inizio ci siamo proposti di cercare un paesaggio terrestre perché ci eravamo detti che la maggior parte degli uomini quando guardano nella natura, hanno in fondo davanti a sé lo stesso paesaggio, almeno nelle sue linee essenziali. Sotto c'è la striscia verde e marrone (la terra) e sopra il cielo azzurro. (13)

> From the beginning, we intended to search for an earthly landscape as we agreed that most people looking at nature ultimately see the same landscape in front of them, at least in its essential lines. Below a green and brown line (the earth) and above the sky.

As Messori writes and as Fossati shows in his photographs, it is the attention to detail and the very physicality of the portrayed landscapes that inspires the authors' reflections as they seek to attune themselves with a place, following the example of the artists who, before them, turned these spaces into literary places. Although each of the nine chapters is important to the book, which should be analysed *in toto* for a fuller appreciation, in the space of this essay I will focus on the four chapters that most powerfully address the book's main issues, convey the artists' aesthetics, and develop their notions of (aesthetic) experience and auratic landscape. These are the third chapter, "Non è ancora buio" ("It Is Not Dark Yet"), on Courbet; the sixth, "I motivi di Cézanne" ("Cézanne's Motifs"); the eighth on Friedrich's "Eldena," and the ninth and final chapter, "A Capri" ("In Capri"). I will analyse the recurrent themes in these chapters, such as the centrality and interdependence of reflection, imagination, memory, sensorial experience, and affectivity in the aesthetic experience of landscape; the consonance with the aesthetics of the artist whose work is being celebrated in each given chapter; and the dialogue of the photographic and written texts, which complement each other in their reflections on landscape. In my analysis, I will refer to a number of photographs and quote various key passages in the written text. I will also comment at more length on three key photographs that encapsulate different visions of landscapes in various chapters.

The coexistence between materiality and vision or reflection strikingly emerges in the third chapter, which depicts Courbet's landscapes of the Loue valley around Ornans. After the journey up to the rocky Julierpass in Engadina, a "zona d'incertezza" (zone of uncertainty; 37) outside of civilized society where the previous chapter ended,[12] we descend to the wet, green *karst* woods of the Jura, a darker, more visceral landscape that allows us to reflect on realism and on a "documentary," photographic approach to reality.[13] Drawing on John Berger's seminal essay on Courbet, "Courbet and the Jura" (1980), Messori and Fossati focus on how the painter uses darkness to render the depth and mystery of this region and how he highlights its abundance of water through a play of reflections and mirror images. We see echoes of this doubling when Fossati turns the photograph *Valle della Loue, Miroir de Scey 1999* (*The Loue Valley, Miroir of Scey 1999*) (51) upside down, thus revealing the centrality of reversal in his work – a theme that also distinguished Ghirri's photography. As in Ghirri's work, here the boundaries between reality and illusion, imagination and representation are blurred; indeed, our authors realize that "capovolti nell'acqua, i paesaggi al Miroir de Scey diventavano più interessanti, affascinanti e compiuti" (turned upside down in water, the landscape at the Miroir de Scey became more interesting, fascinating and complete; 52). Tellingly, Courbet's own musings on the prominent role of imagination in art support the authors' conviction that it is impossible to distinguish between real and imagined places: "l'immaginazione in arte consiste nel saper trovare l'espressione più completa di una cosa esistente. Perciò non si tratta mai di copiare, piuttosto di rendere visibile qualcosa che ci appare in natura dandogli una forma, un'apparenza compiuta" (imagination in art consists in being able to find the most appropriate expression for an existing thing. Thus, art is never about copying, but rather about making visible something that appears in nature, giving it a shape, an all-rounded appearance; 39). Messori's suggestion that we attune ourselves to landscape in order to give it shape points to the effort to compose the different aspects of a natural view into a harmonious image.

Interestingly, although Fossati and Messori set out to find the specific landscapes that Courbet painted, they soon found this impossible and instead resolved to "ritrovare i suoi quadri inquadrati nella natura" (find again his paintings framed in nature; 45). They sought, in other words, to equate Courbet not with specific paintings but rather with a tonality, a style, a perception of the world. In so doing, they realized that they could only discover the essence of Courbet's art by rewriting the landscape they saw through their own imagination – a lesson that informs the rest of their book. Possibly, this is why Fossati does not look for the exact oak in Courbet's *Le chêne de Flagey, appelé chêne de Vercingétorix* (*The Oak of Flagey*) (1864); instead, he photographs another ancient oak near Epeugny. This photograph is titled *Dintorni di Ornans 1999* (*Ornans' Surroundings 1999*) (49) (*Figure 3.1*). Here, the dialogue between word and image is at its clearest: this photograph, which takes up half of a recto page, is introduced by a page of written text that addresses the importance of the motif of the oak in Courbet's painting. Courbet used to recount that he was born under an oak, a piece of self-mythologizing that reveals the importance he attached to being immersed in nature. For Messori, the oak in Courbet's painting symbolizes both natural time and historical time and thus suggests the passing of time and the limits of human life – a theme that recurs in the book, as do images of trees of different shapes and sizes, particularly in this chapter and in the one on Cézanne.[14] Here, Messori compares Courbet's famous *The Oak of Flagey* with Fossati's photograph of a different oak, recounting that the authors were struck by "l'apparizione di una quercia" (the apparition of an oak; 48). This brings us back to Benjamin's definition of aura with reference to landscape. Given that a different oak from Courbet's has been chosen, it also seems to suggest that for Fossati and Messori, all landscapes can be auratic once they have been immortalized through art. As Messori spells out in the text, unlike the oak in Courbet's painting, which dominates the frame with its imposing presence, nearly obscuring the sky, the oak photographed by Fossati is less imposing. It is amply framed by the sky and has mistletoe growing on its branches, that "sembravano [...] volessero ricordarci che adesso la natura è spesso malata" (seemed ... to want to remind us that nowadays nature is often ill; 48). Accentuating the temporal distance from Courbet's era, Fossati's photograph reveals human traces: the broken branches under the tree, a truck diagonally cutting the green; however, as in Courbet's image, no human figure is present, which suggests abandonment. This photograph and the accompanying text constitute one of the many cases in the book where writing and image complement each other; Fossati's photograph and Messori's prose echo each other while reflecting on the themes of landscape and

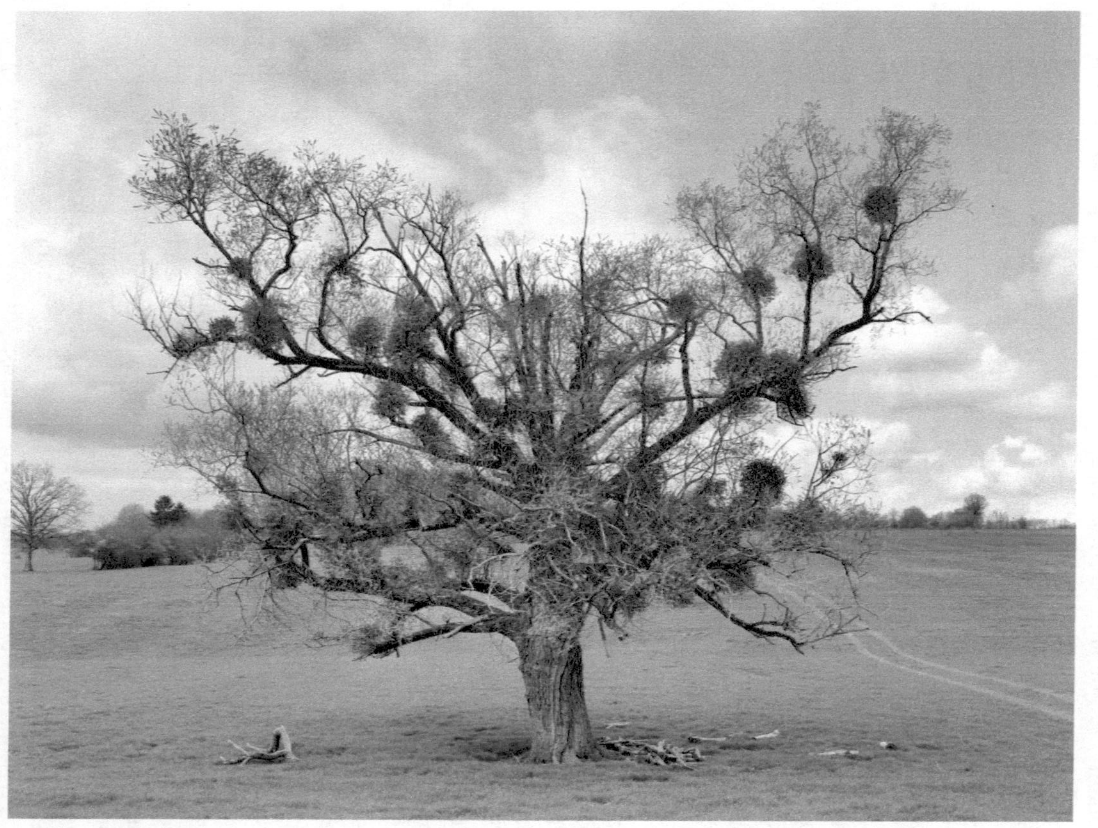

Figure 3.1 Vittore Fossati, *Dintorni di Ornans*, 1999. In *Viaggio in un paesaggio terrestre*, 49. © Vittore Fossati.

nature's decay and on the survival of an auratic dimension to landscape and to art.

The chapter's final photograph, *Valle della Loue, Miroir de Scey, 1999* (53), portrays the tourist park dedicated to Courbet. There, the authors are unable to find the views pictured in his paintings and conclude that "quando vediamo, vediamo anche attraverso dei quadri, o la scena di un film" (when we see, we also see through paintings, or through a scene from a film; 52). This awareness makes them realize that "l'esperienza non è tanto ciò che si vede, ma come si organizza una visione" (experience is not so much what we see, but how we organize vision; 52) and that looking at a landscape through the eyes of an artist is similar to an "esperienza interiore [...] vissuta nel corpo" (interior experience ... lived through the body; 52), not just a mental, abstract experience. For them, an aesthetic experience is both physical and spiritual and also involves affectivity and imagination. This is in line with a long tradition of reflection on landscape that, especially with the Romantics, depicts landscape as a space for solitude that can induce reflection, contemplation, and imagination and thus a deeper relationship with nature and the self. This is also in line with current philosophical thought, which, since the 1970s, has sought to redress a reductive notion of aesthetics by recovering the original meaning of the Greek word *aésthēsis* (combining the senses and the intellect), and which has increasingly recognized the multisensorial experience of being in a landscape.[15]

Another chapter that explores the complexity of landscape representation and the coexistence of an attentive look at the exterior and the power of memory and imagination, thus challenging the existence of purely documentary art, is the sixth, on Mont Sainte-Victoire.[16] *I motivi di Cézanne* (*Cézanne's Motifs*) focuses on the artist's most famous motif, the Sainte-Victoire, which, like its painter, has become a key symbol of modern art and of landscape representation. Messori and Fossati deeply admire Cézanne's art and highlight its essence: its attentive rendering of nature; its handling of colour and composition, which Fossati echoes in his photographs for this chapter by experimenting with greens and reds; and the way it expresses that there is no single version of reality but rather infinite facets of the same thing. This is magnified by the fact that Cézanne painted the same mountain in many different ways over the last twenty years of his life. To convey the artist's obsession with this motif, Messori makes the mountain the focus of his prose and Fossati includes it in nearly all of his photographs, always from a different angle and distance and in diverse colours and lighting conditions.[17] Cézanne's lesson is reflected in Messori's close attention to minor, everyday details, which are rendered in "simple," unassuming prose, and in Fossati's emphasis on geometrical composition, which is part of his effort to find, like Cézanne, "il giusto punto di tensione fra gli elementi che si componevano nell'inquadratura" (the exact balance between the various elements in the frame; 93) or the "accordo reciproco" (reciprocal consonance; 93) of the various elements in a picture. Like Cézanne, Fossati frames his photographs with trees and bushes; in doing so, over the course of the chapter, he refers directly to many of Cézanne's paintings and increasingly exposes the mountain to the viewer's eye. This gradual approach to the mountain recalls another text about the same place, Peter Handke's *Die Lehre der Sainte-Victoire (The Lesson of Mount Sainte-Victoire)*, which this chapter acknowledges as a key intertext. This same approach also reminds us of Petrarch's ascent of Mount Ventoux, the theme of a previous chapter. If in Handke's text the experience of the mountain goes together with the "sparizione dell'io" (disappearance of the I; Bertone 14), in *Viaggio in un paesaggio terrestre* the human subject is completely absent from the photographs, apart from the last picture, *Montagna Sainte Victoire 1999* (*Sainte Victoire Mountain 1999*) (98) (*Figure 3.2*), where Messori, like the mountain, "tornava a stare in mezzo alle cose, senza volerle più dominare" (returned to be surrounded by things, without trying to dominate them; Fossati and Messori 98). Following on Giorgio Bertone's suggestion that both Handke and Cézanne search for a "paesaggio alla seconda" (a landscape to the second degree; 14), the presence of Messori in this photograph testifies that this is a "paesaggio nel paesaggio già dato dalla memoria" (a landscape within a landscape that already exists in our memory; 14). A similar approach informs the rest of this chapter and indeed the entire book.

As before, the written and photographic texts enter into a close dialogue while reflecting on Cézanne's paintings and aesthetics. Messori acknowledges the mediated nature of our reflection on landscape at the end of this chapter where this photograph is placed, at which point he quotes Handke's experience of the mountain as "un'apparizione del cielo" (an apparition of the sky; 96). This is a key theme throughout the book and reveals the artists' auratic view of landscape, echoing Benjamin's definition of aura as an apparition. In the final few pages, Messori reflects on the similarity between Cézanne's mountains and the sky and the clouds with their perpetual mutability (a theme that reminds us of Ghirri's aesthetics). In Messori's words: "E in Cézanne perfino

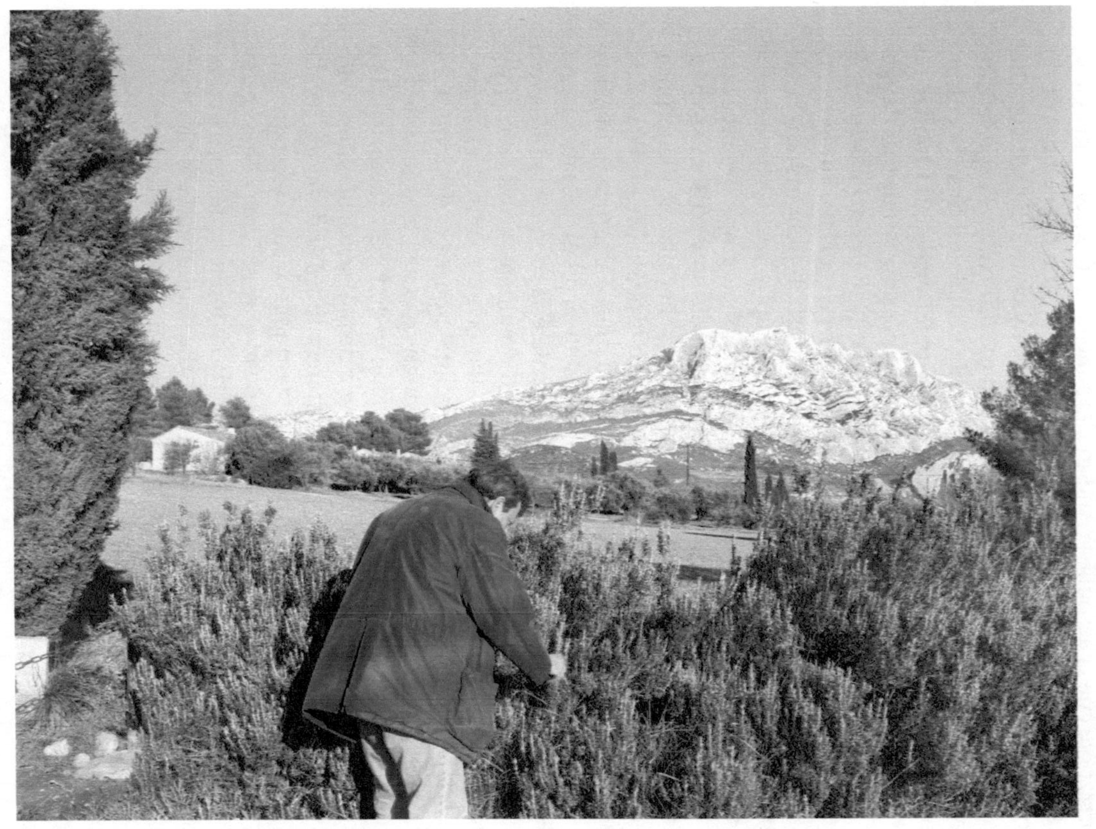

Figure 3.2 Vittore Fossati, *Montagna Sainte Victoire*, 1999. In *Viaggio in un paesaggio terrestre*, 98. © Vittore Fossati.

il cielo, nelle vedute della Sainte-Victoire, ha spesso la consistenza e i colori della montagna; e la montagna diventa la sua nuvola di pietra, l'orizzonte che ci accoglie" (And in Cézanne even the sky, in his views of the Sainte-Victoire, often has the consistency and the colours of the mountain; and the mountain becomes its stony cloud, the horizon that welcomes us; 97). Messori then reflects on the difficulty of experiencing reality sensorily and on the danger that his visual and literary culture (specifically, his knowledge of Cézanne's paintings) could hinder his actual experience of the place. Messori, like Fossati, avoids this danger by contextualizing the mountain within its immediate surroundings, as shown in the photograph on page 98, where the writer is pictured reconnecting with external reality by touching a bush in front of him. Highlighting the close dialogue between photography and writing in the book, Messori's text immediately below this photograph describes the sense of peace felt in this landscape and suggests how sensorial experience can trigger memory and remind us of other places, the implication being that no landscape exists purely in itself. In Messori's words: "Allora se l'attenzione si spostava anche su prati e alberi, la terra ocra e la semplice eleganza dei cipressi e delle casette ai piedi della montagna, allora la visione si pacificava maggiormente e la montagna tornava a stare in mezzo alle cose, senza volerle più dominare" (And then, if the attention shifted to the fields and tree, the ochre-coloured earth and the simple elegance of the trees and the little houses at the foot of the mountain, one's vision became increasingly pacified and returned to being surrounded by things, without trying to dominate them; 98). The sense of peace that results from merging a distant sense of nature with its actual experience, from bridging different times and places, recalls Benjamin's definition of the aura (as "a strange weave of space and time: singular appearance of distance, however near it may be"; Lesley 51). This is what distinguishes the artwork: its unique presence in time and space connects "the two perceptions – the natural and the historical auratic perception" (Lesley 52), giving rise to a sense of serenity.

After their reflections on photography and on the origin of landscape painting in the seventh chapter, dedicated to Vermeer's Delft, the authors continue their journey to their farthest point north, Pomerania – more precisely, the island of Rügen and the ruins of Eldena. Caspar David Friedrich's art, which in this book stands in for the Romantic vision of landscape, is a key influence on *Viaggio in un paesaggio terrestre*. This is evident in Messori's reflection on imaginative places and, particularly, in Fossati's many direct references to Friedrich's paintings – references that, while testifying to his debt to the Romantics, often seek to rewrite the landscape in an ironical key, emphasizing displacement as in the opening chapter. In the seventh chapter, the authors are split between a dislike of the modern and touristy island of Rügen and a sense of belonging to the realm of art and imagination, exemplified by Eldena, which gives the title to this chapter. In line with the other chapters, which present foreign landscapes as spiritual places, this one opens on the myth of the North as a place of imagination and childhood memory, a place where one looks for oneself: "nord, la direzione che spesso l'immaginazione prende quando vuole intraprendere un viaggio interiore. Il nord lo si vagheggia per andare alla ricerca di sé, così come si va al sud per cercare una maggior vitalità, una riconciliazione attiva con gli uomini" (North, the direction that the imagination often takes when embarking on an interior journey. One dreams of the North to look for oneself, just as one goes to the South to look for greater vitality, for an active reconciliation with other human beings; 111). The reference to imagination and memory contrasts with the photographic precision of the previous chapter as the authors set out to find a "spazio di affezione" (space of affectivity), a "miraggio" (mirage; 113), rather than an actual place. Their expectations, however, clash with the modern architecture and hordes of tourists they encounter on Rügen and with the ruins of Nazi architecture, such as the ominous tower block "hotel" "Kraft durch Friede," here pictured in *Stralsund 1999* (115). More welcoming seems the town of Rostock, where Fossati's photograph of a sailboat moored in the harbour (112) reminds us and the authors of some of Friedrich's paintings, as Messori acknowledges in the text. This recurrent intertextuality is spelled out in the photograph that follows, *Greifswald 1999* (113), where Fossati quotes one of Friedrich's paintings of his hometown from a distance, *Wiesen bei Greifswald* (*Meadows near Greifswald*) (c. 1822). As in Friedrich's pictures, in Fossati's photograph the village is a nearly indistinguishable line on the far horizon and the sky occupies two thirds of the frame. This long shot encourages the reader's imagination while reminding us of Vermeer's frontal views and wide skies (discussed in the previous chapter).

The photographs that follow of Eldena (116–19) – a site now emblematic of Friedrich's painting and of Romantic art in general – are accompanied by Messori's reflections on the theme of ruins. Rather than at dusk or at night, on page 118 Fossati pictures the ruins in bright morning light, juxtaposing them, on the following page, with a reproduction of a painting by Friedrich, *Klosterruine Eldena und Riesengebirge*

(*Ruins of Eldena in the Riesengebirge;* 119) (1834), which displaces Eldena onto the Giant Mountains. This was a common practice for Friedrich, who favoured imagination over exact reproduction. As Messori notes, landscape in Friedrich's paintings becomes "il luogo delle rimemorazioni più segrete, una specie di specchio dell'anima, non semplice esercizio dell'occhio" (the place of most secret remembrances, a kind of mirror of the soul, not simply an exercise of the eye; 120). He emphasizes that "per lui il paesaggio doveva sempre aprirsi all'immaginazione contemplativa, evocare lontananze irraggiungibili, nostalgie mute che travalicano il visibile" (for him landscape always had to open to contemplative imagination, evoke unreachable distances, silent feelings of nostalgia that go beyond the visible; 121). The Romantic emphasis on places of imagination, memory, and desire clearly resonates within Messori's and Fossati's aesthetics to the extent that they originally chose Pomerania as their *finis-terrae*, as the book's conclusion, in line with Friedrich's effort to "allargare lo spazio del paesaggio all'incommensurabile" (extend the space of landscape to the incommensurable; 121).

At the end of the chapter, Fossati quotes other paintings by Friedrich, such as *Kreidefelsen auf Rügen* (*Chalk Cliff on Rügen*) (c. 1818 and 1825). Here, these paintings are playfully "rewritten" in two photographs of the same title, *Isola di Rügen, Stubbenkammer 1999* (*Rügen Island, Stubbenkammer 1999*) on pages 120 and 121. Friedrich frames the abyss once with three people looking down and then, in another picture, solely with rocks and trees; similarly, Fossati presents a first photograph devoid of people (a common feature of their art, suggesting a lost link between human beings and nature), and then another, taken from a slightly different angle, where the sea is partly covered by the darkened silhouettes of three figures who, although seen from the front, are unrecognizable. The chapter's final photograph, *Prora 1999* (122), recalls other paintings by Friedrich, such as *Mondaufgang* (*Moonrise*) (1835–7). In the German painting, two figures stand on the shore in front of a vast moonlit sea, thus juxtaposing without mediation forefront and background; whereas in the photograph, a lonely figure stands next to a pillar in front of the sea in broad daylight, suggesting the isolation of the contemporary individual and the loss of a shared sense of landscape. These ironical rewritings testify to the diminishing of human presence in the contemporary landscape and to the impossibility of finding Friedrich's landscapes again except through one's own imagination. Ultimately, this is in line both with the painter's lesson and with the contemporary aesthetics of landscape. The chapter ends with what sounds like a first attempt at a conclusion, as Messori highlights the importance of finding our own place of affectivity and belonging, wherever that may be: "a volte abbiamo bisogno di nomi, luoghi immaginati e immagini che altri ci hanno regalato, nomi e immagini che possono condurci altrove, in Pomerania o in Engadina, solo per sperare di riconoscere nel mondo un luogo a cui volere ancora appartenere" (sometimes we need names, imagined places and images that other people gave us as a gift; names and images that can lead us elsewhere, to Pomerania or to Engadina, only with the hope to recognize a place in the world to which we still want to belong; 123).

After reaching their farthest point north, in 2002, while looking for a publisher, Fossati and Messori resumed their journey, reversing direction and going south to Capri. Although the gap with the previous chapter set in Pomerania is quite clear in time, space, and direction, the final chapter is a coherent addition to the book, for it brings to the fore Messori's philosophical reflections on beauty, art, and landscape and on the place of the human being in that landscape. *A Capri* is at once consonant with and opposite to the preceding chapter on Eldena, in that both explore the theme of the island, but in different ways. The island of Rügen had been busy with summer tourists; Capri, which they visit in winter, is empty and is pictured as a utopian island outside space and time. After finding their space of affectivity in Pomerania, our authors find in Capri a promised land, "l'unico luogo, l'unica ipotesi a cui affidare le speranze di risveglio di una sensibilità altrimenti cieca, atrofizzata" (the only place, the only hypothesis on which to base our hope of re-awakening an otherwise blind, atrophic sensitivity; 133). This chapter also echoes the opening chapter on Villa Minozzo, in that both are set in Italy, unlike the rest of the book. However, while Villa Minozzo is familiar to the authors, who spent a summer together there, and while it has been chosen for the book as an example of a mundane place, neither of them has ever visited Capri. Instead of approaching that island as a tourist site, Fossati and Messori emphasize its mythical, auratic dimension, as if outside of time, eternally present; at the same time, though, they retrace the island's long history from the Greeks and Romans to modernity through the many famous people who spent time there, who include the Roman emperor Tiberius, Walter Benjamin, Maxim Gor'kij, Rainer Maria Rilke, and Bruce Chatwin. For Messori, what unifies all of their journeys to Capri is a search for beauty, however ephemeral; and photography is an ideal means of rendering this contemplative approach in a way not dissimilar to poetry, which is deeply conscious of individual mortality:

> Nella fotografia si può solo rimanere nell'immanenza del creato, non c'è spazio per fantasie che esulino da questa immanenza. In questo senso la fotografia si può imparentare alla poesia, che fra le forme espressive è quella che mi sembra più vicina a questo destino d'immanenza e di fugacità. (130)
>
> In photography, one can only stay within the immanence of creation; there is no space for fantasy that moves beyond this immanence. In this sense, photography can be assimilated to poetry, the expressive form that seems to me to be the closest to this destiny of immanence and fugacity.

Following the example of Rilke, who, like Petrarch, sought to merge a "terrestrial" with an ascetic dimension, and echoing Benjamin's emphasis on the mythical origins of art, by positing Capri as a primordial place, Messori emphasizes the mythopoietic function of art and poetry, namely,

> il compito di dare ordine e compiutezza al mondo frammentato, a una realtà altrimenti caotica. Perciò non si tratta mai di 'descrivere' la realtà, o, come direbbe Vittore, fare 'fotografie'; bisogna piuttosto rintracciare, nella realtà, quelle matrici simboliche che ci permettono di percepire una struttura compositiva della realtà stessa, cioè quasi un suo stato embrionale, originario. (132)
>
> the task of giving an order and a sense of completion to a fragmented world, to an otherwise chaotic reality. Thus, art is never about 'describing' reality, or, as Vittore would say, about taking 'photographs'; rather, one should re-discover in the external reality those symbolic matrices that allow us to perceive the informing structure of the same reality, that is, nearly its embryonic, original state.

In line with Benjamin's aesthetics, Messori here voices his belief that through the aesthetic experience the artist can access a mythical time, albeit momentarily, and thereby move beyond historical life as a "continuum of experience in a state of perpetual disintegration" in order to "produce a fragile image of transcendence" (Wolin 213). Indeed, he desires that the artist do so. This position echoes the aesthetics of

Ghirri, who believed that contemplating nature could bring one peace, albeit momentarily (132) – a conviction shared by Messori and Fossati.

The final chapter's complexity is also evident in the tight interdependence of writing and photography as well as in the many intertextual references to Ghirri's photographs of the island, some of which appeared in *Viaggio in Italia*. These include *Capri 1982*, where a view of the *faraglioni* is framed by a railing and a telescope. Clearly, Fossati references this picture in two photographs of his series *Isola di Capri 2002* (*The Island of Capri 2002*), on pages 126 (*Figure 3.3*) and 127, which omit the telescope and add, in the second image, a portrait of the back of a hooded man – most likely Messori – looking towards the sea. These images recall the opening photograph of the chapter on Eldena, *Isola di Rügen, Wissower Klinken 1999* (*Rügen Island, Wissower Klinken 1999*) (132), in which a group of tourists, shot from behind, gaze out at a sea view over a railing while another tourist examines the sea through a telescope. This shows how various themes recur throughout the book, linking different places and artistic representations so that they form a single albeit multifaceted view of the landscape. As often happens in the book, the two photographs on pages 126 and 127 enter into dialogue with each other, presenting specular views of the seascape, with vegetation and rocks framing the view from the left- and right-hand sides respectively. Notwithstanding the human presence in the second image, these photographs strike us as empty and desolate, a theme reinforced by Messori's text, which reflects on death – the death of all past inhabitants of and visitors to Capri, and the death that distinguishes the "stagione più morta dell'anno" (the deathliest season of the year; 126), when Fossati and Messori chose to visit Capri in order to avoid the hordes of tourists. This desolate, wintry landscape reinforces the theme of ruins that is key to the whole chapter – ruins that come to signify the ruins of a civilization while at the same time recalling a mythical time outside of history, a time of paradise or earthly utopia. At the end of the chapter, Messori's text reflects on the fading of beauty and on the ephemeral nature of photography, which is compared to poetry. The focus on photography on page 130 is reinforced by Fossati's picture on the same page, *Isola di Capri 2002*, which shows a view of the *faraglioni* framed by a doorway – a technique that Ghirri also used to emphasize that framing is intrinsic to photography and to lead the viewer to reflect on the nature of photography. The final photograph, *Isola di Capri, Grotta Matermania* 2002 (133), a close-up of a multitude of footsteps on grey sand, powerfully ends the book by conveying a deep sense of

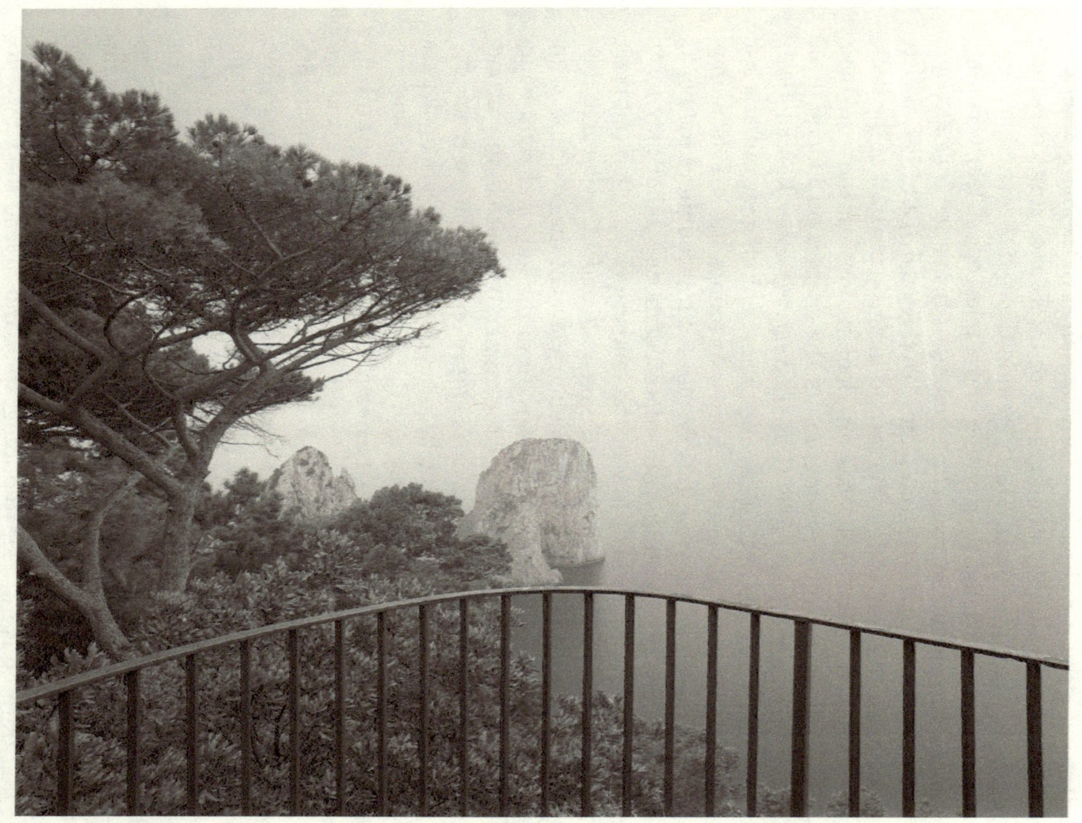

Figure 3.3 Vittore Fossati, *Isola di Capri*, 2002. In *Viaggio in un paesaggio terrestre*, 126. © Vittore Fossati.

ephemerality and a view of landscape as memory, traces, illusions. The book's final page focuses on *risveglio* ("awakening"; 133) and *salvezza* ("redemption"; 133) and thus recalls two key notions in Benjamin's aesthetics. Merging a messianic view of history as based on a notion of salvation or redemption with Marxist thought that strove for awakening from the dream-sleep of capitalism, in his work Benjamin talked about "awakening" from a dream, a utopia, and "becoming conscious." Interestingly, Richard Wolin juxtaposes Benjamin's aesthetics of redemption to postmodernism, which seems devoid of a narrative of redemption and which declares that nothing exists but appearances. Messori and Fossati in their photo-text convey a postmodern sense of displacement, but like Benjamin they still believe in an essentially "Romantic" notion of art and literature, seeing these as means of looking beyond what appears to the senses so as to awaken a sensitivity towards nature and the everyday, which Messori contends is a path to redemption and to finding one's place in the world. In his words: "È probabile che la Terra Promessa, l'Utopia, non siano che le dimostrazioni della storia, momenti appunto, non una durata, ma rimangono pur sempre l'unico luogo, l'unica ipotesi a cui affidare le speranze di risveglio di una sensibilità altrimenti cieca, atrofizzata" (It is possible that the Promised Land, Utopia, are nothing but historical realizations, simply moments that do not last; however, they remain the only place, the only hypothesis on which to base one's hope of reawakening a sensitivity that is otherwise blind, atrophied; 133). Messori closes the book with the notion of redemption, which, devoid of any political or religious overtones, voices the unexpressed intentions of their journey and points to a "via di salvezza nel riscoprire una creaturalità che si realizza solo perdendosi nella natura" (a route for redemption, by recovering a sense of being in the world that is realized only by becoming lost in nature; 133). This message is reinforced in his poetic conclusion, which, while reminding us of our mortality and finitude, exhorts us to seek beauty in nature: "L'importante è riconoscere che il mondo non avrebbe bisogno di noi, e che però noi possiamo essere testimoni di una compiutezza che non ci appartiene ma che a volte si può anche rivelare straordinariamente vicina, amichevolmente vicina" (The important thing is to recognize that the world does not need us, and yet we can witness a completeness that does not belong to us, but that can appear incredibly close to us, as a friend; 133).

With *Viaggio in un paesaggio terrestre*, Fossati and Messori have rewritten the history of Western landscape representation, paying homage to some of its key painters and artists, including the late photographer Luigi Ghirri, to whom both are deeply indebted. By revisiting famous literary landscapes and exploring mundane ones (such as the opening chapter's landscape around Villa Minozzo), the authors have sought to insert themselves into a long tradition of landscape representation, emphasizing the role of memory and imagination in the construction of a "landscape of the mind." Their aesthetics is informed both by earlier notions of landscape and art – from Petrarch and particularly the Romantic approach, which read landscape as compensation for a lost nature and the empathy with landscape through the subject's projection of feelings onto nature as a surrogate for the estrangement of the subject – and by modern art, which voices the subject's loss of control over an increasingly elusive object and focuses on personal, affective ways of exploring marginal objects. Their work – particularly Messori's – is inspired by a notion of contemplation that is triggered by the "apparition" of a landscape, which talks both to their senses and to their memory and imagination as they recognize the aesthetic beauty and immortality of the depicted landscapes and as they seek to recreate an aura for even the most commonplace ones in an effort to recover a sense of tradition and identity in line with Benjamin's thought. While well aware of the deep cultural changes undergone in postmodernity and of the intrinsic displacement of the postmodern subject, Messori and Fossati follow Benjamin's lesson and the aesthetic tradition by recovering a contemplative approach to landscape and art, an approach that could allow time for reflection and for the establishment of a dialogue with the exterior and with tradition. At the same time, their work is in line with contemporary theories of landscape, such as D'Angelo's aesthetics, which posits the inherently aesthetic and culturally complex construction of landscape, emphasizes the dialogue between the human being and landscape (rather than a superimposition of the subject's emotions onto nature), and argues that all places have an aesthetic valence; in this way, they move beyond a restrictive notion of beautiful or picturesque landscapes. While echoing this approach, in their book Messori and Fossati focus mainly on literary landscapes, demonstrating that these are often places of belonging for artists, for this is where they repeatedly practised their close observation of reality in order to transfigure it into art through memory and imagination. Messori's prose and Fossati's photography emphasize the authors' efforts to position themselves in a physical and literary space as much as it does their deep sense of displacement, their inability to recognize a place as familiar. Indeed, as Fossati revealed in Castelnovo, the authors ultimately admit their failure to find in a place what they were looking for at any given time, thus conveying a postmodern sense of anxiety. Yet at the same time, they resurrect an auratic and aesthetic view of the exterior that, drawing on Benjamin's aesthetics, posits the uniqueness of the experience of the artwork and emphasizes a mutual dialogue between the individual and the artwork, as well as with the exterior, with which our authors seek communion. Finally, in this book, Fossati and Messori succeed in appropriating the chosen places through their own art, in establishing a close dialogue between different media, and ultimately in inhabiting their own "spazio dell'anima" (landscape of the soul; 62), their refuge from which to narrate the human experience on earth.

* I would like to thank Vittore Fossati for allowing me to reproduce some of his photographs; Helmut Schmitz for his precious help with Benjamin's thought; Pietro Bevilacqua for his suggestions on Messori's reading, and Giorgia Alù and Nancy Pedri for their kind invitation to contribute to this volume and for their editorial suggestions.

NOTES

1 "Phototext" here refers to a specific type of photobook built around a close relation between words and photographs, which have roughly equal importance. On the photobook, see Parr and Badger; see also Di Bello, Wilson, and Shamir.
2 Sturken and Cartwright define visual culture studies as examining "the shared practices of a group, community, or society, through which meaning is made out of the visual, aural, and textual world of representations" (3). This definition seeks to overcome the sharp dichotomy of word and image.
3 See, among many, Albertazzi and Amigoni; Bryant; Hunter; Montandon; Parr and Badger; and Wagner.
4 Walter Benjamin's collected works began to be published in German in the early 1970s and were systematically translated into Italian beginning in the early 1980s. See Agamben's edition for Einaudi.
5 The notion of "experience" in German is conveyed by two words that for Benjamin express two opposite ideas: *Erfahrung* and *Erlebnis*.

6 See also Benjamin, *Selected Writings* II: 518; see also his "A Short History of Photography" 209.

7 Interestingly, Messori quotes this very passage from Agamben in his own dissertation on "Forme narrative in Peter Handke" (Narrative Forms in Peter Handke), which he wrote under Luciano Anceschi's supervision in 1981–2. He quotes this and another book by Agamben in the bibliography at the end of Fossati and Messori, *Viaggio in un paesaggio terrestre*.

8 Luigi Ghirri (1943–1992) was a leading figure in the revival of Italian photography in the 1970s and 1980s that led to the birth of the so-called Scuola italiana di paesaggio (Italian School of Landscape). Ghirri was a strong catalyst for many interdisciplinary collaborations in the 1980s and until his premature death in 1992.

9 Like Ghirri, Messori was born in the province of Reggio Emilia; Fossati is from Alessandria but has been exploring the Emilian landscape since the 1980s with Ghirri.

10 On the representation of place in Messori's fiction, see my 2011 essay, "Sense of Home and 'Exile,'" in *Romance Studies*.

11 Interestingly, the notion of "paesaggio terrestre" was used in Italian geography texts in the 1960s and 1970s, such as Biasutti published in 1962 and Turri published in 1974 and in a revised edition in 2008.

12 The desolate rockiness of this landscape indirectly reminds us of the sculptures of Alberto Giacometti, to whom this chapter is dedicated.

13 Photography clearly influenced Courbet's art and that of many realist painters of the mid- to late nineteenth century; see Marra.

14 The chapter on Cézanne is, in a way, the natural continuation of the discourse on natural landscape and painting in the third chapter on Courbet, after the chapters on Petrarch and on the ideal city of Chaux.

15 See, in particular, Perniola, *Del sentire* and *L'estetica del novecento*; D'Angelo, *Estetica e paesaggio*; and Brady.

16 This chapter is preceded by two others that explore key themes such as contemplation through solitude and dead times and traces of the past and dust. The first of these is dedicated to Petrarch's vision of the landscape of his Mount Ventoux, a vision that is now considered a milestone in the modern theory of landscape and of subjectivity; the second looks at the ideal city of Chaux and the Saline Royale, as well as at the quarry of the *Chemin des Ocres*, which was also used by Cézanne.

17 In his letters to Emile Bernard, Cézanne revealed that his painting *d'après nature* "presuppone una sempre maggior confidenza col soggetto, senza accontentarsi dell'immediatezza e fugacità dell'impressione" (presupposes a greater and greater familiarity with the subject, and doesn't content itself

with immediacy and fugacity of impression). See Fossati and Messori
92. Cézanne voiced a commitment to "penetrare ciò che si ha davanti, e perseverare nell'esprimersi il più logicamente possibile" (get to the heart of what is before you and continue to express yourself as logically as possible). See ibid. 91. For the full text of Cézanne's letter to Emile Bernard of 26 May 1904, see *Correspondance* 304.

PART TWO

Photography Structuring Narrative

4 The Fiction of Photography: Vittorio Imbriani's *Merope IV – Sogni e fantasie di Quattr'Asterischi* (1867)

SARAH A. CAREY

Neapolitan writer Vittorio Imbriani (1840–1886) has always been consigned to the fringes of the Italian literary canon, a location cemented by the Italian literary deity Benedetto Croce, who categorized his work as "bizzarrie" ("weirdnesses").[1] In his lifetime, his reputation as a polemical iconoclast overshadowed both his literary career and, most unfortunately, the publication of his first novel in 1867, *Merope IV – Sogni e fantasie di Quattr'Asterischi* (*Merope IV – The Dreams and Fantasies of Four Asterisks*). Although it is barely known to Italian scholars – let alone to those abroad – Imbriani's first work is highly unusual in several regards: it blurs generic boundaries distinguishing the novel from the autobiography; its thematic emphasis is on the oneiric and the fantastic; it is characterized by linguistic pastiche; and it is overtly metatextual. Because of its relative obscurity, several generations of critics have failed to see the novel for what it is: one of the first postmodern works of Italian literature.

One of the most original and as yet unexplored aspects of the novel is Imbriani's prominent use of descriptions of photographic objects. The work was published in the mid-1860s, at a time when photographic practice was finally gaining in popularity in Italy. Born just one year after photography's invention in 1839, Imbriani belonged to a generation of writers growing up in an entirely different era of visual representation, one in which the "handmade" tradition of painting found itself pitted against a machine thought to mechanically reproduce reality, or at least its appearance. Imbriani's contemporaries – Giovanni Verga and Luigi Capuana, for example – likewise were attracted to the possibilities of the new technology within their program of literary realism (the Italian movement of *verismo*, which, like photography, aimed to capture "reality"). These writers, however, did not employ photographic description or fully engage in photographic practice until the later 1800s.

Pre-dating them by at least two decades, Imbriani's *Merope IV* is ground-breaking in two respects: it does not treat photography solely as a novelty (indeed, the text relies on described photographs for its organizing principle), nor does it use photography to heighten realism (in fact, it does the exact opposite).[2] In *Merope IV,* photographs are markers of fiction, not truthful imprints of the real world that early practitioners of photography saw as the medium's great achievement. By instead singling out photographs as mere copies, Imbriani's novel stands as a critical reaction against positivism and the *vero* (truth) at the root of *verismo*'s origins. *Merope IV*'s emphasis on the photograph as a simulacrum (especially in the sense of it being an imitation or substitute for something real) further positions this object as a locus of desire – an image that indeed can be possessed, but one also symbolic of an inability to possess the thing it represents.[3] The themes of this nineteenth-century work resonate with many of the tenets of psychoanalysis, and Imbriani's use of photography in his work anticipated many of the critical theoretical discussions of photography and visual representation that would come to dominate the twentieth century.[4] A postmodernist before his time, Imbriani combined his musings on desire with a critique of photographic representation in order to craft an elaborate narrative that played on the overlapping of fact and fiction in photographic objects. In the process, he created a unique metaphor for the art of writing itself.

Portions of *Merope IV* were first published in 1866 in the newspapers *La Patria* (*The Homeland*) of Naples and *Il Secolo* (*The Century*) of Milan, although Imbriani immediately expressed his disappointment with both of these early versions (Cenati 165). Its publication as a complete work in 1867 was likewise greeted with distaste by the author, who openly confesses to the work's incompleteness in the note to the reader that precedes the first chapter. This mode of self-deprecation, however, is Imbriani's clever way of masking his unconventional aesthetic aims. The novel was published on the heels of the *succès de scandale* of Gustave Flaubert's *Madame Bovary,* although neither the polemic of French realism nor the organic structure of the traditional novel suited Imbriani. Imbriani's linguistic experimentation was also at complete odds with the literary program of Italy's own "great" novel: Alessandro Manzoni's *I promessi sposi* (*The Betrothed*). The final, revised version of this epic, published in 1842, was one of the greatest achievements in the standardization of the Italian language. *Merope IV,* by contrast, includes dialect as well as numerous archaic words and *latinismi* ("Latinisms"), in addition to unusual punctuation and conjunctions. Competing against fellow writer Ippolito Nievo's novel *Confessioni di un italiano* (*Confessions of an Italian*), published the same year as *Merope IV*, Imbriani's work is a parody of the historical novel and of Romantic literature more broadly.

The work's title, *Merope IV,* is itself playful, in that it labels Imbriani's work as the successor to three notable theatrical adaptations of the Merope myth: Francesco Scipione Maffei's *Merope: Tragedia* (*Merope: Tragedy*) (1713), Voltaire's *La Mérope française* (*The French Merope*) (1743), and Vittorio Alfieri's *Merope* (1782). In the original myth, Queen Merope's family is murdered by Polifonte, but she is able to save one of her sons, Cresfonte. Now, however, she faces a forced marriage to the tyrant. When Cresfonte returns and his identity is revealed, he kills Polifonte in revenge and saves his mother from the imminent union. The myth of Merope, with its echoes of Oedipal tension, is manipulated and perverted in Imbriani's version: he inverts the role of the tragic heroine and portrays her as a less than admirable character – a superficial and garrulous married woman who comes to embody not a woman to be saved, but one to throw away. Imbriani's sentimental version of the myth is one of forbidden, adulterous love (a common theme in other works of the Romantic period), yet it occupies a minimal part of the work as a whole. Surrounding it, and inserted into it, are the dreams and fantasies of the protagonist, a young military officer named Quattr'Asterischi; long and obscure literary quotations; and even long passages of poetry. This narrative structure is further complicated by the chapter epigraphs, which either allude to the thematic content with frustratingly uneven accuracy or, in conjunction with the chapter title and a page filled with dots, form the chapter's entire content. The work hints at a coherent structure while simultaneously negating one – a tension that ultimately leaves the novel's genre an open question.

Imbriani's suspicion of the traditional nineteenth-century novel and his attempts to undermine facile notions of historical truth are conveyed even more clearly through the blurring of fact and fiction in *Merope IV* (something that also explains why descriptions of photographic objects in the work are used in such an interesting way). Take, for instance, the name of the protagonist: Quatt'Asterischi (Four Asterisks). Imbriani seems to be creating an anonymous character (****); however, the moniker actually refers to Imbriani's own pseudonym, which he used for his 1864 *Versi* (*Verses*) and for his journalism. The love story between Merope and Quattr'Asterischi is based on Imbriani's relationship with Eleonora Bertini, a married woman, in the year before the novel was published. This affair coincided with Imbriani's military service in the Austro-Prussian War of 1866 (which led to his imprisonment in Croatia). That experience served as the basis for the protagonist's profession in the novel; more importantly, it corresponds to some of the key elements of the rather loose plot. Imbriani's first novel, then, is a self-conscious hybrid of autobiography and creative fiction – a hybrid for which there were few previous models in Italian literature. Also, its unconventional style created a space for comic literature that Imbriani felt was lacking in Italy at the time.

The presence of photography in *Merope IV* ties in to the work's status as part autobiography, a non-fictional genre that is problematic with respect to authorship and memory. Critic Timothy Dow Adams states that "just as autobiographies are obviously artificial representations of lives, so photographs are clearly manufactured images" (466). Autobiography and photography share a presumption of unalloyed "truth," yet each form is stained by artifice: they "both by definition and common perception, have a strong felt relationship to the world, a relationship which upon examination seems to disappear" (483). By the early decades of the twentieth century, photographers themselves were warning that photographic images should not be trusted. Photographer Edward Steichen declared in the first edition of the periodical *Camera Work* in 1903 that "every photograph is a fake from start to finish" (qtd in Walton 246). Theorist Philippe Dubois later suggested that the only true thing we can say about a photograph is that it is a contradiction: "Of all the visual arts, photography is the one in which representation is simultaneously, ontologically, closest to the object and furthest from it: closest since it is the direct, physical emanation of the object, its luminous imprint, which sticks quite literally to its skin (the celluloid); furthest because it maintains the object as absolutely separate, distant, *opposite to* the real" ("Photography" 167, emphasis in original).

This opposition marks the essence of photographic ambiguity: the interplay between its objective and subjective aspects (a game that Imbriani seems to take up in the very genre-bending nature of *Merope IV*). Barthes's 1961 essay "The Photographic Message" provides perhaps the clearest explanation of the relationship between these two axes. Working through Saussure's distinction between paradigmatic and syntagmatic meaning, he argued that the signification of images proceeds along two parallel orders: the *denotative* and the *connotative*. Denotative meaning is straightforward, almost tautologically so: a picture of a child shows that child, and the viewer's understanding at this level of meaning requires no exertion. Connotation, however, represents the subjective element within the process of mechanically reproducing the image of a real thing. How it is photographed is driven by subjective, human decisions: what to shoot; how to shoot it; how to crop or frame it. These choices represent the meaningful and ideological connotative properties of an otherwise powerfully denotative art form; the two in tandem constitute what Barthes himself called the paradox of the medium. That is, photographs always already embody a challenge to their seemingly analogous relationship to reality.

A century before Barthes, Imbriani pointed out this paradox with his use of photographic objects in *Merope IV*. In the dedication that opens the work, as previously mentioned, Imbriani self-consciously reveals himself to be the author and explains how it came to be. He is forthright in admitting he is a creator of fiction: "ho creato due personaggi, ho detto loro di levarsi e camminare; poi quel che vidi io scrissi" (I created two characters, I told them to get up and walk; then I wrote down what I saw; 9).[5] What is unique in this description is Imbriani's emphasis on *watching* the fictional characters move before his figurative eyes and how he then captures the imaginary visions through the act of writing. Such an approach is itself photographic: it is a "way of seeing." On this point, it bears quoting art historian John Berger at length:

> An image is a light which has been recreated or reproduced. It is an appearance, or a set of appearances, which has been detached from the place and time in which it first made its appearance and preserved – for a few moments or a few centuries. Every image embodies a way of seeing. Even a photograph. For photographs are not, as is often assumed, a mechanical record. Every time we look at a photograph, we are aware, however slightly, of the photographer selecting that sight from an infinity of other possible sights. This is true even in the most casual family snapshot. The photographer's way of seeing is reflected in his choice of subject. (*Ways of Seeing* 9–10)

If we think of Imbriani as a kind of "literary photographer," we easily become enmeshed in his way of envisioning his fictional world. His choice of subjects – which he sees as if they were based on his own self – presents us with an unusual type of photographic self-portrait. And as we will see, this is only compounded by the presence of photographic objects within the fiction itself. Just as Berger asserts that photographs are appearances rather than records, the novel *Merope IV* is not true, but sometimes "looks like" the truth.

In the first chapter, "Il mio scrittoio" ("My Desk"), the task of narrating is handed over to one of the characters whom Imbriani "saw" – Quattr'Asterischi. The young military officer's story begins as he rifles through the chaos of his desk; in it he happens to find five photographs of a woman. He ponders these objects – which he calls "cinque ricordi" (five memories; 13) – and in the process is inundated with a flood of both bitter and sweet reminiscences. Imbriani's choice of language here is significant: by labelling the images *ricordi*, he is intimating that human memory operates much like photography.[6] In the case of Quattr'Asterischi, seeing a woman whom we assume to be a past lover (albeit in simulated form) is enough to make what he calls "una buona ferita" (a good wound; 13) ache again. The emotional undertones of these *ricordi* are significant; the protagonist still finds some element of pleasure in the pain of the past. This undercurrent of masochism will be a recurring theme in the novel.

After his moment of self-reflection, Quattr'Asterischi invites the reader to "look" at Merope:

> Guardala qui! Svelta svelta, ma bassina; in abito di seta nera con lo strascico e poi de' coturnetti guarniti di lacrime di vetro sull'attaccatura delle maniche. [...] Di profilo, con le braccia intrecciate ed appoggiate alla spalliera d'un seggiolone, spinge distrattamente l'occhio innanzi e si vede che guarda senza vedere. (13)

> Look at her here! Quick and nimble, but a little short; in a black silk dress with a train attached under the sleeves by laces trimmed with glass teardrops ... In profile, with her arms folded and resting on the back of a big chair, she stares absently ahead and one sees that she is looking without seeing.

This command to the reader is problematic, mainly because the images are not reproduced anywhere in the printed version of Imbriani's work. We can only look at her by mentally reconstructing an image based on Quattr'Asterischi's words. Our vision of the woman will be through his eyes; indeed, the ways of seeing in Quattr'Asterischi's entire story will be centred on the male gaze and firmly rooted in the satisfaction of man's subjectivity.

It bears mentioning that this approach to looking at the female figure is perhaps the *only* conventional element in Imbriani's work. It falls right in line with twentieth-century feminist critiques of the objectification of women through visual media. Laura Mulvey was an early and influential analyst of cinema's tendency to be organized by and for the satisfaction of the male subject position. While her seminal 1975 essay "Visual Pleasure and Narrative Cinema" explores how this operates in film, it is just as applicable to Imbriani's use of photographs in *Merope IV.* Mulvey argues the woman is bound by "a symbolic order in which man can live out his phantasies and obsessions through linguistic command by imposing them on the silent image of woman still tied to her place as bearer of meaning, not maker of meaning" (834). In *Merope IV*, the creator of meaning is doubly male: both the character and the author set their gaze on the female character – Imbriani in his mental envisioning of her and Quattr'Asterischi as voyeur to the photographic objects themselves.[7] The enigmatic phrasing Quattr'Asterischi uses to describe this first photograph – "si vede che guarda senza vedere" (one sees that she is looking without seeing; 13) – establishes a pattern for how we will see Merope: as a fragmented and passive object of desire who is not in control of her gaze. As Mulvey would argue, it is the male gaze that is all-consuming.

The narrator's close attention to Merope's stature and attire (the way she "looks") is a recurring and even disconcerting aspect of his descriptions of the remaining five photographs. To use Mulvey's terminology, Merope embodies *to-be-looked-at-ness* (837).[8] The second chapter of *Merope IV*, for example, highlights the role of a woman's appearance in a long, drawn-out scene in which the protagonist waits impatiently while Merope gets ready in her dressing space. She pays close attention to how she looks and to how the delay in being able to be "looked at" will fuel Quattr'Asterischi's desire to see her. Berger emphasizes how women have always been seen (and see themselves) differently from men. A woman has to "survey everything she is and everything she does because how she appears to others, and ultimately how she appears to men, is of crucial importance for what is normally thought of as the success of her life. Her own sense of being in herself is supplanted by a sense of being appreciated as herself by another" (*Ways of Seeing* 46).

Man is in complete control over his own gaze (to use Imbriani's implication, he both looks *and* sees) and is also the primary agent in the shaping of a passive female subjectivity. This, too, bears on the way in which photography can compound the objectification of the female body. "The surveyor of woman in herself is male: the surveyed female. Thus she turns herself into an object – and most particularly an object of vision: a sight" (47). In Imbriani's work, Merope plays the role of object on two different levels: she is at first a photographic vision and then, in the main plot of the novel, the object of desire.[9]

Returning to Quattr'Asterichi's initial description of the five photographs, he looks at and describes at length the photographic objects in his possession. These will be analysed later; however, it bears mentioning here that he concludes the first chapter by explaining how each of the five photographs will form the basis of a separate episode in the story of desire that will unfold as we continue reading the novel:

> Queste cinque fotografiuzze rappresentano altrettanti episodi di una storia che racconterò, quantunque possa costarmi. Si direbbe che come alcune celeberrime attrici si fanno fotografare nelle mosse più spiccate de' cinque atti di una tragedia in cui maggiormente vennero applaudite, così la mia signora nelle cinque principali scene del nostro breve dramma, che seguendo l'uso degli autori di produzioni spettacolose e nuovissime battezzeremo così:
>
> QUADRO PRIMO. Il supplizio di Tantalo ovvero il primo bacio.
> QUADRO SECONDO. Il tentativo notturno.
> QUADRO TERZO. Lo squillo delle trombe ossia la Dama travestita.
> QUADRO QUARTO. Il ferito delle patrie battaglie.
> QUADRO QUINTO. L'addio senza lacrime. (16)
>
> These five naughty little photographs represent just as many episodes from a story that I am about to tell, whatever it might cost me. One might say, just as some of the most renowned of actresses are photographed in their most striking poses during those five acts of a tragedy in which they are most applauded, so too will be my lady during the five principal scenes of our short drama, which, following the practice of the writers of the latest spectacular productions, we will christen thusly:
>
> FIRST SCENE. Tantalus's Torment or The First Kiss
> SECOND SCENE. The Nocturnal Attempt
> THIRD SCENE. The Trumpet's Blare i.e., The Lady in Disguise
> FOURTH SCENE. The Wounded Soldier of the "Patrie Battaglie"
> FIFTH SCENE. Tearless Farewell.

This explication posits the photographs as the novel's structural mechanism; it also alludes to a particular historical debate that has surrounded photography since its inception. Quattr'Asterischi elects to label each of the five scenes of his tragedy a *quadro*, a term in Italian that was used (at least in the nineteenth century) exclusively for paintings. By appropriating this vocabulary, the work gives a significant nod to the debate during Imbriani's time about the relationship between old and new art forms. By the time *Merope IV* was published, photography had become *the* solution to the problem of realistic visual representation. It was somehow "truer" than a painting because, as Stanley Cavell notes, it seemed to remove "the human agent from the act of reproduction" (23). Critic Roger Scruton explains that while we often see what a painting represents (but do not mistake it for the thing itself, as we might a photographic likeness), there is still an element of truth to a painting: the "truth of the painting amounts to the truth of the viewer's perception" (584). When Imbriani posits photographs and *quadri* as interchangeable terms in the novel, he implies that photographs are likewise "true" with respect to the subjectivity of the viewer or "false" in the sense that they – like paintings – only reproduce an appearance. Structuring *Merope IV* around objects that are inherently engaged in this dichotomy between fact and fiction is fitting for a work whose very structure oscillates back and forth between the genres of autobiography and the novel.

The use of the term *quadro* has further implications for a reader of Imbriani's work today. With the advent of cinema in the twentieth century, the word came to be employed in Italian to describe the frames of a film. If we consider the description of the photographs in the first chapter in this way (one right after another), the effect is one of photographic animation – a literary "movie" that unfolds as a series of flashbacks. Temporally speaking, the narrator's viewing of the images takes place in the present, and the later chapters that correspond to each of the photographs are flashbacks to the moments in which they were taken. So, as the reader navigates through the rest of Imbriani's work, he or she must remember (or flip back to the beginning pages) how each of the photographs relates to its corresponding chapter. The rather complicated process we must undertake, therefore, mimics Quattr'Asterischi's own voyage into memory and the subconscious.

Once the first chapter of *Merope IV* concludes with the outline of the five different *quadri* and their titles (the "scenes," as I call them in my translation), we segue into the first flashback (which, as a reminder, corresponds to the photograph of Merope "looking without seeing" that I spoke about at length earlier). Its title, "Tantalus's Torment or The First Kiss," fits well with the storyline's portrayal of desire and makes reference to the "tantalizing" act of viewing a photograph, an object with the promise – although ultimate failure – of accessing the inaccessible. It begins as Quattr'Asterischi waits in Merope's salon as she gets ready. He flips nonchalantly through a photograph album, secretly hoping to find a photo of her in it. The appearance of an album is significant; as Sontag writes: "Photographic collections can be used to make a substitute world, keyed to exalting or consoling or tantalizing images" (162). For Quattr'Asterischi, the album has the possibility of opening up an entire world of fantasy with respect to his object of affection.

This momentary invitation to fantasy is interrupted when Merope finally emerges from her dressing room. Quattr'Asterischi remarks on how she looks identical to the photograph from his desk (the object described in the first chapter). This is just one of many confusing temporal shifts in the novel; if this scene were a true flashback, in other words, the protagonist would not have any knowledge of the photograph that he finds later in his desk. Instead, the protagonist deftly switches back and forth from his role as a character in the scene to his role as the external narrator of the story. The effect apprises us that we have not moved back in time (as we would in a traditional flashback); rather, we are enmeshed in Quattr'Asterischi's own movement between past and present that is orchestrated through the photographic object.

After the protagonist/narrator alludes back to the initial description, the object itself finally appears within the narrative flashback: Merope finds it among the pages of the album and tells Quattr'Asterischi to keep it as a memory of her, which echoes Imbriani's use of the term *ricordi* earlier. She chooses this particular image precisely because she is dressed in the present moment in exactly the same way as she appears in the photograph: "Passando pel salottino prese l'albo ch'io sfogliazzava un'ora prima, ne trasse un suo ritratto e me lo porse: 'Serbatelo per memoria: qui son vestita proprio com'oggi'" (Passing through the parlour, she took the album that I had been leafing through an hour earlier, withdrew her portrait from it and gave it to me. "Keep it for memory's sake: I'm dressed here just the same as I am today"; 30). We know from the first chapter that the protagonist has done just that: it is one of the mementos from his desk. What Imbriani chooses to do so masterfully in this passage is have Merope pick out this image precisely because it is a replication of how she looks to Quattr'Asterischi in person. In some sense, therefore, she is copying her own photographic image – she reproduces the reproduction. The effect is one of rendering the living figure of Merope photographic: a copy on paper, and now a copy in real life.

The next chapter to be based on a photograph is chapter 7, "The Nocturnal Attempt." This photograph, the second of the five, is described in the first chapter as a small image of Merope meant for a locket, which is usually kept close to the body as a memento or apotropaic object:

> Nel secondo ch'è un medaglione, non abbiamo che testa e busto, ma più in grande assai; e si veggono meglio i particolari dell'acconciatura che è la stessa. I capelli un po' scompigliati (era un suo vezzo) ed ha di quegli orecchini che chiamano pompeiani. [...] Il colletto inamidato fa spiccare per tono il collo che invita a' baci e le punte ricamate a foglie della cravattina sembrano indicare le bellezze nascoste. (14)

> In the second, which is from a locket, all we have is her head and bust, though enlarged; one can better observe the particular features of her coiffure, which is the same. Her hair is a little unruly (it was a habit of hers) and she has on those "Pompeian" earrings, as they are called ... Her starched collar brings out the tone of her neck, inviting kisses, and the leafy embroidered tips of her little tie seem to point to beauties hidden underneath.

As the protagonist describes the details of the image, he remarks first on how Merope is framed (one sees just the upper parts of her) and then on her hairstyle, which appears the same as in the first photograph. Quattr'Asterischi's eyes then begin to descend lower and lower, gazing upon increasingly minute details with an equal heightening of erotic language. The way in which the protagonist fragments Merope's body into smaller pieces gives us the keen sense that Imbriani sees the photographic object as fetish. Freud explains in his 1927 essay "Fetishism" that the fetish is a type of stand-in. It is a "substitute for the woman's (the mother's) penis that the little boy once believed in and – for reasons familiar to us – does not want to give up" (152–3). As Christian Metz later pointed out in his seminal article "Photography and Fetish," the Freudian concept of castration anxiety – which is produced when a child finally sees his mother's genitalia and realizes that she, unlike him, does *not* have a penis – is assuaged by a fixation on a particular object. He writes: "The compromise, more or less spectacular according to the person, consists in making the seen retrospectively unseen by a disavowal of the perception, and in *stopping the look*, once and for all, on an object, the fetish" (86, emphasis in original). The implicit impulse of fetishism, therefore, is driven by a need to divert one's attention from the whole and to focus on a fragment. Metz connects this to photography by positing the camera as fixing itself on a chosen object or scene (to the exclusion of all possible others). "In all photographs," he writes, "we have this same act of cutting off a piece of space and time" (85). Quattr'Asterischi's visual dissection of Merope's figure is therefore fetishistic on two levels: he is directing his gaze at smaller and smaller pieces vis-à-vis an object that itself is but a piece of the larger whole.

The description of the locket photograph ends by "hinting" at what lies underneath Merope's clothing, a type of tease that is also at work in the chapter that corresponds to this image. In "The Noctural Attempt," Quattr'Asterischi becomes increasingly frustrated with, yet also titillated by, a coy and hesitant Merope in what he calls a "giuoco d'amore" (game of love; 61). She succeeds in keeping her eager lover at bay for much of the chapter, finally acquiescing to a single kiss. The chapter's emphasis on the chase – the prolonging of actual possession – remains in line with Imbriani's exploration of the nature of desire. It is the impossibility of attaining the woman that continues to attract Quattr'Asterischi. As the chapter's title suggests, the appeal lies in the "attempt," not the conquest.

Jumping ahead to the fourteenth chapter, we find the elaboration of the third photograph in the series. In its description back in chapter 1, the narrator mocks one of his literary predecessors (Alessandro Manzoni and the aforementioned novel, *I promessi sposi*) and references the photographic practice of the *tableau vivant*, which re-creates literary, theatrical, or touristic scenes using costumed and posed sitters.[10] Gazing upon this image, the narrator comments:

> Chi è mai codesta contadinotta vestita come la Lucia de' Promessi Sposi? È dessa; con tutti quegli spilloni d'argento in capo, con quella faccia patita, sembra una delle sante immortalate da' pittori, rozze nelle vesti, gentilissime di volto, circondate da raggi. La mano s'appoggia su d'una panierina di frutta: il guarnellino succinto mostra le gambe ignude; al piede non ha che gli zoccoli. (14)

> Whoever could this little peasant girl be, dressed like Lucia from *The Betrothed*? It's her; with all those silver pins upon her head, and with that pale face, she resembles one of those saints immortalized by the painters – roughly dressed but delicate of feature, encircled by rays of light. Her hand is resting on a little basket of fruit: her scanty petticoat shows her bare legs; mere clogs on her feet.

Imbriani's allusion to the photographic representation of Manzoni's famous heroine could have been based on real examples of theatrical photographic staging that were popular at the time. Quattr'Asterischi's description of Merope's skimpy attire suggests a parodic deformation of the historical novel's notoriously pious heroine. As with his description of the second photograph, the narrator surveys the woman from top to bottom, finally resting upon two familiar *topoi* of fetish, the legs and the feet: "Ah quelle gambette, quei ditini, quella molle curva che gli anatomici con voluttuosa metafora chiaman *collo del piede*, farebbero sospirare chiunque, anche la Statua del Commendatore, figuratevi me!" (Ah those little legs, those tiny toes, that soft curve that anatomists call with voluptuous metaphor the *neck of the foot*, they would make anyone sigh, even the Statue of the Commendatore, believe you me!; 14, emphasis in original).[11] Quattr'Asterischi is drawn to this image because the contents invite fetishist viewing but also because the photograph is itself the fetish object. This becomes clear when he admits to where he used to keep it: in his bedside table or under the covers of his bed (14–15). The protagonist depends on the object (what Metz calls a "pocket phallus"; 89) as a substitute for a woman he cannot obtain and as a defence mechanism against the anxiety that lack creates in him. This is further emphasized in the protagonist's confession that he is jealous of the photographer who took the picture, the man who saw the woman in flesh and blood.

This provocative photograph corresponds to the chapter titled "The Trumpet's Blare i.e., The Lady in Disguise," which is noteworthy for another tumultuous encounter between the two characters in which the moment of coitus is interrupted *in medias res*. It again features a "game" of pursuit and denial; this one quickly digresses into an erotic display that, in keeping with Imbriani's emphasis on titillation and desire in the novel, is drawn out as long as possible (142–3). The passage accentuates, once again, the way in which Merope is attired. Her dress features a laced-up bust that Quattr'Asterischi cannot undo, and in his frustration he finally resorts to cutting the strings with a knife. Finally able to cut her loose, we expect that we have reached the moment of consummation. In fact, Quattr'Asterischi addresses his readers directly, asking us politely to leave: "Lettor mio bello, lettrice mia cara, quanto sarei contento di dovervi ora pregare d'andarvene pe' fatti vostri, stando ché il pudore mi obbligasse a calare il sipario" (My good sir reader, my dear lady reader, how happy I would be to have to ask you to go mind your own business now, as though modesty obliged me to lower the curtain; 143). Quattr'Asterischi feels it is his modest duty to close the curtains on the risqué spectacle, reserving the soon-to-be nude figure of Merope for his eyes only. But in a moment of literary *coitus interruptus*, he tells his readers that they can remain: "Ma nient'affatto, sventuratamente pur troppo potete rimanere" (But no, oh wretched me, unfortunately you can both stay; 143). The young military officer explains that he has heard a call to arms, summoning him to report for duty. The interruption compounds the fact that Quattr'Asterischi is unable to obtain a full vision of Merope. Neither the protagonist nor the readers – shut out as we are by the figurative curtain – will be able to see her. All he will have later on, in fact, are the photographs (partial visions).

The last two photographs of Merope in the series of five signal an important shift in the narrator's mode of description – from eroticization to de-eroticization – as well as in the way the story of the lovers concludes. These images correspond, respectively, to chapters 18 and 23 of the novel, and they merit being analysed together. With the fourth image, the reader detects the beginnings of the process of the de-eroticization of the female figure: Merope stares pensively out a window, leaning with arms crossed upon the threshold (15). Quattr'Asterischi notes with disappointment the details of her dishevelled appearance: her hair is uncombed and her face unmade. He surmises that Merope must have been too busy to care about how she "looked," resulting in her hastily constructed appearance. Noteworthy here is that the protagonist seems to be admitting to us that the woman is a real person who might have had her own obligations, ones that were more important than how she appeared to others. The implication, in Mulveyian terms, is that she no longer exudes *to-be-looked-at-ness*.

As the narrator's tone changes dramatically from desirous to detached, the pleasant memories from his initial descriptions of the photographs give way to more freighted musings on the past. In keeping with this subtle shift away from an eroticized female subject, the corresponding chapter sees Merope morph from lover to caretaker. Quattr'Asterischi has finally returned from the battlefield and is recovering from his war wounds in a hospital. Merope's arrival at his bedside allows the protagonist to remark on the drastic changes in her appearance, which correspond almost directly to his descriptions of the photograph in the first chapter. Quattr'Asterischi marvels at her dedication to his convalescence, although he seems quick to point out that she seems to have "let herself go." His extended musings on the effects of her outward neglect signal the decisive decline in his relationship with her: what he sees now before him no longer corresponds to an eroticized vision of womanhood. His current state of debilitation (his sexual impotence now even more corporeal) thrusts the protagonist into a situation of dependence rather than sexual pursuit.

Just as Quattr'Asterischi begins to recover his strength, and to desire Merope again, he realizes that he sees her more as a maternal figure, which he forthrightly admits borders on the incestuous:

> Poi, quando ebbi cominciato a ridesiderarla, quando già la guardavo con occhio di concupiscenza, uno strano pudore mi allacciava la lingua; io provavo un occulto rimorso di quelle mie brame, quasi mi fossi impaniato in una passione incestuosa: mi ero tanto assuefatto a star con lei in una stanzuccia, in un letto, giorno e notte, senza idea, senza conseguenze, che ora mi figurava un delitto il valicare quella linea stabilita dalla consuetudine. (190)

> Then, just when I had begun to desire her anew, when again I looked on her with concupiscence in my eye, a strange modesty gripped my tongue; I felt an occult guilt over those cravings of mine, as if I had been ensnared by incestuous passion: I had become so accustomed to being with her in a little room, in a bed, night and day, without care or consequence, that now I reckoned it was a crime to cross the line that I had fixed by routine.

The allusion to incest is not just another of Imbriani's taboo themes in the novel: it is a strange part of his own biography and crucial to the overlapping of autobiography and fiction that remains constant throughout the work. After his adulterous affair with Nora Bertini turned sour, he married her eighteen-year-old daughter – his former lover thus becoming his mother-in-law. Through his inclusion of a photographic object as evidence of Merope's shift from lover to mother, Imbriani alludes to his own uncomfortable, non-simulated situation.

The fifth and last photograph of the series depicts the aftermath of Quattr'Asterischi's convalescence. It confirms that the photographic

Merope is fading in the eyes of her former lover, much like an old photograph that yellows with age. In the protagonist's description of the image, Merope's face bears the traces of time and the strain of their relationship. She shows some remnants of her former beauty, but her face now seems cold, her nose is ever so slightly shrivelled, and her lips and chin lightly sneer as if to challenge or reproach the viewer (16). Merope seems, as it were, to finally challenge the male gaze, and as such, Quattr'Asterischi depicts this final image of the woman as frigid, immobile, and even threatening.[12] The description contains no vestige of the pleasure that dominated the narrator's initial viewing of the images; this suggests that the illusion of womanhood has been interrupted. What Mulvey calls the "spell" has been broken; it prevents the spectator from "achieving any distance from the image in front of him" (844). To return to the myth of Tantalus, something is desirable only when it is out of one's reach.

The photograph corresponds to the chapter titled "Tearless Farewell," which details the couple's emotionally detached separation. Quattr'Asterischi describes how, even though he loved her, he was getting tired of Merope in a very *visual* sense:

> E talvolta io mi sentivo stanco di lei e di amarla, come il pittore che s'è travagliato per ore ed ore intorno ad un dipinto, lascia poi cadere spossato i pennelli, la tavolozza, le mani ed il capo, e rimane con un grande indolenzimento a' polsi e con una fiera cefalalgia, e sente proprio il bisogno di stare un secolo senza vedere alcuna pittura od almeno quella pittura. (217)

> And sometimes I felt tired of her and of loving her, just as a painter torments himself for hours and hours about a painting and then, exhausted, lets his brushes, palette, hands, and head fall, and, left with a great soreness in his wrists and a savage headache, feels he really must go a century without looking at any painting whatsoever, or at least not his own.

Like a painter, Quattr'Asterischi has become saturated with the repetitive viewing of the same visual material, and Merope (as image) has lost all her original appeal. The protagonist has reached the limit of the relationship – its breaking point – and his final description of the last photograph in the collection of five reveals this rupture. His concern over his own debilitated state after the war mirrors his disappointment with her, and that aversion again is tied inextricably to the way Merope "looks." He cannot look at her in the same way because the object of his gaze has changed: she is older, vulnerable, accessible. Yet now that he can have her, he does not want her.

Reaching the end of Imbriani's novel, it is clear that the author has employed photographic interpretation in order to investigate and lay bare the nature of desire. Also, the presentation of the images as a series of storyboards in the first chapter is the only equivalent of plot that one can find in this heterogeneous work of autobiographical fiction. Imbriani emphasizes photography's role in fantasy, not (as his contemporaries will do) in literary realism. In keeping with the author's completely irreverent approach to storytelling, however, the novel's conclusion completely undermines the importance of the photographs. The final chapter sees Quattr'Asterischi leave his role of character and return to that of narrator (emerging from memory into the present). He again addresses his readers by warning them not to be hasty in their reaction to the work:

> Non affrettarti ad invidiarmi, umanissimo lettore, e Lei, cara lettrice, non si affretti a stupire del cattivo gusto della Merope, e della buona ventura di questo sciocco Quattr'Asterischi. Ahimè, di quanto ho narrato sin qui, sull'onor mio, non è accaduto nulla, nulla, a me Quattr'Asterischi; v'ho ammannito un sacco di bugie: fate conto che fossi un programma elettorale fremebondo. (232)

> Don't be too quick to envy me, O most humble reader; and you, O dear lady reader, do not be alarmed by Merope's bad taste, nor by the good luck of this fool Four Asterisks; alas, of what I have narrated up to now (on my honor), nothing, nothing happened to me – Four Asterisks; I have subjected you all to a sack of lies: but bear in mind it was a smear campaign.

In this apostrophe, Quattr'Asterischi's roles as narrator and character overlap with little respect for narrative convention: he refers to the character of Four Asterisks in the third person and then clarifies that he is indeed also referring to himself. This shifty figure confesses that the story is a lie, invented by a spurned lover who might just be taking literary revenge on someone who has wronged him. The fact that the plot is false should not really surprise us: we are reading a novel, after all. We even know from the prologue (which is signed "V.I.") that the characters have been created by the author himself. And even though there are many resonances between the story and Imbriani's own biography, the latter too could be rife with fiction. But rarely does one find an author so willing to divulge his own deceit, and to foreground it so strongly, as Imbriani.

He goes even further, in fact: the confessional conclusion of *Merope IV* also reveals that the photographs – the objects that seemed to play such an integral part of the "lie" – are simply "found" objects. They are random snapshots of an unknown woman:

> I cinque ritrattini sono di una ignota e non mi appartengono ... E per non so quale iattura che mi perseguita non ho mai incontrato con alcuna donna: eppure suol dirsi che hanno il gusto tanto bizzarro! Non me ne sono mai accorto. Ho amato è vero, e (credo) come va, ma con una rara disdetta: mai un canchero che consentisse meco; tanto che, non essendovi cosa alla quale l'uomo non s'abitua, ho finito per rassegnarmici. (232)

> The five little portraits are of an unknown woman and they don't belong to me ... And owing to a strange misfortune that hounds me, I have never met any such woman: yet, as they say, their taste is so peculiar! I never realized it. I've loved, it's true, and (I think) I know how love goes, but with one rare exception: never have I consented to call such a nuisance mine; given that it's not something to which we men habituate ourselves, I've finally resigned myself to it.

Imbriani concludes his novel by admitting to using photographic objects as visual pawns in the process of crafting fiction. Such a move is an outright affront to the dominant cultural perceptions of photographs during Imbriani's time: he fervently insists there is *nothing* realistic about them. Furthermore, he undermines their communicative and aesthetic worth by discarding all five of them at the end of the novel as if they were meaningless. The author warns us that we should be wary of putting any trust in photographs as objective proof, even if they succeed in producing a type of "reality effect." The abrupt and unexpected conclusion further shows how an author's ability to create an imagined world affords him the right to undermine its very premise and to reveal the act of fiction in every literary and, as Imbriani implies, every photographic work.

NOTES

1 The generally harsh judgment of Imbriani in literary circles is due to Benedetto Croce's dismissal of him in *Letteratura della nuova Italia* (1922).

Croce expresses disdain for the author's predilection for pseudonyms such as "Italianissimo" and calls his temperament strange and savage. Croce concludes that Imbriani's work was not new or original and that his violent, excessive, pedantic, and cantankerous nature probably impeded his activities as a critic and historian (199).

2 Cenati is one recent critic who has noted that the novel's structure is based on photographic images. Likewise, Pusterla states that the sentimental and autobiographical subject matter is entrusted to the appearance of the images (xxii). But neither of these critics mention the extreme novelty of this approach given the novel's year of publication, nor do they explain how photographs function specifically within the text.

3 Sontag puts it best: "One can't possess reality, one can possess (and be possessed by) images" (163).

4 Here, and in the rest of my argument, I am referring to Freud's theories of scopophilia and fetishism and to Lacan's theory of desire. With respect to criticism on photography, Imbriani's work explores questions of reproducibility, memory, and the gaze. These resonate with later theoretical works ranging from Sontag to Walter Benjamin to Roland Barthes to Laura Mulvey. Despite the vast critical literature on photography in the twentieth century, it is crucial to acknowledge the nineteenth-century intellectuals whose thoughts on the new medium followed more closely on the heels of its invention. Many of these early enthusiasts were themselves important writers: Nathaniel Hawthorne, for example, as well as Mark Twain, Lewis Carroll, Gustave Flaubert, and Émile Zola. All of them, to a greater or lesser degree, seemed absorbed by the question of how photographic practice could help solve the problem of realistic representation.

5 Imbriani's novel has yet to be translated into English. All translations are my own. Special thanks to Harris Feinsod for his assistance.

6 In *The Interpretation of Dreams*, for example, Freud compares the functioning of the human mind to that of a camera: "[We] should picture the instrument which carries our mental functioning as resembling a compound microscope or photographic apparatus" (574). In his very last work, *Camera Lucida,* Barthes too makes explicit the connection between memory and photography. In what is perhaps that work's most poignant moment – when he finally locates a specific photograph of his mother – Barthes writes: "For once, photography gave me a sentiment as certain as remembrance" (70). Yet the link between memory and photography can also be viewed as weak. As Kracauer reminds us: "Memory encompasses neither the entire spatial appearance of a state of affairs nor its entire temporal course. Compared to photography, memory's records are full of gaps" (50). In this vein, Imbriani suggests in his conclusion that – contrary

to Kracauer's implication – photographs never arrive at the truth of the past; they are fragments of it at best.

7 "Voyeurism," Michelle Henning writes, "describes a mode of looking related to the exercise of power in which a body becomes a spectacle for someone else's pleasure, a world divided into the active 'lookers' and the passive 'looked at.' To some extent photography, by the very nature of the medium, invites voyeuristic looking" (171).

8 Berger makes a similar claim: "One might simplify this by saying: *men act* and *women appear*. Men look at women. Women watch themselves being looked at" (*Ways of Seeing* 47, emphasis in original).

9 Without embarking on a completely psychoanalytic rereading of the novel, the figure of Merope does invite a Lacanian interpretation – which, as is well known, Mulvey also relies on in her analysis of the film form. Merope could be considered what Lacan calls the *petit objet a*, the object of the "other" (*autre*) that causes desire (62). The "inaccessible" is at the heart of this theory: it is only when we keep a distance from the object of desire that desire persists. What helps us connect this to the photographic objects within Imbriani's narrative is that they too represent the inaccessible and, as a consequence, are symbols of a certain kind of lacking. As Barthes and others have commented, photographs are absent presences: we can hold them in our hands in the present moment but they represent a moment that is no longer there. We lack access to that past moment. As Lacan argues, however, it is precisely our lack of something that makes us want it; as such, photographic objects function particularly well in discussions of desire.

10 The genre was one of the most popular traditions in Imbriani's Naples around the time of the novel's production, and it achieved nationwide popularity with photographs of Virginia Oldoini (known as the Countess of Castiglione). Oldoini was an Italian courtesan who seduced Napoleon III and was revered for her exceptional beauty and for her theatrical, photographic recreations of famous female literary figures, which were achieved almost exclusively through her collaboration with the Parisian studio of Mayer and Pierson. The Countess's fame and the genre of the *tableau vivant* must have been familiar to Imbriani. For more on Oldoini and on other female icons in the nineteenth century, see Muzzarelli. See Miraglia, "'Genere' e 'Tableau vivant,'" for a discussion of the importance of *tableaux vivants* in Neapolitan culture.

11 According to Freud, this is because of a child's particular vantage point with respect to the female body above him and his aversion to looking up towards the genitalia (which lack the penis). In "Fetishism," he writes:

"[The] subject's interest comes to a half half-way, as it were, it is as though the last impression before the uncanny and traumatic one is retained as a fetish. Thus the foot or shoe owes its preference as fetish – or a part of it – to the circumstance that the inquisitive boy peered at the woman's genitals from below, from her legs up" (155).

12 Even though Mulvey alludes to the female image as, at times, "threatening," what has waned in Imbriani's work is the sense of titillating danger that Freud's castration complex embodies: "Hence the look, pleasurable in form, can be threatening in content, and it is woman as representation/image that crystallises this paradox" (*The Interpretation* 837). At this point in the novel, however, the threat of Merope is no longer one of pleasure but one of resignation.

5 Narrated Photographs and the Collapse of Time and Space in Erri De Luca's *Non ora, non qui*

NANCY PEDRI

Introduction: Photographic Space and Time

Erri De Luca's *Non ora, non qui* (*Not Now, Not Here*) opens with a bold statement about photography and its relation to time and space. Pondering the large collection of photographs taken by his father during a ten-year period framed by the family's first prosperity and the loss of his father's vision, the unnamed protagonist reflects on their documentary status. He states: "Resta così documentata fino al dettaglio una sola età, forse l'unica che sono riuscito a dimenticare. Gli album, gli archivi non mi sorreggono la memoria, invece la sostituiscono" (Thus, only one period remains documented down to the minute detail, perhaps the only period I was able to forget. The albums, the archives do not trigger my memory; instead, they substitute it; 7).[1] The protagonist confesses that the photographic images collected in family albums do not help him recall the details of his teenage years. Instead of preserving and subsequently stimulating memory – a process that would entail recognition through familiarity and an understanding of the photographic image as an *aide-memoire* – the photographs actually *create* memories.

Although it disrupts the photographic image's claims to be evidentiary, substituting remembering with creating nonetheless sustains the documentary work of the photographic image. It does so, however, not by confirming the image's temporal-spatial fixity, which relies heavily on the process of its making, but rather by exposing its documentary status as dependent on the interaction of image and viewer, an interaction that highlights the photographic image's narrative fluidity. So, although in *Non ora, non qui* the emphasis on photographic images' fabrication of memories disrupts their conventional associations with truth, authenticity, and evidence, it does so without dismantling the documentary work that photography is reputed to do. In De Luca's book, the photograph's evidentiary pull, its being "inextricably linked to the real world" (Thompson 3), resides with the viewer's engaged looking, which sees beyond the fixity of photographic details, carrying them through the subjective act of reading into a number of possible spaces and times. Hence, not memory fixed as or in a photograph, but rather possible memories built *across* the photograph.[2]

The building of memories – temporal and spatial pasts experienced anew in the present – is of particular consequence in *Non ora, non qui* given that its narrative universe is one in which past and present temporal-spatial distinctions collapse into one another. They do so through the protagonist's act of looking at the photograph. *Non ora, non qui* is the story of a man in his sixties who, acutely aware of his approaching death, leafs through family albums. As he does so, he contemplates his childhood years, repeatedly stopping on his difficult relationship with his mother, who throughout his youth continually struggled with her son's speech impediment. Impatient with her child's inability to express himself clearly, she often stops him from speaking, thus forcing him to live in the shadow of her words. The old narrator returns to those maternal words – "non ora, non qui" (not now, not here; 44) – that work alongside the photographic images to bridge or (better) collapse what would otherwise be perceived as two distinct temporal planes. One critic describes the narrative's unravelling of time as the product of "un gioco ottico ed una prospettiva quasi filmica, sovrapponendo e scomponendo le dimensioni dell'immagine e del tempo" (an optical game and a quasi filmic perspective, superimposing and breaking up the dimensions of the [photographic] image and of time; Diana n. pag.). By way of the protagonist's viewing, that is, from the point of view of the protagonist who is the present viewer of the photographic image, both subjects – the mother and her son – are fixed in the photographic image, and both are at once old and young, at once in the present and in the past, always completely entangled one in the other. In De Luca's temporally complex narrative universe, memory, which constantly intersects with the photographic image, is paradoxically not confined to events firmly situated in the past. Instead, those events are made to live in the present, to seep into it and affect it and, most importantly, push the present into the future.

Barthes is perhaps the most noteworthy theorist who repeatedly grappled with the lure of photography's instantaneous recording of time and space and its relation to evidence. Throughout his discussions of photography, he accentuates again and again the photographic image's temporal-spatial immobility. In "Rhetoric of the Image," he claims that "in the photograph [there is] a natural *being-there of objects*" (279, emphasis in original). For him, the photograph's unique referential status among the pictorial arts resides not so much in its ability to show *how* something was, but rather *that* it was in a past space and time. The photograph, he argues in *Camera Lucida*, does not allow one to "deny that *the thing has been there.* There is a superimposition here: of reality and of the past" (76, emphasis in original). In this late work, Barthes again theorizes the photograph's temporal immobility, its ability to freeze a precise moment in time, as the locus of its power.[3]

Adherence to the photograph's temporal-spatial fixity informs Marina Spunta's examination of photography in De Luca's short text. She argues that "*Non ora, non qui* conveys space and time displacement through photography" ("A Balanced Displacement" 387). In her analysis, photography in De Luca's text functions as an *aide-memoire,* bringing "alive the past, through an intrinsic spatial and temporal displacement" (389). She argues that photographic images work as indexical forms of witnessing, their meaning and value grounded firmly in the undeniable past existence of the referent. They serve as memory icons, historical records, or authentic documents that "prove that someone was alive at a particular time and place in history" (Sturken and Cartwright 17). As such, they hold reliable clues as to what once was by verifying spatial or historical facts.[4] She thus understands the photographic image in De Luca's *Non ora, non qui* as functioning much like the actual photographs reproduced in the work of Lalla Romano, Claudio Di Scalzo, or Elio Vittorini: as evidence for a past empirical reality that is being narrated.[5]

Although there is a temporal and spatial displacement attached to photographic references in De Luca's *Non ora, non qui,* I would like to suggest that this is not due to a quality intrinsic to the photographic image. The spatial and temporal displacement of which Spunta speaks is not, in other words, dependent upon the photograph's indexicality. Instead, in *Non ora, non qui,* displacement or the collapsing of the narrative's temporal and spatial distinctions between a past, present, and future time and space is set in motion and solidified through the process of reading photographs, a process in which the narrator partakes throughout the text. Displacement occurs by way of the narrator's active and highly subjective engagement with the photographic image, which occasions his reunion with his mother and the claiming of his identity at the time of his own death. Indeed, the reading of a photographic image allows De Luca's narrator to step into the visual and, in so doing, disrupt or (better) expose as false the photograph's highly theorized temporal and spatial immobility. It gives rise, in other words, to what De Luca describes as the photographic image's "durevole momento" (extended moment; 41).

Temporal-Spatial Displacement in *Non ora, non qui*

Non ora, non qui, De Luca's first published novel, is a first person account of a man in his sixties who recalls his past life, paying particular attention to the difficult relationship he had with his mother as a stuttering young boy. As the nameless narrator revisits (and to some extent rebuilds) his past, readers are pushed back in time through flashback techniques and also thrust ahead in time through flash forwards. This temporal structure is complemented with a spatial fragmentation, which is introduced by way of recurrent references to a photographic image of the narrator's mother as a young woman staring into a bus window. The photograph is one among the many his father had taken over a period of ten years that ended when the narrator was nineteen years old. Enthralled by the image, the narrator returns to it, not only to describe what is pictured but also to engage in potential narratives that take shape both within and beyond the photograph's temporal and spatial frame.

In *Non ora, non qui,* the temporal-spatial laws governing the world of the photograph oscillate between two possibilities: that of a fixed viewpoint where time yields to space, and that of a mobile viewpoint where space yields to time. At times, the narrator describes the photographic image as in motion, with people bustling about the city streets. Only the narrator, who looks from one fixed viewpoint, and his mother, who is the object of his gaze, are still. Looking out the bus window, the narrator explains: "a questo vetro d'autobus mi accorgo di essere in un'ora e in un posto a me riservato da tempo. Intorno ferve il movimento. [...] [C]'è trambusto, ma tu e io siamo fermi. [...] Siamo fermi nella fotografia" (at this bus window I am aware of being in a time and in a place reserved for me. Around me, everything is in motion ...

There is bustle, but you and I are still … We are still in the photograph; 44). The narrator, who describes himself as both inside and outside the photographic image – at once viewed and viewer, object and subject – contemplates a possible moment that stands apart from those that were "errori di tempo e di luogo" (errors of time and space; 44). Through the act of reading the visual image, he is able to transpose his self into a space that permits him and his mother to stand still and thus meet in a way that was not possible in the past. He is thus able to overturn the familiar maternal reprimand "non ora, non qui" (not now, not here; 44) that characterized his relationship with his mother when he was growing up. From his newly established viewpoint within the photographic image, from the stillness such a point grants, the narrator sees the possibility of establishing an intimate connection with his mother. "Chi si ferma si incontra, anche una mamma giovane e un figlio anziano" (Who stops will meet, even a young mother and an aged son; 44), he explains. When one can stay still, time loses its weight and cannot be felt as an oppressive force, "non è più la soma che sagoma la schiena" (it is no longer the burden that breaks one's back; 44). Engagement with the photographic image makes time – recorded past time and present narrating time – fade in importance so that it can stand still for the narrator and his mother. Once suspended in time, they are unaffected by everything else in the photograph and in the narrated universe that is in motion.

A different temporal-spatial situation is introduced when the photograph is described by the narrator as portraying his mother standing in front of an old bus on a winter day. From this different vantage point and after some reflection on the scene, the narrator explains, "Tutto è fermo intorno, io solo potrei muovermi. Perlustro con gli occhi i visi dei passanti, tra essi vedo il tuo, mamma" (Everything is still around me; only I could move. I survey the passengers' faces with my eyes; among them, I see yours, mom; 15). Everyone and everything in the photograph is still, yet the narrator enjoys the freedom to move through time and space. This possibility allows him to look from one passenger to another until his gaze stops on his mother: "Guardo la tua faccia: tu guardi" (I am looking at your face; you look; 17). Moving across the photographic image, which portrays his mother in a heavy brown coat as she is "fissando l'autobus" (looking at the bus; 17) or "fissando qualcuno" (looking at someone; 18), the narrator delves deeper into its details, looking across them through a number of screens, each one in a different time and space. He specifies:

> Sento che è già avvenuto, altrove. In altri momenti, so adesso, ti ho visto attraversare il cancello di un giardino di San Giorgio a Cremano da bambina giocare con la terra, o attraverso i vetri di una veranda rincorrere i tuoi fratelli intorno a un tavolo da pranzo ed esserne rincorsa. Ho già visto attraverso. (19)

> I feel as though it has all happened, elsewhere. In other moments, I now know, I saw you across the gate of a garden of San Giorgio in Cremano as a girl playing in the dirt, or across the glass of a veranda chasing after your brothers around a table as they chased you. I have already seen across.

The narrator's looking gives rise to a witnessing of events that took place at a different time and in different places than the one imaged in the photographic image. It is quite plausible that the narrator's witnessing of other times and places is born of or at the very least entangled in the creation of memories by other photographs collected in the family albums. It is equally plausible that he "sees" other times and places that were never photographed but were told through the stories of others or imagined by the narrator. Either way, the photograph's meaning and its evidential power reside with the narrator's viewing, not with the photograph's showing.

By looking across several details to other moments and places, the narrator moves towards creating a past identity as it intersects with that of his mother. Since his past identity is irretrievable through memory because it never was (he insists that as a child he existed only in the shadow of his mother's voice and in the painful stories of others), the photographic image can only hold meaning in the narrator's present viewing time and space. So, although it cannot serve as a trace of his past – "Gli album, gli archivi non mi sorreggono la memoria, invece la sostituiscono" (The albums, the archives don't trigger my memory; instead, they substitute it; 7) – the photograph certainly offers a means for the narrator to occupy the past anew. This begins to explain why, although the photographic image portrays a past moment (his mother is in her thirties), what the narrator sees in it is a future possibility, a possibility that would allow him to meet his mother. When considering that this opportunity may be missed, he exclaims, "Aspetta mamma, non avere fretta anche da ferma in una fotografia" (Wait, mom, don't be in a hurry even when still in a photographic image; 22). The narrator's urgency to see and be seen by his mother, even if across a photograph, cannot be underestimated. Such a meeting is crucial for the creation of his self.

When, however, time yields to space and everyone in the photograph is moving except for the narrator and his mother, it is the present narrative moment – that of the narrator's death – that is being examined. Like death, the photographic image offers the narrator an ideal opportunity for understanding and fully claiming his self, since "solo in morte la vita è interamente di chi l'ha vissuta, e il possesso è senza donatori, senza rimproveri" (only in death does life belong entirely to who lived it, and the possession is without givers, without reproach; 39). Studied at the moment of death, the photograph permits him to situate himself in his present, a present that is entirely his. Like death, it presents an ideal situation for self-reflection, one that permits the exclusion of all others.

This is what lies behind the frame of the window, so often mentioned in *Non ora, non qui*. Just as the window protects the mother from the narrator's words, so the photograph protects him from his mother's words that denied him existence and controlled his body, thoughts, and actions as a child. Now, at his moment of death, he is able to efface her dominance over him and to claim his own identity. The photograph and, in particular, its invitation to imagine possible narratives provide the distance necessary to permit self-awareness. The narrator is thus able to view his self anew and project that self onto a possible future: "Ora nella fotografia che ci ferma io potrei scendere a questa fermata. Ti verrei incontro attraversando la strada. Potremmo ancora avere un seguito. Verrei a darti il braccio. Cosa faremmo? Noi capiremmo. Sottobraccio capiremmo tutta la nostra vita" (In the photograph that stills us, I could get off at this stop now. I would cross the street and come towards you. We could still have a continuation. I would come and give you my arm. What would we do? We would understand. Arm-in-arm we would understand all of our life; 51).

A future interaction between mother and son is possible because the narrator simultaneously occupies two temporal and spatial frames: that of his viewing self as a man in his sixties who is nearing death, and that of the photograph, which portrays his mother in her thirties, looking into the bus window where her aged son (the dying narrator) is looking out at her. Faced with the moment of his own death, De Luca's narrator reads his own self, his own destiny, his own identity into the photograph, which depicts his mother in her thirties. Across the narrator's sustained act of viewing, the photographic image's time and space are repeatedly confounded with those of the dying narrator, who proceeds towards death in both worlds. The closing line of *Non ora, non qui* makes this complex spatial and temporal universe evident. Speaking of his mother, the narrator recalls, "Un giorno di domenica tornasti a casa e raccontasti di avere visto un uomo morire in un autobus" (One Sunday you came home and told us about having seen a man die in a bus; 91). In *Non ora, non qui*, it is possible for the mother to witness the death of her adult son and recount the extraordinary event of seeing a man die to that very son. This "strana condizione" (strange condition; 22) is possible "perché il possibile è il limite mobile di ciò che uno è disposto ad ammettere" (because the possible is the movable limit of what one is prepared to admit; 19).[6]

De Luca's *Non ora, non qui* thus breaks away from understandings of the photographic image as temporally and spatially immobile (cf. Lanslots 239 and Spunta, "A Balanced Displacement" 388). Instead, it highlights how reading and, by extension, the reality – past and present – that comes from reading, together invigorate, expand upon, or literally give life to the photograph's multiple temporal-spatial possibilities. The photograph, which pictures "una mamma giovane e un figlio anziano" (a young mother and an old son; 44), triggers the narrator's reflection on the photographic image's spatial-temporal ambiguity. "Il tempo [time]," he specifies while looking at the photographic image, "fa come le nuvole e i fondi del caffè: cambia le pose, mescola le forme" (behaves like clouds and tea leaves at the bottom of the cup: it changes shapes, mixing forms; 44). Faced with the photographic image, the narrator experiences its temporal and spatial mutability and indeterminacy. Time and space are not locked by the photographic image; on the contrary, they are constantly changing so that *nothing* in the image remains the same.[7] In other words, that which the photograph shows is suspended in the unknowable, in a space that does not stand still, or in what Myriam Swennen Ruthenberg describes as the "non-spazio e [...] non-tempo di *Non ora, non qui*" (non-space and ... non-time of *Non ora, non qui*; 52).

In both possible temporal-spatial combinations, the narrator recognizes his mother, who, as portrayed in the image, is far too young to have an elderly son, and the mother, in turn, partakes in the narrator's world, seeing him looking at her without recognizing him as her own son. Looking at the photographic image, the narrator carries its content, its past time and setting, into his own uncharted future. Photographic time thus collapses into narrative time to document a future event, the narrator's death. In this way, the photograph is a veritable instigator of stories.[8]

Stepping into the Photographic Image

As such, the photographic image in *Non ora, non qui* can be described as the motor of De Luca's narrative: it extends beyond what is pictured to push the narrative forward, announcing past and future events and introducing possible stories. The photograph's narrative function in *Non ora, non qui* is so pronounced that Spunta describes the novel as "revolving on the metaphor of vision and silence" ("A Balanced Displacement" 386). As suggested by Spunta, although the narrator refers to his past difficulties with language – he was "il muto" (the mute one; 27), "balbuziente" (stuttering; 8), and "poco adatto a farsi intendere e forse poco disposto" (not too cut out to make himself understood or perhaps not very willing; 15) – in front of the photographic image, he is not silent. On the contrary, the image triggers his speech, creating "una strana condizione" (a strange condition; 22) where he is able to meet his younger mother. For the narrator, looking at photographs is a looking that refers not so much to the specific scene imaged, but rather to one who is engaged in a process of narration that infuses the image with his highly subjective experience. The photographic image's visual details – all that would otherwise work towards stimulating memory – recede or diminish in significance when such a looking takes place. For De Luca's narrator (and for the story of *Non ora, non qui*), what matters in looking at the photographic image are the uncountable number of stories that the forms or impressions on its surface give rise to, stories that can be of the past or of the future.

Photography critic Serge Tisseron emphasizes that the photographic image is always for someone insofar as it demands commentary (29). What is imaged, in other words, asks to be verbalized, to be expanded into a narrative by the viewer through the very act of looking. Hence, Tisseron concludes that there is no stasis – spatial or temporal – in the photographic image. On the contrary,

> any photograph carries a virtual spatiality and temporality which constantly dislocate its spectator from the spatiality and temporality that belonged to the referent, when the picture was taken. This is why photography is both a space to be explored and a time in progress. (qtd in Louvel, "Photography as Critical Idiom" 33)

Because photographic images separate "the viewer in time and space from the guarantors of this truth – the events and objects that had generated the image" (Osborne 10), they invite spatial and temporal expansion. In other words, they demand from their viewers a type of looking that asks them to "find themselves in imagination" (Elkins, *What Photography Is* 50).

De Luca's narrator articulates two future possibilities as he sees them in the photographic image: his reunion with his mother who is half his current age (22), and his reclaiming of his identity, which occurs at the time of his own death (39). Recognizing himself in the act of looking (14), the narrator performs (i.e., literally embodies) the superimposition of two moments – the past, that of the photographed event, and the present, that of his act of reading the photograph – which conflate to give rise to a future possibility. His reaching into the photographic image openly explores its narrative gesture towards the future. Throughout *Non ora, non qui*, the photographic image to which the narrator returns over and over again is meaningful in relation to his subjective looking practices and narrative voice. As argued above, his looking and speaking identify several temporal-spatial frames at once, thus confirming the photographic image's relation to space and time as undetermined or, at the very least, as less fixed than conventional thinking about photography has allowed.

In "A Short History of Photography," Walter Benjamin remarks on the photograph's imaged subject as resistant to being neatly accommodated or fixed in a past time. The precise technique of photography, as Benjamin thought it to be, can render a past event present, real here and now. Benjamin describes the photograph's reach into a time beyond that which is pictured as something "strange and new" to photography. He writes that in certain photographs, the "spark [of accident] has, as it were, burned through the person in the image with reality, finding the indiscernible place in the condition of that long past minute where the future is nesting, even today, so eloquently that we looking back can discover it" (202).[9] For Benjamin, the photograph's potential to reach into the future is a narrative potential, one where the viewer's imagination is triggered through the process of reading the visual. Indeed, the viewer's interpretative engagement with the photographic image realizes the photograph's complex temporal ambiguity, where the past overlaps with the present and leads into the future. For Benjamin, the photograph's "particular appeal … emerges from an underlying sense of displacement that contrasts with its tangible presence and immediacy" (Duttlinger, "Imaginary Encounters" 84).

In De Luca's *Non ora, non qui*, the photograph's temporal ambiguity is coupled with a spatial ambiguity, where the narrator's looking at the photograph is both a *seeing as* and a *seeing in*, seeing governed by or restricted to what the image is of and seeing as an expansionary process that subjectively engages with what is pictured in the photographic image. Spatial ambiguity can be understood as what Maurice Merleau-Ponty refers to as "double perception" (159–60) or the act of seeing into what is photographed so that at least two spaces are always commingling: that of the photographed event and that of what the viewer sees in the photograph. When the narrator looks at the photograph of his mother in front of a bus, his viewing space overlaps or is confounded with the photograph's space: the narrator occupies simultaneously the photograph's space and a separate narrative space situated outside of, but dependent on, the photographic space. Engaged in a different kind of seeing, a seeing *in* where the gaze penetrates the photographic image's surface,[10] the narrator is transposed into the pictured space so that apparently distinct temporal and spatial realms blur into one another.

This shifting or moving of time and space within and across the photograph is born from the act of looking, an act that has been theorized as proving "yesterday [to be] no more than an endless today" (Rim, qtd in North 3). In its use of photography, *Non ora, non qui* can be said to enact a poetics of photographic looking. To enact a poetics of photographic looking is to distance oneself from notions of photographic fixity and to concentrate instead on the photograph's *present* realization, its actual visualization, its assessment, and all of that has to do with the experience to which reading gives rise.[11] It is to embrace the photographic image's invitation to imagine possible narratives, to expose its claim to a past moment and past event in a past space as stimulating the creation of new memories, and, finally, to accentuate the photograph's inherent entanglement in the present.

Looking at the photographic image, De Luca's narrator experiences his look returned to him by his mother and sees himself being seen. He compares this exchange of gazes to looking at certain types of paintings: "Ci sono occhi in certi quadri che seguono lo spettatore ovunque esso si sposti. È così per me adesso: tu guardi e io ho l'impressione di essere guardato" (There are eyes in certain paintings that follow the viewer wherever s/he moves. This is how it is for me right now: you look and I have the impression of being looked at; 18). In this type of "unusually forceful and sustained" looking (Elkins, *What Photography Is* 211), a looking that excites the drive to look more, to see beyond, the narrator is able to render his absent self present in the photograph. Although he is not visibly reproduced on the photograph's imaged surface, he is nonetheless the principal object to be understood across its reading.

This process of self-objectification through looking makes his present space and time overlap with the space and time of the photograph. The narrator explains what he sees in the photograph as unsurprisingly occupying the actual dimensions of his space, that is, the space of his viewing:

> Guardo la fotografia. Non mi stupisco di come si vada ingrandendo e dei particolari che riesco a cogliere. [...] Dalla via del mercatino viene gente. Il formato di quello che sto vedendo aumenta, decresce la scala: uno a cento, uno a cinquanta, uno a dieci fino a che la dimensione dei passanti raggiunge la mia taglia o io la loro. (14)

> I look at the photograph. I'm not surprised to see that it gets bigger nor of the details that I am able to see ... People are coming from the road where the market takes place. The format of that which I see is growing, decreasing the scale: one to one hundred, one to fifty, one to ten until the dimension of those walking by reaches my own size and I theirs.

That the photograph grows in scale or that the narrator shrinks to the photograph's size indicates a complete absorption in the act of reading the photograph, a stepping into the photograph that eliminates frames, focusing devices and, most importantly, temporal-spatial distinctions. The narrator is at one and the same time within *and* without the photograph. He is both viewing subject and viewed object.

Stepping into the photographic image allows the narrator to work through his inclusion (or exclusion) in the world. The photograph is like a map that permits him to either see the whole picture or focus on one facet of the whole. As De Luca's narrator confirms, the photograph is the element that divides living from understanding even while uniting these. "Ho già visto attraverso" (I've already seen across), he states. "Non è come la vita-dei-giorni, che non cura schermi, è come la vita-improvvisa-dei-momenti che si rivela, ma con la precauzione di un diaframma, sia esso fotografia, cancello, finestra o lacrime agli occhi" (It is not like the day-to-day life, which does not respect patterns;

it is like the unpredictable moment-to-moment living that reveals itself, but with the precaution of a screen, whether it be a photograph, a gate, a window or tears in one's eyes; 19). In *Non ora, non qui,* the photographic image encourages a focused view on the whole as well as on the focusing apparatus that allows one to see the individual components that make up the whole. Through this type of viewing, the "vita-improvvisa-dei-momenti" overlaps with the "vita-dei-giorni" so that temporal and spatial ambiguity propels the narrative forward, inviting the formulation of unpredictable narratives.

The photographic image offers up to its viewers an open space, one where each viewer is invited to imbue the photographic image with meaning. Some, like Max Kozloff, claim that this invitation to "step through the [photograph's] surface" rests on the apparent absence of an author (17). Others, like Michael North, suggest that the invitation to enter into the photograph rests upon the image's possibility of visual maladjustment, that is, of its forcing an improper or strange seeing. Either way, as De Luca's *Non ora, non qui* suggests across its treatment of photography, the photograph is a space full of details about a past, details that need to be fattened in order to render meaningful the photograph and the past to which it lays claim. Each reader, then, steps into the image, ultimately thrusting the present into the past of the image as well as into the past of his or her own personal history. It is thus "bello scendere in una fotografia, bello stare fermi" (nice to descend into a photograph, nice to stay still; 41). To descend into the photograph is to experience its ability to "establish a hold on the past in which history is sealed, so to speak, in a continuous present" (Clarke 11–12).

As indicated by the unique viewing experience presented in De Luca's *Non ora, non qui,* the photographic image's ability to document the past has little or nothing to do with the objective recording of reality. Instead, it has everything to do with the subjective. By presenting something of the past, the photograph offers the occasion for viewers to imagine beyond it. It is in the subjective that its power lies, a power that transposes readers into a past space and time that is not clearly separate from their present space and time.[12]

Conclusion

Unlike in many other literary texts that make use of photography, the temporal and spatial displacement set in motion in *Non ora, non qui* by the narrator's looking practices actually exposes the photograph's ontological deception. Although certainly produced by a mechanical process, photographic images contain ambiguous, complex, and contradictory narrative possibilities.[13] Their meaning is determined in the present through the viewer's practices of looking, so that what is imaged actually has more to do with the reader than it does with the past object placed before the camera, mechanically imprinted and imaged on the photographic image's surface. Once the messiness informing the photographic representation of space and time is recognized and accepted or, indeed, performed as it is in De Luca's text, the photographic image's narrative role is one of bridging the past and present so to carry them into the future. What De Luca's text shows is that because a photographic image is, as John Berger says, "weak in intentionality" (Berger and Mohr, *Another Way of Telling* 90), its meaning resides not so much in what it shows, but rather in what its reader makes, wants, or believes it to show.

Looking creates a narrative link between distinct temporal spaces. It also exposes what the photographic image means as actually standing somewhat, but nonetheless significantly, apart from the time and space of that which is pictured. Through the act of looking, the neat distinction of two worlds, that of the photographic image and that of the narrator, collapses. So, although the viewing narrator exists separate from the time and space of the photograph, his present time and space also coincide with that of the photograph. Because of the spatio-temporal ambiguity born of photographic reading practices, photographic images in *Non ora, non qui* create memories, draw forth possible stories, and bear witness to future events.

NOTES

1 This and all subsequent translations are mine.

2 Time and again, photographic images have been described as "honest, realistic likness[es]" (Abbott 181), as "faithful pictorial records" (Arago 17), as "plastic verification[s] of a fact" (De Zayas 125), as "pure, almost meaningless factuality" (Stahel 13), as "evidence" (Struk 5). Even today, when revisionist practices and theories continue to "question the assumed idea that photographs depict some pro-filmic event" (Edwards 182), it is difficult to dispel belief in the photograph's evidential status, a status that understands the photographic image as an absolute objective record of things as they are. Despite the gathering distrust of a documentary

objectivity inherent in the camera, the photographic image and its power to provide a "deeply meaningful record," a truthful document of life that brings "into the open hidden facts," has come "roaring back" (Goldberg 13–19). In short, the photographic image continues to trade on its claim to optical truth, asking viewers "to accept as real the existence of the object reproduced, actually, re-presented, set before [them], that is to say, in time and space" (Bazin 241). Indeed, recent work by Marianne Hirsch relies heavily on this influential assumption about the photographic image's documentary status.

3 Photography has been described repeatedly as freezing time and space. As early as 1839, Fox Talbot harked on the instantaneity of photography, emphasizing that "all that is fleeting and momentary, may be fettered by the spells of our 'natural magic' and may be fixed for ever in the position which it seemed only destined for a single instant to occupy" (qtd in Prodger 34). Talbot's articulation of photography as a process in which fleeting time is arrested in the space of a single moment has been echoed and expanded upon by a number of critics of photography, including Sontag (17), Swinnen (178), and Weston (171).

4 See Watt 57.

5 For an alternative reading of Romano's use of photography in her autobiographical texts, see my "From Photographic Product to Photographic Text" and "Reading the Photographic Text with Lalla Romano."

6 A more conservative reading would not conflate the two temporal–spatial frames so completely; instead, such a reading would argue that one frame designates the intradiegetic fictional world where the narrator is looking at the photograph and the other the imaginative domain within the fictional world born of the narrator's viewing. This reading is in line with the reader's reality (i.e., the extradiegetic empirical world) but does not fully account for the book's closing line, for its sustained spatial–temporal ambiguity, or for its unique reading experience, in that readers are uncertain as to where imagination begins and intradiegetic reality ends. It does, however, bestow upon the act of reading the photograph the same creative power as my slightly different reading does. I would like to thank the two reviewers of this article for stimulating this discussion.

7 James Elkins argues that through viewing, "nothing [imaged in the photograph] is the same, everything has moved. There is no duration, nothing remains" (*What Photography Is* 61).

8 Ulrich Baer argues that the transfer of the photographic referent into the future is implicit in every photograph (23). I would emphasize that it is implicit not in the photograph but in the act of reading the photograph. It

is the viewer, not the image, that pushes the photographic referent into the future.

9 Benjamin's description of the photograph's power is tellingly similar to Barthes's definition of the photographic punctum.

10 See Elkins, *What Photography Is* 19–21.

11 See Louvel, "Photography as Critical Idiom" 33; and Ortel 254.

12 For an extended analysis of the importance of the subjective for photographic meaning, see my "Documenting the Fictions of Reality."

13 Critics who have stopped on the photograph's ontological deception are numerous; they include Damisch (88); Solomon-Godeau (169–83); and Tagg, *The Burden of Representation* (187–9).

PART THREE

Narrated Photographs and Photographs Narrating

6 Photo-Poems: Visual Impact Strategies and Photo-Story in the Work of Mario Giacomelli and Luigi Crocenzi

MARCO ANDREANI

Nel corso di un sogno [...] non si racconterebbe a se stessi, ma si fantasticherebbe un quadro, una situazione statici, espressivi di uno stato psicofisico, la 'passione dominante.' L'apparente svolgersi di azione in sogno, nascerebbe dalla successione degli inconsci tentativi volti a definire sempre meglio la visione [...]. Come chi vi mostrasse un quadro; poi subito dopo lo stesso quadro con personaggi mutati e ritoccati. Se ciò fosse fatto con velocità e come si deve – ecco il racconto cinematografico, ma un racconto dove ogni sequenza è un tentativo rinnovato di dire la stessa cosa.

Cesare Pavese, *Il mestiere di vivere*, 14 February 1941

During a dream ... you would not tell a story to yourself, but rather you would envisage a static painting or situation, expressions of a psychophysical state, the "dominant passion." The apparent unfolding of the action in a dream arises from the succession of unconscious attempts to bring greater and greater clarity to the vision ... As if someone showed you a painting; then right afterwards the same painting with the figures altered and retouched. If that were done quickly and correctly – it would be cinematographic narration, but a narration where each sequence is a renewed attempt at saying the same thing.

In the column "Il giornale dei peccati" ("The Journal of Sins") in the literary review *Il Caffè politico e letterario* (*The Political and Literary Café*), Luigi Crocenzi (1923–1984) published a few episodes of a photo-novel between December 1954 and April 1955. The novel – which was never actually completed – was based on a written outline and set in a timeless and culturally hidebound Italian province.[1] One episode in particular, called *Un seminarista* (*The Seminarian*), tells the story of a young man who, bored with life in a seminary, runs away to Rome to throw himself into everyday life in a working-class neighbourhood. There he meets a woman with whom he eventually falls in love. A few years later, prompted by a poem by Father David Maria Turoldo, Mario Giacomelli (1925–2000) completed *Io non ho mani che mi accarezzino il volto* (*No Hands Are There to Caress My Face*) (1961–3), his famous series of "little priests" photographed running and dancing in the snow in the seminary of Senigallia.

These two works are central to a fascinating yet little-known episode that illustrates the relationship between Italian literature and photography. They allow us to shed some light on the historical links between Giacomelli and Crocenzi – links that are as interesting as they are under-researched.[2] Many of Giacomelli's sequences were born out of the evocative power of a poetic text[3] and have their origins in theories and activities promoted by Crocenzi in the 1950s and 1960s.

Both Giacomelli's sequence and Crocenzi's *Un seminarista* are based on written texts and examine similar subjects. Also, both highlight the rift between a life of disciplined seclusion in a seminary and life on the outside. In each case, the conflict centres on the physical and emotional world of the protagonists and triggers a form of escapism. However, there are profound structural differences between the photographic sequences and the figurative solutions arrived at by each of the authors. The two works, therefore, offer fertile ground for a comparative study highlighting two different and paradigmatic views of photography and its relationship with written language.

Inspired by democratic ideals and neorealism, Crocenzi sees photography both as a means of investigation and as a tool of mass communication. In his photo-stories, his photographs work like written words, which have been carefully assembled in a precise diegetic order in order to convey a clear and truthful message. Giacomelli, by contrast, seems to work with no practical goal in mind; in the semantic ambiguity of photographic images, he sees a chance to shape the deep and unresolved tensions unleashed by the poetic text. Each photograph represents, for him, an attempt to express as much as possible, thus revealing ambiguous, conflicting, and ever-changing meanings so that the final sequence, in whatever order it is ultimately constructed, always results in a circular structure that repeats variations on an unchanging theme.

Crocenzi's Democratic Notion of the Photographic Language

The two photographers met in 1954, when Crocenzi invited Giuseppe Cavalli – who was Giacomelli's teacher – to join him in creating a cultural movement to renew photography in Italy.[4] Crocenzi, an eclectic photographer as well as an avid reader and cinemagoer, came into contact with some of the key features of postwar cultural renewal during his years as a student. At that time, Italy was brimming with ideas, rediscovering its identity, and recovering from Fascist oppression. In 1946 and 1947, Crocenzi was in Milan, where he met Elio Vittorini, editor of the magazine *Il Politecnico* (*The Polytechnic*), who was deeply committed to disseminating culture "per la rigenerazione della società italiana" (in order to regenerate Italian society; qtd in Forti and Pautasso 6). Crocenzi published various photo-stories in *Il Politecnico*, all of which treated working-class subjects,[5] with photographs arranged in columns on the page as if they were frames from a movie. In 1948, he moved to Rome, where he took courses on film directing at the *Centro Sperimentale di Cinematografia* (Experimental Centre of Cinematography), which was run by Luigi Chiarini and Umberto Barbaro, both of whom aimed to create a realist cinema capable of conveying an idea of "la vita vera e i personaggi concreti dell'Italia contemporanea" (real life with actual characters from contemporary Italy; Laura et al. 30). Chiarini and Barbaro emphasized the social and educational value of such work. At the centre, Crocenzi experienced neorealism first-hand and encountered the theories of montage developed by Eisenstein, Pudovkin, and Béla Balázs. Finally in 1950, with Vittorini, he travelled to Sicily, where he took about 180 photographs for the illustrated edition of *Conversazione in Sicilia* (*Conversations in Sicily*) (1953).

In the mid-1950s, with Alvaro Valentini[6] and other collaborators, Crocenzi founded the *Centro per la cultura nella fotografia* (Centre for Culture in Photography; CCF) in Fermo. That group promoted an approach to photography that linked together various snapshots in rapid sequence, treating each photograph as equivalent to a word of text. For Valentini, "ogni fotogramma" (each frame) was a "*parola da vedere*" (*word to be seen*) (*Premio Annuale* n. pag., emphasis in original). This concept lay at the heart of an ambitious project whose aim was to democratize culture by making it more accessible to the working classes at a time when there was a heated debate over how intellectuals could best further social reform in Italy. This debate coincided with the publication, between 1948 and 1951, of Antonio Gramsci's prison diaries, *Quaderni del carcere* (*Prison Notebooks*).

For Crocenzi, photographic language differed from written language in that it could be understood and used by anyone, given its uncodified immediacy and simple technology. When planning the exhibition "Il giorno degli italiani" ("The Day of the Italians") with Cesare Zavattini, Crocenzi invited everyone, not just professional or amateur photographers, to use photography to document the everyday life of Italians, whatever their social background.[7] At the same time, Crocenzi dreamed of creating a new form of literature based on images: "I fotografi saranno gli scrittori, gli storici e i poeti della nostra società" (Photographers will be the writers, historians, and poets of our society; CCF, "Discussione" 44). Thoughts and ideas disseminated in this way would be accessible to millions of people all over the world.

As Valentini put it, the language of photography would be able to take on "tutte le funzioni, da quella artistica a quella didascalica" (all of the functions, from artistic to didactic; *Mostra di fotografia* n. pag.) by juxtaposing one image with another "come di sostantivo ad aggettivo, [...] soggetto a verbo" (like that of a noun to an adjective ... a subject to a verb"; *Premio annuale* n. pag.). But according to Crocenzi and Valentini, the language of photography still lacked an established tradition and had neither the precise grammar and syntax nor the communicative flexibility of written language. For this reason, the CCF's publications highlighted the need to study the sequences of the great photo-journalists; the editing techniques, image compositions, and layouts developed within the fields of cinema, painting, and graphics; and texts about visual semiotics and the psychology of form. For the same reason, the CCF ran a column in the review *Ferrania* that focused on photographic language, with contributions by people such as Herman Craeybeckx, Albert Plécy, and Paul Sonthonnax.[8] Often working alongside photographers, graphic designers, writers, and linguists, Crocenzi began several publishing projects. Between 1959 and 1969, the CCF organized exhibitions dedicated to photo-stories, photo-reportage, and photo-books.

The correspondence between Crocenzi and Giacomelli began in 1956 and lasted until 1983.[9] The period of their most intense collaboration, however, was from the late 1950s to the early 1970s. Documents indicate that after 1959, Giacomelli took part more and more frequently in the exhibitions and editorial projects promoted by the CCF and that Crocenzi himself inspired Giacomelli to create series such as *Un uomo una donna un amore* (*A Man a Woman One Love*), a kind of photo-novel, and "La buona terra" ("The Good Land"), a story about the life of a farming family. Most importantly, it was Crocenzi who provided Giacomelli with the detailed storyboards for the sequences *A Silvia* (*To Silvia*) (unpublished) and "Caroline Branson," based on the poems of Giacomo Leopardi and Edgar Lee Master respectively.[10]

A Silvia was part of a project that aimed to popularize great works of literature by recasting them as photographic works. On 8 November 1963, Crocenzi wrote to Giacomelli to tell him about the launch of a new review that, in a column titled "Testo a fronte" ("Parallel Text"), would contain prose and poetry texts "translated" into photographic language through the "concatenazione" (concatenation; CRAF, Crocenzi Fund n. pag.) of images. On 13 November, Crocenzi further explained that these translations would be created by following a series of steps: "sunto della storia" (story summary); the development of a "soggetto" (storyline) and a "sceneggiatura" (storyboard; CRAF, Crocenzi Fund n. pag.); the making of the images; and the final editing and layout. The storyboards, developed from poems by Eugenio Montale, Giuseppe Ungaretti, and Giacomo Leopardi, were subsequently turned into a series of photographs by Giacomelli himself and by Ugo Mulas, Ferdinando Scianna, and various other photographers. In the end, these works were not published; instead, they were filmed and broadcast by RAI in 1964 as part of "Telescuola" ("TeleSchool") programming for schools. This indicates why their final editing outlines also specified frame times; the movements to be followed by the television camera; fade-ins and fade-outs; and the soundtrack.[11]

Crocenzi chose written language as his theoretical frame of reference, which suggests equivalence, at a structural level, between photographic, linguistic, and cinematographic discourse. Thus, the photographic image was to be considered "alla stregua della inquadratura nel film, parola (Pudovkin) da articolare e comporre nella pagina" (just like each shot in a film, like words (Pudovkin) articulated and composed on a page; CCF n2). As Pudovkin wrote, for a director "each shot of the finished film subserves the same purpose as the word to the poet … [He pieces] together the "phrases of editing" from which a film will gradually emerge step by step; 24).

For Crocenzi, the storyboard, the editing, and the photographic layout were the principal concerns when it came to constructing a photographic sequence, whether this involved visually transposing poetic or prose works (in the letters dated 8 and 13 November 1963, no distinction is made between the two) or describing or narrating real situations or events. For the photo-stories and photo-reportages of "Storie italiane" ("Italian Stories"), for instance, Crocenzi recommended dividing the creative process into the following stages: interrogating the main theme, developing the story, rendering the story photographically, developing the narrative montage, and, finally, creating the final layout of words and pictures on the page ("Storie italiane" 18).

Each time, in fact, the final sequence was conceived and articulated in the same way as a written text. Thus, it emerged from a rigorous process of selecting and combining images, a process that reflected the paradigmatic and syntagmatic axes of Saussure's linguistic theory.[12] Through the association of images, wrote Crocenzi, "il discorso si forma" (speech takes shape; "Storie italiane" 20); and while each of these images in its own right has its own meaning, those meanings vary as a function of how the images are arranged in sequence. The *syntactic* component is vital to an understanding of the work. For this reason, Crocenzi urged the editor of *Il Caffé* to publish his photo-stories "nelle sequenze complete da me preparate" (in the complete sequences I have prepared); otherwise, he continued, it would be as if "dei suoi articoli [...] pubblicassero frasi staccate e con il senso alterato" (your articles ... were published in disjointed sentences and with an altered meaning; Letter to the Editor). Similarly, Nazareno Taddei, one of the CCF's theoreticians, associated photographic sign with verbal sign, referring to the concepts of "denotation" and "connotation" formulated by Barthes in "Le message photographique" ("The Photographic Message") (1961). In the case of a photo-story, the author expresses his own thoughts not only at a connotative level, through the way he structures every single image (frame choice, angle, lighting, etc.), but also through the choices he makes when sequencing the photographs, so that the images stand for "vocaboli di una sola frase" (words of a single phrase; Taddei n. pag.). For a photo-story, therefore, to be defined as such: "1) ogni fotografia deve dire qualcosa [...] 2) la fotografia successiva deve dire qualcosa di nuovo sulla precedente; 3) tra la fotografia precedente e quella successiva ci deve essere un rapporto di sviluppo" (1) every photo must say something ... 2) the next photo must say something new about the one before; 3) from the one photo to the next there should be a progressive relationship"; n. pag.).[13]

Photo-Story and Variations on the Same Theme

Giacomelli was fascinated by the breadth of a project that saw photography as crucial for human progress. His letters to Crocenzi contain positive comments about him and, as he put it, about the "fotografia intesa come quella per la quale giustamente ti batti" (kind of photography that you are justly fighting for; 22 September 1965, CRAF). Furthermore, except for a few portraits and still lifes from the early period, Giacomelli would always work through cycles of photos consisting of tens or hundreds of prints, usually completed over several years. However, between the two men, notwithstanding these periods of collaboration, there are certain clear and important differences in terms of theory.

Crocenzi's works are based on the principle of maximum intelligibility. They emphasize the visual – an emphasis he derives from neorealism. For Crocenzi, however, a visual text is subordinate to the theoretical supremacy of a written one insofar as its message is more immediately "readable." Reality is a book to be read, one that tells the truth and can be understood by everyone. However, the members of the CCF never succeeded in elaborating an organic and original theory of the language of photography. They equated it with a system of signs, and they made it comparable to a language – but these are key building blocks in linguistics and structural semiotics. Thus, the sense of a photographic image coincides with the meaning it conveys; there is a perfect overlap of visible, readable, and intelligible knowledge (Ronchi, *Il pensiero bastardo* 257).

Since the late 1970s, several theoreticians of photography, including Barthes himself, Rosalind Krauss, Philippe Dubois, Henri Van Lier, and Jean-Marie Schaeffer, have strongly challenged such assumptions, finding in Charles Sanders Peirce's semiotics an alternative to those of Ferdinand de Saussure. For them, the indexicality of the photographic image is its most distinctive trait, one that cannot be reduced to the paradigms of alphabetic writing and the mimesis of reality to which Crocenzi himself refers. Peirce distinguishes signs depending on how they are produced and, thus, on their relation to the referent. Such relations can be conventional (symbols: words, numbers, signs), of resemblance (icons: paintings, statues), or of physical connection (indices or traces: imprints, symptoms, clues, photographs). Any of these relationship types may be represented by any given sign – for example, a photograph may *also* look like its referent (and while this is often the case, it need not necessarily be so, as in the case of abstract photography or photos that have faded over time), or it may come to take on a symbolic meaning (Robert Capa's famous photo of the instant a Republican soldier is killed by a bullet, which came to stand for the Spanish Civil War). In this way, photography has strong ties to both the mimetic arts (icons) and written language (symbols), as in the case of Crocenzi. But before becoming an icon or a symbol, a photograph is an imprint left on the film emulsion by a fragment of reality that, for an instant that is gone forever, has found itself (*ça-a-été*, in Barthes's words) before the lens. And whatever it becomes later, it will always remain so. From this perspective, a photograph can be considered a "mute presence," one that is not mediated by the symbolization and internal organization processes[14] that demarcate the languages of traditional arts.

It was this aspect of photography that interested Giacomelli most of all. In his library there is a copy of Barthes's *Camera Lucida* – a key text for this theoretical turning point – copiously underlined by the photographer. The French theorist's well-known distinction between *studium* and *punctum* – which goes back to Peirce's distinction between icons, symbols, and indices – neatly summarizes Crocenzi's and Giacomelli's contrasting views on photography and its relationship with writing. Commenting on this distinction, Ronchi writes that on the one hand, there is a type of photograph "che *dice*" (that *speaks*), allowing itself to be read "come un testo" (like a text; "Immagine vita" 59, emphasis in original).[15] This type of photograph refers to a reality that meets our expectations, where nothing ever stands in the way of the order of the discourse (60). This is exactly how Crocenzi viewed photography. On the other hand, there is a "fotografia-indice" (photograph-index) that, instead of explaining what kind of object it refers to, documents its presence, giving us a "presente puro estraneo all'ordine diegetico della narrazione" (pure present unrelated to the diegetic order of narration; 60), where things, escaping any sense of judgment "che le scopre *come* questo o *come* quello, si mettono, grazie al *punctum*, a oscillare" (that reveals them *as* this or *as* that, begin to waver, thanks to the *punctum*; 62, emphasis in original).

This is the type of photography to which Giacomelli aspired, as we will see in the pages that follow: unlike the photo-story of Crocenzi (*Un seminarista*), Giacomelli's series *Io non ho mani che mi accarezzino il volto* completely lacks a narrative structure; instead, the work is resolved through the repetition of monothematic images that forever balance contrasting meanings and that are presented over and over again in a different order.

Un seminarista (see *Figures 6.1 and 6.2*) – a visual transposition of a short story outlined in preliminary form by Crocenzi in a series of notes[16] – consists of a preamble anticipating the main themes, followed by photographs and captions, all of which are set together in a precise order.

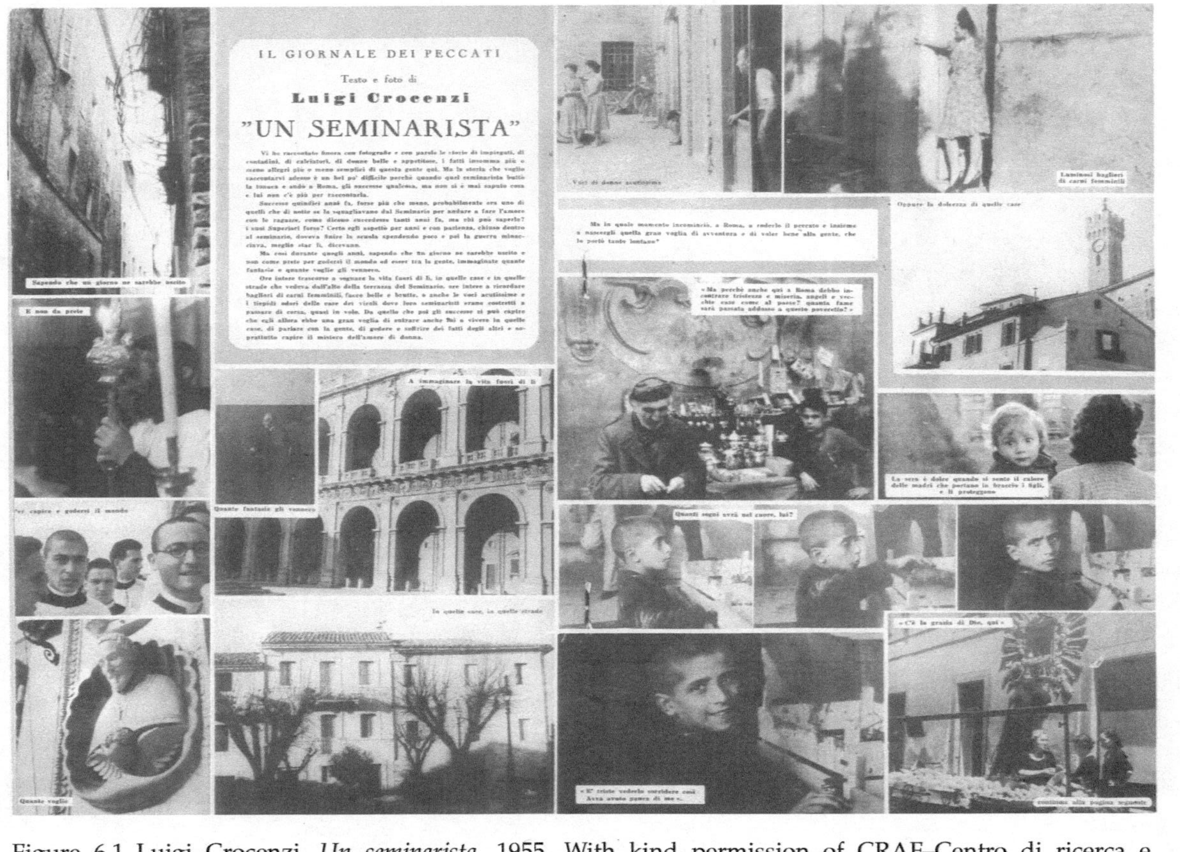

IL GIORNALE DEI PECCATI

Testo e foto di

Luigi Crocenzi

"UN SEMINARISTA"

Vi ho raccontato finora con fotografie e con parole le storie di impiegati, di contadini, di calzolai, di donne belle e appetitose, i fatti insomma più o meno allegri più o meno semplici di questa gente qui. Ma la storia che voglio raccontarvi adesso è un bel po' difficile perchè quando quel seminarista buttò la tonaca e andò a Roma, gli successe qualcosa, ma non si è mai saputo cosa e lui non c'è più per raccontarla.

Successe quindici anni fa, forse più che meno, probabilmente era uno di quelli che di notte se la squagliavano dal Seminario per andare a fare l'amore con le ragazze, come dicono succedesse tanti anni fa, ma chi può saperlo? i suoi *Superiori* forse? Certo egli aspettò per anni e con pazienza, chiuso dentro al seminario, doveva finire la scuola spendendo poco e poi la guerra minacciava, meglio star lì, dicevano.

Ma così durante quegli anni, sapendo che un giorno ne sarebbe uscito e non come prete per godersi il mondo ed esser tra la gente, immaginate quante fantasie e quante voglie gli vennero.

Ore intere trascorse a sognare la vita fuori di lì, in quelle case e in quelle strade che vedeva dall'alto della terrazza del Seminario, ore intere a ricordare bagliori di carni femminili, facce belle e brutte, e anche le voci acutissime e i tiepidi odori delle case dei vicoli dove loro seminaristi erano costretti a passare di corsa, quasi in volo. Da quello che poi gli successe si può capire che egli allora ebbe una gran voglia di entrare anche lui a vivere in quelle case, di parlare con la gente, di godere e soffrire dei fatti degli altri e soprattutto capire il mistero dell'amore di donna.

Ma in quale momento incominciò, a Roma, a vederlo il peccato e insieme a nascergli quella gran voglia di avventura e di voler bene alla gente, che lo portò tanto lontano?

Figure 6.1 Luigi Crocenzi, *Un seminarista*, 1955. With kind permission of CRAF–Centro di ricerca e archiviazione della fotografia, Spilimbergo.

IL QUADERNO DEL SABATO SERA

I VICOLI DI FERMO

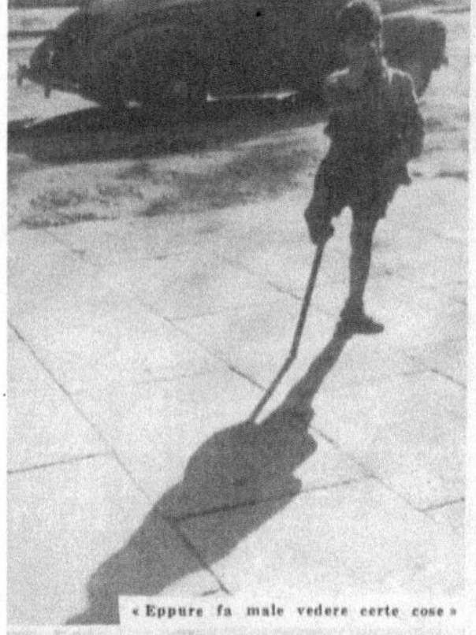

« Eppure fa male vedere certe cose »

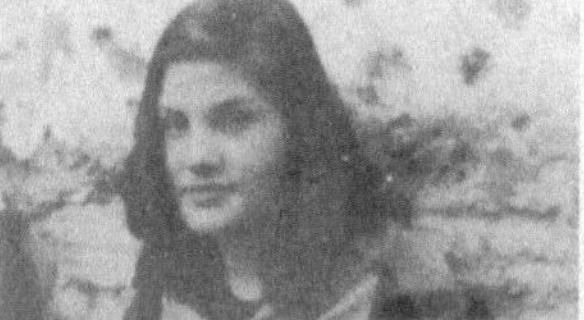

In questi occhi sogni, attese, speranze

Giro il mondo, le strade dei paesi, prendo a destra, a sinistra, imbocco un vicolo striminzito: chi cerco lo trovo sempre; lo fiuto a un miglio se è un allocco o un ladro, una ragazza forastica o un bocciolo, che la greve ombra vuol pungere e aprire.

Un uomo mi salta agli occhi, non perchè sta a grattarsi la schiena ai cardini delle porte; una donna può sedere su una panca nana o si spidocchia al sole, io le chiedo senza guardarla dove è per un sorso d'acqua. Sempre risponderà, saggia, con moderazione.

Così interrogo le città, carico di capricci, senza guida, né mete. Magari un quadro di Rubens mi contento saperlo in una chiesa, un museo non lo visito; ma la gente, le mani, le bambine, quelle che giuocano nei vicoli verdi, i vecchi, i gesti delle donne sui muri, le creature vive o morte negli androni, tutto questo me lo stampo davanti agli occhi per sempre, a riviverlo quando mi pare.

Ed ecco ora Fermo, la buffa e gonfia città, matura e bionda come un grappolo, dai cento vicoli digradanti dalla grande piazza, e dal Duomo altissimo sui tetti.

Cento, mille vicoli: un intrico di labirinti, di stretture, di graziose intricate meraviglie. C'è che i vicoli qui a Fermo non sono come nelle altre città d'Italia; qui, una volta che ti ci avventuri, è certo non li scordi più.

Prova a camminarci di giorno con il sole, verso sera al tramonto, poi la notte nei silenzi più aperti; àlzati sotto il mattino a respirarci il primo albore; può capitarti la storia di un contadino che sale per il dottore, ci parli della stagione, di sua moglie impedita dalla paralisi. Tutto può accadere: si raccontano storie di fanciulle rapite dietro grandi finestre, agguati con mantelli neri, pugnali dietro la schiena, poi esili castellane che appaiono sul fondo bianche ed aeree.

Credetemi, qui a Fermo tutto può accadere.

Un amico mi fa: — Vedi quella? — Io guardai la ragazza.

— E' l'angelo della città.

— Capisco, tu non m'imbrogli. — Pensai di correre, scappare sotto un arco, buttarmi dentro uno sdrucciolo.

Fermo è così, la più bizzarra e lunatica città delle Marche. Se l'abbracci ti dà l'anima, perchè i vicoli, cercate di capirlo, non sono strade aperte, sfacciate a tutti i venti; disdegnano la vita rumorosa, falsa, avvelenata delle piazze. Un vicolo è come il cuore, tutto chiuso, è un segreto. Una piazza è la mano, che all'ora stabilita si distende come una prostituta, spalanca il formicaio delle creature che s'odiano, si amano, si corrodono; la mano che a volte è vaiolosa, putrida, a volte splendida di vernici, lucida di pomate.

Basta un passo per sentirsi fuori, e la piazza la vedi là, come un piccolo campo da fiera.

A Fermo sali su dal corso o dalla strada nuova, appena entri in piazza, i primi a dirti eccomi, sono amici. Qui è il punto per ritrovarsi, poi scappare. Fermo credo sia l'unica città del mondo dove gli amici l'incontri a tutte l'ore, nevica o bruci il sole.

Ma la piazza è impostora; meglio i vicoli: un vicolo è carpirgli l'anima, tirargli giù i panni che lo coprono; le pietre, gli angoli, una piega che increspa una facciata, tutto ha sapore agrodolce. Un vicolo ha la sua storia, le sue verginità, il suo caldo pudore, i suoi santi da proteggere.

Un vicolo non si concede che per amore; solo allora puoi aprirlo come un frutto, crederci al suo sangue, alle sue tenerezze. Varcata la sua soglia, allora puoi camminare dove crude sono le verità, dove una donna puoi capirla cattiva, i figli tristi, uno che esce dalla galera col pensiero fisso di tornarci.

La vita d'una città sta nei vicoli, tra i muri di certe case che trasu-

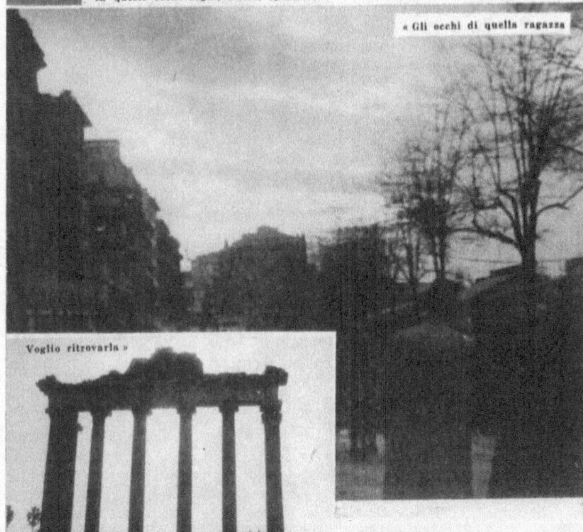

« Gli occhi di quella ragazza

Voglio ritrovarla »

Figure 6.2 Luigi Crocenzi, *Un seminarista*, 1955. With kind permission of CRAF–Centro di ricerca e archiviazione della fotografia, Spilimbergo.

On a first level, guided by the captions, reading the images is like reading a written text, from left to right and from the top to the bottom of each page. In the layout, the photographs are bound together by logical, spatial, and temporal relations and follow one another in a way that determines the gradual unfolding of descriptions and events: first we see the young man at the seminary (first page; see *Figure 6.1*); next, following his escape, in the backstreets of Rome (second page; see *Figure 6.1*); and then, in front of the girl with whom he eventually falls in love (third page; see *Figure 6.2*). The captions, which have both a narrative function and an explanatory one, alternate between the narrator's voice and the character's thoughts, where citation marks are used. This alternation makes for a continual shifting from an external view of the events to images conveying the main character's own perspective.

The photos on the first page are also juxtaposed with those on the second page by means of a kind of parallel montage that expresses the contrast between life in the seminary and that in a working-class neighbourhood.[17] The presence of seminarians in isolation and the bleakness of the seminary's inner courtyard on the first page are set against scenes of a mother holding her child, of prostitutes, and of varied aspects of humanity on the following page; the portrait of the seminarians is set against that of the urchin stealing fruit; the statue of the monk, in solitary isolation, is set against popular religion represented by such details as the tabernacle shown above the women in the marketplace. Clearly, if the layout were changed, or the number or type of images, the story's meaning would also change.

Nothing similar to this can be found in Giacomelli's series *Io non ho mani che mi accarezzino il volto*, nor in the equally well-known series *Vita d'ospizio* (*Hospice Life*) (1955–7), *Lourdes* (1957, 1959, 1966), or *Scanno* (1957, 1959, 1962),[18] even though these works kept the author busy for years and seem to be close to the genres of photo-story and photo-reportage. First of all, Giacomelli never began his work with a storyboard, either written or imagined, nor did he edit or create a layout for the photographs following a preconceived scheme. In 1964 and 1965, he published his work about the "little priests" in at least four magazines, always showing it through a sequence of images while varying the number (from eight to ten), the order, and the types of images in each case (see *Figures 6.3; 6.4; 6.5*). Indeed, none of the photographs is simultaneously present in all of the four publications.[19]

Things did not change when, in the following decades, the author published this and other series in catalogues and monographic essays.

SURREALIST SEMINARIANS

Who are these young men in black, who run through the snow like children, play with puppy dogs, toss each other in a blanket, sprawl in poses of an odalisque, read the breviary amidst a mock fist-fight? Actors from an Italian movie, future Cardinals of the Curia? They are actually seminarians in Italy, where photographer Mario Giacomelli caught them in these playful, uncensored moments.

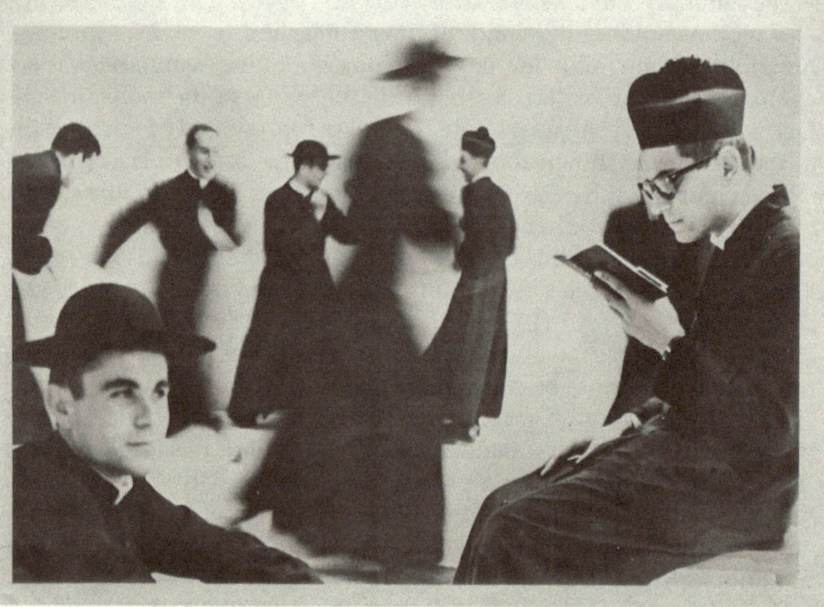

Figure 6.3 Mario Giacomelli, *Io non ho mani che mi accarezzino il volto*, "Surrealist Seminarians." *Jubilee* (March 1965): 45–9. With kind permission of Archivio Mario Giacomelli, Senigallia.

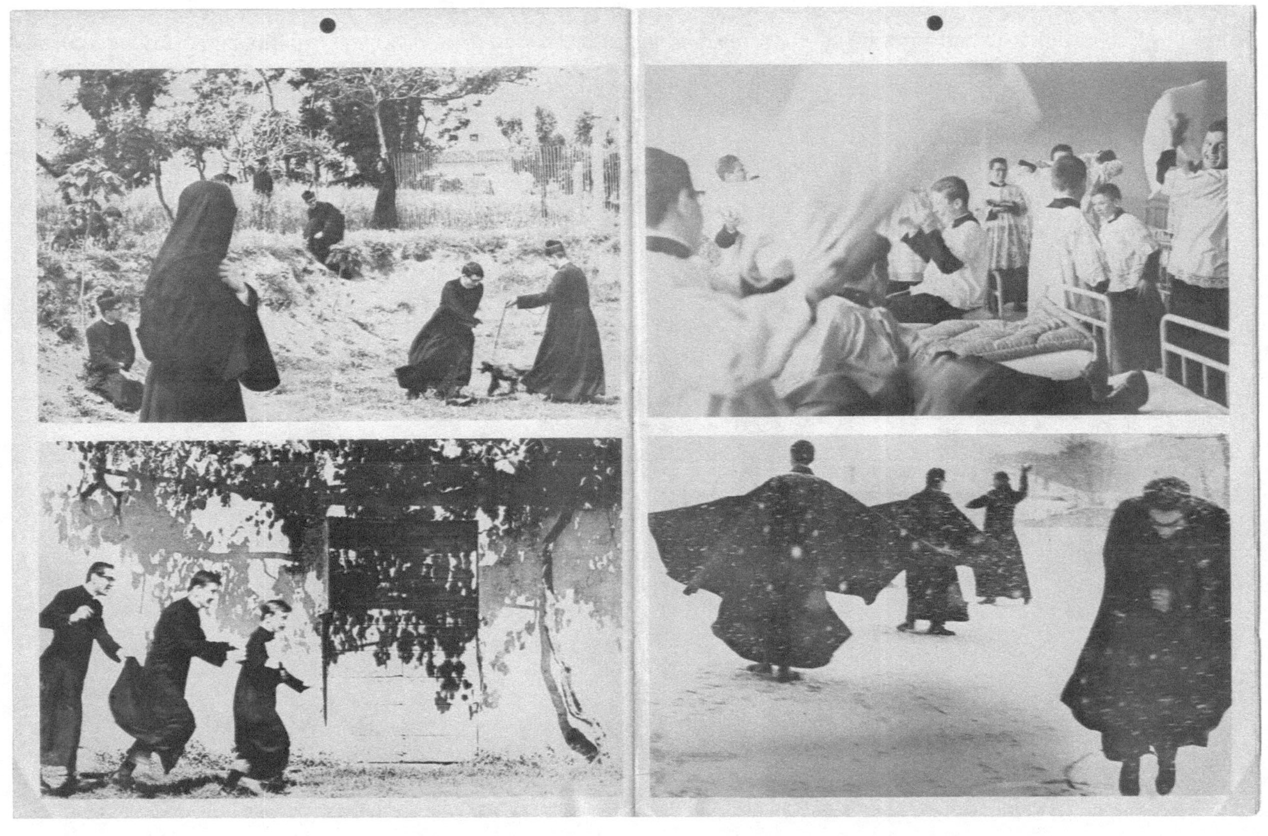

Figure 6.4 Mario Giacomelli, *Io non ho mani che mi accarezzino il volto*, "Surrealist Seminarians." *Jubilee* (Mar. 1965): 45-9. With kind permission of Archivio Mario Giacomelli, Senigallia.

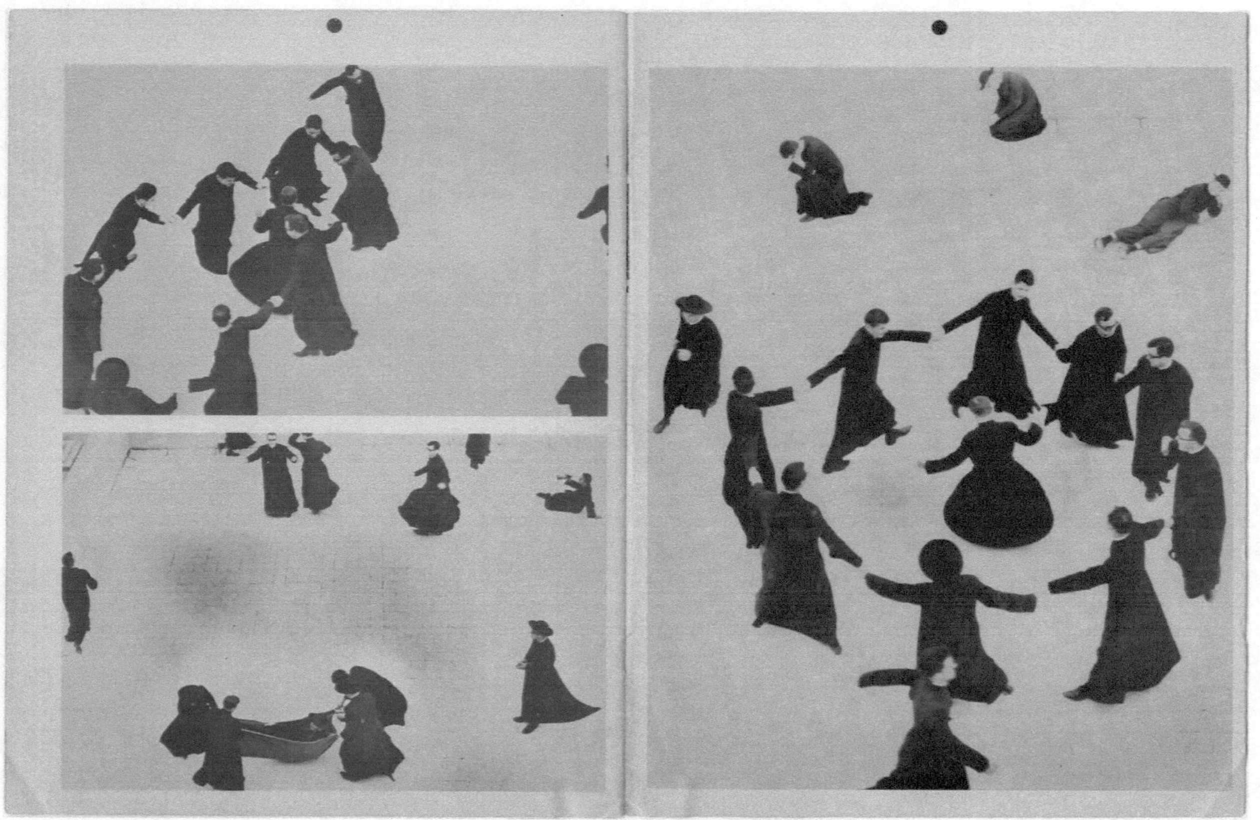

Figure 6.5 Mario Giacomelli, *Io non ho mani che mi accarezzino il volto*, 1965. With kind permission of Archivio Mario Giacomelli, Senigallia.

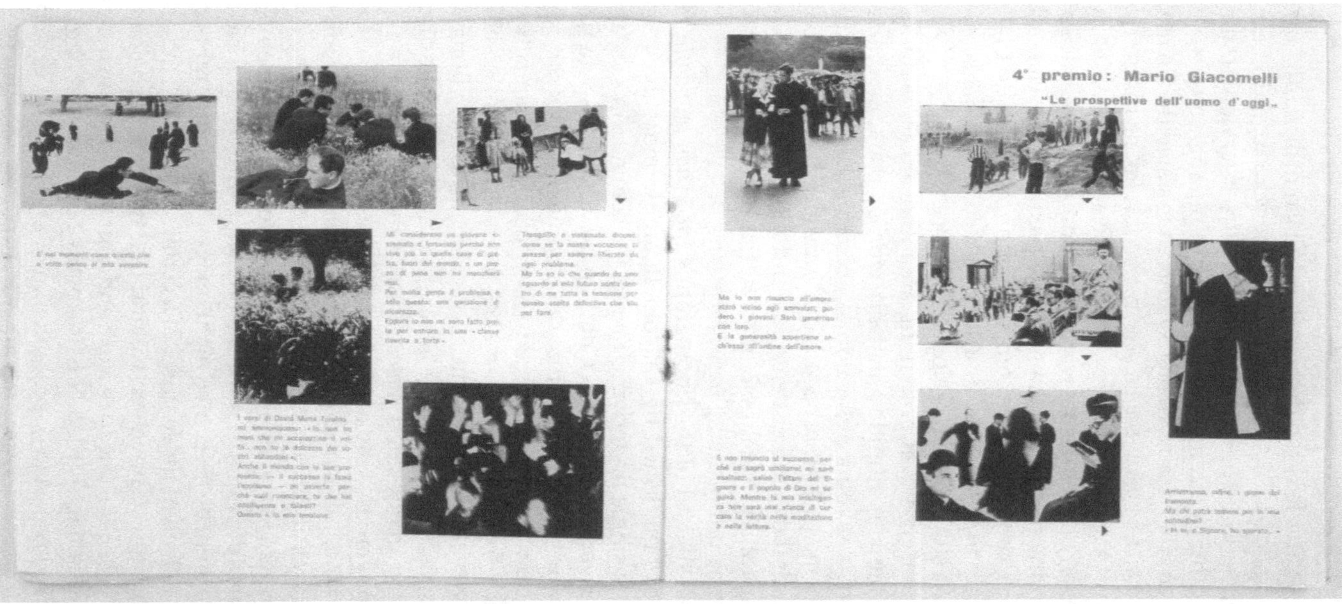

Figure 6.6 Mario Giacomelli, *Le prospettive dell'uomo d'oggi*, 1963. CRAF-Centro di ricerca e archiviazione della fotografia, Spilimbergo.

A significant example is the first essay on Giacomelli, edited by Arturo Carlo Quintavalle in 1980, the most complete with regard to the works of the earlier period. The artist gave a lengthy interview to the editor and provided him with a different series of photographs but without any instructions for editing. In fact, Quintavalle stated that in the case of *Scanno* and *Io non ho mani che mi accarezzino il volto,* he himself decided the sequence of the images, following the chronological order in which they were taken or moving forward "dall'immagine realistica a quella mitica" (from the realistic to the mythical picture; 226). The order was "fissato rigorosamente da Giacomelli" (rigorously dictated by Giacomelli; 226) only for "Caroline Branson," which, like *A Silvia*, had been prompted by a storyboard developed by Crocenzi.

Crocenzi himself, when presenting an anthological exhibition dedicated to Giacomelli, admitted that his works "risultano chiaramente non progettati a tavolino; essi non si aprono e non si chiudono secondo uno schema [...] di sceneggiatura" (are clearly not planned at the drawing board; they neither begin nor end following the outline ... of a storyboard); rather, "sembrano quasi tutti non conclusi" (nearly all of them seem to be unfinished; *Storie di terra*, n.p.).

The point is that all of the photographs for *Io non ho mani che mi accarezzino il volto* published by Giacomelli are no more than continual variations on a single underlying theme: the seminarian's escape from study and prayer. According to Chini, in the visual passage from one image to another there is no actual development of a theme, no direct progression from an initial image to a central section and then to an ending.[20] Such superabundance makes the selection and combination processes irrelevant: whatever the choice, whatever the editing and the layout of images, they will never generate a logical or poetic discursive development, a many-sided description of the subject, or a narrative that moves forward by way of visual references and counter-references. At the same time, it is symptomatic that when Giacomelli took part in photo-reportages and photo-story competitions organized by the CCF, needing to adhere to a similar structure, he would often assemble photographs from different series for the occasion. In 1959, in the compulsory theme section, he presented eight images. The photographers were required to catch all of the features of a certain place.[21] When we examine the photographs,[22] however, we find that two of them belong to the series *Il mare* (*The Sea*), one to *Scanno,* and four to *Puglia*. Even more significant is the "collage" titled "Le prospettive dell'uomo d'oggi" ("The Attitudes of Today's Man"), presented in 1963. The point of departure was again Turoldo's poem, but this time Giacomelli made a photo-story out of it "in the manner of Crocenzi" – a style he never used again – complete with captions, arrows directing the reading sequence, and images in contrast with one another. It is significant, however, that when composing it, he was forced to alternate the photographs of the "little priests" with those from other series, such as *Puglia* (*Apulia*), *Lourdes*, *Un uomo una donna un amore*, and *Vita d'ospizio*.

Giacomelli and Symptomatic Structure of the Image

What gives rise, then, to the structural differences between *Io non ho mani che mi accarezzino il volto* and *Un seminarista*? In other words, how does the poetics of Giacomelli differ from and diverge from that of Crocenzi?

Crocenzi seeks to highlight the contrast between the pureness of a faith lived within the walls of a seminary in the exterior acceptance of abstract rituals and phrases and the religious sentiment embodied in the concrete and "impure" daily life of the poor. This is the meaning or subject of *Un seminarista*, as the author wrote in his notes. Giacomelli's series sprang from a similar conflict, as is clear from the poem that inspired it and from which its title is derived. The text, completely ignored by the critics, was composed by a priest, Father Turoldo:

> Io non ho mani / che mi accarezzino il volto, / (duro è l'ufficio / di queste parole / che non conoscono amori) / non so le dolcezze / dei vostri abbandoni: ho dovuto essere / custode / della vostra solitudine: / sono / salvatore / di ore perdute. (55)

> No hands are there / to caress my face, / (harsh is my role / with these words that do not know love) / I do not know the sweetness / of your fond abandonments: I am forced to be / custodian / of your solitude: / I am / the saviour / of lost hours.

This verse gives the title – *Io non ho mani* – to a collection of poems (and lies at its very heart) published by Turoldo in 1948 (illustrated with black-and-white plates).[23] In the poem, as in Crocenzi's photo-story, we find references to love outside the church and, above all, to the conflict faced by a man of the cloth, who is torn between spiritual practice, which estranges him from the lives of other men, and his own overwhelmingly earthly dimension, which reconciles him with human weaknesses and the physical experience of others. Indeed, in the foreword to this collection, Turoldo speaks of a religious experience lived as the joy of living "al margine delle cose" (on the fringe of things) without experiencing them "perdute né veramente perdibili" (as lost or truly able to be lost; 7), to regain "nelle immagini di Cristo quel tanto di natura, di sensibilità e di tempo che a nessuno è concesso di rifiutare nell'irrimediabile giuoco della propria esistenza" (in the images of Christ that little bit of nature, sensibility, and time that no one is allowed to refuse in the inevitable game of human existence; 7).[24] Such a dilemma is historically ascribable to the age-old rift between the contemporary sociohistorical reality and the Catholic Church, which is entrenched in conservatism and closed to the outside world. Pope John XXIII was to address this ten years later by establishing the Second Vatican Council, in full session between 1961 and 1963, around the time when Giacomelli created this series.

Crocenzi's photo-story enunciates this theme through subsequent scenes (see *Figure 6.1*). At first, the young man is in the seminary, eager to "delight and suffer" together with others and to understand "the mystery of women's love." He abandons ecclesiastical life; then the moment of crisis arrives while he is in Rome as sin begins to torture him and at the same time he develops a strong desire for adventure. Finally, the "impasse" is overcome through a synthesis of conflicting needs: "The grace of God is here," the young man exclaims in front of the tabernacle in the marketplace. He discovers the spectacle of misery and beauty in the maze of alleys of a working-class neighbourhood. Similarly, the dilemma expressed by Turoldo in his opening lines – the regret and suffering of a priest who has never experienced the embrace of love – is finally resolved through an analogous and symmetrical compromise. Turoldo did not leave the priesthood; nor did he leave sinners to their own destiny; rather, he planned to be there for them and pray for their salvation.

Focusing on the first part of the poem – "No hands are there … of your fond abandonments" – in which the bewildering ambivalence of Turoldo's lines remains unresolved, Giacomelli attempts to give tangible shape to that very same tension. In the captions of "Le prospettive dell'uomo d'oggi" (Prospectives of Today's Man) you can already read (in the words of one of the seminarians):

> I versi di David Maria Turoldo mi ammoniscono: "Io non ho mani che mi accarezzino il volto […] non so le dolcezze dei vostri abbandoni." Anche il mondo con le sue promesse […] mi avverte: perché vuoi rinunciare, tu che hai intelligenza e talenti? *Questa è la mia tensione* […] per questa scelta definitiva che sto per fare. (20, emphasis added)

> The lines of David Maria Turoldo's poem warn me: "No hands are there to caress my face ... I do not know the sweetness of your fond abandonments." Even the world with its promises ... is a warning for me: why do you want to give up, you who are intelligent and talented? *This is my conflict* ... for this final choice that I'm about to make.

In this specific case, however, according to Crocenzi's dictates, Giacomelli follows the logical development of Turoldo's lines all the way through. On the first page, for instance, he shows the initial tension by juxtaposing pictures of the seminarians lying on a meadow against those of lovers flirting in the bushes. Then he, too, overcomes the "impasse" with a summary that refers to the reform movement of the Vatican Council. Thus, the caption introducing the following page reads: "Ma io non rinuncio all'amore: starà vicino agli ammalati, guiderà i giovani" (But I do not give up on love: I will comfort the sick, I will give guidance to the young; 21). And while on the left-hand page the seminarians are still portrayed in their carefree and solitary moments of abandon, in the photographs on the right they are shown tending the sick and young children, going to mass, or reading the scriptures.

It is significant that the most famous photographs from *Io non ho mani che mi accarezzino il volto*, those of the seminarians playing "Ring around the Rosey" on the snow, have not been chosen for *Le prospettive dell'uomo d'oggi*. Conversely, some of those included there were never published again by Giacomelli (like the one taken during mass). The real challenge Giacomelli faced with *Io non ho mani che mi accarezzino il volto* was not so much a matter of transposing Turoldo's lines into images, by arranging various photos in contrast with one another, as that of creating an image that, paradoxically, could take on two diametrically opposed meanings at the same time, thus giving texture and depth to the profound and unresolved conflicts of Turoldo's text. Giacomelli said that wherever he went, he "creava molte contraddizioni, rompeva la pace di ogni seminario" (created many contradictions, and disturbed the peace at every seminary; qtd in Quintavalle 172). The choice of subject, in that respect, was completely apt. By definition, a seminarian finds himself caught in a highly unstable and in some senses intensely paradoxical condition. He is no longer part of the secular world, but neither is he yet a priest; in a sense, he occupies both worlds and neither at the same time. The question is how to reveal the dilemmas arising from the continual flux of identity, which the seminary education seeks to normalize by repressing the earthly aspects of this conflict.

It is surprising that despite the redundancy of the series, Giacomelli visited the seminary in Senigallia for about two years. He did not have a storyboard with him. At first, he documented the most common everyday activities such as the seminarians attending mass or saying the rosary. However, Giacomelli was not really interested in narrating the everyday life of a seminary. In a few interviews, in fact, he explained that during the first year he did not achieve anything of any value.[25] He settled in, became acquainted with the seminarians, and watched them "[fare] gli spiritosi per le ragazze della colonia" (joking around with the summer camp girls; qtd in Carli 35). He got to know their natural and secret desires. Then one day, it began to snow. Suddenly the seminarians poured into the courtyard and, in an uncontrollable transport of child-like joy, began to dance and throw snowballs at one another. That day, he took some of the most famous photographs in the series (Giacomelli, *Io non ho mani* 176).

Giacomelli was so fascinated by this image that over the next few months, after the snow had melted away, he continued to explore its basic framework. "Le mie foto," he explains, "diventano dei racconti, delle serie, perché la mia è una ricerca mai appagata" (My photographs become stories, series, because my research is never finished; Interview 34). The subject would be abandoned only when it "non mi stimola più" (no longer inspires me; Interview 34). In a sequence of variations on the same theme, he reconstructed the visual dynamics of those photographs both re-creating the white of the snow inside the darkroom and most of all by acting like a real director while shooting. As one of the seminarians would reveal later, "la foto in cui facciamo il girotondo l'ha richiesta lui" (it was he who asked us to pose for the photograph of us playing "Ring around the Rosey"), while for other snapshots, "ci faceva vestire con delle mantelle nere" (he made us all wear black cloaks) and "ci chiedeva semplicemente di giocare" (he just asked us to play; qtd in Guerra 99).

To grasp the meaning of these images, we cannot simply read them at face value. As Dubois writes, as an "index" of a "piece of world," the photographic image, unlike traditional visual languages, is inseparable from the specific action that produced it and from the context in which it occurred. To understand its originality, one must examine "*il processo* molto più che il prodotto" (*the process* far more carefully than the finished product; *L'Atto fotografico* 68, emphasis in original). Apart from the specific shooting strategies and the development of the series during the years of production, the actual context of the images should be considered. In the seminaries of that era, it was not unusual to have rules for performing daily rituals of personal care and hygiene without removing one's clothing, as well as prohibitions such as those against assembling in small groups during leisure time, sharing confidences with fellow seminarians, entering their rooms, or even touching them.[26] Inside a seminary, where life is governed by rigorous precepts centred mainly on the control of the body and contact between the young men, these photographs represent not so much (or not only) a violation of the rule, but rather an actual compromise-formation in the Freudian sense: "a cleverly chosen ambiguity with two completely contradictory significations" (*A General Introduction* 369).[27] The "Dionysian" vitality of those "possessed" young men dancing in pairs or circles as they hold each other's hands, with their robes billowing up as they spin round, certainly contravenes every idea of priestly composure and propriety; it is also contradicted by the innocence of these games and by the starkness of the black cassocks against a white background – an unambiguous reference to Christianity. In this sense, the photographs can be considered as a symptomatic and "displaced" expression of that physical and emotional desire that is explicit in both Crocenzi's and Turoldo's work. On a few rare occasions, this subtle equilibrium was broken, for example, when Giacomelli photographed the seminarians after giving them cigars – in 1964, as a result of these photos, he was permanently banished from the seminary – or when he portrayed them playing instruments and singing at the tops of their voices in the seminary attic surrounded by wine bottles and overturned chairs.[28] Yet, such variations[29] confirm the presence, in this series, of the "Dionysian" element.

In any event, Giacomelli does not slip into the one-way banality of an irreverent transgression, nor does he attempt to reconcile opposites with a problem-solving synthesis; rather, he gives shape to the paradox of an image that simultaneously encompasses the two aspects of a contradiction. The resulting photos are highly ambiguous; they were published by Christian magazines[30] but at the same time were used by magazines and newspapers to illustrate articles about the crisis that was affecting seminaries and the Catholic Church and in pieces about the phenomenon of homosexuality among priests.[31] Jean Claude Lemagny was right when he wondered why "questi giochi innocentissimi hanno qualcosa di diabolico" (these absolutely innocent games have something diabolical about them; 13), just as Michela Vanon was right when she associated the ingenuity of the seminarians' "giochi puerili" (puerile games) with the sensual mischievousness of their "tenerezze e impulsi femminei" (tenderness and feminine impulses; 120).

The character created by Crocenzi is *first and foremost* a seminarian, until the moment he ceases to be a seminarian; he experiences a crisis, which he overcomes. Once the story had been written, following a classic beginning–middle–end pattern, Crocenzi put together the pieces needed for his visual rendition. The photographs needed to have both a narrative and a documentary function: each needed to show "lo svolgersi degli avvenimenti del racconto" (how events in the story unwind; "Storie italiane" 19) and to be bound together by "associazioni logiche – causa ed effetto, prima e dopo – e suggestive" (logical associations – cause and effect, before and after – and evocative associations; 18), and they always had to be taken "dal vero" (from life) and with the utmost "immediatezza" (immediacy; 18). All of this so that the photographic sequences would provide a clear and solid discourse. In this regard, it is interesting to note the frequent use in the captions of *Un seminarista* of deictic words ("*this* poor man," "how many dreams has he got in his heart, *this* man?," "it's painful to see *such* things," etc.) and the fact that many of the people shown are looking directly into the lens. Such devices plunge the reader into the middle of the story. It is as if the narrator and the character were wandering along the streets of Rome with a handheld camera, giving a running commentary on unfolding events. This technique was defined by Crocenzi as the "soggettivazione narrativa delle immagini" (narrative subjectification of images; "Soggettivazione narrativa" 16), which for him could guarantee greater adhesion to the irrefutable truth of visible facts. Crocenzi's narrative techniques fully embrace neorealist aesthetics as defined by Alberto Asor Rosa, who sees the "concezione dell'arte come *racconto di storie*" (conception of art as the *telling of stories*) as being "il nocciolo più caratteristico del fenomeno neorealistico" (the most characteristic core feature of neorealism; 92, emphasis in original). Such a conception results from mixing the typical narrative features of literary language with the typical documentary visuals of the language of film (which in this case is virtually identical with the language of photography). Vasco Pratolini argues, for instance, that film and literary fiction are uplifting and evocative "in misura dell'*immediatezza*, della *logicità* e *inconfutabilità* ottenute nel riprodurre la *successione degli eventi*" (in proportion to the *immediacy, logicality*, and *irrefutability* obtained in replicating the *sequence of events*; qtd in Asor Rosa 95, emphasis in original).

Crocenzi proceeds by amassing images with captions that give ever more detailed descriptions of place, time, and meaning for each story.

Giacomelli goes in completely the opposite direction, moving towards an ever more radical decontextualization of his subjects. Fully exploiting the temporal and spatial potential of photographic framing, his vision slowly becomes more and more essential and intense but at the same time increasingly ambiguous and difficult to decipher.[32] After a year of research, he decided to select only moments of recreation, after each day's regular activities were over and the grip of censure from higher authorities had been relaxed. He then removed all references to location, both when taking photographs (he often photographed the young men from above, eliminating perspective and cutting out details of the seminary surroundings) and when in the darkroom, where he heightened contrasts and masked background details so that the dark silhouettes of the "little priests" could float on a flat surface of absolute white (see *Figure 6.5*), as can be seen when comparing variations in the prints.

These images therefore constitute enlargements of detail. But the details are not revelatory, that is, they do not help us grasp the context; rather, they disrupt our view of the path of study and prayer, through which young men gradually abandon their secular lives to become priests. Such details point to moments of crisis during which conflicting desires find expression; clearly decipherable meanings are replaced by the bewilderment caused by images fluctuating before our eyes. What exactly can we see? First, the seminarians' explosion of relief as they escape the oppressive dogma to return to the material world; then, in contrast but with equal clarity, the uncontrollable joy of those who have just discovered their true vocation, who have become children again – in the ideal condition to enter the "kingdom of heaven" – and who sing the glory of the Lord. These men seem to be dancing to a hymn praising the Lord; but their dances could equally be read as the Dionysian dances of ancient pagan maenads, as Georges Didi-Huberman might have put it.[33] No semiotic or iconological study, however meticulous, could decipher these photographs or the story told in this series. There is nothing to help us either determine the place and time of the action or sense what is happening. There is no point in scrolling through any sequence of images, since they do not point to a "before" and an "after," a "here" and a "there," a "cause" and an "effect." Giacomelli does nothing to resolve this ambiguity; on the contrary, he reinforces it to give it the utmost expressive power, asking the young men to strike different poses within the same scene. What are these seminarians doing together, one lying on the floor drinking from a bottle, another standing with his hands joined together, and others dancing and joking? And why are some of them praying on their knees while others are playing Ring around the Rosey? The posture of devotion – typically Christian – and its meditative immobility stand each time in clear contrast to the uninhibited corporeal exuberance of the dancers (see for instance *Figure 6.5*). A strange atmosphere permeates these photographs, clouding their apparent spontaneity and consistency.

Looking at Crocenzi's sequences, the viewer's eye glides from one photo to the next, just as the seminarian's eye travels over the surface of the world in which he moves. Crocenzi minimized the formal elaboration of his images – as well as the complexity of his plots – to emphasize their mimetic and above all "transitive" properties. Instead of individual photographs, we see the diegetic structure that organizes and permeates all of them, until we arrive at their complete and clear meaning. Giacomelli's photographs, by contrast, are points of resistance that impede our faculties of interpretation, tampering with our codes for reading reality and with our need to attribute significance to what we see. In his sequences, each transition from one photograph to the next only intensifies the impasse: his "little priests" are eternally suspended between Christian and pagan rites, between the earthliness of their dancing bodies and the spirituality of the heavenly light in which they float, between the vitality of their kinetic exuberance and the alienating fixity of a photographic snapshot, on the paradoxical threshold of images uniting "ciò che, seguendo la linea retta del discorso, andrebbe invece disgiunto" (that which, following a straight line of discourse, would instead be disjointed; Ronchi, *Il Pensiero Bastardo* 26).[34]

Conclusion

Crocenzi takes the side of visible reality and human progress, of the knowledge and transparency offered by a universal means of communication; Giacomelli, by contrast, inhabits a realm of estrangement and uncertainty, of obsessive reiteration of whatever cannot be completely defined: the dark side where each image is "un tentativo rinnovato di dire la stessa cosa" (a renewed attempt at saying the same thing), as his beloved Pavese wrote in his 14 February 1941 diary entry (220).

Krauss has ably shown how photography, taken in its indexical dimension, was pivotal for members of the historical avant-garde in their efforts to debunk idealist Romantic and Renaissance conceptions of art. So it is no wonder that Italian culture, with its deeply entrenched literary tradition, which long venerated the written word after centuries of humanism (not to mention a good dose of Crocean idealism), had always looked askance at photography as a method of expression, viewing it as if it were "tainted" by material reality and technology. The most that could be hoped for, usually, was ambivalence. Vittorini was a case in point: on the one hand, he saw the photographic image as a mechanical reproduction of real life almost devoid of artistic merit, and the photographer as a mere technician; on the other, he was clearly fascinated by photography, and he used a great number of photographs in the pages of *Il Politecnico* and to illustrate *Americana* and *Conversazione in Sicilia*. Whatever his limitations, Crocenzi deserves credit for helping bring together two worlds that seemed hard to reconcile, for calling on great photographers such as Giacomelli and Ugo Mulas to work alongside intellectuals and writers, who included not only Vittorini but also Cesare Zavattini, Vittorio Sereni, and Franco Fortini. When we examine the relationship between literature and photography in Italy, it becomes clear that a careful, in-depth examination of Crocenzi's work would enable us to look closely at how Italian culture responded to the provocations and challenges of contemporary art, a field in which photography plays a key role.

Translated by Massimiliano Marconi and Alison Bron

NOTES

1 See Amodeo et al. 7–28.
2 Crocenzi has been the subject of a few brief monographs. See for instance Zannier, and Amodeo, Giusa, and Turrin. Like Giacomelli's archives, Crocenzi's archives in Spilimbergo (PN) at the *Centro di ricerca e archiviazione della fotografia* (C.R.A.F.) are awaiting systematic study. Similarly, despite the vast amount of literature on Giacomelli, there are very few references to his association with Crocenzi.
3 Besides the sequences produced during the 1960s, which we are going to analyse, other works, among the ones published as monographs, include these: *Il teatro della neve* (*The Theatre of the Snow*), *Felicità raggiunta si cammina* (*Happiness Is Achieved Walking Thus*), *L'Infinito* (*Infinity*), *Passato* (*Past*), and *Bando* (*Bando*). These were created during the 1980s and 1990s, having been inspired respectively by the poems of Francesco Permunian, Eugenio Montale, Giacomo Leopardi, Vincenzo Cardarelli, and Sergio Corazzini.

4 As can be seen in their correspondence held at the C.R.A.F., Crocenzi Fund. Cavalli was a key figure at that time in Italian amateur photographic circles.
5 See Amodeo et al. 7–28.
6 Essayist, writer, translator, and professor of Italian Literature at the University of Macerata, Alvaro Valentini (Fermo, 1924–1991) was a prominent figure in the C.C.F.
7 See C.C.F., "Notizie del Centro" (Notices of the Centre) 44.
8 Between 1955 and 1958, almost all the articles written by Valentini and Crocenzi, the programs, and the columns of the C.C.F. were published in the review *Ferrania* (Milan: SAES).
9 See C.R.A.F, Crocenzi Fund, and Giacomelli Archive.
10 See C.R.A.F., Crocenzi Fund.
11 Italo Zannier 68–9.
12 Roman Jakobson refers to these concepts (22–45), which constitute one of the cornerstones of structural linguistics.
13 The volume containing Taddei's essay provides a wide selection of photo-stories and theoretical contributions published in the catalogues of the C.C.F. photo-story awards in the 1960s.
14 See Krauss, *Le photographique*.
15 For critical analysis of Barthes's *punctum*, see Attridge and Sliwinski.
16 See C.R.A.F., Crocenzi Fund.
17 Crocenzi openly draws on the work of American director D.W. Griffith (*Storie italiane* 20), inventor of this type of editing, which consists in alternating scenes taken from different situations or events set up one against the other in some respects.
18 See Quintavalle 85–106, 107–16, 120–32.
19 See Giacomelli, "Fotografias de Mario Giacomelli" and "Surrealist Seminarians." See also Giacomelli and Racanicchi, and Turroni.
20 See Chini, "Tutto nel Fototesto" (All in the Phototext) and *Linguaggio fotografico* (*Photographic Language*) 50.
21 See Valentini, *Mostra di fotografía* (*Photographic Exhibit*).
22 The photographs of the competing works taken by Crocenzi during the final exhibition are kept at C.R.A.F., Crocenzi Fund.
23 Actively involved in the Resistance in Milan, Turoldo was the author of successful poetry collections. Moved by a religious sentiment as profound as it was restive and innovative, in 1953, following pressure from the Holy Office, he was banished from Italy. He returned permanently in 1964, at which time he founded *Casa di Emmaus*, a religious community that was open to atheists and Muslims as well. There, he established the Ecumenical Studies Center Giovanni XXIII.

24 Giacomelli owned a first edition of the collection, kept at the archive of Senigallia.

25 See, for example, Quintavalle 172 and Celant 15–16.

26 See Napoli 9–12.

27 According to Freud, parapraxes (or Freudian slips), dreams, and neurotic symptoms are compromise-formations through which a repressed desire, which the ego opposes, is finally satisfied by making itself unrecognizable as such to the consciousness.

28 It is no coincidence that these images, with a few rare exceptions, were not published by Giacomelli until the 1990s.

29 See Celant 240 and Mauro 236.

30 See Giacomelli, "Surrealist Seminarians." See also Bovo et al.

31 See Giacomelli, "I Seminaristi"; Napoli; Di Stefano; and Sorge.

32 Sontag wrote: "Through photographs, the world becomes a series of unrelated, freestanding particles … It is a view of the world which denies interconnectedness, continuity, but which confers on each moment the character of a mystery" (22–3).

33 Drawing on Warburg's lecture on the survival of ancient art and referring to Bertoldo di Giovanni's Magdalene sculpture, which portrays her in the act of tearing her hair out at the foot of the crucified body of Christ, the author writes that "pur devota" (though devout), she dances "come una Menade antica danzerebbe corpo a corpo con la nudità del satiro che sta provocando" (as an ancient Maenad would dance body to body with the nudity of the satyr whom she is provoking); 247. The "formula gestuale, qui" (gestural language here) expresses "un momento d'intensità" (a moment of intensity) that preserves the memory, in the body of the Magdalene, "di un paganesimo cui tutto il contenuto simbolico – il sacrificio del Verbo incarnato – è assolutamente estraneo. Si tratta dunque di una sorta di sintomo" (of a Paganism whose whole symbolic content – the sacrifice of the Word made flesh – is completely extraneous. It is, therefore, a sort of symptom); 264.

34 The author refers back to a late Greek myth. On the plain of Thebes, the Teumessian fox and the Cephalus dog challenge each other. One is said to be impossible to catch, the other to catch all it chases. How could these two animals engage in this challenge without giving up their conflicting nature? How to picture this paradox? In this world, Cephalus could do nothing but catch his prey; Teumessia could do nothing but evade capture. Not even the myth can narrate this challenge because it does not belong "all'ordine delle cose che si possono dire seguendo la linea retta del discorso" (to the order of things that can be narrated following the straight line of discourse); 10. Zeus, then, turned the two opponents to

stone at the beginning of this challenge. His wisdom was not "discursive" but "figurative." "Egli optò per una *istantanea*" (He chose a *snapshot*); 10, emphasis in original. In this way he made solid, in the form of a statue, elements that knowledge and predicative speech would find a pure contradiction (71).

7 What the Writer Saw (and the Camera Didn't): Antonio Tabucchi's *Notturno indiano* and Daniele Del Giudice's *Lo stadio di Wimbledon*

DONATA PANIZZA

In his semiotics, the American philosopher Charles Sanders Peirce distinguished among three types of signs: the icon (linked to the object by a relation of similarity), the index (which maintains a relationship of physical connection with the object), and the symbol (which relates to the object according to a conventional code). While Peirce defined the photograph now as an indexical sign, now as an iconic one, and at other times as both at once,[1] since the 1970s a line of theoretical studies has focused on Pierce's interpretation of photography as an indexical sign, that is, as a material imprint of the real.[2] Two works relevant to this line of thought are Henri Van Lier's *Philosophie de la photographie* (*Philosophy of Photography*) (1983) and Jean-Marie Schaeffer's *L'image précaire: Du dispositif photographique* (*The Precarious Image: Of the Photographic Scheme*) (1987). Both theorists complicate the notion of photography as an index, stating that the medium's very indexicality makes photographs elusive to any stable readings and independent of both the represented scene and the photographer who tried to fix it. Photography has such a close link to reality that whatever a photograph captures of the outside world, it cannot produce a mediated and codified representation of reality. Starting with similar assumptions, Van Lier and Schaeffer reach different conclusions: while the former acknowledges photography's sufficiency and autarky, the latter focuses on its inability to produce a semiotic double of reality.

Van Lier's and Schaeffer's theories help us appreciate the rich thematic and structural role that photography plays in Antonio Tabucchi's *Notturno indiano* (*Indian Nocturne*) (1984) and Daniele Del Giudice's *Lo stadio di Wimbledon* (*Wimbledon Stadium*) (1983), as well as its relationship to the metafictional elements and themes in these novels.[3] Both novels are travel accounts in which the protagonists/narrators are searching for a certain individual. In *Notturno indiano*, Roux is searching for Xavier, an old friend who has been for some unspecified time lost in India. In *Lo stadio di Wimbledon*, the unnamed narrator seeks answers about a man he never met, an intellectual and friend of such writers and poets as Saba and Montale; this somewhat mysterious figure, now deceased, is based on a real person named Bobi Bazlen. A gifted writer, he had decided not to write anything. The narrator's journey is instigated by a desire to understand this wilful refusal to put pen to paper.

In following the tracks left by the two characters, the two protagonists are privy to scattered pieces of evidence: a letter and some vague, contradictory information in the first case; the testimony of friends, acquaintances, and surviving lovers in the second. Both are compelled to travel abroad. Roux goes to India, while the protagonist of *Lo stadio di Wimbledon* takes several trips to Trieste and a final one to London. In both works, the search is called off and replaced by writing as the discourse becomes increasingly reflective and philosophical.

Writing is explored in the final chapter of *Notturno indiano*, in which Roux imagines recounting his journey from the perspective of the one being sought. In the fiction of the book within the book, the protagonist thus becomes the *other*, retracing in reverse the journey he has just undergone. In this way, the search exhausts itself even while offering a hypothetical solution to the problem of his disappearance. In Del Giudice's novel, the act of writing does not enter the text in so blatant or direct a way; instead, it is writing as vocation that emerges and matures in the mind of the protagonist. As he decides to become a writer himself, he abandons his quest to determine what brought another to leave his artistic destiny unfulfilled.

In very different ways, the art of photography enters both texts in complex juxtaposition to the act of writing. In *Notturno indiano*, there is the book of photographs whose author describes to the protagonist in the final chapter; in this way, the book of photographs and Roux's imagined novel confront each other as different approaches to dealing with reality, only one of which – namely, literature – is able to solve the contradictions of reality. In *Lo stadio di Wimbledon*, some of the characters whom the protagonist visits show him old pictures, which he rejects as inadequate representations of the past he is trying to dig out. Although in *Lo stadio di Wimbledon*, photography and writing do not confront each other in as direct a way as in *Notturno indiano*, the rejection of photography is a step in the process that will lead the protagonist to become a writer.

In both novels, photography offers a specific way of relating to reality, a mode of action quite its own, one that responds to its own laws and needs. Indeed, the photograph is irreducible to written locutions, despite being incorporated – or, rather, transformed – into writing in the course of each narrative; thus, the theory of photography seems the only proper approach to addressing the significance and function of the photographic in these contemporary novels. Photograph as artefact emerges from the comparison with the written as an essential device, as a necessary stage that must be explored and then overcome for literature to show its unique potential. In *Notturno indiano*, the photographer tries to produce *the* photograph that faithfully represents an event, but such an attempt is doomed to failure. Literature, however, has the capacity to rearrange reality through a web of suppositions and hypotheses that solve the inconsistencies of reality without any countercheck in the outside world. In *Lo stadio di Wimbledon*, the photographs cannot help the protagonist find the answers he is looking for since – following Schaeffer's theory – photography is unable to produce a semiotic double of reality. This is what literature achieves both throughout and at the end of the novel: it transposes reality onto a more condensed, self-evident, and rigorous level, that of representation.

Notturno indiano

In *Notturno indiano*, photography appears in the final chapter, after a few short references in the first chapters. It is introduced when the protagonist meets Christine at the Oberoi Hotel near Bogmalo Beach in Goa. Over dinner, the two exchange the usual information that two strangers share when they first meet: Christine is a photographer, while the main character reveals that he is writing a book. His work in progress, I argue, can be compared to Christine's own work: it is a book called *South Africa* that reproduces a sequence of photographs, almost all without captions. The first picture, Christine specifies, is the image of "un giovane negro, solo il busto; una canottiera con una scritta pubblicitaria, un corpo atletico, sul viso l'espressione di un grande sforzo, le mani alzate come in segno di vittoria: sta evidentemente tagliando il traguardo, per esempio i cento metri" (102) (a young negro, just his head and shoulders, a sport singlet with a sales slogan, an athletic body, an expression of great effort on his face, his arms raised as if in victory;

obviously he's breasting the tape, in the hundred metres for example; 106). The second photograph, which is the earlier, cropped image shown in its entirety, turns the tables on the viewer:

> sulla sinistra c'è un poliziotto vestito da marziano, ha un casco di plexiglas sul viso, gli stivaletti alti, un moschetto imbracciato, gli occhi feroci sotto la sua visiera feroce. Sta sparando al negro. E il negro sta scappando a braccia alzate, ma è già morto: un secondo dopo che io facessi clic era già morto. (102–3)

> On the left there's a policeman dressed like a Martian, a plexiglass helmet over his face, high boots, a rifle tucked into his shoulder, his eyes fierce under his fierce visor. He's shooting at the negro. And the negro is running away with his arms up, but he is already dead: a second after I clicked the shutter he was already dead. (106)

The only caption in the book is linked to the first image, the cropped one: *Mèfiez-vous des morceaux choisis* (*Don't Trust Selected Works*). Christine is warning the reader that it is possible to change the meaning of an event by showing only a part of it. The act of violence represented in the second photograph, which according to her is the accurate reproduction of a real event, can easily be turned into something completely different by cutting out part of the picture.

Van Lier's theory of photography sheds some light on Christine's point of view. In *Philosophie de la Photographie*, he asks us to understand a photograph as depicting something that only apparently reproduces a real scene: photography's technical characteristics make what is photographically depicted a quasi-scene, even a non-scene. In Van Lier's words, a photograph "creates a kind of non-scene through its superficiality of field, its matter of fact framing, its relentless isomorphism and synchronism, its negative-positive alternations, its ostensible digitality, its informational subcharge and surcharge, and its monocular and cyclopean capture" (40).[4]

In the photographic image there is constant tension between clarity and abstraction, information and background noise. Moreover, Van Lier renders problematic Pierce's notion of indexical sign, insofar as it is not the objects that imprint themselves on film, but the photons that emanate from them: the photograph is then an imprint of an imprint, a trace of a trace. Its relationship with reality is tenuous, elusive, and difficult to determine. Van Lier distinguishes between *indices* and *indexes:* indices are "the physical effects of a cause they physically signalize [*sic*], either through monstration … or demonstration" (17). They are neither intentional nor conventional nor systematic; therefore, he contends, they are not signs. Indexes, by contrast, are conventional, intentional, and systematic: "they indicate objects much in the same way the index finger or an arrow might point to an object" (17). Translated into photographic terms, indices are the footprints of the photons on the film and then on photographic paper (i.e., what we see and recognize, or rather, what we claim to understand in a picture), while indexes are means to enhance or direct the indices, which include the choice of film stock, the framing, the depth of field, the brightening or darkening of certain parts of the photograph, and so forth. Indexes are all those things on which the photographer can act, but they can only refer to something, that is, to the indices – they have no relationship to the referent. Indices, by contrast, do have content – albeit a flexible one – with respect to the referent; however, they are not intentional or dependent on the photographer. They are a vague mass of information that can be variously interpreted and combined. Van Lier argues that in photography, one encounters "fearful sufficiency; its autarky; the way in which it constantly eludes our grasp" (20).

Christine's operation of contrasting an entire picture with its own part and highlighting the change in meaning (only one of which is established as true) is but an attempt to capture what Van Lier calls "autarky," the quality of photography that keeps it always beyond human grasp. Cropping *a posteriori* the photograph (i.e., here, cutting away a piece of it) is an operation on the level of indexes, which according to Van Lier does not affect the nature of the photograph. As he specifies, "the reframing of a photograph is not inevitably more illegitimate than its framing" (32). The entire photograph is no more related to the outside spectacle than the cropped one: both represent non-scenes. Christine claims instead that, unlike a true, complete picture, a "false," mutilated one cannot possibly reflect the truth of the event. By reframing the photographic image, she attempts to control the production of its meaning. As noted above, for Van Lier all photographs have been mutilated by the original framing process; they are in any case "chosen bits," to use Christine's expression. The choice, however, has not happened solely on the basis of human initiative, but rather by a series of efforts, among which the photographer's intervention is not the most relevant. Indeed, the photographer's intervention "only takes place after other initiatives, namely those of the technician, of natural light, and of the spectacle with its structure and actors" (53). The blending or composing of indices, in unstable and shifting combinations, alters with each development. According to Van Lier, this hinders one from defining precisely and once and for all what any given photograph represents. Similarly, it is impossible to define precisely the indices, which are, in *Notturno indiano,* all of those elements that Christine lists in her description of the two photographs. Uniting them around a single coherent and final reading, Van Lier argues, is effectively impossible.

In light of Van Lier's theory, Christine's attitude can best be described as an attempt to control the elusive photographic image in order to establish a single acceptable meaning. It thus constitutes a test of his central contention, according to which a photograph is but the sum of infinite indices "in overlap and perpetual emergence from a background in which they submerge" (32) and indexes that try to orient the indices but are not related to the outside scene. The control over reality can merely be apparent, since it is possible to hypothesize the presence of other photographs that, by acting on the indexes (in the case of Christine, the cropping of her photograph), affect the perception of the image and potentially create an infinite number of other readings of the same image, derived from the continuous mixing and combining of indices. The notion that photography attempts to establish power over reality was stressed by Sontag, who in *On Photography* wrote memorably, "There is something predatory in the act of taking a picture" (14).

The book of photographs can be compared to Roux's imagined book, which serves as the novel's keystone. "Supponiamo che stia scrivendo un libro" (100) (Let's suppose I'm writing a book; 104) are the words that introduce this imagined novel. And here begins the account of what happens in this imaginary book:

> La sostanza è che in questo libro io sono uno che si è perso in India [...]. C'è un altro che mi sta cercando, ma io non ho nessuna intenzione di farmi trovare. Io l'ho visto arrivare, l'ho seguito giorno per giorno, potrei dire. Conosco le sue preferenze e le sue insofferenze, i suoi slanci e le sue diffidenze, le sue generosità e le sue paure. Lo tengo praticamente sotto controllo. Lui, al contrario, di me non sa quasi nulla. (102-3)

> The central idea is that in this book I am someone who has lost his way in India ... There is someone else who is looking for me, but I have no intention of letting him find me. I saw him arrive and I have followed him day by day, we could say. I know his likes and his dislikes, his enthusiasms

> and his hesitations, his generosity and his fears. I keep him more or less under control. He, on the contrary, knows almost nothing about me. (107)

This is soon followed by a short account of the movements of this other who is seeking the protagonist, who obviously corresponds to the real protagonist of *Notturno indiano*. The end of the story returns to this thematic unfolding:

> Proprio così, per scenario prendo questo. Supponiamo che sia una sera come questa, calda e profumata, albergo molto fine, sul mare, grande terrazza con tavolini e candele, musica in sordina, camerieri che si aggirano premurosi e discreti, cibo scelto, naturalmente, con cucina internazionale. Io sono a un tavolo con una bella donna, una ragazza come lei, con aspetto da straniera, stiamo a un tavolo dalla parte opposta a quella in cui ci troviamo noi ora, la donna è rivolta verso il mare, io invece guardo gli altri tavoli.
>
> A un certo punto lo vedo. È a un tavolo in fondo, dall'altra parte della terrazza. È girato nella mia stessa posizione, siamo faccia a faccia. Anche lui è con una donna, ma lei mi gira le spalle e non posso sapere chi è.
>
> Mi ha cercato tanto, e ora che mi ha trovato non ha più voglia di trovarmi, mi scusi il bisticcio ma è proprio così. (105–7)

> You've got it: I'll take this as the set. Let's suppose that it's an evening like this evening, warm and spicy, a first-class hotel, by the sea, a big terrace with tables and candles, soft music, waiters who move about attentively and discreetly, the best food, naturally, with an international cuisine. I am sitting at a table with a beautiful woman, a girl like yourself, with a foreign look to her; we are at a table on the opposite side to the one we're sitting at now, the girl is facing the sea while I, on the other hand, am looking toward the other tables.
>
> At a certain point, I see him. He's at a table toward the back on the other side of the terrace. He's sitting the same way I'm sitting; we are face to face. He's with a woman, too, but she has her back to me and I can't see who she is.
>
> He has been looking at me for a long time, and now that he has found me, he no longer has any desire to find me. I'm sorry to split hairs, but that's how it is. (111–12)

Thus ends the book: the imagined one and, a few lines later, the one we are reading. The imagined book is the mirror of the real one: not only does it present the same events from the point of view of the sought-after character, but the former's omniscient narration brings resolution to the protagonist's failing quest. The search can be abandoned because it ends with the fiction of the hypothetical book. And this makes the search, the real one, obsolete.

It is important to note that Roux, in recounting the plot of his book, uses the word "control" to refer to the knowledge that the protagonist of the imagined book has of the person who is looking for him. With Christine, photography tries to control reality, and apparently Roux tries to do the same. However, Roux's control is confined to his book: it is a virtual, potential, and momentary control. It does not seek to affect or direct reality, but only to solve its contradictions on another level, that of literature. The photograph turns out to be self-sufficient and impervious to any secure relationship to a stable reality; literature seems to offer a less ambitious task and, at the same time, greater possibilities. Literature corrects reality, offering an alternative to it. It is no coincidence, surely, that during the dinner the two characters, Christine and the protagonist, are arranged in such a way that only the protagonist can see the rest of the room and his alter ego, while Christine faces blindly towards the sea, unable to participate in the unveiling of the mystery, and not only because "l'inseguitore e l'inseguito si sono fusi completamente nel riflesso della finzione del libro immaginato, tanto che anche le due donne per loro possono essere sia l'una che l'altra" (the hunter and the hunted have so completely fused together in the creation of the imaginary book, so much so that to them the two women could be the same woman; Livorni 452). This viewing position further deprives the photographer of her predatory gaze and hence of the possibility to verify the truth of Roux's version of the story. Literature, unlike photography, employs only methods of virtual imagery to rearrange reality. This book is only suggested; it is the idea of an idea, imagination to the second power. Through literature, the writer creates "un altrove che abbia radici nel reale e che ne sfugga, ma muovendo da quello. [...] [Un] mondo alternativo che mantiene le tangenze col nostro, seguendo le piste dei tracciati inattuati [...], una leggera correzione del vero, un irreale che sarebbe potuto esistere" (another place rooted in – but still able to escape – reality, but moving from it ... An alternative world that remains tangential to ours, following paths not actually traced ... a small correction on reality, an inexistence that could have existed; Dolfi, *Tabucchi* 15–16). The task of narrative is in this respect a "correzione del definitivo" (correction of the definitive; Dolfi, *Tabucchi*

19). As such, it is a simple task, a subtle web of hypotheses that covers reality with assumptions without upsetting it and without claiming to act upon it.

This idea of literature is at work in the whole novel. Each of the twelve chapters has a different setting, the rubric of which guides the reader before the book begins. These are the places where the protagonist travels following the ephemeral traces that his old friend has left behind: the hospital and the train station in Bombay, the Theosophical Society in Madras, the beach at Goa, some hotels, and the bus from Madras to Mangalore. The rubric of places, with its precise topographical information, contrasts sharply with the enigmatic environments and characters encountered. Places are always dark or dimly lit, and the characters, situations, and dialogues seem wrapped in a dream. Following his old friend's traces, Roux meets peculiar characters who provide him with more questions than answers: a jainist who is going to Varanasi to die, knowing he has only a few days left to live; a monstrous fortune-teller who tells Roux he is actually someone else and that his real self is on a boat; a member of Madras's Theosophical Society, who engages Roux in an intellectual contest while refusing to give him detailed information about Xavier. It is difficult to interpret their words and expressions: language helps create a kind of indeterminacy.

One could define the language of *Notturno indiano* as a neutral or baseline language or a sort of "*vox media*" (Arvigo 101). Very often, the narrative voice collects the words, taking them in some direction or other. However, words remain at the threshold of possible interpretations. Consider all the moments in which the protagonist ventures some supposition or reports his impressions on what he sees or hears without bothering to check the accuracy of his hypothesis: "il lamento lontano riprese con maggiore intensità, ora molto acuto, per un attimo pensai che fosse uno sciacallo" (29) (the distant cry picked up again and with greater intensity; it was really shrill now. For a moment, I thought it might be a jackal; 33); "passò qualche minuto, mi parve che le luci delle banchine si fossero affievolite" (40) (a few minutes went by; I had the impression that the platform lights had grown dimmer; 35); "mi parve di sentire il ticchettio di un orologio" (59) (I thought I heard the ticking of a clock; 55); "ebbi l'impressione che fosse un paesaggio di palmeti e risaie, ma il buio era troppo profondo per dirlo con sicurezza" (62) (I had the impression that we were going through a landscape of palm groves and paddy fields, but the darkness was too deep to be certain; 59); "in una poltrona fra le due finestre, dall'altra parte della sala, la massa scura che quando ero entrato mi era parsa un vestito buttato disordinatamente sulla spalliera della sedia, si voltò lentamente" (75) (in an armchair between the two windows at the other end of the room, the dark mass, which when I came in I had thought was a cloak carelessly thrown over the back of the chair, turned slowly; 73).

Sometimes the "correction of the definitive" works the other way around: instead of telling the reader what could have happened, it leaves out what actually took place. When, in the first chapter, Roux meets Vimala Sar, a prostitute who had an affair with Xavier, the narrator does not let the reader hear their story from her own lips: "Lei bevve e cominciò a raccontare. Fu un racconto lungo, prolisso, pieno di dettagli. Mi parlò della loro storia, delle strade di Bombay, di gite festive a Bassein e a Elephanta. […] Era una storia che lei aveva accuratamente mondato da bruttezze e da miserie. Era una storia d'amore" (21–2) (She drank and began to tell. It was a long, rambling story, full of details. She talked about their affair, about the streets of Bombay, the holiday trips to Bassein and Elephanta … It was a story she had carefully purged of any ugliness or misery. It was a love story; 12). Interestingly enough, here the narrator corrects something that the character herself had already modified, taking out of her (love) story all that could be unpleasant to hear or remember. It is, in a way, a second degree correction.

Throughout the novel, the narrator provides the reader with a fragmented narration that can always be developed into a hypothesis that, in contrast to Christine's photographs, does not need to be tested and compared to reality. The world is a series of signals that do not unfold in a set, predefined direction, but rather offer a fragmented and inconsistent scene that can transpire in a multitude of ways. Readers are faced with possibilities rather than certainties. These possibilities are precisely what literature takes pains to investigate.

Lo stadio di Wimbledon

In *Lo stadio di Wimbledon*, photographs appear on several occasions but always follow the same pattern. Some of the characters the protagonist enlists in his search show him pictures of the character in whose footsteps he has taken four trips to Trieste and one to London. Although they believe this will be of some help, the protagonist's reaction never alters. Photographs are for the protagonist a foreign body, something that must be kept at a distance and away from view. He thinks that photographs will be unable to help him; indeed, he considers them an obstacle to his quest. As the following excerpts indicate, by refusing to focus on the photograph (quote 1), by willingly blurring the image (quote 2), and by flipping the picture on the table (quote 3), the protagonist denies the effectiveness of photography as a means to represent reality:

> (quote 1) Non me l'aspettavo: ho la cornice d'argento quasi contro la giacca, girata dal mio verso, e con dentro la fotografia. È impossibile non prenderla. Allontano la fotografia distendendo il braccio e spingo la testa all'indietro, come fanno i presbiti. Spero che tutto questo possa apparire in qualche modo naturale. Lei dice "Eccolo, Bobi." Io guardo un punto astratto fuori della cornice. (39)
>
> I didn't expect it: I have the silver frame almost against my jacket, turned towards me, with the photograph inside. It's impossible not to take it. I pull the photograph away extending my arm and I push back my head the way far-sighted people do. I hope all of this can seem natural somehow. She says, "Here is Bobi." I look at some abstract point outside of the frame.
>
> (quote 2) Questa volta ho avuto il tempo di prepararmi, anzi, ho messo a punto un mio sistema. È impossibile non guardare le fotografie ma ogni volta che lei gira pagina io sfoco l'immagine, piegando gli occhi verso l'interno, verso il naso e la bocca. [...] Lei dice: "Eccolo." È inequivocabile, e io ho sfocato al massimo. Il foglio diventa una specie di guazzo scuro, moltiplicato e indistinto. (62–3)
>
> This time, I had time to prepare; actually, I put into action a method of mine. It's impossible not to look at the photos, but every time she turns the page I blur the image, crossing my eyes towards my nose and mouth ... She says, "Here he is." It's unmistakable, and I've blurred my vision as much as I could. The paper becomes some sort of dark puddle, multiplied and indistinct.
>
> (quote 3) Piano piano la fotografia arriva dalla mia parte. Non so, non vorrei fingere, e poi non me la sento di sottopormi alla tortura dell'altra volta a Trieste. Capovolgo la foto sul tavolino, piano; dico: "Senta, non posso vedere le fotografie. È così, mi dispiace." (100–1)
>
> Little by little, the picture comes my way. I don't know; I wouldn't want to lie, but then I would not want to undertake the torture from last time in

Trieste. I turn the photo over on the table, slowly; I say: "Excuse me, but I can't look at the photos. That's how it is; I'm sorry."

Before openly rejecting the photographs in the last excerpt, the protagonist affects them precisely by denying their capacity to visually represent a scene: first, he looks at an "abstract" point outside the frame, then the photographs themselves become "blurry" and "indistinct" thanks to his desperate method for avoiding them.

To understand such a reaction to photography, it is useful to turn to Schaeffer's theoretical considerations in his study *L'image précaire*. Schaeffer's starting point is similar to Van Lier's:

> Puisque la photographie est une empreinte à distance, elle est située d'entrée de jeu dans une tension spatiale qui implique l'absence de tout contact direct entre l'imprégnant et l'empreinte. [...] [L]'empreinte ne peut jamais étre rendue à son context d'extraction, donc l'image, conçue comme construction receptive, est incapable de le restituer 'tel qu'en lui-même.' (17)

> Since the photograph is an imprint at a distance, from the beginning it finds itself in a spatial tension that prevents any kind of direct contact between the printer and the imprint ... The imprint can never be returned to the context it has been taken from, and therefore the image, considered a construction of reception, is not able to return the context "as it is intrinsically."[5]

Schaeffer defines the photograph as an iconic index because the iconic aspect – that is, the likeness of the visual representation – is added to the indexical one. The photograph creates a quasi-perceptual view, independent of both the actual scene it represents and the particular intentions of the photographer: "si le savoir et la visée peuvent en effet motiver la prise de l'empreinte," he writes, "il n'en reste pas moins qu'ils ne sont jamais transférés dans l'image" (if knowledge and intent can actually motivate the recording of the imprint, this does not take away from the fact that these are never transferred into the image; 84). This leads Schaeffer to foreground the role of the recipient, who must insert the image into an interpretative universe. What comes to the recipient is not the intention codified in the picture but rather "la trace visuelle physico-chimique qui lui sert de support: or, la trace laisse le signe largement indéterminé, en sorte que souvent elle s'accomode de substances sémiotiques qui s'excluent les unes les autres" (the chemical-physical visual trace that supports it: but the trace leaves a largely indeterminate sign, so as to often admit semiotic substances that exclude each other; 104). According to Schaeffer, therefore, the photograph is to be considered essentially as a sign of reception. Hence, the relationship that must be investigated is the one between photographic image and observer, not the one between the photograph and the photographer. This seems to fit with the fact that in *Lo stadio di Wimbledon*, as opposed to *Notturno indiano*, photography is presented as an object, not in terms of its genesis and artifice.

Schaeffer considers the photograph to be a precarious and intermittent sign, erratic and opaque, partly irrational, in short, an image that "est toujours légèrement décalée par rapport à notre vision, par rapport à toute poussée sémantique aussi" (has always a slight deviation from our vision, and with respect to any semantic drives as well; 170). A photograph is "cet entre-deux ambigu qui n'est dejà plus une parcelle du monde physique dans lequel nous vaquons à nos plaisirs et peines, et qui n'est pas encore la 'réalité,' ce double sémiotique, ce filet que nous jetons autour de nous pour nous construire une niche sémantique et qui est l'horizon au-delà duquel nous sommes aveugles" (170) (that ambiguous intermediate space that is no longer a fragment of the physical world in which we attend to our pleasures and pains, and is not yet "reality," that semiotic double, that net we throw around us to build a semantic recess, and that constitutes the horizon beyond which we are blind; 149). How can we forget, at this point, the efforts made by Del Giudice's protagonist to escape from the photographs that are put before his eyes, by blurring the image as much as possible to attain an indistinct *gouache*, a mere set of shadows? Similarly, the sideways gaze the protagonist makes to avoid seeing the images brings to mind that photographs, in Schaeffer's words,

> dégagent une sorte de tremblement très fin grâce auquel elles se positionnent légèrement *à côte* de la "réalité," ouvrant une faille microscopique dans laquelle le signe se fracture et grâce à laquelle elles ouvrent notre regard à la manifestation de traces visuelles pures, organisées certes, mais d'une organisation "gratuite," toujours contingente et fragile dans son individualité irréductible, sans "finalité," donc sans intégration globalisante et idéelle. (204, emphasis added)

> emanate a sort of extremely light flickering thanks to which they stand slightly *to the side* of "reality," opening a microscopic crack in which the

> sign crumbles and through which they open our gaze to the manifestation of pure visual traces, organized to be sure, but "gratuitously" so, still contingent and fragile in their irreducible singularity, without "finality," in other words without an ideal and totalizing integration.

Following Schaeffer, one can assume that what the protagonist of *Lo stadio di Wimbledon* rejects in the photograph is that it is not reducible to a language insofar as it remains semiotically mute.

To test this hypothesis, we must examine the rest of the novel and consider the metaliterary vocation ascribed to its protagonist. The novel has six chapters: in the first four, the protagonist recounts his four trips to Trieste and his consequent encounters with five of Bobi's old friends; the last two are devoted to three days he spends in London, where he twice meets with one of Bobi's ex-lovers. The wanderings towards the six characters he meets in the novel are apparently casual; he visits libraries, stores, bars, and restaurants before getting to where he is going. However, the protagonist never misses the target, and his wanderings turn out to be trajectories whose apparent confusion is only part of a complex and accurate process, halfway between chance and necessity, chaos and order:

> forse non c'è un percorso, ma solo un'intermittenza tra la probabilità e l'improbabilità. È come se ogni spostamento lo decidessi lì per lì, per vedere dove porta, e questa scoperta, poi, non fosse altro che l'inizio che cercavo. Vorrei mantenere una certa inerzia, con spinte indispensabili e sufficienti. (9)

> Maybe there isn't a path, but only intermittency between probability and improbability. As if I decided each move off hand, just to see where it leads, and this discovery were but the starting point I had been looking for. I wish I could stay inert, with essential and sufficient pushes. (9)

Over the course of the novel, things slowly but progressively unfold their nature. In the second chapter the protagonist makes an appointment with one of Bobi's old friends within one hour. He comments: "è già un passo avanti poter distinguere il tempo, pensare 'un'ora morta.' È come se dall'indeterminatezza in cui non c'erano anticipi o ritardi spuntasse finalmente una pausa, con quello che ne consegue" (being able to dissect time and think "a dead hour" is a step forward. Like a break springing out of indistinctness, with no advances or delays, and all the consequences that follow; 24). As the trajectories become clearer, all things take on a shape, an order, a possibility of being perceived, distinguished from one another, and penetrated.

The trajectories towards the characters replicate on a smaller scale what happens in the novel as a whole, in which the apparently contradictory versions of the sought-after character finally blend together, but more to affect the protagonist's self-awareness than to form Bobi's coherent personality. Through the characters' stories, Bobi emerges as a playful spirit who enjoys life without actually being happy; as a man who continually changes his life, starting from scratch over and over again; as a puppeteer who arranges people's lives; and, finally, as someone who helps people find their own destiny without them even realizing it. At this point, the protagonist loses interest in the quest: after Bobi has solved his life, he decides to become a writer. The process whereby objects – and people – find their places is the same process that leads to literature: in the end, the protagonist discovers his vocation as a writer, and he does so through his own telling – that is, through a novel. In other words, literature is both a process whereby reality becomes graspable by the human mind and the result of that same process. That literature is a means of codifying reality, condensing it, and giving it meaning is expressed in the novel through the metaphor of Mercator's Map:

> la più antica Carta di Mercatore [è] la carta con cui si costruiscono quasi tutte le altre, dato che si può immaginare come la proiezione della terra su un cilindro tangente alla sfera dell'equatore, sul quale il mondo tagliato con le forbici venisse arrotolato e poi srotolato e messo in piano. I meridiani restano equidistanti; i paralleli si piegano convessi verso i poli, bocche sempre più sorridenti al Nord e sempre più tristi al Sud. Ma la Carta di Mercatore non è una proiezione geometrica, è inventata con un calcolo preciso, e con una matematica quasi perfetta. Il suo secondo nome è Rappresentazione. (82)

> The oldest Map of Mercator [is] the map on which nearly all other maps are modelled, since one can imagine it as the projection of the Earth on a cylinder tangential to the equator's sphere, on which the world cut with a pair of scissors could be rolled up and then unrolled and placed on a plane. The meridians remain equidistant: the parallels bend convexly towards the poles, mouths that smile more and more to the north, bigger and bigger frowns towards the south. But the Map of Mercator is not a

> geometrical projection; it is invented with a precise calculation, and with almost perfect mathematics. Its second name is Representation.

This excerpt describes the process through which the world is turned into a map. Similarly, representation is the process that translates reality into literature.

It is no wonder that, as Colummi Camerino has noted, Del Giudice's prose is full of "strumenti che potenziano la [...] percezione, la reduplicano, la incorniciano. Carte, foto, immagini monitorate, [...] forme di riproduzione e rappresentazione del reale" (instruments that strengthen, re-duplicate, and frame perception ... Papers, photos, images from monitor screens ... forms of reproduction and representation of reality; 63). As for *Lo stadio di Wimbledon,* there are all the navigational tools on the French warship anchored in the port of Trieste, as well as those on the airplane the protagonist takes to London. The tools are not just listed, but incorporated into larger events. Regarding the warship, the protagonist, after watching two young people board it with the commander, imagines (without being able to verify) their subsequent actions. Regarding the airplane, the protagonist imagines it crashing into Mont Blanc as a result of pilot error and various circumstances. The two hypothetical narratives diverge from the text with respect to the verb tense with which they are presented: the future perfect in the first, the conditional in the second, emerging from a substratum of present and past tense. As the switch to a different verb tense reveals, words bring reality to another level, one that is not, as in *Notturno indiano,* a hypothesis. The narrator is not simply imagining something that could happen; he is producing *another* kind of reality, a more rigorous and intellectual one that can only be arrived at through words. All of these tools are incorporated into the narrative as a *mise en abyme* of what is unfolding at a broader, thematic level. Representation is not a simple transcription of reality but a method for codifying it through calculation – something that photography cannot do.

But this calculation is only "almost" perfect. At first glance, the trajectories towards the characters resemble random wanderings, and the quest for Bobi only seems to produce confused images of a dead man, as much as words themselves are in constant tension between accuracy and uncertainty, precision and vagueness. Every word in the novel is a representation *per se* but at the same time just one step further towards building the whole novel, the complete representation.

Words are like "trajectories" and "directions" – two terms that recur often in Del Giudice's prose. His words "tendono, oscillando, ora al rigore della descrizione, ora alla fluttuazione dell'instabilità" (tend to and waver between both exactness of description and fluctuation of instability; Antonello 134). These words produce "un'immagine netta eppure senza contorni, sfigurata per dinamismo interno" (a clear-cut but edgeless image, disfigured by intrinsic energy; 134). This energy is exactly what sets in motion the process towards representation. The reader often encounters this change of levels, from simple account to a sort of hyperreality where everything becomes clear, where everything is, as it were, self-evident:

> Dai quattro angoli della piattaforma venivano fuori dei cavi d'acciaio, li hanno serrati ai martinetti e poi hanno cominciato a tirare. Tiravano lentamente, con molte grida. Il cemento prima si è compresso poi si è dilatato, alla fine c'è stato uno schianto secco, un boato nella valle e il ponte è andato a posto. All'ufficiale non ho detto che era stato un momento di assoluta simultaneità, in cui tutto appariva compresente. (5)

> From the four corners of the platform steel cables emerged; they were shut at the jim-crows and then they began to pull. They pulled slowly, with much shouting. The cement first contracted, then dilated, and finally there was a dry snap, a roar in the valley and the bridge went back into place. I did not tell the official that it had been a moment of absolute simultaneity in which everything became present at once.

As this quote indicates, there is a trajectory that suddenly turns the description of a real event into a moment of hyperreality. The temporal succession of events (first … then … finally) creates and at the same time is replaced by a flash of "absolute simultaneity" that overcomes the causality of the scene. But this simultaneity (another common word in the author's prose) does not imply a return to indeterminacy. It is, rather, a moment when the energy that pervades the whole novel reaches both its climax and its moment of stasis, embracing all things in a synthesis that does not affect their specificity.

The metafictional tension of the novel, which ends with the protagonist's (somewhat implied) decision to become a writer, opposes the use of photography because, as discussed above, it is incapable of forming a semiotic double of reality. This is confirmed in one of the novel's last scenes, in which the protagonist visits Wimbledon Stadium. At a certain point, he feels the need to take a picture:

> Vorrei solo vedere, e sentire; e per la prima volta è spiacevole, proprio adesso, non poter fotografare una visione di insieme, o un particolare che conta solo per me. Prendo un quaderno dalla borsa, per disegnare; nel movimento ho l'impressione di una piccola forma nera sulla destra. Lo sguardo torna indietro da sé: sulla panca al di là dei gradini c'è un cinturino che pende a terra, e un astuccio con un naso pronunciato, e dentro può esserci solo una cosa al mondo: una macchina fotografica. (113)

> I would only like to see and hear; and for the first time, it is unpleasant, right in this moment, to not be able to photograph an overall view, or a detail that means something only to me. I grab a notebook from the bag, to draw; in moving, I get the impression of a small black form on the right. My gaze shifts there on its own: on the bench past the steps there is a strap hanging, and a case with a pronounced nose, and there can only be one thing in the world inside: a camera.

After developing some hypotheses of action with the camera, the protagonist decides to wait and do nothing until another person takes the object away, but not before he has engaged in a visual duel with the main character. Right after this scene, the protagonist meets with Bobi's ex-lover. During their dialogue, he feels that the whole quest has lost its meaning and that the only thing that counts for him is writing. Thus, the dismissal of the camera as a way to produce a general view of things or to gain an accurate representation of a single detail makes sense if it is seen as the last step in the long process of becoming a writer. It is the last wandering before the literary vocation is revealed and the last acknowledgment of photography's inability to produce an enhanced representation of reality.[6]

It is interesting to note that here, as in *Notturno indiano,* there is a sort of reversal of roles: the photographer in the one case, and here the camera itself, are deprived of vision, which becomes the prerogative of the writer. The protagonist looks at the camera, which is unable to look at the world. And the protagonist looks at the camera with a sideways glance, out of the corner of his eye. Once again we are reminded of Schaeffer's observations on photography and its role alongside reality. The vision through which reality must be represented (i.e., projected on another level) is not linked to the camera, but rather to the literary itself, which is born out of an imaginative vision expressed through language.

Conclusion

In *The Politics of Postmodernism*, Linda Hutcheon argues that "photography may be the perfect postmodern vehicle in many ways, for it is based on a set of paradoxes inherent in its medium, general paradoxes which make it ripe for the particular paradoxes of postmodernism" (116). Photography resides halfway between simulacrum and the work of art, art and mass culture, technique and form, objectivity and subjectivity. A photograph is an index – albeit an unstable and imperfect one, as both Van Lier and Schaeffer describe it – but even more, it is a paradox, a hybrid that takes something out of reality but cannot fix it as a controllable, codified, and meaningful reproduction. However, in both *Notturno indiano* and *Lo stadio di Wimbledon*, photography is more than a step on the path towards a higher level of representation; it also has something to teach. In a photograph, a confused and vague mass of information comes from reality: this constitutes, in Van Lier's terms, the *indices*. Because of this close link to reality, photography finds itself somewhat compelled to produce a fixed and faithful representation of an event. In *Notturno indiano*, Christine tries to accomplish this by controlling the level of the *indexes*. However, indexes cannot turn indices into clear information about an event; they can only highlight or accentuate those indices. Tabucchi's prose represents reality as a fragmentary and enigmatic realm as well. However, unlike in photography, the result is not an entrapment but rather its opposite: thanks to the shortcomings of reality, literature is free to produce its own truth, exploring what could or could not have happened.[7] This provisional and potential truth explores possibilities and hypotheses that need not be proven outside the fictional world and that are consistent with themselves. As noted earlier, control is a key term for understanding the difference between Christine's and Roux's books. In the fiction of his imagined book, Roux does control what happens, but the effectiveness of his control is limited to fiction: he does not expect to find any confirmation in the outside world, and he does not offer his solution as the only possible one or even as the definitive one. Literature is not intended to capture reality, but rather to produce a hypothetical and momentary reality that exists solely on a fictional level. Roux's book draws its strength from the mere fact of being narrated fiction that, because of this, "propone un suo tasso di autenticità più forte di qualsiasi verifica extratestuale" (offers a rate of authenticity stronger than any extratextual test; Ravazzoli 31). It is precisely through his "supponiamo che" (let's suppose) – a kind of "performative utterance" that, following

J.L. Austin, implements what is said in the saying, thanks to the very fact of saying it (6) – that his words take on life, potentially creating the imagined scene in front of his eyes; Christine, by contrast, is unable to verify the truthfulness of Roux's words.[8]

In Del Giudice's novel, it seems that everything is born by a rigorous procedure akin to a laboratory experiment[9] through which literature translates reality into the hyperreality discussed earlier. Again, the link between writing and reality is made clear through photography, whose rejection forces the protagonist to seek out a different kind of confrontation with things. Following Schaeffer's theories, photographs are imprints that, because they are closely yet uncontrollably linked to reality, cannot be reduced to a systematic and totalizing language. Because photography fails to produce a rigorous double of reality and never crosses the threshold to a codified representation of it, the protagonist rejects photographs – in his view, they cannot help him in his quest. *Lo stadio di Wimbledon* reflects precisely the process that goes beyond that threshold and leads to the production of a rigorous representation. In *Notturno indiano*, the representation of a confused and enigmatic world allows the narrative voice to create an elsewhere that replaces reality with a web of possibilities and hypotheses. In *Lo stadio di Wimbledon*, the disorder is only apparent, or at least momentary. This disorder is a manifestation of the energy that pervades the whole novel and pushes it towards its resolution (i.e., the transposition onto reality into another, more abstract, level). That happens in the novel at different levels. Sometimes an image or a thought or just a single word suddenly pops out of the narrative as a clear, neat, and self-evident element. At other times, a whole episode overcomes the circumstances that have led to it and takes its own path outside reality towards a rigorous and intellectual representation of it. However, on an even broader level, the novel itself is a long process towards Representation: a Representation that coincides with the novel, getting to its end right at the end of it and that at the same time lives outside of the novel in the protagonist's literary vocation.

NOTES

1 See *Of Reasoning in General* (1895), in which Peirce states that "an icon is a sign which stands for its object because as a thing perceived it excites an idea naturally allied to the idea that object would excite. Most icons, if not

all, are likenesses of their objects. A photograph is an icon, usually conveying a flood of information" (11). In *Nomenclature and Divisions of Triadic Relations, as far as they Are Determined* (1903), Peirce writes instead that "the fact that the latter [a photograph] is known to be the effect of the radiations from the object renders it an Index and highly informative" (297). Finally, in *What Is a Sign?* (1894), Peirce observes that "photographs, especially instantaneous photographs, are very instructive, because we know that they are in certain respects exactly like the objects they represent. But this resemblance is due to the photographs having been produced under such circumstances, that they were physically forced to correspond point by point to nature" (5). All essays are collected in *The Essential Peirce*, vol. 2.

2 The recent history of such theory can be traced to Sontag's *On Photography* (1977), to the more systematic work of Rosalind Krauss in "Notes on the Index" (1977), with its explicit references to Peirce, and finally to *L'act photographique* by Philippe Dubois (1981), a work that explores the photographic sign understood as index. Also relevant is Barthes's *Camera Lucida* (1980), which emphasizes that the photograph is an emanation of the referent.

3 Quotations in English from Tabucchi's novel are from the 2013 translation by Tim Parks. Quotations from Del Giudice's book have been translated into English by the author.

4 According to Van Lier, isomorphism occurs when a real place is replaced with a purely localizable space. Synchronism refers to the fact that a photograph has no duration, but only the datable time of the arrival of the last photons. Furthermore, a photograph is both analogical (since the forms it shows share proportions with the forms of an outside spectacle) and digital (since each grain is converted according to a choice between darkened and not darkened). Finally, subcharge and surcharge refer to the amount of information a photograph conveys, which is always bigger or smaller than what humans can see with their own eyes.

5 Quotations in English from Schaeffer's essay are the author's translation.

6 Before visiting the stadium and then Bobi's ex-lover, the protagonist reads and describes a novel in which "c'è lui come personaggio" (he is a character); 108. Like *Notturno indiano, Lo stadio di Wimbledon* has its own book within the book. In the inner novel – written after the Second World War and set in Rome during the occupation – there are two characters, Sebastiano and Ans, and plenty of "discussioni esistenziali" (existential discussions); 108. Sebastiano, as *Lo stadio di Wimbledon*'s protagonist explains, writes everything that happens and then reads it to the characters involved. This novel is based on *Manoscritto* (*Manuscript*) by Sebastiano

Carpi (1948), where "troviamo tracce di Bazlen nel personaggio di Ans" (we find traces of Bazlen in Ans's character); Curreri 162. Ans complains about the way Sebastiano describes him. At one point, he tells his friend, "Devi correggere Sebastiano. Io non sono così" (You have to correct Sebastiano. I'm not like that); 109. The presence of this novel within the novel stresses one more time the elusiveness of the character that *Lo stadio di Wimbledon*'s protagonist is investigating. However, its presence at this point in the novel is also a farewell to a type of literature focusing on significant and existential themes and a supposedly realistic representation of reality – that is, far from what *Lo stadio di Wimbledon*'s protagonist is looking for.

7 It is interesting to compare Roux's imagined book to Umberto Eco's notion of possible worlds as expressed in *The Role of the Reader: Explorations in the Semiotics of Texts*. According to Eco, a possible world "is a possible state of affairs expressed by a set of relevant propositions," and "since [it] is not actual, it must depend on the propositional attitudes of somebody; in other words, possible worlds are worlds imagined, believed, wished, and so on" (219). Any fictional world is a possible world that "picks up pre-existing sets of properties (and therefore individuals) from the 'real' world, that is, from the world to which the reader is invited to refer as the world of reference" (221). Roux's world is a possible world, both because it is imagined and because it is a (potential) work of fiction. It takes something from the world of reference, which in this case is the novel itself, and turns it into something else.

8 One notes that "like the performative, the literary utterance does not refer to a prior state of affairs and is not true or false. The literary utterance too creates the state of affair to which it refers" (Culler 95).

9 Paolo Mauri defines Del Giudice's novel as a "romanzo-laboratorio" (novel as laboratory); 90.

8 Photographs Illustrating and Photographs Telling: Exercises in Reading Lalla Romano and Elio Vittorini

EPIFANIO AJELLO

I propose to compare two novels that incorporate photographic images in their pages: *Nuovo romanzo di figure* (*New Novel of Images*) (1997) by Lalla Romano and *Conversazione in Sicilia* (*Conversations in Sicily*) (first published in 1937) by Elio Vittorini. I will reflect on the different relationships that images establish with their respective narrative texts.[1] Considering that these novels offer different montages of photographs and written narrative, I suggest some close readings so as to highlight two different ways of combining photographs with literary text.

Nuovo romanzo di figure is a novel comprised of photographs taken by Lalla Romano's father at the beginning of the twentieth century. The author found them by chance after her father's death. In it, photographs are accompanied by written notes that do not merely interpret the images but actually become part of them so that the narration grows out of her comments on the photographs. In Romano's *Nuovo romanzo di figure*, the writing follows the images as well as the childhood memories to which they give rise. By contrast, Vittorini's *Conversazione in Sicilia* was initially published without images. Only after being asked about a new edition did the author decide to add photographs of Sicily to his story. The photographs thus arrived after the verbal text, but not as illustrations for the novel. Rather, they amplify the text and become its allegory in a relationship of both complementarity and collision. In both books, the results hover between life and imagination, reality and fiction, realism and allegory.

Nuovo romanzo di figure: Fragments of Past Stories

Nuovo romanzo di figure is a masterful montage of photos taken by the writer's father, Roberto, from 1904 to 1914.[2] The photos are divided into neat chapters, with commentary provided by Romano in the form of *brevi appunti* (short notes). The writer had taken up this multimodal genre in the past – for example, in *La Treccia di Tatiana* (*Tatiana's Braid*) (1986) – and would return to it in *Dall'ombra* (*From the Shadow*) (1999) and in her most recent novel *Ritorno a Ponte Stura* (*Return to Ponte Stura*) (2000).[3] Indeed, the relationship between word and image, verbal and visual codes, runs throughout her work, beginning with the early oneiric *Le metamorfosi* (*The Metamorphoses*) (1951) and becoming increasingly evident in *La penombra che abbiamo attraversato* (*The Penumbra*) (1964) and in two other noteworthy texts: *Nei mari estremi* (*In the Extreme Seas*) (1987) and *Le lune di Hvar* (*The Moons of Hvar*) (1991). As Romano explains:

> Il mio criterio (o ispirazione) fu il seguente. Accostai al testo fotografico un testo letterario in funzione illustrativa, non informativa. Quello che intendevo illustrare non era l'esteticità – anche se mi presi qualche libertà a questo proposito – ma la pregnanza dei significati, una prospettiva di lettura delle immagini stesse in quanto simboli o metafore [...]. Scelsi di prescindere dalle informazioni di cui disponevo, per interpretare liberamente (creativamente) i segni delle immagini. ("Il mio primo romanzo di immagini" 1597–8)

> My criterion (or inspiration) was the following: I placed a literary text alongside the photographic one for purposes of illustration, not information. What I wanted to illustrate wasn't the aesthetic quality – although I took some liberties in this regard – but the wealth of potential meanings, the perspective of reading the images themselves as symbols or metaphors ... I chose to set aside the information available to me and interpret the signs of the images freely (creatively).

Leaving aside the oxymoron "signs of the image," it is clear that Romano has no didactic intention. To explain means to comment, and one usually comments on a text by staying outside of it. Romano's *appunti* do not comment on or interpret the images; rather, the short notes become part of the photographs themselves without adding any new meaning to them – her words only integrate the photographs into the telling. Thus readers wonder: When does the writing stop explaining an image and instead start broadening its meaning?

The written texts in *Nuovo romanzo di figure* do not name or expose the figures; hence, we cannot consider this book a family photo album *tout court*. Precise information does not seem to be essential to the narrative. The result is a strange text that is neither an autobiographical novel nor a diary, much less an epistolary novel or a collection of tales, but rather an unusual kind of synopsis that links a series of visual details with a minute mosaic of written tesserae. In *Nuovo romanzo di figure*, a paratactic discussion comprised of short, essential sentences is held together with just one punctuation mark, the dash, which links and at the same time distinguishes each clause and accentuates the breathlessness of their concatenation. One clause seems to influence the other without a narrative plot being constructed. The clauses are all subordinate to the images; as Romano writes: "In questo libro le immagini sono il testo e lo scritto un'illustrazione" (In this book the images are the text and the writing is an illustration; *Nuovo romanzo di figure* vi).[4] One could, however, share Vilém Flusser's view, which is that "texts admittedly explain images in order to explain them away, but images also illuminate texts in order to make them comprehensible" (11).

It is this paradoxical intention of the writing to "illustrate an image" that I want to examine. But let me be clear that I am not interested in the implied filmic montage, which Romano described as "vaguely narrative."[5] What interests me is the role played by the notes – or better still, the relationship established between a given image and a given piece of writing. I want to ask what happens with these micro-narrations that are placed alongside the photographic images and that arise from their clash with the photographs.

"Notes" seems to be the right term: it is as if we were underscoring the lines of a text in pencil in order to highlight its parts and grasp what they are telling us. Romano's eye does the same: it isolates or points out a reflective and impressionistic passage. Taking notes, like underlining, is a way to choose, to quote, and to summarize. Giorgio Manganelli has observed that to take notes by highlighting passages of a book is to extract from it a different imaginary path. So the singular process in *Nuovo romanzo di figure* is to underline and stress some aspects or details of the image and isolate them. If this particular text makes use of the photographic images, it is not to increase their emphasis; paradoxically, it is to portray another image: a story not *of* the photograph but *from* the photograph. There is no ekphrastic intention here, and the notes set aside the image soon after observing it; they identify some details and rebuild alongside the image a sort of simulacrum (the text) that no longer has anything of the image yet needs it to exist. The story, if we can define the writings in *Nuovo romanzo di figure* as such, is not in the succession of images, or in the plot, but beside it. A symbiosis is thereby established: the photographs need the writing, and the notes need the images. As suggested by Pier Paolo Pasolini in another context: "La fotografia è lo sforzo estremo del testimone che cerca di ricordare il particolare di un'azione a cui ha assistito senza parteciparvi. È poi attraverso l'immaginazione che integriamo la fotografia di ciò che manca, ossia il movimento" (The photograph is the extreme effort of a witness trying to remember the detail of an action he has seen without taking an active part in it. Then through imagination we integrate the photo with what is missing, that is to say movement; 296). Instead of critically engaging with the narrative movement of individual images as derived from their sequence in a montage, I propose to examine the written "animation" of the individual image. Not so much the probable *consecutio* of a photographic image, but what the photo is able to say, starting from itself but *differently* from itself.[6] I recall (and apologize for the inappropriate comparison) a particular manufacturing process for hats to make their felt thicker, referred to in everyday parlance as *felting*. Well, in the pages of *Nuovo romanzo di figure* a similar process takes place: a thickening of the image's denotations, that is, an increase in the ability to *felt* the photograph.

A theoretical reference can be found in the short passage of *Camera Lucida* where Barthes mentions, briefly, the concept of the "blind field," which "constantly doubles our partial vision" (57). A blind field refers to the capacity of the photograph to be "animated" by an eye and to go on recounting itself *out of* or *beyond* the actual image. What emerges from the photograph has a seemingly incoherent meaning, neither communicative nor symbolic of the photograph to which it refers. Once a blind field is created, readers can extract any plot from the image (55–8). This space may be called the off screen, which gives rise to a kind of story without any (predetermined) plot. Of course, a regular lexical fabula, one with a planned causal-temporal relationship, cannot arise from photographic images, as Boris Tomasevskij has taught us (307–50). The motifs or themes in an orderly classification are not related to the images' "clauses." Instead, they work in a disorderly fashion, making sense out of the photographic exposures. Where this is possible, such as in a private dimension, something of the image (involvement, passion, nostalgia) reminds us of a sort of Joycean epiphany or even, perhaps, of the radiance of Proust's *madeleine*.

The notes in *Nuovo romanzo di figure* move in syntactical streams that are without causality or temporal succession and are not always congruent. In rhetorical terms, this writing is similar to an allegory: "Il risultato non è propriamente un racconto; né un romanzo" (the result is neither a real story nor a novel), writes Romano, "se è proprio necessario catalogarlo in un genere, penso di poterlo definire un'allegoria" (if it is really necessary to classify it in a genre, I think I can define it as an allegory; *La treccia di Tatiana* vi). Allegory does not mean speaking in a different way about a hidden meaning, but rather illustrating a concept hidden in the portrayal. It is evident that Romano's notes are devoid of plot. The short texts are woven together only with free motifs, that is to say "replaceable without any damage to the integrity of the causal-temporal link with the events" (Tomasevskij 316). The verbal material is organized not according to overarching dynamic themes, those that develop the action of a story, but rather according to static themes, descriptions of landscapes and characters that are more important to the narrative than dynamic ones. Presenting them simultaneously on the same narrative level, Romano loosely links the static descriptive elements together and assigns them to the images, with which they begin a dialogue. In this way, her short notes amplify the images, elaborate and invent different meanings for them, and, most importantly, trace the connotations, which are hidden in every photograph. All of this is possible because the writing reconstructs the image in such a way that nothing in the photograph is prearranged.

So, what should we make of the connotations that arise from focal points? In Romano, photographic meaning is far from symbolic. The photographic image takes on a documentary role; essentially, it communicates only what it represents, offering a focal point and, perhaps, a surprise. The photograph can allow another kind of thinking to emerge independently, and that thinking is gathered up in short notes, as in this case, only when the viewer is fully engaged in a reading of the entire image or a particular detail in it. In relation to this process, Flusser speaks of a "scanning" effect:

> One has to allow one's gaze to wander over the surface feeling the way as one goes. This wandering over the surface of the image is called "scanning." In so doing, one's gaze follows a complex path formed, on the one hand, by the structure of the image and, on the other, by the observer's intentions. The significance of the image as revealed in the process of scanning therefore represents a synthesis of two intentions: one manifested in the image and the other belonging to the observer. It follows that images are not "denotative" (unambiguous) complexes of symbols (like numbers,

> for example) but "connotative" (ambiguous) complexes of symbols: they provide space for interpretation. (8)

Scanning, as theorized by Flusser, moves the image in a connotative way. This expansion of connotative meaning happens if the photograph is duly moved via the *punctum*, which requires an eye driven by a private attraction, as well as an affinity with the image, a desire to go beyond what is shown. This process is necessarily born of a seduction of the reader-viewer, a singular delight in the text, an enjoyment of the image (or one of its details), and a delving into what intrigues the viewer about it.

But this type of engagement is possible only for the writer, notwithstanding that she writes, "Presumo che se avessi incontrato quelle immagini in un album di ignoti mi avrebbero incantato allo stesso modo" (I think that if I had met those images in an album of unknown persons they would have fascinated me in the same manner; *Nuovo romanzo* v). Romano reflects on this engagement in a text titled "Il frutto del grano" ("The Wheat's Fruit") after a photographic album dedicated to the Cottolengo in Turin. This text is a commentary on a photographic image portraying the interior of a pasta factory run by nuns for the benefit of orphan children: "Ciò che muove questi macchinari non è, come in tutte le fabbriche, uno scopo di produzione e di interesse, anch'essi vitali [...], ma qui è la Carità. Tutto l'album testimonia questa cosa grande: umana e più umana" (What moves this machinery isn't production and profit as it is in all the factories, though these are vital as well ... but here it is Charity. The whole album testifies to this great thing: human and more than human; 1602). Now, the theological virtue of charity, or pity, is not visible in the photographic image; it is only traceable. Such feelings cannot be photographed, yet somehow they "wound" (using Barthes's word) the writer's eye. Charity is thus the *punctum* that gives life to the photograph; its meaning continues beside it and allows a meaning to surface that condenses around the static image of the nuns who are being photographed – a very rapid reflection on a gesture, telling the sense of an everyday morality. Here "telling" is used with a different meaning than its usual one: it is an account of facts, minor thematic elements that do not exclude a narrative subtext that is the tale of what happened, slight though the plot may be.

Certainly in *Nuovo romanzo di figure* the photograph's magic could have played a role, but it would have produced different notes. The written text is Romano's, and it is the result of a relationship, of an experience shared with what is portrayed privately. Unlike the readers, Romano identifies with the images and the characters photographed; she remembers the landscapes, the events, and it is this *a priori* knowledge that allows her to complete the images. It cannot be otherwise, for in the writing of the short notes another element of perspective is evident, as if the writer's eye were constantly looking through the lens of her father's camera. Romano explains:

> Nell'ordinare per temi e in una progressione vagamente narrativa queste immagini, ho visto trasparire e prendere consistenza quasi un ritratto di mio padre; mentre mi ero accinta a una lettura esclusivamente visiva, come se le fotografie fossero senza autore. In realtà non c'è immagine che non sia in qualche modo una cifra del suo animo. (*Nuovo romanzo* vii–viii)[7]

> As I was arranging these images by theme and in a vaguely narrative progression, I watched a portrait of my father almost taking shape, whereas I had set about doing a visual reading only, as if the photographs had no author. Actually there is no image that is not somehow a cipher of his soul.

The writer engages with the photographic image in the present. She writes of her experience of looking at her father's images: "È un riguardare, guardare di nuovo, come farebbe uno che rivive, [che] è la maniera migliore, anzi l'unica, per guardare con verità i fatti e le cose" (It is taking a second look, as only one who lives over again would do, [which] is the best or the only way to look at facts and things truly; *L'eterno presente* 4). Two narrators, then, meet within the image. However, only one of them (the daughter) attempts to find the original intention of the other's (the father's) choice of poses and framing. Giacomo Debenedetti wonders: "È proprio sicuro, per esempio, che l'obiettivo sia un occhio indifferente? O non è piuttosto un occhio disponibile a captare tutte le immagini che gli vengono proposte, ma quelle soltanto?" (Is it absolutely certain, for example, that the lens is a disinterested eye? Or is it rather an eye ready to catch all the images that are offered to it, but only those?; 83); and Mario Praz points out that "la fotografia ce la può dir lunga sulla persona ritratta, ma una cosa è certa; che non meno di una pittura ce la dice lunga sul fotografo [...]. E qui sta il nocciolo della questione. Il giudizio umano ha una qualità sottile, contagiosa, è un grano di anilina che può colorare un'intera vasca" (A photo can tell us a lot about the person portrayed, but one thing is certain: that no less than a painting, it tells us a lot about the photographer ... And this is the heart of the matter. Human judgment has a fine, contagious quality; it is a grain of aniline that can colour a whole bathtub; 194). The photograph is, for this reason, like a mirror. It also portrays the one who does not appear in it: the photographer. By choosing a pose or a particular frame, the photographer is part of the image that retains his/her judgment and desire.

It is a question of tracing the contours of what the photographer chose to see and, later, fixing it in a photograph. Romano explains: "Mio padre, come ogni altro artista, per quanto minore, faceva delle scelte: libere, in quanto non professionali, né sottoposte ad obblighi sociali; però appassionate, e in questo senso rivelatrici" (My father, like any other artist, even though a minor artist, made choices. His choices were free, not professional, and not subjected to social obligations; but they were full of passion and in this way they were revealing; *Nuovo romanzo* vii). In the tallying, Romano tries to reveal the invisible intention of her father's original look as well as his passionate search for a telling detail.

We have, then, a process that attempts to retrace another process. The short notes, as they *repeat* the image, attempt to uncover the chosen perspectives the photographer wanted so long ago. For instance, when reviewing some of her father's photographs made with a self-timer, Romano fairly easily finds in them signs that lead her to the author – to his melancholy, his pride, his severity, but also to his dreams. Examining the perceptual data of the photographic image makes the datum in question – the frame or pose or glance – reveal something about an existential experience, thus bringing it to light. But above all, in Roberto Romano's obsessive act of taking photographs, the images become little questions through which he nurses illusions in order to muse on them (and also on himself). To reveal, in this sense, is to discover, to show, to take cognizance, to give a value, or to establish a relation and thereby show the self. Hence, the photographer is the true protagonist of the novel and the principal character in his images. For Romano, the portrait "è l'equivalente di un romanzo: complesso, ambiguo, segreto come ogni vita; e insieme rivelatore" (is equivalent to a novel: complex, ambiguous, secret like every life, and at the same time revealing; "Introduzione" 9).

In Romano's notes there is only the writer's wish to understand or make real in the present what happened in the past in the hope of giving a deeper and more memorable meaning to what *was*. For Romano, taking photographs and writing go hand in hand. The writing lingers over her father's framings to become more than a reading of an image born of an imagination. The result is a transparent revision that does not alter the photographic images but rather passes over them in search of something special. To borrow from Stefano Agosti, Romano's writing sets out to capture "l'inquietudine e l'affanno [...] di un uomo che attraverso l'occhio dell'obiettivo cerca inutilmente di avvicinarsi alla donna amata" (the anxiety and the sorrow ... of a man who tries vainly through the eye of the lens to approach his beloved woman; 3). Of course, this sort of writing results from a quest that lacks not only an orientation but also a beginning and an end. From this perspective, from this groping movement, emerges a writing that, as the writer tells us, can be seen as something like an image, a second look.

And this is how the writing experiments with a paratactic, questioning style; it is spare, hidden prose. According to Romano, inspiration "non è qualcosa che 'precede,' ma quella grazia che opera intanto che il travaglio tecnico si compie, e non esiste al di fuori di esso" (isn't something that "comes before," but the grace that operates while the technical labour is in progress and doesn't exist without it; "Poesia della pittura" 1577). It is, then, the "grace" of "technical labour" that enables the writer to discover the conditions for a particular image: the destinies of the people depicted and their relationships, as well as the judgment, the irony, the choices the photographer makes. As Romano specifies, "Dove fosse in gioco la fatuità, una blanda ma sottile canzonatura è leggibile nelle immagini stesse: è il giudizio che ne dava mio padre" (Where there was fatuousness, a gentle but subtle mockery can be read in the images themselves: this is the judgment expressed by my father; *Nuovo romanzo* viii).[8] This is the intricate (temporal and spatial) framework that Romano wants to penetrate. It is a difficult path because it is not conventional: "È facile rintracciare in queste immagini i segni del costume e non difficile quelli di un gusto figurativo; ma la ricerca essenziale è quella di scoprire chi era l'uomo che vi ha espresso se stesso e il suo mondo nel modo indiretto, lucido e insieme allusivo che è quello dell'arte" (The signs of their customs and those of a figurative nature are easy to find in these images; but the essential quest is to discover the identity of the man who expressed himself and his world in the indirect, clear and at the same time allusive manner that belongs to art; *Nuovo romanzo* vii). So it is no coincidence, therefore, that words such as "expression" and "allusion" are the focus of her search. This creates a dialogue between the narrator's parents, as well as an overlapping of her father's interpretation of the world and her own, as Segre notes ("Introduzione" lvi).

The snapshots, no longer precious occasions for nostalgia or documents of an epoch, appear only as fragments of stories, not as a history. They are allegories of individual destinies, "of dead or nearly dead lives," where the word strikes the surfaces of the portraits to extract an emblematic meaning from them.[9] Romano specifies:

> [...] l'importanza di quelle foto non è dovuta tanto alla raffigurazione del gusto di un'epoca, e nemmeno alla sensibilità visiva del fotografo: consiste nella contemplazione della natura e nell'intuizione dei destini da parte della coscienza di un uomo. Lo dimostrano [...] la scelta dei soggetti, il rispetto e l'ironia sulla vita. (*Nuovo romanzo di figure* v-vi)

> The importance of those photographs isn't due so much to the portrayal of the taste of an age, nor to the visual sensibility of the photographer, but to the contemplation of nature and to the intuition of their destinies by the conscience of a man. The choice of subjects, the respect and irony on life prove this.

Along with the horror for what is irrevocably lost, the horror of death and disappearing lives, we sense a persistent moral lesson. Romano's father's conscience is felt everywhere, and the photographs constitute immediate evidence of this: they are stories of a life.

Consequently, the book is not comparable to an impressionistic work; it is a compromise with the love of History and life. As Romano writes: "Le figure e la loro storia [...] appartengono all'irrevocabile segreto del passato, ma tutte ho sentito emblematiche di qualcosa di noi, del nostro tempo" (The figures and their stories ... belong to the irrevocable secret of the past, but I felt that all of them are emblematic of something of us, of our time; *Dall'ombra* 9). Her father's photographs attempt to preserve an ephemeral dimension of harmony.

The world portrayed so far could belong, then, to a real novel and those bodies to characters, making her work a novel with *real* illustrations. A realist novel then? Or a novel made only of appearances, of non-existent or no longer existing places; hence, an imaginary novel? It is difficult, here, to establish the border between reality and imagination. At the end of the reading, there is the feeling of having always been on a barely discernible border between images and words. It is a border on which it is impossible to remain, just as one cannot remain on the one invoked here, that is, between the past (the images) and the present (the writing). These are two incomparable times and registers.

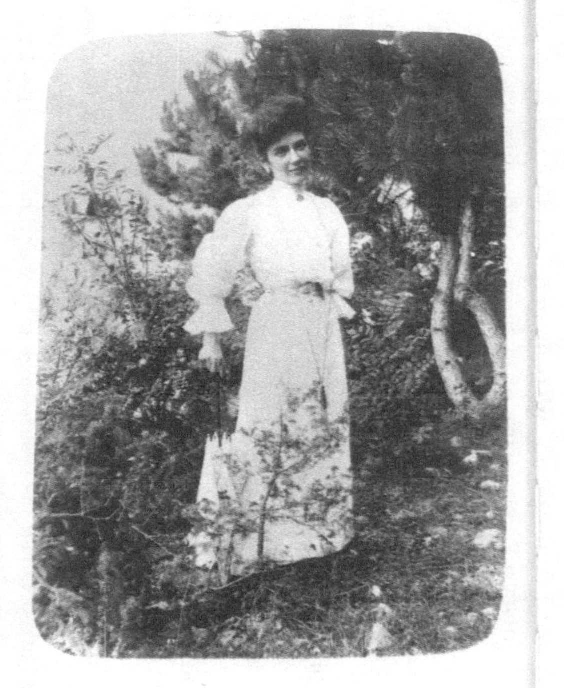

– il bianco rende la figura incorporea, senza peso, sul fondo mosso e confuso – il «ramage» del ginepro spinoso contro l'abito bianco accentua il carattere di fiore dell'immagine – la forma è affidata alla linea – si rispondono le curve del braccio e del tronco sdoppiato – un accenno di profondità è dovuto al movimento ascendente nel bordo dell'abito, nelle linee della faccia – sul fondo scuro del pino e dei capelli la faccia ha un rilievo plastico – il sorriso è accennato, quasi concesso – c'è abbandono: da un fondo di malinconia affiora la fiducia – lei sapeva che quella foto era un atto (per quanto contemplativo) di adorazione; ma non poteva sorridere piú di cosí – nel linguaggio di quella contemplazione c'era anche «l'aurora di bianco vestita» (era un canone del gusto dell'epoca), ma non c'è romanza nell'immagine: la sua grazia è severa –

49

Figure 8.1 Photograph by Roberto Romano. In Lalla Romano, *Nuovo romanzo di figure*, 48–9. With kind permission of Antonio Ria.

What remains, then, of this particular novel, we wonder, but to make us reflect? To read *Nuovo romanzo di figure* is to engage in a revision of things and destinies without the sentimental trick of a non-existent, innocent, and happy village to return to. The book is not elegiac at all; it does not distract us as if those bodies, still full of life, were there as emblems of outraged social justice – humble creatures driven up to us through the deception of an emulsion (and a writing) bound for oblivion and recovered for a time (for readers). It is, indeed, a *real* novel.

Conversazione in Sicilia: Photographic Stillness and Silence

In contrast to Romano's novel, Vittorini's *Conversazione in Sicilia* was published in instalments. After being run in September 1937 by the review *Letteratura* (*Literature*), it was published as a book in 1941, by Bompiani, with minor changes.[10] Two reprints were issued in 1942; and finally the gift edition, illustrated with Luigi Crocenzi's photographic images, appeared in 1953, again published by Bompiani.[11] Thus the author had written a novel, to which he later decided to add photographs "a commento o accompagnamento o integrazione d'un testo letterario" (as a commentary, to accompany or to supplement, a literary text; "La foto" 365).[12] These photographs, then, were additions to an existing literary text; the author saw them as pictorial enrichments that would simultaneously engage in their own narrative.

By the time Vittorini published in *Letteratura,* he had completed the anthology *Americana* (1942), which had been enriched with illustrative columns of photographic images. Vittorini wrote:

> Così i risultati che andavo ottenendo nell'illustrare l'*Americana* mi portarono presto a riflettere che se mi fosse riuscito di illustrare *Conversazione* con gli stessi criteri mi sarei presa la migliore delle rivincite sull'in piú di reticenza che m'ero dovuto imporre. ("La foto" 367)
>
> The results I was getting, illustrating the *Americana,* soon made me think that if I had been able to illustrate *Conversazione* using the same criteria, I would have obtained the best revenge for the additional reserve I was forced to impose on myself.

The Sicilian writer was animated by a sort of revenge against the Fascist censorship that had compelled him to add a note when the novel was first published saying he had set the story in Sicily only because "il nome Sicilia mi suona meglio del nome Persia o Venezuela" (the name Sicily sounded better than the name Persia or Venezuela; *Conversazione* 1941, 225). It gave him real satisfaction to explain the genesis of the book in a note to the illustrated edition, which he had been thinking about since 1941:

> È stato nel 1950, tredici anni dopo la comparsa della prima puntata di *Conversazione* sulla rivista *Letteratura* di Firenze, che sono tornato in Sicilia a fotografare, con l'aiuto non solo tecnico del mio amico Luigi Crocenzi, gran parte degli elementi di cui il libro s'intesse. (*Conversazione* 1941, 225)

> It was in 1950, thirteen years after the publication of the first instalment of *Conversazione* in the Florentine review *Letteratura*, that I returned to Sicily to photograph most of the elements contained in the book, with the technical help of my friend Luigi Crocenzi.[13]

So, some thirteen years after Vittorini had written the first edition of *Conversazione in Sicilia*, he went to take photographs of the places it narrated with photographer Luigi Crocenzi, a contributor to his review *Il Politecnico*. The author acted in a fashion similar to Silvestro, the novel's protagonist, meeting his parents and friends and tracing the same trajectory, walking through the beloved places of his childhood: from Scicli to Enna, Nicosia, and Sperlinga, as far as Siracusa and onward to Caltagirone and Vizzini. These places have magical and mythical names, and it seemed to Vittorini that the environment, and the daily life of the miners and the farmers, was essentially unchanged since the mid-1930s.

The writer, therefore, is the main executor of the images: "Non volevo correre il rischio di trovarmi il libro ingombrato da una 'interpretazione' che gli si sovrapponesse e ne ostacolasse, con delle pretese autonome la lettura" (I didn't want to run the risk of finding my book encumbered by an "interpretation" superimposing itself and inhibiting the reading with irrelevant pretentions; "La foto" 368). Vittorini was possessive of his work: "Ne sono geloso come può esserlo, della sua creatura più diletta, il più tenero dei padri" (I am possessive of it just like the most loving of fathers is of his dearest child; 368).[14] But how did this tendency to nurture the project affect Vittorini's engagement with taking the photographs? As he explains, he would select

> gli 'oggetti' da fotografare e i punti di vista, tenendo presente, insieme ai filoni del libro e alla Sicilia che avevo sotto gli occhi, quali accostamenti avrei poi potuto operare tra foto e foto. Ma sceglievo, stavolta, tra fotografie da fare, non tra fotografie già fatte; sceglievo direttamente nella vita; e così quello che in *Americana* e in 'Politecnico' era stata regìa a posteriori, montaggio, qui era regìa anche a priori. (368–9)

> objects and perspectives, keeping in mind, along with the threads in the book and the Sicily that I had before my very eyes, which photos I could juxtapose with which. But this time I was choosing from photos yet to be taken, not from those already existing. I chose directly from life, and so what in *Americana* and *Politecnico* had been direction *a posteriori,* montage, here was direction *a priori.*

Vittorini had arrived at a process: after memorizing the whole novel, he would visit the places it narrated and choose the subjects, faces, landscapes, and perspectives to be photographed. He even organized some scenes as if shooting a film ("La foto" 369). At the end of the journey, he found himself with some sixteen hundred photographs scattered on a table, from which he would be able to choose only 169. He compared this selection process to buying second-hand furniture:

> M'interessava solo che ogni fotografia avesse un suo contenuto materiale (che cioè riproducesse un certo 'oggetto'), e procedevo alla scelta delle fotografie proprio come avrei potuto scegliere, presso dei rigattieri, gli oggetti di cui ammobiliare una stanza. ("La foto" 366)[15]

> I was only interested in the material content of each photograph (namely, that the photograph reproduced a certain object), and I went about the selection in the same way as I might have chosen objects from a second-hand dealer to furnish a room.

What, then, were his criteria for "furnishing the rooms" of his novel? The answer to this question is not simple, and perhaps it is better to adopt the reader–spectator's point of view and examine the photographs, those precise pieces of reality, the landscapes and men's and women's faces that accompany the chatter of the narration. If we cover the photographs with our hands and follow only the written words, the narration lulls us with a sonorous tone that is almost whispering or singsong-like. Doubts engulf every question, almost evoking a reality where elves, myths, and archetypes suddenly appear and then vanish amidst other details that express real pain, difficulties, and miseries. Everything seems to exist between factual description and myth. The result is a sort of existential fairy tale – true and magical at the same time – that accompanies the reader like a ceremonial journey of initiation to Hell, to the realm of the Mothers,[16] among ghosts and real characters, on the "risky double thread of straight report and magical allusion" (Contini 877) full of "terrible abstractness" (Pintor 97).[17]

But what happens when we take our hands away and allow the photographs to appear? The first impression is that the pages have been filled with creatures, strange presences, or things that have nothing to do with the photos. On seeing the photographs, we start to look for just that person or just that village mentioned in the prose, as we do when reading a newspaper article illustrated by photographs. We also realize quickly that something is wrong: the photographs do not correspond to the written text – there is a disharmony between the visual and the verbal. Indeed, not all of the tale's motifs correspond to or visually "prove" the photographic images. It follows that the text does not serve as a caption for the images and that the photographs do not illustrate the text. They do not adorn it – but they clearly do something else. Vittorini explains: "A me non importava nulla del valore estetico o illustrativo che la fotografia poteva avere singolarmente, ciascuna per sé. M'interessava solo che ogni fotografia avesse un suo contenuto materiale" (I wasn't at all interested in the aesthetic or illustrative value that the photograph could have individually, each one separately for itself. My concern was only that each photograph should have a material content; "La foto" 365–6). The photographs, in fact, neither beautify nor inform the text; instead, each has its own material content, and together they provide a separate narrative that unfolds in tandem with the verbal text. The photographs, then, accompany the verbal narrative while simultaneously breaking away to tell their own story.

In another context, Vittorini used a symphonic term to describe this coming together: *crescendo.* He believed that "il miglior modo di condurre i motivi stessi (in correlazione al carattere del testo) fosse di darne le note fondamentali in un gran numero di varianti che facessero un 'crescendo'" (the best way to use the tones themselves (in correlation with the nature of the text) was to give the essential basic notes in a large number of variants or in a *crescendo* form; "La foto" 369). Perhaps this is why, as we leaf through the pages of *Conversazione in Sicilia,* we find

> diversi tipi di madri siciliane in corrispondenza della madre-sintesi raffigurata nel testo; diversi tipi di spose e di bambine in corrispondenza della sintesi moglie-bambina raffigurata nel testo; diversi tipi di bambini in corrispondenza del mito dell'infanzia raffigurato nel testo; [...] diversi tipi di uomini indomiti e inquieti in corrispondenza del Gran Lombardo favoleggiato nel testo; diversi tipi di città contadine, o di aspetti, di sezioni di esse, in corrispondenza della sintesi d'ogni città contadina siciliana che si articola nel testo. ("La foto" 369–70)

> various kinds of Sicilian mothers according to the mother-synthesis portrayed in the text; different kinds of wives and girls corresponding to the child-bride of the story; different sorts of children corresponding to the mythical childhood portrayed in the story; different types of indomitable, restless men like the Gran Lombardo described in the text; different depictions of country towns or aspects or sections of them, which corresponded to the synthesis of every Sicilian country town depicted in the story.

The text, therefore, "opens" towards the images, spreads out in relation to them, and becomes broader with an allegorical *crescendo*, despite their late arrival.

Vittorini compares *Conversazione in Sicilia* to a patterned cloth whose pictures are the photographs. It seems as if Vittorini compares the unrolling of the cloth with the rolling of a film, a sort of unmovable film that plays in the fast turning of the pages, in the matching of the photographs using the method of a director. He states his intention to insert the photographs into the book according to a "criterio cinematografico e non già fotografico, non già vignettistico, e che dunque riproponga, secondo un suo filo di film, almeno uno degli elementi del testo, allo stesso modo in cui accade che il cinema riproponga (in sede documentaria o in sede narrativa) certi elementi d'un certo libro" (film criterion, not a photographic or cartoon one, thus offering again at least one element of the text, following a film thread of its own, in the same way as cinema sometimes repeats (in documentary or fiction form) certain elements of a given book; "La foto" 366).[18] The question is not as simple as the parallel between the book and the film suggests. But the particular act of putting together images and words in a kind of parallel text does not produce real cinematography: the movements of the people and of the photographs follow independent itineraries, even if they are not quite autonomous because they are necessarily constrained within a book.

As suggested by Vittorini's use of two key words – *accostamento* (juxtaposition) and *riverbero* (reverberation) – when explaining his method ("La foto" 366), he is not interested in the possible cinematography resulting from the subsequent montage among the images, but rather in the relationships between the images taken one by one in correlation only with the text and in the reverberation of the text in the images. Moreover, the photographic images are not assembled in a vertical sequence, as for a film – an approach that Vittorini had already attempted (with the help of Crocenzi) in *Il Politecnico*. Here, he does not straightforwardly adopt the method of a story in photographs. The unique placement of the photographs and Vittorini's remarks regarding their role in an already existing verbal text strongly suggest that he had written the story *for* photographs. The book's various sections and its individual incidents are, in turn, grouped into very specific themes: the journey, the meeting with his mother, the dialogues with symbolic characters (with or without facial hair, the knife sharpener, Ezechiele, Porfirio, and others), the walk in the village with his mother, a nurse, and the meeting with Gran Lombardo and the ghost of his dead brother at the cemetery. It seems that all of these situations were thought of as if already captured in photograms or well-defined visual frames. And at this point, the running titles that open the individual paragraphs seem to stand in for the intertitles used in silent films.

Counter-intuitively, it was the writing of the novel – its narrative motifs, its characters, its moods, and the figures already in the "cloth" – that produced the photographs. These, in turn, were merely reverberations of the text. The photographs are arranged in the correct sequence, placed at specific points like pieces of a puzzle. *Conversazione in Sicilia* is the story that *waits* for the arrival of the images and then fixes them in a jigsaw puzzle between the pages, not vice versa.

Contrary to what Eugenio Montale noted in a review of the most recent edition, there is no contrast between the "fictions imagining Sicily" described and "the real isle" of the photos (1615–20). Instead, they are the same thing – writing an image – because it is the writing itself, through Vittorini's *a posteriori* layout, that looked for those images and linked them, anchored them, made them as they are, and is ultimately echoed in them.[19] The verbal text goes towards the images and expands within and across them, correcting itself by way of them. These images inevitably heighten the story's allegory but at the same time engage in their own distinct narrative, calling forth evidential proof, the *ça-a-été* that is the incontrovertible matrix of every photograph. They become necessary captions, as Italo Calvino states, indicating the "allusiveness" and "responsibility" of the images ("Vittorini").

Vittorini used the 169 photographs to strengthen the *mise en scène;* the writing that previously contained them has now expelled them. In this way, Vittorini's text sets the photographs in a frame that is in stark contrast to the role photographs play in Romano's *Nuovo romanzo di figure.* In Romano, the narrative expands the *fabula,* almost running away from the images. By contrast, *Conversazione*'s verbal text does not function as commentary on the photographs, nor do the images illustrate the story. Instead, there is only the productive work of the story, which chooses the places or the faces of the people and their gaze. It chooses, in other words, a particular photograph, deciding where it can be placed and where to continue with the narration in all of its auxiliary visual elements.

In Vittorini's work, the images thus build a kind of visual continuation of the plot. They illustrate its meaning; they also inject social statements, a political function, the aura of an offended world, the idea of a revolution to be made, and the extreme difficulty of political liberation for mankind. The photographs raise old ideological questions without proposing solutions. Not only the iconography but also the stylistic-linguistic choices of the photographic language conduct an intensive dialogue with the novel's structure (Rizzarelli xvi–xvii).

Perhaps it is not by chance that the book is not rich in words that designate colour or chromatic variation. As Falaschi observes: "La cosa più sorprendente è che questo paesaggio è sotto il sole, e pur tuttavia è in bianco e nero" (the most astonishing thing is that this landscape is under the sun, and yet it is in black and white; 18–19). The black-and-white photograms portray a dark atmosphere that matches the situation. Furthermore, they convey the quite dark atmosphere of the whole fiction despite the actual presence of the sun, the dazzling light that is necessary so that a photograph can be exposed, even if in black and white. There is a constant contrast between the light of the roads and the countryside and the darkness of the interiors of houses and other places. There is dazzling light everywhere, yet that light emphasizes the anguish that slips into all of the novel's dark spaces. Moreover, the things or objects as they are portrayed in the written text do not appear in the photographs, and the characters are not identical in the words and images. Hence, there is no analogy between things written and things seen, with the consequence that the photographs become emblems of the story itself. They expand it into all-inclusive signs, allegories vast in their metonymy. Every village, despite the caption that names it, stands for all villages, just as every person portrayed in the photographs stands for all characters. The villages, faces, eyes, and people photographed are only symbols for all that happens in the described world (and, above all, in the unwritten world).

Paradoxically, *Conversazione in Sicilia* is more real than the photograms, and the photographs are more allegorical than the prose. The words explain the events more faithfully, while the photographs remain in the background. Enrico Falqui, perplexed by the illustrated edition of the novel, has observed that the photo-illustrations most in tune with the spirit of the work are the less documentary, less realistic ones. Richer in imagination than in real explanation, their fascination lies more in what they suggest than in what they declare (172). Although Falqui is accurate in his assessment of the photographic images in *Conversazione in Sicilia*, those images do not deceive, nor do they allude to anything. Indeed, the illustrated edition is a completely different book, utterly organic, whose images are no less important than the prose. The writing points to other places than those addressed by the photographs, yet this does not weaken the reader's attention to or engagement with the narrative.[20]

Seen in this light, the photographs function as testimony: they document a story and show what they understand from the recorded events. They fix these events as testaments, as limited pieces of geography and history. If the writing moves, unrolling like a film, the photographs are still, deliberately repeating themselves. If there is a possibility of beginning again (the final departure of Silvestro vaguely suggests an escape), this is pointed out in the writing. Like a fairy tale, the narration enables a proposition that works against itself in its circularity, and from this we can perceive a subtle optimism. By contrast, the photographs are dry and absolute, implicitly confirming an unalterable condition.

If it is true that the novel has a theatrical form (Panicali 155), it is like a piano score comprised of dialogues and voices; it is a conversation with few descriptions, quite talkative and colloquial (Sanguineti xiv). At the same time, there is the silence of the images, accentuated by the dull interplay of black and white. So there are two conditions: the sonority of the written story, with its filmic meaning and its questions and answers, and the obstinate silence of the photograms. It is a relationship of both complementarity and collision; one does not exclude the other. In the whole book, in fact, contiguousness is produced by

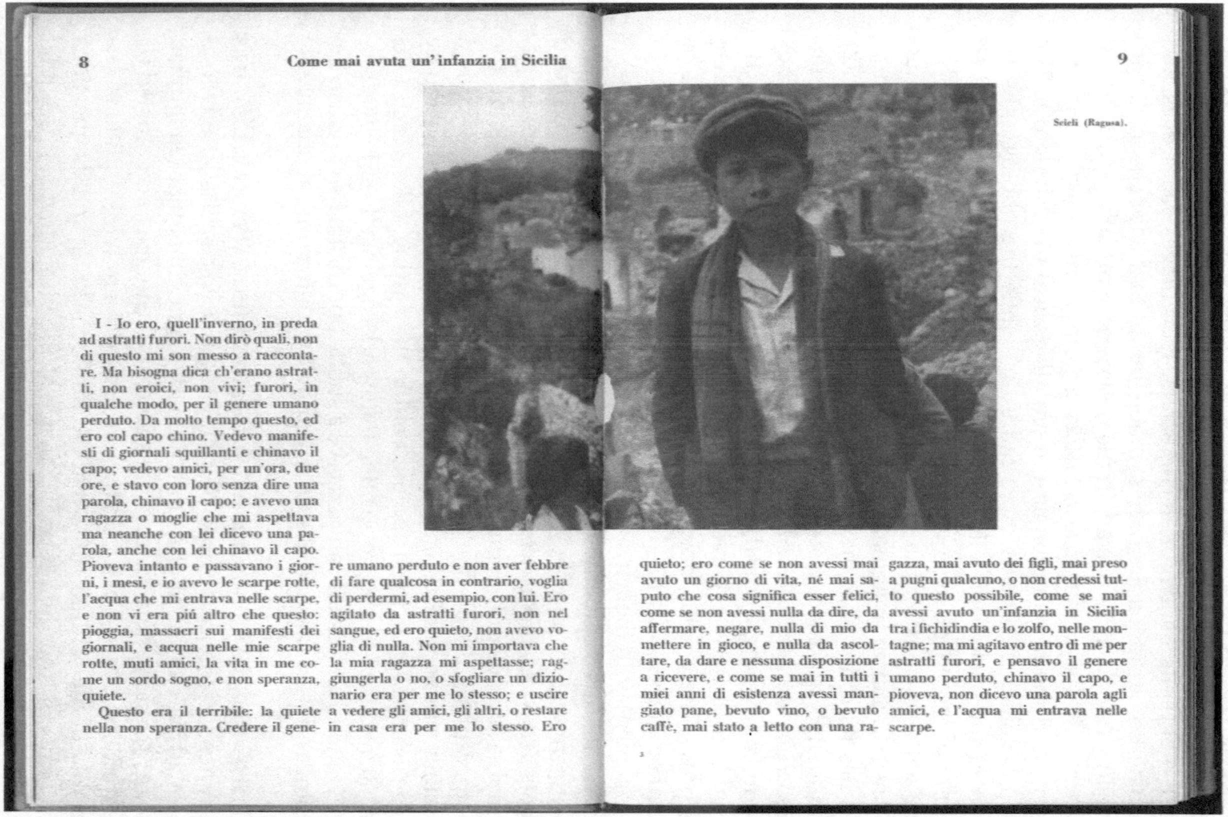

8 Come mai avuta un'infanzia in Sicilia

I - Io ero, quell'inverno, in preda ad astratti furori. Non dirò quali, non di questo mi son messo a raccontare. Ma bisogna dica ch'erano astratti, non eroici, non vivi; furori, in qualche modo, per il genere umano perduto. Da molto tempo questo, ed ero col capo chino. Vedevo manifesti di giornali squillanti e chinavo il capo; vedevo amici, per un'ora, due ore, e stavo con loro senza dire una parola, chinavo il capo; e avevo una ragazza o moglie che mi aspettava ma neanche con lei dicevo una parola, anche con lei chinavo il capo. Pioveva intanto e passavano i giorni, i mesi, e io avevo le scarpe rotte, l'acqua che mi entrava nelle scarpe, e non vi era piú altro che questo: pioggia, massacri sui manifesti dei giornali, e acqua nelle mie scarpe rotte, muti amici, la vita in me come un sordo sogno, e non speranza, quiete.

Questo era il terribile: la quiete nella non speranza. Credere il genere umano perduto e non aver febbre di fare qualcosa in contrario, voglia di perdermi, ad esempio, con lui. Ero agitato da astratti furori, non nel sangue, ed ero quieto, non avevo voglia di nulla. Non mi importava che la mia ragazza mi aspettasse; raggiungerla o no, o sfogliare un dizionario era per me lo stesso; e uscire a vedere gli amici, gli altri, o restare in casa era per me lo stesso. Ero

9

Scicli (Ragusa).

quieto; ero come se non avessi mai avuto un giorno di vita, né mai saputo che cosa significa esser felici, come se non avessi nulla da dire, da affermare, negare, nulla di mio da mettere in gioco, e nulla da ascoltare, da dare e nessuna disposizione a ricevere, e come se mai in tutti i miei anni di esistenza avessi mangiato pane, bevuto vino, o bevuto caffè, mai stato a letto con una ragazza, mai avuto dei figli, mai preso a pugni qualcuno, o non credessi tutto questo possibile, come se mai avessi avuto un'infanzia in Sicilia tra i fichidindia e lo zolfo, nelle montagne; ma mi agitavo entro di me per astratti furori, e pensavo il genere umano perduto, chinavo il capo, e pioveva, non dicevo una parola agli amici, e l'acqua mi entrava nelle scarpe.

Figure 8.2 Photograph by Luigi Crocenzi. In Elio Vittorini, *Conversazione in Sicilia*. Milan: Bompiani, 1953. With kind permission of Demetrio Vittorini, and CRAF-Centro di ricerca e archiviazione della fotografia, Spilimbergo.

the constant rubbing up against each other of words and photographs. It is a conversation (comprised of disputes and silences) between two different languages. One is left to ask if this silent estrangement of the images alters the documentary task in an emblematic, symbolic, and impressive way. Also, is the aim of these photographs to remind us that life is elsewhere, beyond words in the silence of an unwritten world? Here, the obviousness of the photographic account is as awful as it is insensitive.

Conclusion

To conclude, in Lalla Romano's book the *punctual* narrative elaborations provide flashes of insight into the personality of the photographer and, therefore, into the intimate relationship between the author and the photographer. The narration is born out of the images and develops with them through a relationship of interdependence. I see these photographs, therefore, as a sort of paradoxical visual syntax that a reader can develop by adding other perspectives, reflections, or personal images. In this way, readers *read* the photographs not only according to what they *should* say but also according to the potential stories they hold. By contrast, the role of the photograph is inverted in Elio Vittorini's novel: the images move towards the narration in order to complete it. Thus, the photographs emerge from the narration. Yet they do not have an illustrative function and do not represent their subjects. Rather, these photographs derive from the descriptions of people or places, building out of and rubbing up against those very descriptions.

Surprisingly, reflection on the encounter between visual and written representation, fiction and reality, the imaginary and the quotidian in two different books brings us to a common thread. In their union of words and images, both Romano's *Nuovo romanzo di figure* and Vittorini's *Conversazione in Sicilia* formulate a position constantly on the border between "realism" (literary and generically defined) and allegory. Despite significant differences in how the photographs were selected and at what stage they were united to verbal text, an analysis of how they come together in *Nuovo romanzo di figure* and *Conversazione in Sicilia* accentuates the role of imagination, fiction, and allegory in the writing and showing of the real world.

Thanks to Roberta Delli Priscoli and Barbara McGilvray for their help with translation from Italian.

NOTES

1 On this juxtaposition see Di Fazio 93–108.
2 In 1975, Romano published *Lettura di un'immagine* (*Reading of an Image*), which was reprinted in 1986 with the title *Romanzo di figure* and then again in 1997 as *Nuovo romanzo di figure.*
3 See also Romano's photographic album *Terre di Lucchesia* (*Lands of Lucchesia*) (1991). Romano's comments on her own paintings gathered in *Lalla Romano, pittrice* (*Lalla Romano, Painter*) (1993) would merit different and broader treatment. See Segre, "Lalla Romano fra pittura e scrittura" (207–9). On Romano's use of photographs, see Pedri, "Reading the Photographic Text" and "From Photographic Product to Photographic Text"; and Sarah Hill.
4 From now on, Romano's quotes will be taken from this text. Romano's specification regarding the role of images in her text follows Calvino's description of Japanese gardens in Kyoto: "I giardini venivano composti come illustrazioni a poesie e le poesie venivano composte come commento ai giardini" (The gardens were composed as illustrations of poems and the poems as notes on the gardens); "Il rovescio del sublime" 576.
5 Segre states that in Romano's photo-novels, "dalla connessione e dal montaggio delle immagini una storia viene ben fuori […]. Le storie saranno eventualmente intuite dal lettore, cui è affidata la costruzione" (a story derives from the link and the montage of the images […] The stories will be understood by the reader, to whom the building is entrusted); "Introduzione" xxi.
6 According to Peirce, the index, by which he specifies that a photograph has a relative role, in fact indicates a real datum ("a weathercock is an index of the direction of the wind"), not relying solely on analogy as does an icon. Since it physically coincides point by point with the object in nature, the photograph ends up being closely connected to the object without replacing it completely. It is not fully in the place of the object; instead, it tries to be indicative, movable, not static, not "frozen like a mirror," but *ready to act* in its referentiality ("Logic as Semiotic" 98–119).
7 The father's presence is constant in Romano's photographic books. She writes exemplarily in her introduction to the latest "little visual novel," *Ritorno a Ponte Stura* (*Return to Ponte Stura*): "Questo libro vuole essere ancora, da parte mia, un tardivo – ma il tempo dopo la morte non conta – pensiero per mio padre. Ho scritto di lui e della sua arte di fotografo in *La penombra che abbiamo attraversato* e nei vari 'album fotografici'" (This book is intended as another thought for my father, a late one, but the time after

death doesn't count. I wrote about him and his art as a photographer in *La penombra che abbiamo attraversato* and in the various "photo albums"); 5–7. On Romano's father as a photographer, see Cassanelli.

8 At times, the short notes of *Nuovo romanzo di figure* take on the same characteristics as the dreams in Romano's *Metamorfosi* (*Metamorphoses*). According to Segre: "Chi legge questi sogni opera una 'lettura di immagini,' abbastanza vicina alla lettura di vecchie fotografie a cui, decenni dopo, si dedicherà la scrittrice" (Those who read these dreams are carrying out a "reading of images" that is quite like the reading of old photos to which the writer would devote herself decades later); "Introduzione" xix–xxi).

9 See Bazin on the charm of family albums (242).

10 *Conversazione in Sicilia* was published by Parenti in Florence on 1 March 1941 in a volume titled *Nome e lagrime* (*Name and Tears*). To avoid censorship, it appeared as a sort of short second tale following the first one, which gave the volume its name. In a subsequent edition by Bompiani, published in Milan on 6 October 1941, *Nome e lagrime* is not reproduced although it remains as a subtitle in brackets. It was in this 1941 edition that the famous note was printed for the first time: "Ad evitare equivoci o fraintendimenti avverto che, come il protagonista di questa *Conversazione* non è autobiografico, così la Sicilia che lo inquadra e accompagna è solo per avventura Sicilia; solo perché mi suona meglio del nome Persia o Venezuela. Del resto immagino che tutti i manoscritti vengano trovati in una bottiglia" (In order to avoid ambiguities or misinterpretations let me point out that the protagonist of this *Conversazione* is not autobiographical, just as the Sicily that provides his setting and accompanies him is Sicily only by chance, simply because it sounds better than the name "Persia" or "Venezuela." Besides, I imagine all the manuscripts are found in a bottle); *Conversazione* 270. In 1943, the book was confiscated.

11 In 1973, another illustrated edition – with photographs by Enzo Ragazzini – was published by Giorgio Soavi for Olivetti; and in 1986, one with illustrations by Renato Guttuso was first printed. Quotations will be taken from the 2007 edition reprinted by Rizzoli with an additional postscript by Maria Rizzarelli.

12 The article appears in the form of a letter to Guido Aristarco, the founder and editor of the journal *Cinema nuovo* (*New Cinema*).

13 This could make us think that for the author, taking photographs of Sicily was a way to state forcibly, and also visually, that the geographical setting of the novel was just his island and not an imaginary place. (That then Sicily could become a metaphor for the world is a different matter, however.)

14 Vittorini repeated this again during an interview with Raffaele Crovi that appeared in *La Notte* on 5 February 1954. Crovi 18–20.

15 He also used seven photographs by Pozzi Belli, twelve pictures, and postcards. In addition, he asked Luchino Visconti for other images used in his film *La terra trema* (*The Earth Trembles*). See Rizzarelli (13–37).

16 According to David, *Conversazione* might seem to conform to the epic scheme of the descent to the Mothers (454).

17 It is no accident that Pintor, albeit with caution, compares the novel's characters to the figures in *Alice in Wonderland* as well as to the actors in a melodrama or in one of Shakespeare's plays (97).

18 For a comparison between the photographic edition of the novel and the edition of *Conversazione* illustrated with drawings by Guttuso, see Falaschi (12).

19 Spinazzola writes: "Qualunque sia l'interesse da annettere a questo apparato iconografico, non è inutile constatare che la sua funzione era di rafforzare l'ancoraggio del testo a una realtà ambientale siciliana ben determinata" (Whatever interest is to be attributed to this iconographical apparatus, it is not without value to note that its function was to strengthen the anchoring of the text to a quite specific Sicilian environment); 410.

20 For Falqui, the only useful function of the photograph is that of being linked, *there*, to the memory of the writer (174–5). But here the opposite is true, since the writer looks for the images *after* having written the book. Also, Antonelli's point of view is quite reductive in that he sees the illustrated novel as a case of literature with photo-caption commentary (89–91).

PART FOUR

Through the Lens

9 Narrative Scopophilia as Seen through the Lens of a Photographic Camera: Intersemiotic Translation and Voyeurism in Alberto Moravia's *L'uomo che guarda* (1985)

MARIARITA MARTINO

This chapter analyses a case of photographic practice as a translative process of scopophilia, which is the twofold tendency indicating voyeurism and exhibitionism, in Alberto Moravia's *L'uomo che guarda* (*The Voyeur*). The translative process, understood as the move from a source text (ST) to a target text (TT), occurs within a novel that narrates the story of a voyeur, Dodo, who is a professor of French literature at an unidentified university in Rome. The protagonist is also a hobby photographer and defines himself as a voyeur and as someone who is obsessed with vision. He specifies, "io vivo soprattutto attraverso gli occhi" (I live most of all through my eyes; 7). Voyeurism and photography are crucial elements in Dodo's story, for he likes wandering around Rome in search of images, which he then fixates upon. He takes pictures with a Polaroid and then describes meticulously both the photographic process and the pictures themselves. In *L'uomo che guarda*, photography as a practice is important, for it supports Dodo's voyeuristic instinct.

In one of his lectures at the university, Dodo refers to Stéphane Mallarmé's poem "Une négresse par le démon secouée" ("A Negress") (published in 1887 in *Poésies* [*Collected Poems*]) to illustrate a theory of literary scopophilia. Later in his story, Dodo is offered the opportunity to, as he himself observes, "tradurre in pratica la [...] teoria sulla scopofilia nell'arte" (translate the ... theory on scopophilia in art into practice; 59). The translation with which this chapter is concerned involves Mallarmé's poem – included in Moravia's novel in Italian, and used as a pretext to develop a theory about voyeurism and exhibitionism in literature – as an ST, and a fictive photograph (and the process of taking it) as a TT, which is inspired by Edward Manet's painting *Olympia* (1863), and which is taken and described by the protagonist as the translation of his theory. My aim is to discuss how this literary theory of scopophilia illustrated through the poem is translated into the photographic process described in the novel and how this translation involves the scopophilic mechanisms that characterize the photographic medium. However, before analysing this translation in Moravia's novel, it is necessary to identify what kind of translation is explored in the present discussion and what methodology needs to be adopted for the analysis that involves an ST and a TT occurring in the novel.

In *L'uomo che guarda*, Dodo exploits photography as a means of translating his theory of narrative scopophilia from a literary text (used to illustrate this theory) into the description of a photographic process and the image he takes with his Polaroid (which he considers a translation of his theory). After delivering a lecture on literary scopophilia in French literature and art, Dodo wanders around Rome with his camera and meets a stranger, Pascasie, who invites him to her place, for she wants him to take a picture of her. Dodo and Pascasie try but fail to re-create the composition of Mallarmé's scopophilic scenario – in which two women are engaged in intercourse – before the picture is taken. Pascasie is alone in her apartment, so she is the only model available to pose for Dodo, which makes it impossible for them to re-create the image described in Mallarmé's poem. In the end, Dodo photographs Pascasie in a different posture. He describes this image as a photograph inspired by Manet's *Olympia*, a painting that portrays a female nude and represents a sexualized scenario.

The shift narrated in Moravia's text, from an ST (the theory communicated across the poem) to a TT (the theory translated in the photographic practice in the novel), can be defined – using Roman Jakobson's linguistic terminology – as a curious case of intersemiotic translation (understood as the move from one semiotic system to another). But unlike with *proper* intersemiotic translation, where the transmutation involves two different semiotic sign systems, in the case under analysis the shift occurs within the *same* semiotic system, that is, within the novel's verbal narration of the novel. Nevertheless, the ST and the TT are concerned, respectively, with a theory illustrated through the written text of the poem and the process of photographing a woman. In the novel's written text, this episode is narrated in a style that evokes a visual dimension, a different *semiotic* dimension.

Moravia's novel engages deeply with vision as expressed through *chosisme* (thingness), which is a literary style that reflects the author's ability to tell a story as if through the lens of a camera.[1] The scenario in Mallarmé's poem is used to illustrate the theory of narrative scopophilia; later, the protagonist-voyeur translates this theoretical insight into a photographic process, producing an image inspired by a painting and that the protagonist describes in a written narrative. What we have, then, specifically, is a written text – provided by the case study of the poem used to support a literary theory – translated into a fictive photographic practice described in the written narrative and defined as a translation of the theory. The method of analysis to be adopted in this discussion, then, involves comparing the texts in a kind of intersemiotic translation process as described and contained within a novel.

In his triadic definition of translation, Jakobson mentions three categories and defines them as:

> 1. Intralingual translation or *rewording* is an interpretation of verbal signs by means of other signs of the same language.
> 2. Interlingual translation or *translation proper* is an interpretation of verbal signs by means of some other language.
> 3. Intersemiotic translation or *transmutation* is an interpretation of verbal signs by means of signs of non-verbal sign system. (139, emphasis original)

For Jakobson, translation is synonymous with the interpretation of signs and their rendition into other signs. From this perspective, the sign changes but the meaning – that is, the essence of the word – "is its translation into some further, alternative sign" (139). This semiotic approach considers language in terms of signs and meanings that must be interpreted and translation as conveying "all cognitive experience and its classification" (139). The cognitive experience linked to the translation is related to meaning as perpetuated and intersubjectively recognized in the shift from one sign to another within the translation process. Given that in Moravia's novel the texts involved in the translation are a description contained in the text of a poem and the description of a photographic process and its outcome, we can say that the type of translation processed and described falls into the category of intersemiotic translation (although this is not literally carried out, but rather described in the verbal context of the novel). In this translative context, any kind of equivalence needs to be interpreted and analysed according to a semiotic method that considers the meaning of the signs of the ST that are translated as other signs in the TT.

Furthermore, in his definition of intersemiotic translation, the semiotician Nicola Dusi echoes Jakobson's theorization of the shift between the different signs of the ST and the TT; like the Russian linguist, Dusi emphasizes the cognitive and intersubjective interpretation of the signs in the analysis of the texts involved in the translation. According to Dusi, intersemiotic translation targets the structures of the two means of communication, and it is intended as the shift from one semiotic system to another in the totality of the translation process between two different media. This means that translation is a shift involving both levels of language: that of content and that of expression (9). The analysis of the intersemiotic translation in Moravia's text will consider not only *what* elements of Mallarmé's poem are shifted in the photographic image described by the protagonist as adapting Manet's painting, but also *how* these elements are translated from the point of view of the expression.

In highlighting the example of scopophilia, Dodo provides in full, in the novel, the Italian translation of "Une négresse par le démon secouée," also known as "Une négresse" or "Image grotesque."[2] This is one of Mallarmé's most pornographic poems; it depicts a paedophilic lesbian scene between an African woman, described with animal imagery, and a young girl of a lower class who is subordinate to her:

Una negra invasata dal demonio
Vuole assaggiare una bimba trista dai frutti acerbi
E anche criminali sotto la veste bucata.
Questa porca si appresta ad astuti travagli.

Al ventre, felice, strofina due piccole tette
E così alto da non arrivarci con la mano
Dardeggia l'urto oscuro degli stivaletti
Come una lingua inabile al piacere.

Contro l'impaurita nudità di gazzella
Che trema, simile ad un folle elefante, riversa
Sul dorso, aspetta e intanto si compiace con zelo
Ridendo con i suoi denti ingenui alla bimba.

E fra le cosce dove la vittima si stende,
Sollevando la pelle nera dischiusa sotto il pelo
Ecco avanza il palato di quella strana bocca
pallida e rosa come una conchiglia marina. (Moravia *L'uomo che guarda,* 41)

A negress possessed by the devil
Wants to taste a little girl saddened by the new
And evil fruits underneath her tattered dress;
This glutton contrives some cunning tricks.

Against her belly she rubs two blithe young tits
And higher than hand could reach
She thrusts the dark shock of her boots
Like some tongue unskilled in pleasure.

Against the frightened nudity of this gazelle
That trembles, like a mad elephant, laid down
On her back, waits whilst eagerly admiring herself,
Smiling ingenuous teeth at the girl.

And between the legs where the victim stretches,
Lifting the black undisclosed skin beneath the hair,
she pushes out the palate of that strange mouth,
Pale and pink like a seashell.

The lesbian intercourse in the poem is narrated as if seen through the gaze of a hypothetical voyeur, who, according to the literary theory delivered by the protagonist in his lecture, is an implicit narrator/observer who visually records and reports in the medium of the poetic written text the subtle exhibitionism of the two women seen from a voyeuristic perspective. As we will see in the analysis of the translation, a number of changes have occurred in the shift from the ST to the TT if the content of the texts – that is, the characters involved in the narration and the situation – is considered. Notwithstanding these changes, however, I intend to demonstrate that it is still possible to identify points of coherence in the shift that occurs in the verbal context of the novel as we move from the narrative scopophilia illustrated in the ST to the photographic process as a TT.

The analysis of the translative shift focuses on the notion of scopophilia as the pivot around which the equivalence between the ST and the TT can be construed. The two episodes selected portray scopophilic scenarios that seem different when their compositional elements are considered. As with any intersemiotic translation, the shift from one text to another is not linear and precise, and various changes may occur. Here, I intend to analyse how the topography of scopophilia is translated (intersemiotically) and described (textually) in *L'uomo che guarda* by comparing written texts that evoke a visual dimension. In the novel, Dodo illustrates a theory that he applies to literary examples of narrative scopophilia before (as he himself declares) translating them into art. By Dodo's definition, which seems to conflate voyeurism with scopophilia,

> la scopofilia, o se si preferisce, il voyeurismo sarebbe all'origine di gran parte della narrativa. [...] ... il voyeur non tanto spia l'oggetto quanto il suo movimento cioè il suo comportamento. Per giunta questo comportamento deve essere strettamente privato cioè quale a nessuno, a meno di essere scopofilo, può avvenire di spiarlo senza consapevolezza di commettere un'indiscrezione. In altri termini, e tenendomi alla sola narrativa, il romanziere oltre a farci vedere ciò che tutti potrebbero vedere, spesso ci fa vedere ciò che nessuno potrebbe vedere, a meno di essere, appunto, un voyeur. (39)

> scopophilia, or preferably, voyeurism, seems to lie at the source of much narrative writing ... Voyeurism does not seem to be in painting and sculpture, since these forms of art lack movement; the voyeur does not peep at the object of desire, so much as at its movement, that is its behaviour. Furthermore, its behaviour must be strictly private, that is to say that no one, except a voyeur, could peep at it without the awareness of committing an indiscretion. In other words, and as far as written narrative is concerned, the novelist not only allows us to see what anyone could see, but often allows us to see what no one could see, unless of course they happen to be voyeurs.

Moravia's theoretical insight is an attempt to summarize scopophilia as the desire to look actively at sexually stimulating scenes, or voyeurism. By this definition, scopophilia is related to the secrecy of the position of the voyeur, who is usually hidden from the object desired, and to the distance between that object and the voyeuristic subject, who, driven by the desire for knowledge, craves to unveil and discover it. Yet this description excludes the passive pleasure involved in being looked at, or exhibitionism, which constitutes the second tendency in scopophilia, which is two-sided in nature. Scopophilia can be both active (voyeurism) and passive (exhibitionism), and these two tendencies may be enacted jointly or independently; a certain slippage between the two is possible, since the voyeur does to others what he/she desires for him-/herself (he/she is driven by the desire to look at, and in turn subtly desires to be looked at) and in this way implicitly manifests a desire for exhibitionism. In practice, for each voyeur there is usually an exhibitionist, and this coexistence makes the two-sided phenomenon of scopophilia a broader phenomenon than voyeurism, which is generally and sometimes exclusively identified with it, wrongly so.

The term *scopophilia* combines two Greek words: *scopeein*, "to look," and *philos*, "loving." The linguistic combination *scopo-philia* clearly delineates the two frames in which this psychoanalytic phenomenon operates: the contexts of vision and fixation upon visual scenarios (especially sexualized scenarios) from which the subject of the look derives enjoyment (both active and passive). The identification of the visual and the sexual spheres as the domains of scopophilia orients the investigation towards a psychosexual context, especially when we consider the German noun *Schaulust*, coined by Sigmund Freud. Freud's term combines the German word *Lust* ("lust" or "sexual desire") with *Shau* ("looking" or "seeing"); thus, scopophilia is *sexual pleasure in looking*. In "Instincts and their Vicissitudes" (1915), Freud divides the activity of scopophilia into three main stages: in the first, the subject finds satisfaction in looking at the external object; in the second, the subject turns towards the self; this second stage advances into a third one in which the subject's desire to be looked at – or exhibitionism – is heightened (562–8).[3]

The main characteristics of scopophilia are therefore as follows: it involves (a) the secrecy of the position of the subject voyeur, who is usually hidden from the object desired; (b) the object's (un)awareness of the voyeur's compulsive look; (c) a distance between the voyeuristic subject and the object of desire; (d) an instinct for knowledge that drives the voyeuristic subject to unveil, to reveal, and to discover the object of desire; and (e) the object's passive pleasure in being looked at. These characteristics of scopophilia will be crucial as we identify and investigate the equivalence to be constructed in the analysis of the translative process involving the context represented in the poetic text and the one in the fictive photograph described in the novel.

These psychoanalytic features are recognizable, in the first instance, in the poem Dodo takes as an example of narrative scopophilia (see the poem above). The four quatrains of alexandrines describing the sexual assault correspond to a scopophilic scenario, which Dodo interprets as peeped at by an unmentioned implied author and voyeur (internal to the diegesis of the poem). To support his theory, Dodo describes and imagines this supposed voyeur/author/narrator:

> Non è difficile immaginare che è un ragazzo inesperto e curioso delle cose del sesso, figlio del padrone di casa: il modo con il quale è presentata la scena lo fa supporre. Egli capita, forse non casualmente, all'ultimo piano, dove si trovano le camere della servitù, e, passando per il corridoio, sente parlare e ridere dietro una porta socchiusa. Allora si avvicina, spinge un poco la porta e guarda. (43–4)

> It is not difficult to imagine him as an ingenuous but curious boy, as the son of the master of the house; the way the scene is described supports this view. He happens to be, and perhaps it is not casual, on the top floor where the servants live, and, walking down the corridor, he hears talk and laughter coming from behind a door left ajar. So he approaches, pushes the door open a little further and looks in.

In Dodo's theory, the poem is the scene of desire with respect to an implied scopophilic subject that the text itself demands. The nineteenth-century poem becomes the vehicle for Dodo's theoretical speculation on scopophilia as characterizing a narrative that involves both the author/narrator and the reader of the poem in the scopophilic dynamic between subject and object. The theory of scopophilia presented in the novel is thus explored from a psychoanalytic perspective; this is followed by the illustration of its applicability to narrative and of how the narrative of a specific poem enacts scopophilic scenarios with respect to both a scopophilic author/narrator (who creates that same scenario) and the audience/reader (who is offered a scopophilic scenario).

Dodo associates the active voyeuristic subject with the author/narrator who has created the scopophilic scenario for a voyeuristic audience. Indeed, Mallarmé's text portrays two women who, while engaging in sexual intercourse, are described from the point of view of an implied intradiegetic voyeuristic author/narrator. This association of subject – author/narrator – and object/scenario re-creates the topography of scopophilia between the extradiegetic subject-reader as a metaphorical observer/voyeur and the diegetic object-scenario described in the poem: the voyeur is the reader, the poet, the enunciator, or the person who is describing the scene and who is supposed to be looking at these (apparently) unsuspecting lovers. As a metaphorical voyeur, the reader – here, Dodo – is hidden behind the page of the poem, which functions as an element that hides and shelters him and thus separates the subject from the object (while the literal voyeur is hidden behind a curtain or peeping through a keyhole or a crack in a door).

With respect to the verbal written scene, the position of the implied reader is then associated with Dodo the voyeur, who is experiencing the voyeuristic scenario while reading the poem and illustrating the theory of scopophilia through it. Moreover, the association of the reader with the scopophilic subject position raises questions regarding the extent to which this implication is already enacted by the text of Mallarmé's poem. How is the perceptive dimension created for a fictional voyeur such as Dodo? Can a written text be made metaphorically visible for a voyeur? It is interesting that Mallarmé's use of language implies the context in which the verbal representation is described and also forges this context. In his study of Mallarmé's style, Ross Chambers writes that Mallarmé's text "includes us [readers] by addressing itself to us to be read" (190). The analogy between the reader and the implied voyeur is supplied by the fact that the voyeur comes to coincide with a scopophilic subject position that places him/her behind the screen of the text – a screen that, in the poem, is an imaginary curtain, a keyhole, or a crack in a door.

Moreover, the analogy may also be developed through what the text implies on a formal level. Chambers clearly refers to the audience's active role in the text, a role that in this case coincides with that of the scopophilic subject. This active role is constructed through an ingenious employment of phonetics and of visual indicators in the poem's written language (indicators that are present in the French and also conveyed in the Italian translation), which positions the audience of the text firmly within the diegesis. Mallarmé's treatment of language as active and as capable of creating vision in a verbal context makes the poem a dynamic scenario and offers the reader/voyeur that same movement that is fundamental for the enactment of scopophilia in narratives, as suggested by Dodo's already quoted definition of narrative scopophilia at the beginning of his story.

The language expresses and evokes the voyeuristic scenario not only through the sexualized content of the poem but also through its "visual" stylistic features, which support the scopophilic dimension that is being narrated. In its Italian translation, Mallarmé's text seems to be visible and audible in the verbal context. On the phonetic level, in fact, the Italian translation employs words constituted by a number of alveolar phonemes: the polyvibrant /r/, the lateral /l/, and the fricative /s/ and /z/, referring to the vibrating and rustling sounds respectively that alternate in the quatrains. The poem not only represents a scopophilic contextual scenario but also performs the movement and the sound of the two women portrayed and of their Sapphic encounter. Words like *invasata, assaggiare, veste, appresta, astuti travagli* (possessed, to taste, dress, contrives, cunning tricks), and *ventre, strofina, dardeggia, urto oscuro, trema, sollevando, folle, gazzella, dischiusa* (belly, rubs, thrusts, dark shock, trembles, lifting, mad, gazelle, undisclosed),[4] convey the movement of the two bodies rubbing against each other in the feast of textiles, of the two silhouettes trembling in the ecstatic moment – two figures described as if the scene were being recorded from the subjective perspective of the intrusive voyeur. Hence, the poem narrates, as Dodo highlights, an obscene scenario that may stand for a scopophilic narrated scene, both for its sexual nature and for its expressive characterization.

In Moravia's novel, Dodo then translates the theory explored through the poem into a photographic process, which he describes verbally. The description of the photograph reproduces his scopophilic interaction with his object of desire, Pascasie. During their conversation, Dodo and Pascasie talk about Mallarmé's poem, which is also evoked by the two characters in connection with the photographic process: "Come vuoi che ti fotografi?" (How do you want me to photograph you?), Dodo asks, and Pascasie answers: "Se vuoi, come l'africana della tua poesia" (Like the African woman in your poem, if you want; 57). During their meeting, Dodo repeatedly associates Pascasie with the African character in the poem. His comments range from noting the physical similarities between the African woman in the poem and the African woman he meets to referring explicitly to the poem in relation to Pascasie. For example, from the very first moment, Dodo points out that Pascasie "ha alluso al Mallarmé della poesia" (alluded to the Mallarmé of the poem; 48) while interacting with him. Then he compares the two African women on a physical level: the one trembling like a mad elephant (verse 10), and Pascasie's hips reminiscent of the "'folle elefante' di Mallarmè" (Mallarmé's "mad elephant"; 52). Finally, he sees Pascasie's gaze as enacting the desire to be looked at that is only implied in the poem's scenario of desire: "Mi guarda e vedo nei suoi occhi la curiosità fredda e indiscreta che è propria del voyeurismo: in realtà, mentre si esibisce, spia in me un possibile turbamento" (While she looks at me I can see the cold and intrusive curiosity typical of voyeurism; the truth is that while exhibiting herself, she spies in me a possible excitement; 59). Pascasie flirts with her new acquaintance and openly shows interest in being photographed like the African woman in the poem, thus inviting Dodo to enact the voyeurism and exhibitionism implied by that scenario. But Dodo changes his mind and decides to photograph her in a different posture:

> Ti fotograferò come l'Olimpia di Manet, un contemporaneo del poeta che ha scritto la poesia sull'africana. Anche nel quadro di Manet c'è un'africana, la cameriera di Olimpia, che stringe al petto un mazzo di fiori. Io invece ti metterò al posto di Olimpia. (58)

> I will photograph you like Manet's Olympia; he was a contemporary of the poet who wrote the poem about the African woman. In Manet's painting there is also an African woman, Olympia's maid, who holds a bouquet of flowers to her breast. But I will put you in Olympia's place instead.

In photographing Pascasie as an African Olympia, Dodo deviates from his original intention, which was to photograph her like the African woman of the poem, which has offered him a pretext for the picture and for interacting with his new acquaintance. When we compare the poem's content with that of the painting that inspires Dodo, we find a conspicuous number of differences between them. For example, in the poem, the scenario involves two women engaged in the sexual act. In the painting, there are two women, but these are the nude courtesan, who is looking off-canvas, and the servant, who is holding flowers in a dutiful gesture.[5] Moreover, in the poem, exhibitionism is not as explicit as in the painting: the reader of Mallarmé's text does not actually know whether the two women are aware of the voyeur's implied gaze; in the painting, Olympia's posture is particularly exhibitionist. In the photograph taken and described by Dodo, Pascasie is alone in her bed, looking exhibitionistically at the photographer while he is taking a picture of her. It is true that the choice of Olympia as an inspiring text is not an innocent one, since this text is characterized by exhibitionism and nudity: the confrontational attitude and the gaze oriented towards the off-frame space informs the composition, creating an immediate link between the external observer and the internal one. But unless Dodo had in mind Larry Rivers's *I Like Olympia in Black Face* (1970), the pop art sculpture that interculturally reinterprets Manet's painting, it is true that there seems not to be a one-to-one correspondence between the scenario portrayed in the poem and the one in the photograph.

All in all, Dodo creates a different image in his photograph. Why, then, does he define his photographic experience with Pascasie as the opportunity to "tradurre in pratica la [...] teoria sulla scopofilia nell'arte" (translate the ... theory on scopophilia in art into practice; 59)? Is it possible to identify or construct points of equivalence between the poem and the photograph? How is the equivalence between a scenario shown in a poem and a photograph described in the verbal text of a novel constructed? And why does Dodo use photography to enact his translation?

Dodo is not interested in reproducing the scenario described in the poem in another medium. What Dodo translates is the articulation of scopophilia identified and illustrated in the poem, which is reproduced in the photographic process as a scopophilic practice. Scopophilia is translated intersemiotically from the poem to the (fictive) photograph, and the process of photography allows Dodo to do this translation. In the poem, the lesbian scenario is described by an implicit intradiegetic narrator/voyeur. The novel, through the taking of a photograph, recreates a similar interaction between the scopophilic subject and object: the photographic adaptation is described as if through the eyes of the internal narrator, Dodo, who is positioned as a voyeur with respect to the exhibitionist Pascasie; the dynamics of scopophilia are constituted by the interaction between Dodo, the photographer/narrator/voyeur, and Pascasie, the photographed object/scenario/exhibitionist. What is translated here is not just the sexualized scenario evoked in the poem, but also the enunciation and expression of scopophilia as articulated by the poem's voyeur, who looks at the scene of desire through a hole or the crack in the door in the ST; in the TT, Dodo looks at the object of desire through the lens of the photographic camera and is positioned as a voyeur with respect to the photograph he takes. In the novel, both the poem and the photograph demand a scopophilic subject whose curious gaze is interpellated by the texts.

As Olga Ragusa points out in her study of Moravia as a voyeuristic storyteller, the writer fixes his eye on the scene while this is taking place. To paraphrase Ragusa, Moravia is a novelist who conveys a "peeping Tom" effect: an eye is fixed on the scene taking place in the bright light at the end of the dark passageway, and the novelist is the eye that sees it (128). In *L'uomo che guarda*, this "peeping Tom" effect is supplied at a macro-level by the visual dimension that informs the narrative. As the diegetic first person narrator, Dodo is the vehicle of a visual narrative described in a written context, a narrative that can be defined as visual for its conspicuous emphasis on vision and for the generous descriptions it contains that are processed by the internal narrator.

In the episode concerning the photographic process, this visual emphasis can be seen at work on a micro-level as well. Dodo describes Pascasie meticulously, using visual indicators such as verbs that pertain to a visual semantic domain: "Pascasie si tira giú i pantaloni [...] il triangolo del pube è di un nero diverso [...] curiosamente piccolo e ridotto" (Pascasie pulls down her trousers ... the triangle of her pubic hair is a different black ... strangely small and under-sized; 58). And again, Dodo/Moravia records Pascasie's movements: "Eccola muoversi per la stanza. [...] [V]a all'armadio a muro, l'apre, ne estrae un paio di stivali" (There she is moving around the room ... She goes to a wall wardrobe, opens it and takes out a pair of boots; 58). The whole episode is centred on a conspicuous use of words that describe the setting, the *mise en scène,* the enactment by the object of what will become the photographic scenario: "Mi avvicino e con gesti discreti dispongo il suo corpo alla maniera del corpo di Olimpia" (I approach her and discreetly arrange her body in the pose of Olympia; 59). Like Mallarmé, Moravia – via Dodo – also works on the perceptival aspects of the text. This is a clear example of Moravia's use of *chosisme* – that is, a verbal narrative style in which people, events, and settings are recorded as though seen by the author through the lens of a camera. Like the poem, the novel abounds in these sorts of examples. The text engages with narrative voyeurism and more generally with vision in different ways, such as through the deictic use of spatial adverbs and the conspicuous use of descriptive adjectives and verbs of movement often used to describe a sexualized scenario.

Dodo translates the theory illustrated by Mallarmé's poem into his own art through photography by transposing the features of scopophilia from the ST to the TT. What is equivalent between the poem and the photograph is not their respective content, but rather how the content engages with the scopophilic subject in a scopophilic dynamic. Thus, it is the methodology of narrative scopophilia and how narrative scopophilia can be read in the two texts that are translated. The texts represent scenarios that are normally defined as scenarios of sexual desire, which is the kingdom of scopophilia: on the one hand, sexual intercourse between two women; on the other, an unknown naked woman observed through the lens of the camera. Scopophilia informs both the ST and the TT as it invites the voyeur to a scenario of discovery. As we have seen, the poem engages with a gradual discovery of the "bocca / pallida e rosa come una conchiglia marina" (a mouth / pale and pink like a seashell) and with the representation of an unusual scenario of desire; in the TT, curiosity is satisfied by discovering an unknown woman who is undressing. The fact that the woman represents a different culture from the voyeur's, and clearly constitutes a novelty for the male character, adds to the scene's scopophilic quality. Finally, Dodo translates the articulation of the scopophilic subject implicit in the poem (the unseen voyeur engaged in describing a scopophilic object) into the articulation of the scopophilic subject implicit in the novel (Dodo, who describes his scopophilic object through the fictive photographic image and process). Like the internal voyeur of Mallarmé's poem, who peeps at a sexual scenario from an imaginary point of vision, Dodo explores and discovers his object of desire through the concealing lens of the photographic camera. As objects, the scenario described in the poem and the fictive photograph described in the "literary snapshot" allow the voyeur to possess and thus control the scopophilic object and therefore satisfy the voyeuristic instinct.

In conclusion, the analysis of two related episodes in Moravia's novel has investigated points of coherence between different texts linked by a complex translative relationship. We have moved from a theory of scopophilia illustrated in a poem (understood here as the ST) to a fictive photograph and its process described in the novel and inspired by a painting (presented as the TT). The identification of the type of translation occurring between the texts involved has allowed us to in turn identify a methodological trajectory that highlights the complex shift from the verbal text of Mallarmé's poem to the fictive photographic process described in the novel. The intersemiotic approach to the analysis of the translation of scopophilia from the ST to the TT has identified not only similarities and differences between the contents of the texts involved, but also and especially the expressive features of the texts and how these texts have engaged with a scopophilic discourse and articulation. The result of the analysis is the identification of isotopic coherence in the expressive characterization of scopophilia as enacted in the enunciative structure of both texts (ST and TT). Given the verbal context and Moravia's narrative style in which the shift occurs, it can be argued that the specificities of the verbal language evoke vision and voyeurism both in the written dimension of the poem and in the implied visual dimension of the fictive photograph. In highlighting points of coherence between semiotically different texts described in Moravia's novel (on the one hand, the narrative scopophilia that informs a poetic text; on the other, that which informs the written description of the photographic process), I have shown how the texts share their intrinsic scopophilic enunciation. Moravia's text is permeated with scopophilia, and this characteristic is also the pivot around which the equivalence between a poem and a fictive photograph – both described from the point of view of a voyeur – has been hermeneutically constructed.

NOTES

1 The term *chosisme* refers specifically to a writing style adopted in the context of the *nouveau roman*, or the new novel, a literary genre that developed in the 1950s in France. The most influential writers of the new novel, such as Alain Robbe-Grillet, Michel Butor, and Nathalie Sarraute, were highly experimental, and their writing style diverged significantly from the one adopted by classical realist writers such as, to name a few, Balzac, Stendhal, and Flaubert. *Chosisme* privileges meticulous descriptions of the objects that inhabit the diegesis, while the plot and the characters and their psychological traits are de-emphasized. For a study on the interpretation of *chosisme*, see Barbu; for further references to the study of *chosisme* in the context of *L'uomo che guarda*, see Ragusa.

2 The original text in French reads: "Une négresse par le démon secouée / Veut goûter une enfant triste de fruits nouveaux / Et criminels aussi sous leur robe trouée, / Cette goinfre s'apprête à de rusés travaux; / À son ventre compare heureuses deux tétines / Et, si haut que la main ne le saura saisir, / Elle darde le choc obscur de ses bottines / Ainsi que quelque langue inhabile au plaisir. / Contre la nudité peureuse de gazelle / Qui tremble, sur le dos tel un fol éléphant / Renversée elle attend et s'admire avec zèle, / En riant de ses dents naïves à l'enfant; / Et, dans ses jambes où la victime se couche, / Levant une peau noire ouverte sous le crin, / Avance le palais de cette étrange bouche / Pâle et rose comme un coquillage marin." Mallarmé 6.

3 For a schematic illustration of Freud's three developmental stages of scopophilia, see Eidelberg.

4 Note that the French original already contained these linguistic features, which have been kept in the target text of the Italian translation. What could be described as the "phonetics of the erotics" can in fact be identified in the generous employment of words containing alveolar phonemes like the polyvibrant /r/, the lateral /l/, and the fricative /s/ and /z/ (e.g., "négresse," "secouée," "triste," "fruits," "criminels," "trouée," "goinfre," "s'apprête," "rusés travaux," "ventre," "heureuses," "langue inhabile," "plaisir," "peureuse de gazelle," "tremble," "renversée," "zèle,"

"coquillage," just to name the most significant words that convey the erotic movement of the two women in the French original).

5 In his comprehensive study of Manet's *Olympia*, in drawing the main contextual and hermeneutic coordinates of the painting, Theodore Reff points out that although it rocked the audience of the time for its content and its realism, it also drew from an established art tradition, as well as influencing painters who followed the model. *Olympia* was inspired by the major painters involved in the representation of Venus and of female nudes: Giorgione (*Sleeping Venus*, 1510), Titian (*Venus of Urbino*, c. 1538), Velásquez (*Rokeby Venus*, 1647-51), and Ingres (*Odalisque with a Slave*, 1842). Furthermore, the painting's legacy is evident in the years that follow its completion, as well as in the twentieth century. We must mention at least Cézanne's *A Modern Olympia* (c. 1870) and *Olympia* (1875--); Picasso's *Parody of "Olympia"* (1901); Dubuffet's *Olympia (Corps de Dame)* (1950); and Larry Rivers's *I Like Olympia in Black Face* (1970), which juxtaposes the original with a reversed version in which the two characters, the courtesan and the servant, appear as black and white, respectively, as if they were changing roles. For further references, see Reff 28–38.

10 Photography into the Limelight: Andrea De Carlo's *Treno di panna*

SARAH PATRICIA HILL

Andrea De Carlo's experience of working as a photographer had a profound effect on the subject and style of his first published novel, regarded by many critics as his best. *Treno di panna* (*Cream Train*) (1981) contains both descriptions of photographs taken by the narrator and an intensive use of photographic analogies, metaphors, similes, and terminology, as well as a meditation on the connection between photography and celebrity. The novel's protagonist experiences the world in fragments and as surface: a result of the way his camera mediates his relation to experience and the cause of his ultimately fruitless attempt to use his camera as an epistemological tool. The tension this creates echoes the contrast between the two major ways in which photographic seeing is usually defined: that is, either the eye of the camera is equated with that of the photographer, so that the photographer comes to be equated with a detached "objective" and objectifying gaze, or the camera is seen as providing access to what is invisible to the naked eye, the "unconscious optics" of which Walter Benjamin speaks (*The Work of Art* 237).[1] *Treno di panna* makes use of both these approaches but suggests that the protagonist's "photographic" vision of the world ultimately provides him with neither objectivity nor insight and that seeing can only ever be limited and fragmentary.

Critics immediately praised the novel for its remarkable verbal representation of "photographic" effects, but without defining what that meant. This chapter therefore analyses what these effects are, how they are achieved, and what their function is within the novel. It argues that De Carlo's use of photography in *Treno di panna* provided him with an inventive means of describing the experience of a world of surface and celebrity, one that is rooted in a postmodernist concern with the fragmentary, contingent nature of knowledge and experience. As Jane M. Rabb has argued, the late 1970s and early 1980s were a period during which "photography appeared to be the art form that best reflected postmodernist concerns" ("Introduction" xlviii). From this perspective, De Carlo's decision to employ photography as a decisive feature of his novel's content and style is at the same time highly original and very much in tune with its historical context.

Treno di panna is based in large part on De Carlo's experience of life in Boston, New York, and Santa Barbara, where he worked in various temporary jobs, including, like his protagonist, teaching Italian. De Carlo also worked as a photographer before writing his first published novel. While at university, he carried out various photographic projects and assignments; later, he was employed to work on publicity photographs for design magazines in Milan by the photographer Oliviero Toscani, perhaps best known as the communications strategist and photographer behind United Colours of Benetton's controversial advertising campaigns from 1982 to 2000.[2] The experience of working as a photographer, particularly in a commercial context, had a profound effect on the subject and style of De Carlo's first literary work. The novel focuses on the superficial – in both senses of the word – and makes use of a language whose emotional detachment from the world it describes echoes that of the "cold eye" of the camera. As such, it can be read as an attempt to translate the photographic rendering of surface effects (particularly in the slick images of most advertising photography) into verbal language. In a postmodern context in which seeing is no longer believing, but is rather a process through which beliefs are constructed, De Carlo does not use words to attempt to render an unattainable photographic realism. Rather, he employs a style that seeks to replicate the detachment of technological seeing and adopts a narrative approach that concentrates first and foremost on questions of visibility.

Although De Carlo has said that he tried to create a character as unlike himself as possible, one who was "antipatico, frivolo, cinico, superficiale" (unpleasant, frivolous, cynical, superficial; "Alter Ego"), *Treno di panna* is clearly grounded in personal experience.[3] It recounts the adventures of twenty-five-year-old Italian photographer Giovanni Maimeri, who comes to Los Angeles to visit friends who are trying to make it in Hollywood. Although their world seems alien to him in many ways, he ends up staying on, working at a variety of dead-end jobs, before eventually leaving his friends behind and breaking into the world of movie actors and directors. He does so through meeting a movie star with the improbable name of Marsha Mellows (perhaps a reference to the sickly froth often produced by Hollywood), who supposedly starred in a movie called *Treno di panna* made in Venice in 1971.

As Stefano Tani points out, the narrating voice in *Treno di panna* is above all "a look" that is "always slightly alien, emotionally detached from the world it describes," to the extent that Giovanni recounts even his own feelings as though they were "objective data" (164). At the same time, Tani argues, De Carlo does not aim for neutrality: "the look is objective in the sense that it offers the reader mainly physical objects, but does so through original angles, emphasizing its own subjectivity … The point of view is selective, often idiosyncratic, sensitive to particular details" (164). While De Carlo's style has been linked by some critics to the *nouveau roman* with its focus on externals and surfaces, the detached gaze that characterizes the novel is not impersonal. Rather, it is an active gaze that selects and processes images in a very individual way and that can be paralleled to the active gaze of the photographer selecting and framing fragments of the world with a camera. In a piece posted on De Carlo's website discussing the influence of photography on *Treno di panna,* the author writes that he wanted to tell a story "partendo dagli elementi di superficie, per arrivare a quello che c'è sotto" (starting from the surface to reach what is underneath; "Fotografia"). He claims that his approach was halfway between photography and ethology, and influenced also by hyperrealist painting (itself based on photography). While De Carlo claims that he was starting from the surface to reach down to what lies below, in my view the interest of the novel lies precisely in its depiction of surface and superficiality and its expression of its protagonist's gaze more than with his voice.

A number of critics praised *Treno di panna* for its stylistic innovations and the originality of the detached voice of the narrator and his selective and zoom-like point of view. In a contemporary review, Mario Barone praises De Carlo for offering readers "un'indagine diversa di una letteratura giovanile che credevamo ancorata ormai del tutto a certi clichés o ad alcune note linguistiche" (a different investigation of a youthful literature that we thought was by now firmly anchored to certain clichés or linguistic notes; 3). He argues that, refreshingly, De Carlo's novel is without "sfoghi esistenziali o manierismi" (existential outbursts or mannerisms; 3). In a review quoted on the back cover of the 1996 edition of the book, Italo Calvino likewise admires it for its representation of what he called "un'insaziabilità degli occhi che bevono lo spettacolo del mondo multicolore ingigantiti come attraverso la lente d'un teleobiettivo" (the insatiability of eyes that drink up the spectacle of the multicolored world, enlarged as though they were looking through a telephoto lens) and its depiction of a gaze that "afferra e registra un enorme numero di particolari e sfumature" (grasps and registers an enormous number of details and subtleties). Calvino was also the first of many critics to link the protagonist's selective choice of visual information, with its extreme focus on individual fragments of the external, and his distinctive narrative style to the work of American hyper- or photo-realists ("Introduction"), which De Carlo mentioned in the quotation above.[4] Martin McLaughlin argues that Calvino, who identified the primary focus of De Carlo's novel as "la superficie della coscienza che sfiora un mondo tutto in superficie" (the surface of consciousness brushing against an entirely superficial world; 78), must have connected this concentration on surface detail to his own *Palomar*, which he was writing at the time.

As we shall see, there are also points of contact between Calvino's "L'avventura di un fotografo" ("The Adventure of a Photographer") and De Carlo's work, although De Carlo himself had a closer involvement with photographic technology than Calvino.[5] It seems likely, though, that De Carlo would have been familiar with Calvino's short story, published in 1970 as part of *Gli amori difficili* (*Difficult Loves*). Given the strong role played by photographs and what I am calling photographic style in the novel, it is also plausible that he would have had at least some awareness of the theoretical debates over representational self-reflexivity (as in the photographing of photographs explored in Calvino's short story, for example) and photography's relation to knowledge – debates that dominated many discussions of photography at the time.[6] Again, De Carlo's novel lacks the extreme self-reflexivity of many of Calvino's works, but he does share with the older author an interest in seeing as a key narrative theme.

In De Carlo's novel, this is expressed as a fascination with photography's mediation of seeing. The influence of a photographic approach to representation is also reflected in the immediacy of De Carlo's language, with its paratactic constructions and striking use of photographic terminology. Maria Pia Ammirati argues that De Carlo's prose reflects the fact that for him the camera is no longer a useful means of documenting reality, but rather a tool that allows for a mutual contamination of different languages, transforming literary language "da uno stato di polisemia a quello superficiale dell'iconografia" (from polysemia to the superficiality of iconography; 61). "Contaminated" in this way, De Carlo's writing functions in a similar way to photography, proceeding in snatches, representing space in brief, sequential scenes that focus on external details. This valorizing of everyday moments from ordinary life reflects the author's interest in how photography conditions ways of seeing and interpreting the world by offering it to viewers as a series of fragments. By capturing a succession of individual moments, each of equivalent value, photography offers an alternative model both to the traditional linear flow of literary narrative and to film's seamless flow of images. It is particularly interesting that De Carlo should have chosen to employ this photographic model in writing a novel about the world of cinema.

Indeed, many critics agreed that the most exciting and original aspect of the novel was its narrator's fragmented, "photographic" point of view, with its sharp focus on sequential, external details and an almost purely visual Los Angeles.[7] This represented a response to a world in which the human relation to the environment was increasingly becoming a question of visual perception. Giovanni's experience of photography makes him particularly sensitive to effects of light and darkness and the arrangement of surfaces. For him, photography functions as a metaphor for fragmentation and superficiality, for the artificiality of life in a large, modern American city, and for the desire to be a detached observer. But above all, in *Treno di panna* it serves as the protagonist's primary means of understanding his environment. He employs photography to try to make sense of the new space in which he finds himself and the jumble of images and impressions that flash by him. Giovanni perceives his new world through a series of lenses, reflections, and artificial and environmental filters. For example, he describes how the car window through which he sets up his shots in turn frames him, at the same time hiding him from the view of those he photographs behind the frame of the windscreen and the reflections on its glass (138). Even when he is not looking through the lens of his camera, there are constant references to what he sees or imagines seeing through or reflected by windows and glass doors (7, 138, 148, 190, 205–7), mirrors (4, 31, 45, 100, 154), water (141, 187), panes of glass and shop windows (29, 76, 81, 91, 129), and sunglasses (136–7). Looking into and through fish tanks (126, 185, 206), shop windows (76, 108, 114, 129), car windows (29, 41, 43, 75), supermarket display cases, two-way mirrors (23, 205), and glass spheres, Giovanni sees Los Angeles through a series of transparent surfaces and fragmented by the changing effects of light.

This is clear from the beginning of the novel, which opens with the protagonist gazing down on Los Angeles from the window of his descending airplane. It is night, and from that perspective, he sees the city only as a network of bright points, an incomprehensible swirl of flickering lights below him. His inability to comprehend this space continues even after he lands. On the freeway with his friend Tracy, who has come to pick him up from the airport to take him back to the house she shares with her boyfriend Ron, he enters a stream of headlights, and the rest of the landscape seems to dissolve:

> Davanti a noi si percepivano solo luci rosse di automobili nella stessa nostra direzione, fari bianchi di quelle che venivano in senso opposto. C'era intorno questo vuoto, riempito di luci e strinamenti di luci, curve di fanali, lampeggiamenti di frecce. Solo a tratti apparivano visioni più ampie, avvolte in un alone opaco; confuse nel buio e l'acqua che scorreva sui finestrini. (6-7)

> In front of us, only the red tail lights of the cars going the same way and the white headlights of those coming towards us could be seen. All around was this emptiness filled with lights and streaks of light, curves of headlights, flashings of indicators. It was only in snatches that broader vistas appeared, enveloped in a dull aura; blurred by the darkness and the water streaming down the car windows.

The effect of these descriptions of Giovanni's disorientation is quasi-cinematic, an example of one of the points in the novel where the incomprehensible cinematic intervenes and overwhelms the analytical photographic. At this point, he experiences the space of the city as a dark void traversed by lights, almost as though the whole of Los Angeles were one giant movie theatre filled with competing movies, none of which he can understand as he is rushed past them. Even when they stop, he realizes that Ron and Tracy's house – in an unpleasant suburb far from the centre of the city – is almost directly under the freeway, with cars passing practically overhead: "Da sotto si vedevano i fari che schizzavano avanti; si trascinavano via intere strisce di buio nella distanza" (From below we could see the headlights spurting ahead; trailing whole strips of darkness away into the distance; 9). The bewildering lights and movement continue incessantly right above and beside them, creating "un riflesso di luminosità innaturali in continuo spostamento" (a reflection of unnatural, ever-shifting luminosities; 12) in the darkened apartment. He can make no sense of these cinematic reflections, and it is only once he uses photography to still the movement around him that he begins to orient himself.

The next day Giovanni sets out on a walk with Ron through the urban wasteland of the neighbourhood, and again his experience is one of complete disorientation. It is a gloomy day, and both the light and the landscape create a monotonous, monochromatic effect in which "tutti i colori tendevano al grigio" (all colours tend toward grey; 21). As the two walk on, they seem to make no progress and the landscape remains essentially unchanged, apart from subtle differences in the details of the little houses along the roadside, otherwise barely distinguishable from one another (21). These differentiating particulars are so minimal that they are only noticeable to a macrophotographic gaze that can capture apparently insignificant details and lend them a new importance. In noting these details, then, Giovanni can use them as a means of orienting himself in this confusing and almost entirely artificial new environment. He goes on to describe how the only truly notable element to emerge from this background is the sign of a service station in the distance. As they progress, however, it appears larger but also farther away: "Dopo venti minuti che camminavamo era immensa, ancora a qualche chilometro di distanza. Questo dilatava lo spazio, lo appiattiva e spampanava nel mattino tardo" (After we'd been walking for twenty minutes it was huge, though still kilometres away. This dilated the space, flattening and stripping it in the late morning; 21). Here, too, the description recalls photographic effects, but in this case the distortion caused by the use of a very strong telephoto lens focused on a distant object. This shift from the macroscopic to the telescopic in De Carlo's descriptions of the landscape once again reveals his interest in using verbal language to represent a photographic rather than a "natural" or even "cinematic" way of seeing.

A few mornings later, Tracy takes Giovanni to Beverley Hills, where they walk around the stores together. Giovanni's encounter with this new area is described once more in purely visual terms. The description is completely dominated by the verb *guardare* (to see) and other verbs of seeing, and by a sense of disconnection and anxiety:

> Guardavo i negozi italiani di abiti che si affacciavano sulla strada in forma di immense scatole di confetti [...]. [G]uardavo in giro in preda a una strana ansia morbosa [...].

> Guardavo la gente davanti e dietro alle vetrine; le grandi macchine che passavano raso al marciapiede e si fermavano per qualche minuto senza aprire le portiere. Fermo a un angolo ho osservato una signora mentre parcheggiava una Rolls Royce grigia in uno spazio ristretto tra due altre automobili. [...]
>
> Guardavo gli oggetti esposti nelle vetrine: mi colpiva la loro consistenza, la loro densità nella luce.
>
> Guardavo ragazze che camminavano veloci, con calzoni larghi chiusi alle caviglie e guance arrossate; signore di mezz'età con occhiali pesanti e sandali sottili; uomini con pance e abbronzature di diverso spessore. Non riuscivo bene a capire chi faceva davvero parte della scena, e chi invece era ai margini e si limitava a indossare modi di fare e abiti di ruolo. (29)

> I looked at the Italian fashion shops that faced onto the street like great chocolate-boxes ... I looked around, prey to a strange, morbid anxiety ...
>
> I looked at the people in front of the shop-windows and behind them; at the big cars that passed close to the sidewalk and stopped for a minute without the doors opening. Standing at a corner, I watched a lady park a grey Rolls-Royce in a tight space between two other cars ...
>
> I looked at the goods on display in the shop-windows: I was struck by their concreteness, their density in the light.
>
> I looked at swift-moving girls, in baggy pants gathered in at the ankles and with rouged cheeks; middle-aged ladies with heavy glasses and flimsy sandals; men with paunches and tans of varying thickness. I couldn't quite work out who was really part of the scene and who was merely on the margins, donning mannerisms and apparel to play the role.

In describing a sequence of fragmentary glimpses, these paragraphs create the impression of a series of photographic details. Yet, without the aid of a camera to fix them, Giovanni still finds himself "preda a una strana ansia morbosa," unable to understand the roles being played out before him. At this point, the city of Los Angeles and its occupants remain exotic and impenetrable to him. Their poses, too, are unintelligible, and he is initially unable to distinguish between those who really belong and those who are faking it, constructing an image of belonging in the hopes that it will become a reality. Again, a contrast is drawn between the protagonist's longing for photographic clarity and his immersion in cinematic uncertainty.

Giovanni only starts to form a clearer mental picture of the geography of Los Angeles more than halfway through the book, once he gets his own car and uses it to drive around taking photographs. In control of his own movement, he uses his camera to still the movements around him; this gives him a way of understanding and negotiating his surroundings: "Con la macchina ho cominciato a girare la città. Mi sono reso conto che fino ad ora non ne avevo percepito che frammenti: atolli isolati nel mare di strade e costruzioni. Poco alla volta le relazioni tra i diversi punti sono divenute chiare" (I began driving around the city. I realized that up until now I had perceived only fragments of it, isolated atolls amid the ocean of streets and buildings. Little by little, the relation between one point and another became clear; 113). Giovanni begins to make sense of the city especially once he begins taking his camera with him on his drives and his gaze is doubly mediated by technology. Ironically, the camera, often a symbol of the world's fragmentation, and the car, often thought of as symptomatic of the isolation of the modern individual, provide Giovanni with his only means of mapping Los Angeles. Examining the mansions of Bel Air and Beverly Hills from multiple angles, he tries to absorb their overall aspect, their constitutive details, the consistency and thickness of their walls and hedges, putting together images from magazines and television with the ones he gathers in his travels with his camera (113–14). In this way, slowly, his mental map of the city takes shape.

But his map consists of discontinuous surfaces. He forms an idea of the city as made up of overlapping spheres that share the same space without touching. He uses the same metaphor of coexistent but not contiguous spheres to express the separation between the person he would like to be and the one he actually is: "La sfera di quello che avrei voluto essere e fare diventava spessa e stagna; lontanissima da quella che conteneva invece la mia vita. Il vetro delle due sfere diventava così denso e opaco da schermare del tutto la luce" (The sphere of what I would like to be and do was becoming solid, airtight; a world away from the one that actually contained my life. The glass of the two spheres was growing so thick and opaque as to screen out the light entirely; 148).[8]

Incommunicability is fundamental to Giovanni's relationship to the world around him and to the others he encounters. Ammirati describes De Carlo's gaze in *Treno di panna* as one that "testimonia l'avvenuta separazione fra il mondo e l'uomo, per cui la rappresentazione della realtà si pronuncia come la catalogazione disarticolata di ciò che esiste al di fuori dell'uomo [...] senza più legami d'intesa" (testifies to the separation between the world and human beings. Because of this separation the representation of reality emerges as the disarticulated cataloging of what exists outside the human ... no longer with any connections based on mutual understanding; 60). Yet the situation is more complicated than Ammirati implies, since photography – despite its flaws as a hermeneutic tool – constitutes the protagonist's main way of relating to and interpreting the world. As such, it represents his method of dealing with his sensation of separation from the world, rather than a symptom of it. Massimo Cacciari has argued that photography does not provide a means of representation, duplication, or capturing of some kind of external truth, but rather a means of creating a "new" reality. In Giovanni's case, photography enables him to create just such a "reality," a world he feels he can interpret at least in part.

Giovanni's imaginative world is also populated by photographic images. Infected by the desire to "make it" that dominates the lives of everyone he encounters in Los Angeles, he imagines a successful future for himself in the city made up not of "confused sensations," but rather of

> immagini, film o fotografie mentali: io in una grossa automobile che rispondevo ai saluti di gruppi di persone in strada; io sul bordo di una piscina in conversazione con diverse ragazze molto belle; io che parlavo davanti a due o tre telecamere, abbagliato dai riflettori.
>
> Quasi sempre queste visioni erano ricche di dettagli, definite nei particolari più minuti. Mi bastava addentrarmi nel loro tessuto con una lente di ingrandimento per osservare lo sviluppo di immagini secondarie. A volte stavo per ore di seguito a guardarle da vicino: le ripercorrevo decine di volte, senza riuscire ad abbandonare il tepore irreale che producevano. (147)

> images, mental films or photographs: me driving a large car and waving to groups of people greeting me in the street; me in conversation with various beautiful girls by the edge of a swimming pool; me speaking in front of two or three television cameras, dazzled by the spotlights.
>
> These visions were nearly always richly detailed and well-defined, down to their most minute particulars. I had only to explore their fabric with a magnifying glass to detect the development of secondary images. At times I would spend hours on end studying them closely: I would go over them dozens of times, unable to give up the unreal warmth they produced.

These mental slides of the future are unconnected to any attempt to realize them (unlike the American characters like Ron and Tracy and

Jill, who are all trying in vain to achieve success in show business) and have no value for Giovanni as photographs of a possible reality. Rather, the power of the images and the specificity of their details provide him with a kind of escape, which nevertheless leaves him feeling dejected when the images finally dissipate and he is left to contemplate their impossibility, "come uno guarda un muro abbastanza alto da non poterlo superare" (as one might look at a wall too high to get over; 147).

De Carlo's extreme attention to photographic detail recalls John Szarkowski's claim that with photography's invention, "the compelling clarity with which a photograph recorded the trivial suggested that the subject had never before properly been seen, that it was, in fact perhaps not trivial, but filled with undiscovered meaning" (8–9). As mentioned above, De Carlo is very much concerned with the way in which photography suggests and conditions ways of seeing. Yet this conditioning of vision is problematic. Despite the protagonist's close scrutiny of his images, the meanings they yield are at best difficult to interpret, since they, like the world of appearances in which he exists, partake of the mysteries of vision and what John Berger calls "the enigma of appearances," which are always read in different ways depending on mood, emotion, circumstances, and so on (Berger and Mohr, *Another Way of Telling* 116–17). As Berger goes on to point out, however, the photographer's choices differ from those of just "someone looking." While the former singles out particular details of appearances for attention, or fragments of reality, the latter's gaze is absorbed into a continuum of appearances that flow into and out of one another seamlessly, without the interruption of a photographic frame. In Giovanni's case, the fragments he assembles piece by piece constitute his main way of relating to his surroundings and the people he encounters, providing him with insights he might miss without the aid of photographic technology. At the same time, his focus on surfaces and fragments prevents him from seeing things the way others do, both literally and metaphorically.

Likewise, Giovanni prefers to remain literally and metaphorically distant from others. He makes use of a telephoto lens, which enables him to take close-up photographs of people while remaining unseen himself, spying on them from a distance. Giovanni's photographic focus, both literal and metaphorical, is most often one of extreme close-up or aerial distance – perspectives that reveal the gap between what the human eye and the camera lens see while emphasizing the protagonist's ethical as well as physical distance from those around him. While preparing the 1000 mm lens, he recalls the salesmen who sold it to him in Italy telling him it was more suited to photographing wildlife or the craters of the moon than to photographing people. Giovanni replied that "mi bastava appena; che anche così dovevo avvicinarmi troppo" (it was barely adequate; that I would still have to get too close; 120).[9] By using his car in conjunction with the telephoto lens in order to remain hidden while taking pictures, Giovanni manages to maintain even more of a distance between himself and his photographic subjects. His use of the vehicle recalls Sontag's comparison of cars and cameras as "predatory weapons" (14). While the detached predations of photographers may take place without the awareness of their "victim," Sontag goes on to argue that photography represents a kind of violation because it turns its subjects into "objects that can be symbolically possessed" (14) and allows photographers to have privileged knowledge of them that the subjects themselves do not and cannot have.

Giovanni's first efforts to photograph people rather than just places in Los Angeles frustrate him precisely because they do not provide him with this kind of privileged knowledge – a knowledge similar to that sought by Calvino's photographer Antonino in "L'avventura di un fotografo." These photographs fail to break through the carefully arranged surface appearances of his subjects: "Ho fatto centinaia di fotografie inutili. Quando le ho viste mi sono sentito idiota. Sarebbe stato lo stesso andare direttamente da loro con una Istamatic in mano e chiedere se per piacere potevo scattare qualche foto" (I took hundreds of useless shots. When I saw the prints, I felt like an idiot. I might as well have gone straight over to them with an Instamatic and asked if I could please take a few snaps; 121). So he expands his hunting ground from the luxurious mansions of Bel Air to more secluded homes and places of work, searching for moments of unbalance, the slippage of the mask:

> Capitava che un attore e un'attrice che erano stati amanti si incontrassero per caso davanti a un negozio di mobili, e rimanessero per un attimo imbarazzati, senza difese. Oppure un divo anziano doveva convincere il proprio cane a rientrare in casa dal giardino, ed era costretto a richiamarlo scompostamente: agitando le braccia. Era questa momentanea sbilanciatura di tratti, questa increspatura non prevedibile in una superficie omogenea che mi attirava. (121)

> An actress and an actor who had been lovers would chance to meet outside a furniture store and stand for a moment in embarrassment, defenceless. Or else an aging star might have to persuade his dog to come back in

> from the garden and be forced into undignified behaviour in summoning him: waving his arms. It was this momentary disturbance of features, this unforeseeable ripple on a homogenous surface that appealed to me.

These are precisely the kinds of moments that for Marcel Proust indicated photography's greatest inherent flaw: its preservation of an untruthful moment of a person's life that provided no information about his or her usual behaviour and personality (815). De Carlo's protagonist, however, inhabits a postmodern world in which Proust's notion of photography's betrayal or distortion of a person's "true" character no longer has meaning. Nor can his photographs be seen as a Pirandellian process of "unmasking." While Giovanni's camera captures an "increspatura non prevedibile in una superficie omogenea" (ripple on a homogenous surface; 121) by preserving it in a photograph, this ripple in fact reveals nothing lasting about what lies below the surface – not even the existence of yet another mask. Rather, it emphasizes that the surface is all there is. In Giovanni's world of surface and simulacra, photography's unveiling of Benjamin's unconscious optics – the workings of visual and social codes, practices and rituals that shape everyday social interactions – holds no lasting revelatory or revolutionary potential (*The Work of Art* 237).

Looking from a distance at the pile of his black-and-white photographs spread out on the kitchen counter, Giovanni sees them as a single black-and-white mass. This again recalls the self-reflexive photography of Calvino's Antonino, who ultimately decides that photographing his photographs is the only "true" photography. For Giovanni, however, the case is different. Spread across the kitchen bench, his photographs look like a single black-and-white figure, but when he picks up his magnifying lens, details spring into view, like an older woman in a white Cadillac, with "gli zigomi di persona soddisfatta e gonfia di benessere; gli occhi distratti, persi in immagini autoriferite" (the cheekbones of smug affluence; the eyes distant, lost in self-engrossed images; 137). Looking at a series of other photographs, he notes details of body parts and apparel. The closer he brings his eye to the lens, the more the details take on other meanings and the more he finds connections among them: "Pensavo a cosa li collegava tra loro, come perle di una collana" (I thought about what linked them all together, like a pearl necklace; 137–8).

From the distant view of the mass of images, Giovanni passes – in the style of Antonioni's *Blow-Up* – to a series of extreme close-ups, through the use of a magnifying glass. The fetishistic description of body parts like wrists and feet juxtaposed with that of the eye pressed to the lens recalls Christian Metz's famous description of photography as "a cut inside the referent [that] cuts off a piece of it, a fragment, a pan object, for a long immobile travel of no return" (84). The details that strike him as he moves over the photographs with the magnifying lens also bring to mind Barthes's description of the contrast between *studium*, the shareable cultural appreciation of an image, and *punctum*, the "accident which pricks me (but also bruises me, is poignant to me)" (*Camera Lucida* 27). Yet De Carlo ends the episode by having his protagonist meditate on the connections among the details he studies so intently, using the metaphor of the contiguous spheres of the pearl necklace rather than the more violent imagery of Metz's cut or Barthes's *punctum*. Once again, there is a shift from an extreme distance, which reduces a mass of images to a single form, to an extreme close-up, which disintegrates bodies and shapes into their constituent fragments. Studying the photographs, Giovanni explores their unconscious optics with ever-greater intensity, not in search of any inner meaning, but rather in the aid of a photographic poetics that explores and creates connections between disparate images.

Giovanni studies his own photographs in an attempt to gain a clearer idea of his surroundings and the people he encounters; he makes use of other people's photographs in similar ways. For example, when he moves in with Jill, who is the cashier at the restaurant where he works, he looks through her boxes of letters and photographs while she is out. Although he reads the letters, the photographs seem to provide the details he is really after. Having read a letter in which Jill's friend Ray tells her euphorically about the possibility of working with a big record producer, he finds a photograph that seems to confirm its contents and to provide further clues: "Quella [fotografia] di Jill e Ray sull'amaca doveva risalire a poco dopo la lettera: era nello stesso spirito" (That [photograph] of Jill and Ray on the hammock must have been taken shortly after the letter was written: it was in the same spirit; 96). After one of his many quarrels with Jill, Giovanni goes back to the photographs to try to get a better mental picture of her: "Sono andato a frugare nella sua scatola di vecchie lettere e fotografie, per aggiungere qualche particolare al quadro che mi ero fatto di lei" (I went and rummaged through her box of old letters and photographs so as to add some more details to the picture of her I had built up; 111). Giovanni goes to the trouble of finding and going through Jill's letters and photographs, yet he is unable or unwilling to try to find out about Jill from actually talking or being with her.[10]

This inability or unwillingness points to one of the limitations of Giovanni's photographic relational mode: it reinforces to an extreme the notion of point of view and its assumption of dominance. The camera's monocular mode of vision corresponds to Giovanni's monologic discourse.[11] Although he recounts his story in a detached language that appears to take as its non-verbal model the ostensible objectivity of the camera, this seeming detachment functions as a symptom of what Ammirati calls the "assoluta autorità del suo pensiero, come espressione del suo unico e particolare punto di vista sul mondo, e sull'estraneità ugualmente assoluta di partecipare o condividere o capire un altrui punto di vista" (absolute authority of his way of thinking, as an expression of his unique and personal point of view of the world, and of his equally absolute inability to empathise with or understand another point of view; 55). For Giovanni, being the object of another's gaze does not guarantee any sort of reciprocity – quite the contrary.

For example, while working in the "Italian" restaurant (where all the other waiters are Mexican), Giovanni feels himself disappear from the visual field of his customers as the lens of their attention moves away from him, coming back into focus as soon as they need something from him:

> Era una sensazione quasi fisica: la scomparsa graduale della mia presenza in termini visualmente percepibili. Mi pareva di essere sullo specchio ribaltabile di una macchina fotografica mentre chi la tiene in mano gira l'anello della messa in fuoco su una distanza ravvicinata. I miei contorni si dissolvevano progressivamente. La mia giacca rossa era una macchia di colore; si allargava sempre più sfumata, fino a diventare un'ombra labile, che vibrava sul piano estremo del campo visivo, assorbita nei chiari e gli scuri dello sfondo. [...] Ma questo stato invisibile non durava mai molto: a tratti la lente girava verso di me e venivo improvvisamente a fuoco, stagliato sullo sfondo di tavoli e sedie. (67-8)

> It was almost a physical sensation: the gradual elimination of my presence in terms of visual perception. I felt as though I was on the view-finder of a camera while the person holding it was adjusting the focus to close-up. My outlines dissolved progressively. My red jacket was a splash of colour; it spread wider and wider, more and more blurred, until it had become an evanescent shadow, quivering on the very edge of the field of vision,

> absorbed into the lights and darks of the background ... But my invisibility never lasted long: from time to time the lens would swing round towards me and I would spring into focus, outlined against a background of tables and chairs.

Here, he describes himself as part of the focusing mechanism of a camera, but he also uses similes related to photographic film to describe his relationship to the clients of the restaurant, relating, for example, how "a volte il singolo gesto di un singolo cliente mi restava impresso come un episodio significativo per tutto il giorno dopo" (sometimes a single gesture by a single customer would remain imprinted on my mind as a significant occurrence for the whole of the following day; 88), like the impression of light on a photographic negative. He would then break these gestures down into separate photographic details:

> Questi dettagli perdevano proporzione durante la notte, si ingrandivano come fotografie, si sgranavano fino a che era impossibile averne un'immagine d'insieme, o capirne l'origine. Mi restava in mente la porzione di un gesto; un'espressione isolata dal contesto di mille espressioni che avevano costituito l'intera recitazione facciale di una giovane donna a cena con un pretendente. (88–9)

> These details would lose their true dimensions during the night, becoming magnified like photographic enlargements; they would grow grainy until it was impossible to grasp any overall image or understand how they had originated. My mind would retain a fragment of a gesture; one expression isolated from the context of a thousand expressions which had made up the complete facial performance of a young woman dining with an admirer.

This description creates an almost Cubist faceting of reality that would be unimaginable without photography's capacity to still movement and to fragment space, as the explicit references to photographic enlargement make clear. Giovanni's description seems to echo the great American photographer Edward Weston's definition of the photograph as closer to mosaic rather than drawing or painting. The photograph is made up not of lines, but of "tiny particles" whose "extreme fineness ... gives a special tension to the image, and when that tension is destroyed – by the intrusion of handwork, by too great enlargement, by printing on a rough surface, etc. – the integrity of the photograph is destroyed"

(172). De Carlo, like Calvino, takes this notion a step further not just by considering the individual photograph as akin to a mosaic, but by also regarding collections of photographic moments as like a mosaic whose pieces have been shuffled and disassociated from one another.

Giovanni, by turns photographic eye and photographic negative, contrasts his own invisibility and impressionability with the visibility of Marsha Mellows, wondering if it is possible for her to go anywhere "per conto suo, senza essere notata, fermata, fotografata" (on her own, without being noticed, stopped, photographed; 189). Her extreme visibility means that Giovanni has the impression that he cannot see her directly, without the mediation of all of the photographic images of her he has seen. Meeting her for the first time, he feels that he is seeing the event as though "attraverso un filtro: attraverso un vetro zigrinato" (through a filter: through rippled glass; 130). He watches her as though he is looking at a series of photographs of her, taken from far away but in extreme close-up, like those he lays out on the kitchen counter:

> Guardavo Marsha Mellows a trenta centimetri da me, e mi sembrava solo di vedere delle sue fotografie, disposte in successione così da creare un'idea di movimento. Guardavo queste sue fotografie di fronte e di tre quarti e di profilo, e mi sembrava di conoscerle bene. Mi sembrava di poter anticipare e accompagnare e concludere ogni suo gesto o espressione. Non vedevo molto nitido. (131)

> I was looking at Marsha Mellows from thirty centimetres' distance and I seemed to see only photographs of her, arranged in sequence so as to convey the impression of movement. I looked at these pictures full front, half on, and in profile, and they looked very familiar to me. I felt I could anticipate, accompany and follow through her every gesture and expression. I could not see very clearly.

Eventually, he manages to fight his way through this succession of simulacra, and details come into focus: her blue pants and jacket, her crocodile belt, the shirt she wears, her hair tied back in a yellow ribbon, the shape of her eyebrows, and the colour of her eyes. He describes how these details "venivano a fuoco poco alla volta, man mano che riuscivo a vederla al di là delle fotografie che avevo in mente" (came into focus little by little as I slowly managed to see her outside the photographs I had in mind; 131). The details of the "real" Marsha must compete with the photographic images of her that Giovanni already has in his mind.

This doubling effect continues as they begin their lesson: "Quando prendeva fiato, o girava gli occhi, ricalcava immagini che mi ricordavo dai suoi film. Adesso venivano fuori più tridimensionali che in anticamera; appena più vere del vero" (When she drew breath, or moved her eyes, she traced images that I recalled from her films. Now they appeared more three-dimensional than in the reception room; just a bit more real than real; 133). The still photographs and cinematic images of Marsha the star that Giovanni recalls continually interpose themselves between him and the flesh-and-blood Marsha. When he goes to her house to teach, he is surprised to find her in the kitchen, baking, and tries to think of an image to help him interpret her presence there: "Mi chiedevo se l'avevo vista in qualche film in una scena di cucina, ma non riuscivo a ricordarmene" (I wondered whether I'd ever seen her in some film in a kitchen scene, but couldn't recall one; 156). Without the mediation of his camera lens or the recollection of other photographic images, Giovanni is profoundly uncomfortable. He is so conditioned by photographic seeing that he finds himself at a loss when confronted by the possibility of a gaze that is not technologically mediated. For Giovanni, in a world of simulacra and surface, the concept of a "naked eye" is an absurdity: mediated vision is the only possible basis for consciousness.

Nevertheless, the encounter in the kitchen turns out to be decisive for Giovanni's ability to break through from one "sphere" to another, for it leads to him becoming a photographer in Marsha's eyes and hence to becoming "visible" in her world. This shift in identity takes place not because of any efforts on his part, but rather because of a chance remark he makes to Marsha Mellows as a conversational gambit in response to his discomfort about seeing her in the kitchen: "Ero in leggero imbarazzo [...]. Le ho descritto alcune fotografie che avevo fatto il giorno prima" (I was slightly embarrassed ... I described to her some pictures I'd taken the day before; 157). Marsha replies distractedly that she would like to see them, but she does not seem particularly interested, and to Giovanni it sounds like an empty phrase. Nevertheless, from then on she apparently thinks of him as "the photographer." Despite never having seen any of his photographs, she introduces him as "un fotografo bravissimo" (an excellent photographer; 161) to her husband and friends (165), much to Giovanni's embarrassment. He tries to explain that he is not really a professional photographer, but no one pays any attention. Giovanni's voyeuristic hobby thus comes to validate him as a "fellow artist" to the group of actors, directors, and producers of Marsha Mellows's circle.

Although Giovanni's situation has changed, at the end of the novel he finds himself in a similar position to where he was when it opened. Once again, he is looking down on the city, not from an airplane this time, but from the even dizzier heights of the Hollywood home of a famous actor where Marsha Mellows has taken him:

> Ho guardato in basso, e di colpo c'era la città, come un immenso lago nero pieno di plancton luminoso, esteso fino ai margini dell'orizzonte. Ho guardato i punti di luce che vibravano nella distanza: quelli che formavano un'armatura sottile di paesaggio, fragile, tremante; quelli in movimento lungo percorsi ondulati, lungo traiettorie semicircolari, lungo linee intersecate. C'erano punti che lasciavano tracce filanti, bave di luce liquida; punti che si aggregavano in concentrazioni intense, fino a disegnare i contorni di un frammento di città e poi scomporli di nuovo, per separarsi e perdersi sempre più nel buio. Li guardavo solcare gli spazi del tutto neri che colmavano inerti il vuoto, in attesa di assorbire qualche riflesso nella notte umida. (209–10)

> I looked below me, and suddenly, there was the town, like an immense black lake full of luminous plankton, stretching as far as the horizon's edges. I looked at the points of light that shimmered in the distance: the ones that formed a flimsy framework of landscape, frail and trembling; the ones in motion along undulating pathways, along semi-circular trajectories, along intersecting lines. There were points that left trails behind them, dribbles of liquid light; points that clustered together in intense concentrations, tracing the outline of a fragment of the town and then shattering it once more, dispersing and receding and vanishing ever more into the darkness. I watched them slice through the dead, solid black spaces that filled the void, waiting to absorb some reflected gleam in the humid night.

This time, however, he too is a fixed point of light, having perhaps himself absorbed a little reflection from the stars that surround him. As Tani points out, in *Treno di panna,* "light becomes above all the light of appearance, spotlight and limelight," something that creates both "illusions and disappointments" (166). While Giovanni's "success" is an ironic one, the legitimizing of his identity as "a photographer," combined with his peculiarly photographic way of seeing, has enabled him to break through one of the transparent walls that separate one sphere from another and achieve a longed-for visibility. Yet the view turns out to be much the same view of points and surfaces: the patterns of light on dark that make of the night cityscape a kind of photographic negative, endlessly reproducible, full of multiple meanings but ultimately leading to only a limited kind of knowledge.

Treno di panna is very much a novel of its time in its concentration on surface effects and the perceived need to interpret the world in visual terms because of a crisis of faith regarding what lies beyond the visual. These elements are fundamental to De Carlo's approach to photography and to his analysis of what might be called the "limelight effect" of an ever-increasing desire for photographic visibility. The question of what photography can actually reveal is central to the novel, but it is one that is resolved only by doubt about photography's ability ultimately to offer more than a limited perspective on the world. Belying its author's claim that it is a novel that starts from the surface to reveal what lies beneath, in the final analysis *Treno di panna* represents an in-depth investigation of surface in a world in which photographic seeing limits any other type of exploration. It suggests that, particularly when the glare of celebrity creates distorting reflections and refractions, the fragments of knowledge photographs can offer are at best fragile and contingent.

NOTES

1 On the eye/camera analogy, see also Scott 9.

2 De Carlo claimed that he was originally attracted to what he saw as the glamour of photography, but changed his mind about it once he actually began working as a photographer: "La prima volta che ho visto *Blow up* di Antonioni, mi ha affascinato l'immagine del fotografo, dinamico e irregolare quasi come un musicista rock. Qualche tempo dopo ho fatto il secondo assistente a un fotografo di moda. Ma visto da dentro era un mondo molto meno affascinante di come sembrava da fuori: i fotografi spesso erano servi arroganti agli ordini di stilisti e art director e redattrici ancora più arroganti. Tutti si rifacevano sulle modelle, che erano vittime compiaciute e mi facevano venire la nausea con i loro sorrisi finti e le loro braccia troppo magre" (The first time I saw Antonioni's *Blow Up*, I was fascinated by the image of the photographer, dynamic and erratic almost like a rock musician. A bit later, I worked as second assistant to a fashion photographer. But seen from inside it was a much less fascinating world than what it had seemed like from outside: the photographers were often arrogant slaves to the orders of even more arrogant stylists and art directors and editors. Everyone took it out on the models, willing victims who made me feel

sick with their fake smiles and too-thin arms); "Fotografia". De Carlo also worked in the world of cinema. In 1982 and 1983, he was Federico Fellini's assistant on *E la nave va* (*And the Ship Sails On*) (1983), and he worked as a director's assistant for Michelangelo Antonioni. He directed a film version of *Treno di panna* in 1988, for which he also wrote the screenplay. Of his film, he wrote: "Se ci penso adesso, credo di avere concentrato in un solo film tutti gli errori che un regista può fare in anni di lavoro" (Thinking about it now, I believe I concentrated all the mistakes a director could make in years of work into just one film); De Carlo, "Cinema".

3 He goes on to say, however, that "ogni volta che mi addentro in una storia finisco per identificarmi con i suoi protagonisti: i filtri saltano, la distanza svanisce, i nostri sguardi e pensieri coincidono. Divento loro" (every time I get into a story, I end up identifying myself with its protagonists: I lose my filters, distance vanishes and our gazes and thoughts merge); "Alter Ego."

4 See also Biondi and Pandini.

5 In Calvino's words, "the world of drawing has always been closer to me than that of photography." "Cinema and the Novel" 78.

6 Calvino's own essay, "La follia del mirino" (The Madness of the Viewfinder), originally published in 1955, was an important early precursor to these debates. On this topic, see also Marra.

7 See, for example, McLaughlin and Ammirati.

8 These are also the terms he uses to describe the worlds of those few who have "made it" and the many who are trying to do so.

9 There is a long history of theorizing about "taking" photographs as opposed to "making" them. Photographers themselves are often eager to make this distinction, which opposes the notion of a voyeuristic, exploitative taking to that of a more collaborative making. On this topic, see, for example, Szarkowski.

10 It is telling that he uses a visual metaphor ("al quadro che mi ero fatto di lei" – to the picture of her I had built up) to describe his understanding of the kind of person she is.

11 On the question of monologic form in the novel and its connection to aesthetic activity as a form of seeing, as opposed to the shift from seeing to hearing in the polyphonic novel, see Bakhtin 270–4.

11 Looking through Coloured Shards: Words and Images in Ornela Vorpsi's Works

GIORGIA ALÙ

We live in a time obsessed by visual images: we remember, imagine, and (re)construct places, objects, people, experiences, and ourselves through images. Photographs, in particular, respond to our desire to stop, frame, and freeze the world, to possess it and secure it in space and time. Yet we live in an era of significant geographical mobility and displacement where notions of space, time, and identities are also constantly called into question in relation to the way we perceive ourselves and others visually. By the recording, display, and narration of personal and collective experiences of travel, migration, and exile, every day we are provoked and encouraged to experiment with new ways of seeing and being. What happens, then, when photographic means and products (traditional and digital) come to influence or complement tales of displacement? In what way does the writing of present and past experiences of departure reflect and respond to photographic images? How are identity, memory, and nation expressed through the interlacing of written and photographic texts? And how does what we see photographically, and then narrate, reflect gender – in particular female identity – and displacement?

In the field of Italian Studies, academic work on the relationship between photography and the genre of migration and travel literature still needs to be developed.[1] Moreover, when we look at women's writing, attention to the gendered politics of exile, decolonization, migration, and immigration has recently led scholars to explore issues surrounding the transmission of experiences and memory across spatial and generational boundaries.[2] Yet investigations focusing on women as both active and passive users of visual means – in particular photography – with regard to questions of identity and dislocation are still scarce in Italian Studies.[3]

In this chapter, I examine works by Albanian migrant writer and photographer Ornela Vorpsi and the intertwining of writing and images in her artistic production. A particular concern will be the way the act of writing and that of taking photographs interact within her experience of exile and estrangement. How does photography enter the act of her (self-)writing? And how does the preoccupation with the body inform both the content and the form of her texts? By drawing evidence from her short novels *Il paese dove non si muore mai* (*The Country Where No One Ever Dies*) and *La mano che non mordi* (*The Hand You Don't Bite*) and from her collection of short stories *Vetri rosa* (*Pink Shards*), I will analyse the interaction between words and visual images in Vorpsi's writing and her creation of a photograph-style narrative. I will then briefly examine the epistemological value of Vorpsi's photographic production and the way her photographs serve as agents of empowerment and reappropriation. Seen as a trace, the photograph begs not only for a meaning and an "intentionality" but also for a context, a before and an after that only verbal descriptions can provide.[4] The interpretation of Vorpsi's photographic work is, therefore, illuminated by her own written stories. At the same time, whether inserted in her novels, added on the covers of her books, or gathered independently in photographic volumes, her photographs are used as a space for a more intimate way of thinking about female identity, displacement, and, above all, the body.

Vorpsi was born in Tirana in 1968 during the national-communist regime of Enver Hoxha and just after the declaration of state atheism. In 1991, when she was twenty-two years old, she moved to Milan together with her mother; at the time, her father, a political dissident, was imprisoned in the Spaç gulag. She studied Arts at the Brera Academy. In 1997, she moved to Paris, where she devoted herself first to the visual arts and then to writing. In 2001, she published *Nothing Obvious*, a photographic monograph displaying a series of female nudes. *Il paese dove non si muore mai* was her first narrative text and was first published in France by Actes Sud.[5] In 2005, it was edited and published in Italian by Einaudi; the following year it won the Grinzane-Cavour Prize. In 2005, Actes Sud also published her collection of thirteen stories with the title *Buvez du Cacao Van Houten!* (*Drink Van Houten Cocoa!*)[6]. The same year, Vorpsi completed *Vetri rosa*; in 2007 Einaudi published her *La mano che non mordi* and in 2012 *Fuorimondo*.[7]

Together with Vesna Stanic (Croat), Kenka Lenkovic (Croat), Tamara Jadrejcic (Croat), Sarah Zuhra Lukanic (Croat), Bozidar Stanisic (Serbo-Croat), Ingrid Coman (Romanian), Gezim Hajdari (Albanian), Anilda Ibrahimi (Albanian), and Ron Kubati (Albanian), Vorpsi belongs to the group of authors who migrated to Italy from the Balkans, mostly during the late 1980s and early 1990s in the aftermath of the collapse of the Soviet Union.[8] Vorpsi's work belongs to that body of texts that can be broadly defined as "literature in Italian," "Italophone literature," or "migration literature."[9]

Although Vorpsi moves away from confessional "ego-documents" (typical of works produced in the early stages of migration literature in Italian) by exploring a more sophisticated way of writing, her texts are unquestionably autobiographical. The experience of the repressive socialist regime – in particular, the experience of being marked by the state's appropriation of the body and its effects – pervades the form, content, and linguistic choices of her narration. For Vorpsi, the only way to remain "inside" Albania is by looking at and framing – with words and lens – her own people and culture from a linguistic, temporal, and spatial distance. Literary and photographic practice allows Vorpsi to respond to the confining, judgmental, authoritarian gaze of the others and thereby create a site for resistance.

In a number of his writings, Michel Foucault describes domination in terms of "relations of power" and rejects the assumption that "power is a system of domination which controls everything and which leaves no room for freedom." For Foucault, instead, in all relations of power "there is necessarily the possibility of resistance" (124), which can be accomplished by returning the gaze. As stated by Frantz Fanon: "This look, from – so to speak – the place of the Other, fixes us, not only in violence, hostility and aggression, but in the ambivalence of its desire" (109). bell hooks terms this an "oppositional gaze" (94–105). For Vorpsi, agency exists if she can interrogate the insistent look of the Other on herself. In her case, however, the Other is not essentially the host culture (in this case French or Italian), as in most post-colonial and migration literature, but primarily the culture of her origins. As I will explain, from a distanced perspective, Vorpsi can interrogate and return that gaze by "seeing photographically"; through the visualization techniques she adopts, things and people appear framed, immediate, as well as blurred and uncanny, as if from the angle and viewpoint of a camera. According to Edward Weston, the photographer learns "to see his subject matter in terms of the capacities of his tools and processes" (173). Vorpsi then translates past faces, bodies, places, and objects into the photographic images she wants to make. I will argue that these images express subjectivity while at the same time claiming an observational representation of reality. In this way – in looking back and "freezing" the Other as from behind a camera – she turns Albania into the object of her own control, power, and knowledge as well as her desire. In addition, she sees herself photographically. She accomplishes this in her visual (and hallucinatory) writing and develops it further through the practice of taking material photographs and eventually looking at them. Photographs, in particular, become acts of self-extension, what Celia Lury calls "prosthetic culture" (148) following Barthes's view, the "advent of myself as other." As I will discuss, Vorpsi's photographic (self-)portraits, together with her fragmentary visual writing, are sites for cognition, for memory as well as resistance against the totalitarian – and very often phallocentric – politics of spectatorship and control.[10]

Writing Photographically

Vorpsi's first short novel, *Il paese dove non si muore mai,* consists of harsh autobiographical sketches of her childhood and adolescence during Hoxha's dictatorship in Albania. The book narrates her discovery of the world, of her female fragility, of the secrets of her own body, and of the fascinating mystery of death in a society subdued by the regime by alternating between first and third person singular. The author represents her own country as oppressed by the "Madre-Partito" (Mother-Party), whose historical materialism regulates everybody's life, and by what she calls the "questione della puttaneria" (the issue of whoring): women's beauty is seen as a sort of curse. As she reveals when talking about her experience at school and with her teacher: "Ero figlia di un condannato politico, quindi dovevo impregnarmi d'educazione comunista più degli altri perché ero a rischio, anche a causa della mia avvenenza, che mi stava conducendo alla perdizione" (19). (I was the daughter of a political prisoner, so I had to make sure that I – even more than the other students – got a good communist education. I was at risk – not only because I was pretty. It seems that I was constantly on the brink of damnation; *The Country* 16).

In Vorpsi's various stories, the spectre of *puttaneria* (whoring) haunts every aspect of women's lives. From the perspective of the totalitarian regime, beauty is an enemy of society, which must free itself from class struggle and from any aesthetic antagonism: "la bellezza non doveva turbare lo spirito. Se in una società comunista si poteva essere uguali in tutto sarebbe stato meglio" (Beauty was not allowed to upset the spirit. In a communist society it would have been better if we were all the same; "L'Albania"). This is further developed in *La mano che non mordi,* in which the female protagonist-narrator, now living in Paris, travels to Sarajevo to visit a friend; this journey also marks a return to her own Eastern European culture. Once she arrives, she becomes an object of curiosity and judgment because of her decision to live in Paris, her new manners, and her attractive appearance: "Sono diventata molto *straniera*" (I have become very *foreign*; 65, emphasis in original). She also runs the risk of becoming like her friend from Sarajevo, who after moving to Milan felt "con il corpo messo a nudo" (my body stripped of cover), "senza pelle" (skinless), with the organs "a vista d'occhio, fuori, come esposti a una mostra, tutti li possono toccare, curiosare, osservare, spostare, pizzicare" (visible, on the outside, as if on display; everybody can touch them, pry into them, observe, move and pinch them; 52). According to Abdelmalek Sayad, the immigrant discovers the "individuation" of his body as it is a "body that is socially and *aesthetically* designated as a foreign body" (204, emphasis in original). This happens both in Vorpsi's native land and in her guest country.

But Vorpsi devotes most of her pages to the insisting, penetrating, and controlling gaze that her people direct at others – especially women. In her books, secondary characters repeatedly stare at and gaze into other people's lives, their tragedies, and their bodies. This behaviour is embodied in their customs, such as the *sehir:* "Guardare gli altri, vivere nel guardare gli altri. Voluttuosità del guardare. *Big brother. Sehir* è di eredità turca" (To gaze at the others, to live by gazing at others. The voluptuousness of the gaze. Big brother. *Sehir* has got Turkish origins; *La mano* 29). This piercing, disturbing gaze of both men and women affected both her mother and herself in Albania: "Quando passi per la strada, i loro sguardi t'incrociano penetrandoti fino al midollo, così in fondo che il tuo essere diventa trasparente" (*Il paese* 8). (They stare so hard as you pass by, it's as though you're becoming transparent. As soon as you're penetrated by one of their stares, it transfixes you forever; *The Country* 4). Vorpsi draws a direct link between this intense staring and her mother's exceptional beauty:

> Mia madre è molto bella [...]. Lei passava sotto gli sguardi ammirati degli uomini e quelli invidiosi delle donne. La mostruosa invidia delle donne l'ho vista in concreto dietro di lei. Sarebbe bastato uno sguardo fatto d'amaro – di quell'acido che corrode le vene e lo stomaco – a far bruciare castelli e paesi interi. L'avrebbero spolpata o mangiata viva, l'avrebbero gettata in pasto ai cani. (*Il paese* 15)

> My mother was beautiful ... The eager eyes of our men and the jealous glances of our women following her every step down the road. I could see the envy in their eyes. There was something very bitter in them, corrosive like an acid eating through their veins and intestines. One small dose would have been enough to destroy a castle, a whole town. If they could have, they would have torn the flesh off her bones and eaten her alive ... or thrown her to the dogs. (*The Country* 12)

The verbs *penetrare, bruciare, corrodere, spolpare, mangiare* (to penetrate, to burn, to corrode, to tear the flesh off, to eat) express the moral, visual, and almost physical violation of women's bodies. The narrator's mother too is represented as a victim of her people's voyeuristic gaze and surveillance. Vorpsi, however, develops strategies to return and respond to this gaze. As an expatriate, by practising writing and visual arts, she is able to look at and frame her past from an ideal distance and thereby re-create images of her native country. As she puts it: "Sopravvivo solo con e tramite la distanza. [...] Lontano da tutto ciò che mi è vicino" (I survive only with and through distance ... Far away from everything that is near me; *La mano* 66, 86). This is also the distance of the viewer-photographer, who, simultaneously inside and outside the portrayed object, re-creates visions and projections of a world that does not physically exist in her present time and space. This distanced look manipulated in opposition to structures of domination makes resistance possible. And one way of achieving this is through a visual writing.

Vorpsi is a photographer and painter, and as she says, "Io provengo dalle arti plastiche e sono di formazione frammentaria, la mia struttura è fatta di immagini" (I come from the plastic arts; my artistic background is fragmentary and my cast of mind is visual; "L'Albania"). Thus, she fragments her narrative into images by focusing – as if through a camera lens – on specific moments and scenes. This is attained, first, through fragmentary writing and an episodic structure. In most of her books, the narrative breaks with linear chronology, disintegrating into a series of short sentences, paragraphs, and sections. Also, her short chapters often hold visual titles – for instance, in *Il paese dove non si muore mai,* "Macchie" ("Stains"), "Tuorli d'uovo" ("Egg Yolks"), "Acque" ("Water"), "Sangue rosso sulla neve bianca" ("Red Blood on White Snow"). Vorpsi's visual perception of life is particularly evident when we analyse her use of language. The Italian language epitomizes the culture she secretly idealized during childhood and becomes the means through which she can express herself creatively.

Her writing is characterized by bluntness and plain syntax, largely a consequence of writing in a language that is not her own. For instance, *La mano che non mordi* opens this way:

> Viaggiando, ho capito *profondamente* di non essere un viaggiatore. Non che prima non lo sapessi. Con il pensiero ho sempre voluto viaggiare l'intero mondo e al di là, se possibile. Con il corpo mi riusciva difficile. Mi sono detta poi che se sforzo un po' la mia carne, forse lei può trovare piacere unendosi al pensiero che ama viaggiare. Magari era solo pigrizia. Così che mi sono mossa. (3, emphasis in original)

> By travelling I have *profoundly* understood I am not a traveller. It's not that I did not know this before. With my mind I have always wanted to travel the whole world and beyond, if possible. This was difficult for my body. I have always told myself that if I force my flesh, maybe it can find some pleasure by joining the mind that loves travelling. Perhaps it was laziness. Thus I got a move on.

The transitive use of the Italian verb *viaggiare* (to travel) in the second line, the hypothetical sentence constructed with the present tense (in both the main and the dependent clause), and her beginning the last sentence with the adverb *così* (thus) without the auxiliary *essere* (to be) (for *è così*) are all imperfections that add to the starkness of her already colloquial language.[11] Italian loses its literariness and becomes essentially an instrument of austere, crude narration and resistance; its structure evokes and conjures the brutality and hardship of life in Albania under the dictatorship.

Rather than implying the loss of her origins, her adoption of Italian enables her to express feelings (anger, rebellion, grief) and stories that had been repressed.[12] Yet her use of Italian evokes distance. Only occasionally does a subtle nostalgia for the objects, foods, or smells that characterized her childhood pierce through Vorpsi's pages, as in *La mano che non mordi,* where she momentarily indulges in memories of drawers full of family objects (64), a brand of chewing gum (81), green water glasses, and the exotic aroma of hot, sweet *salep* (25) or the flavour of *byrek:* "Mastico mentre sono mangiata dai ricordi. [...] Il cibo dell'infanzia è magico: ho riempito la bocca, ho chiuso gli occhi e sento i passi della nonna dietro le spalle, l'odore dei cachi maturi, la luce forte del sole di Tirana che mi penetra le palpebre." (I chew while I am devoured by memories ... Childhood food is magic: I have filled up my mouth with it, I have closed my eyes and I can hear my grandma's steps behind my shoulders, the smell of ripe persimmons, the strong light of the sun in Tirana which penetrates my eyelids; 78). Seeing, smelling, hearing, and tasting are all present in this description together with verbs suggesting bodily possession and violation (the passive use of *mangiare* with the first person singular and the recurring use of *penetrare*). Thus, although often observational and essential, Vorpsi's language is laced with sensations and corporeality.

Julia Kristeva's concepts of the symbolic and the semiotic can be used to highlight how sensations and the body infiltrate Vorpsi's writing. According to Kristeva, the symbolic is associated with language and separation and is understood as the linear, syntactic, and representational discourse of a socially constituted reality. The semiotic, by contrast, is controlled by the maternal influence at the pre-Oedipal stage and is characterized by the use of words for their rhythm, intonation, musicality, and irrational signification rather than for their meaning or what they represent (*Revolution* 27). In Vorpsi's stories, the bare yet grammatical language (the symbolic) interacts with the enigmatic, dreamlike narrative (the semiotic). According to Kristeva, this latter language allows the representation and verbalization of feelings and thoughts that have remained unspeakable – although close to the body – because the ordinary (native) language has not been able to express them (*Histoire d'amour* 16–17).[13] For Vorpsi, the Italian language breaks silences and taboos in the name of a subjectivity that is, nevertheless, expressed through verbal essentiality. Therefore, in her *Il paese dove non si muore mai* we read: "Ed ecco che il suo sguardo m'incenerì vestendomi di sporco" (12) (She threw me one of her withering glares, reducing me to ash, covering me with dirt; *The Country* 9); "La pancia le si era gonfiata. Togliere aveva voluto. Sangue, e poi sangue e ancora sangue le era colato tra le cosce finché si era svuotata tutta" (26) (Her belly had already swollen up. She wanted to get rid of it. Blood, blood, and more blood had flowed down her thighs until she was empty; *The Country* 23); "La gonna va stretta a Ganimete, i suoi seni negano con fierezza la gravità della terra, i capelli godono una libertà selvaggia" (42) (She always wore tight-fitting dresses, her breasts proudly resisting the force of gravity. Her hair she left loose and wild; *The Country* 40); "D'estate […] mentre il sole stuprava ogni poro della sua pelle scaldandola tutta fino al calar della sera (45)" (In the summer … while the rays of the sun raped her every pore, keeping her warm until evening; *The Country* 43). The descriptions – in particular, the verbs she chooses – convey the humiliation, violence, and isolation but also the sensuality and carnality of the female condition through a stark bodily language. As Vorpsi herself admits, the use of Italian is crucial for her to achieve a linguistic distance and to abandon abstraction: "per evitare il viscerale e il melodrammatico, per scrivere con secchezza" (to avoid the visceral and the melodramatic, to write with dryness; "Fahrenheit Radio Interview"). And this verbal "aridity," which can be identified with the "symbolic," facilitates the production of a visual, oneiric writing (the "semiotic") that has, however, been released from any sentimentality. This is also often conveyed with vivid metaphors (which for Kristeva belong to pre-verbal enunciation and are agents of the semiotic) and similes, like these: "Nella via che porta il nome di Durazzo, fa bella mostra una casa di due piani tinta di giallo ormai invecchiato. L'edera l'assale, come le vene di una mano in piena estate" (*Il paese* 42). (There was a lovely two-story house on Durrës Street – named after the town of Durrës – though the yellow plaster on its walls was crumbling in places. Ivy covered most of the façade like the veins that bulge on the backs of your hands in summer; *The Country* 40). Sentimentality is also absent when she writes of cities from her past: "A Tirana, Sarajevo e Creta, ti addolora vedere gli animali ridotti pelle e ossa, il loro ventre che cola contro la spina dorsale. Le chiazze di sangue fanno sparire il pelo. Sembra di vedere delle cartine di non so quale paese, cartine di sangue in cammino" (In Tirana, Sarajevo and Crete, it hurts to see the animals reduced to skin and bone, their bellies stuck to their backbones. Their fur is invisible under stains of blood. It is like looking at maps of some unknown country, walking maps of blood; *La mano* 17).

Imagery functions much like photographic close-ups. Vorpsi's metaphors and similes attempt to provide tangible representations of things that are not present to the senses. Like photographs, imagery offers immediacy even while claiming "objectivity." Her country and its people are also represented in these terms:

> È il paese dove non si muore mai. Fortificati da interminabili ore passate a tavola, annaffiati dal raki, disinfettati dal peperoncino delle immancabili olive untuose, qui i corpi raggiungono una robustezza che sfida tutte le prove. [...]
>
> Di polvere e fango è fatto questo paese; il sole brucia a tal punto che le foglie della vigna si arrugginiscono e la ragione comincia a liquefarsi. Da qui nasce una specie d'effetto secondario (temo irrimediabile): la megalomania, delirio che in questa flora germoglia come un'erba pazza. (*Il paese* 2)

> Albania is a country where no one ever dies. Fortified by long hours at the dinner table, irrigated by *raki*, and disinfected by the hot peppers in our plump, ever-present olives, our bodies are so strong that nothing can destroy them …
>
> This country where no one ever dies is made of clay and dust. The sun scorches it until even the leaves on the grapevines look rusty, until our minds begin to melt. Living in this environment has one inevitable side effect: megalomania – a condition that sprouts everywhere, like a weed. (*The Country* 1)

The *fortificati* (fortified), *annaffiati* (irrigated), and *disinfettati* (disinfected) bodies, the melting minds, and the final simile all provide the reader with visual effects that enrich the subject matter with other levels of meaning (just as a photograph does with the object it represents); but they also empty the representation of Albania and its people of any strong emotion.

Just as Vorpsi the photographer distances herself from events through a camera standing between her and her object, so in her written works she distances herself (in space and time) from facts and people through a language that allows her to freeze images and to be basically observational. Thus some scenes, such as those that portray brutality against women, are barely described (for instance, in *Il paese dove non si muore mai*, the young protagonist suffers under the teacher's heated metal ruler, and her mother is repeatedly beaten by her husband). In such instances, it is up to the reader to complete or reconstruct the stories. The reader is constantly left with the feeling that some detail has been deliberately omitted. On various occasions, characters are described only vaguely, remaining incomplete and blurred. As through a steamy window, they are made to appear and disappear in the text. It is the reader's task to complete their features and to bring their physical details into focus. For instance, in *Vetri rosa*, at the beginning we read that only the thought of the friendly features of a little girl could settle the protagonist's disturbed nights: "Ogni volta che mi svegliavo col cuore all'impazzata, cercavo di ricomporre nel buio il faccino di Bardha" (Every time I woke up with my heart racing, I tried to recompose Bardha's little face in the dark; 6). A few lines later we read of Nardi, a thirty-year-old man the young protagonist fell in love with when she was only six: "la sua presenza mi faceva del bene […]. Anzi, per essere più precisa, a calmarmi erano i bianchi denti di Nardi, quelli che vedevo mentre lui sorrideva" (His presence was good for me … To be precise, however, it was Nardi's white teeth that calmed me down, the ones I could see while he was smiling; 9). Years later, the protagonist meets Nardi, only to be disappointed:

> Lo riconobbi dai suoi nei [...]. Nardi rallentò e sollecitato dal mio sguardo cominciò a seguirmi. Faceva quello che fanno gli uomini quando vogliono fermare una donna per strada e chiedere un po' di sesso. Non mi aveva riconosciuta. Quel giorno Nardi per me morì. (10–11)

> I recognized him from his moles ... Nardi slowed down and encouraged by my staring started to follow me. He was doing what men normally do when they want to stop a woman in the street and ask for sex. He did not recognize me. For me that day Nardi died.

Many of Vorpsi's characters (or some of their physical features) come temporarily into view, emerging through memories of pleasure and pain only to fade away. The effect is that of precariousness. This is another photographic strategy, by means of which Vorpsi seems to keep a distance from her subjects and to interrogate them. Such appearance and disappearance, rather than distorting the representation, increases the characters' credibility. Just as a blurred photograph can be associated with directness (while an extremely sharp photograph taken with a high-tech camera may look artificial and manipulated), so the vague descriptions of her characters increase the reader's active (visual) perception of the subject.[14]

This sense of incompleteness is emphasized by the presence of bodies that, alive or dead, are often in pieces. For instance, in *Vetri rosa* a woman loses her eyeball, and in *Il paese dove non si muore mai* the protagonist's father's teeth are knocked out after a beating from the secret police, and the thighbones of an uncle shot in his youth by Madre-Partito are hidden in the garden in a terracotta amphora. Her female characters, in particular, have suffered multiple breakages because of their social and political context as well as their daily struggle and dislocation (Cattani 177–94).[15] Also suggesting fragmentation of the Self – especially of the female and expatriate identity – are frequent changes in name. In *Il paese dove non si muore mai,* the main protagonist is a young girl whose name changes continually as the story progresses: she is called Elona, Ormira, Ornela, Ina, and Eva. Through both her language and these (strongly autobiographical) female characters, the author simultaneously constructs and hides herself. According to Derrida, "there is no writing which does not devise some means of protection, to protect against itself, against the writing by which the 'subject' is himself threatened as he lets himself be written: as he exposes himself" (278–9). And it is through photographic "exposure," in fact, that her own image appears and disappears in her narrative, also with hallucinatory effects. Throughout her writing, she is all of her female characters (with different names) who come into view and then fade away.

Many of Vorpsi's narrated scenes, however, as photographs, deliver hallucinations even while delivering facts:[16]

> Le mamme ci lasciarono davanti alla porta della scuola. Là conobbi la grande solitudine. Quella piccola la conoscevo già. Conobbi l'aguzza, la spietata che ti getta contro un muro di cemento armato per poi farti giacere a terra dolore e sangue. Mamma, urlavo, mentre la sua cara visione cominciava a scomparire. […] Di nuovo contro il muro di cemento armato. Di nuovo colavo sangue e le mie ossa si frantumavano. (*Vetri rosa* 21)

> Our mothers left us in front of the school's main door. There I experienced great solitude. I had already experienced little solitude. There I met the harsh, pitiless one which flings you against a cement wall and then makes you lie on the ground, in pain and blood. Mum, I was screaming, while her beloved image faded … Again I was against the cement wall. Again my blood was oozing and my bones were crumbling.

> Allora vidi una cosa che mi fece orrore; lei piantò a un tratto un dito nel suo bell'occhio nero e cercò di farlo uscire dall'orbita. […] Senza nessun grido di dolore e con una calma sconcertante, Arta cavò fuori il suo occhio e volle regalarmelo. […]
>
> L'occhio di Arta giaceva nella mia mano. Nella confusione mentre volevo ridarglielo, il globo ruzzolò per terra. Con un rumore cristallino si aprì a metà. (*Vetri rosa* 34–5)

> Then I saw something that horrified me; she suddenly stuck her finger into her beautiful black eye and tried to take it out of its orbit … Without screaming in pain and with a disconcerting calm, Arta pulled out her eye and offered it to me as a gift …
>
> Arta's eye was lying in my hand. In the confusion when I wanted to give it back to her the eyeball tumbled down. With a crystalline sound, it split in half.

Vorpsi creates a sort of surrealist visual experience (amplified by references to vision and seeing, as in "la sua cara visione" and "occhio") that links perception and imagination, objectivity and subjectivity, the rational and the irrational, and that parallels the meeting between the Kristevan symbolic and semiotic.[17]

This perspective is also constructed through some of her main characters. These are usually women and young girls (as already seen in the case of her first book) who observe, scrutinize, and narrate their own lives and those of others. In particular, one main character should be considered: a dead girl. In *Vetri rosa,* death needs to be understood as an oneiric, privileged status. It is by looking at life from this position that everything that was originally forbidden or stolen can be claimed back and made to reappear mysterious, fascinating, and desirable: sexuality, the body, childhood, adolescence, solitude, and death itself. From this strategic position, things, people, and events are observed with detachment and fascination, as well as through random changes of focus, as if looking through a kaleidoscope. At the beginning of the book, Vorpsi writes:

> La morte è pacifica, ti lascia l'animo in quiete e, se vuoi, puoi essere un ottimo osservatore. Da morti non si ha più paura di dire quello che si pensa. Il pensiero è oggettivo perché si è distaccati dal terrestre. Sono un perfetto spettatore. Niente fa male, contemplo solo come da bambini si contemplano i disegni luminosi e geometrici che creano il movimento del caleidoscopio nelle mani. Così faccio ruotare piano i vetri colorati della mia esistenza. Preferisco quando la geometria dei disegni è bagnata dal colore rosa. Dai vetri rosa. In questo punto mi fermo sempre un po' più a lungo. Ho l'eternità per scrutare, è vero, stato che non mi annoia perché è uno spettacolo che cambia di continuo. (7)

> Death is tranquil; it leaves your heart at peace, and, if you so wish, you can be a very good observer. Once dead, you are no longer afraid to say what you think. Your thoughts are objective because you are detached from earthly things. I am a perfect spectator. Nothing hurts; I just gaze, just like children who contemplate the luminous, geometric patterns created by the movement of the kaleidoscope in their hands. In this way, I slowly turn the coloured shards of my existence. I prefer it when the geometry of the patterns is tinted rose. When the shards are pink. At this point, I always linger a bit. It is true that I have all eternity to contemplate it and this does not bore me, because it is an ever changing spectacle.

Like her first work, *Vetri rosa* – a sort of pamphlet – focuses on childhood and adolescence in Albania. As already mentioned, this is, however, characterized by a recurrent hallucinatory atmosphere. Its structure is even more fragmented than *Il paese dove non si muore mai,* for there are no clear connections among the various episodes, each only a few pages long. They are titled "Purgatorio" ("Purgatory"), "Giochi" ("Games"), "Il colore blu" ("The Colour Blue"), "Lenzuolo bianco" ("White Sheet"), "Vasco" ("Vasco"), "Arta" ("Arta"), and "Ritrovi" ("Reunions"). In *Vetri rosa* the main protagonist and narrator is a dead seventeen-year-old girl. At the beginning of the book, in the passage quoted above, she presents herself as a privileged spectator of things and facts. Her stained shards function like an enchanted lens through which she can select, filter, capture, colour, and scrutinize the world: family, young friends, prohibited sensual games, first love, school, and the demise of a grandmother. To the (immobile) observer, people and things appear in endless, complex, and variegated patterns. They also seem to belong to a time past; in Barthes's famous phrase, to a *what has been*. They set up a relationship between the viewer in the present and the past moment of space or time that they are supposed to represent. People and things are, nevertheless, traces left by the disappearance of something else. They are traces leaving "the illusion of a particular object shining forth, the image of which becomes an impenetrable enigma" (Baudrillard, *Within the Horizon* 131). It is from the radical exception of this enigma that one can enjoy an "unobstructed vision of the world" (131).[18] Characters and events in *Vetri rosa* appear as if suspended between reality and reverie.

Much like photographic images (as understood by Baudrillard), each scene in *Vetri rosa,* rather than representing or illustrating events, is an event in itself; the reader does not know if it happened or precisely when, as we are not given any information about the time of each fact narrated. Such a fragment of life conveys strangeness and distance; every scene remains "a fiction and hence echo[s] the unaccountable fiction of the event" (Baudrillard, *The Intelligence* 99). Furthermore, the coloured shards as the mirrors of the kaleidoscope, or even photographic lens, function like a screen behind which the viewer can examine, "freeze," and oppose her gaze to the Other undisturbed.

Photographs of Selfhood

As Vorpsi stresses on various occasions, the idea of beauty as evil is also rooted in the spirit of her people, in its "machismo" and "istinto di proprietà molto sviluppato" (its very developed ownership instinct;

"L'Albania"). Unfortunately, abroad, the condition of women is not exactly how the protagonist had imagined. At the end of *Il paese dove non si muore mai*, the young protagonist escapes with her mother to Italy, where she soon learns that the country of her dreams is a land of disappointment and dislocation, another place where women – especially if they are foreigners – are essentially seen as sexual objects (*Il paese* 108–10). Nevertheless, it is outside Albania that beauty, rather than being a crime, can be slowly transformed into an agent of reaction and knowledge: rediscovering the beauty and mysteries of life and of the body through the arts, especially the figurative ones, is a way to respond to the uncertainty, prohibitions, and confinement of the past.

The structure and codes of the written language – the inseparability of the semiotic from the symbolic – can prevent the female artist from fully expressing herself and her individuality. Material photographs, by contrast, can provide a non-verbal totality and a space where the artist, through embodiment, can further express and develop her own subjectivity.[19] It can be argued that in Vorpsi's artistic productions, the photograph, being both instantaneous and indexical (unlike the word, which is symbolic), provides a locus for a new self-identity based on reiteration and performativity. Through photography, the displaced woman can express her uniqueness. According to Lury, subjectivity results from a mimetic experimental and sensual relationship with the visual; this is "a metonymic relation operating both within and outside representation, within and outside the frame" (5). Mimesis here is intended as self-extension conceived in terms of performativity. According to Lury, identity is thus performative in relation to a process occurring as a result of and subsequent to the encounter with the photographic image (31–6). I am applying this to Vorpsi in relation both to the process of taking photographs (i.e., choosing subject, setting, pose, light, focus, and angle) and to the act of looking at the final product. Vorpsi is simultaneously the maker and the viewer of her works. These photographs mirror her image back to her and become a prosthetic extension of her Self; they allow her as an individual to reconfigure her identity experimentally. In this way, she lives inside the photographs and their constructed space.

Vorpsi's photographs are either self-portraits or portraits of (usually) her female friends. The images in her first photographic book, *Nothing Obvious*, and in the photographs added at the end of *Vetri rosa* are female nudes. Female bodies appear decentralized and multiplied; they are curled up in wooden boxes (see *Figure 11.1*), next

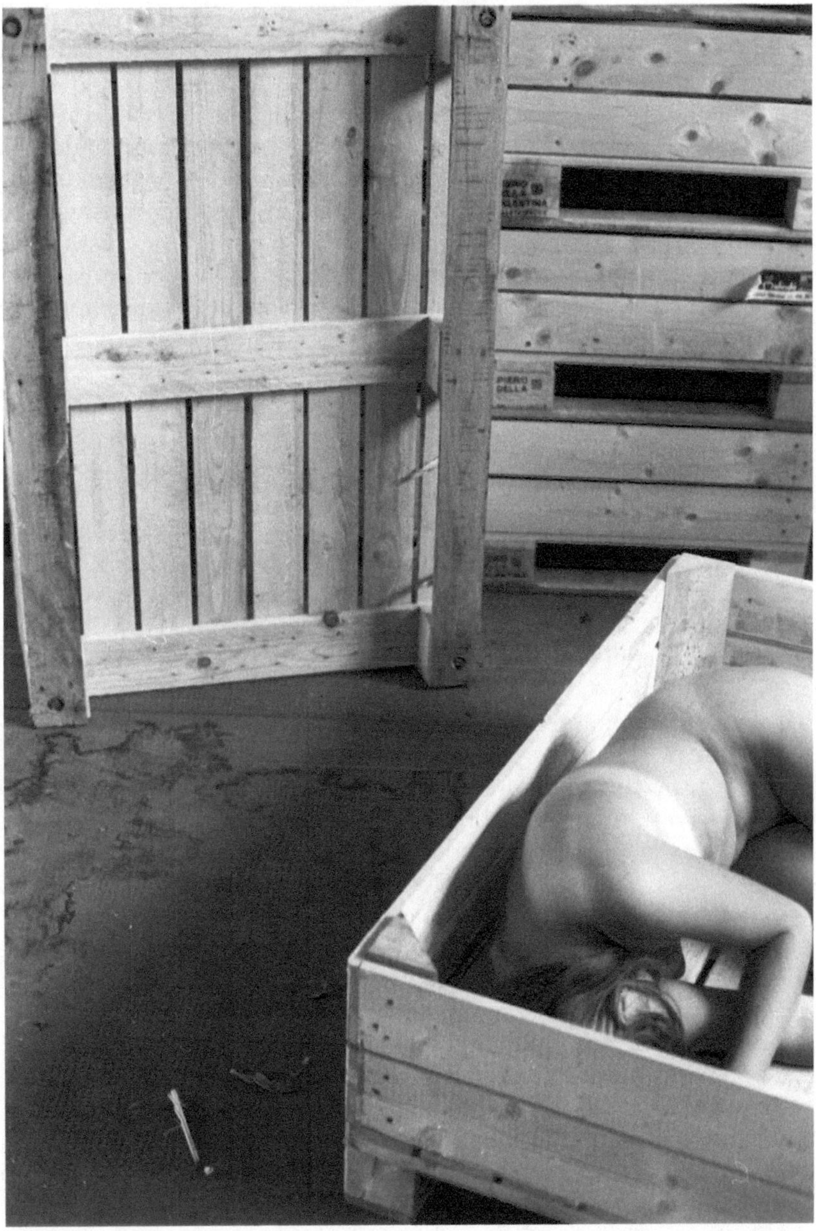

Figure 11.1 Ornela Vorpsi. "Pomeriggi." In *Vetri rosa*, 40. © Ornela Vorpsi.

to windows, against walls, or on stairs, or they are laid down in empty industrial buildings or in bedrooms, bathrooms, or other unidentified places.

Some of these images are in black and white (like the ones added as a coda in *Vetri rosa*); others are characterized by lush colours. Red, in particular, recurs in her pictures – in dresses, in details, or surrounding the figures with a blurred patina – reflecting the frequent references to blood in her books. This is the colour of the Albanian flag, of physical and psychological suffering, of patriotism, and of the partisans' resistance to dictatorship. At the same time, in Vorpsi's photographs the colour red refers primarily to childhood dreams and desire:

> I nostri ideali erano rossi [...] la rivoluzione e il sangue degli eroi era rosso. [...] Se mi chiedevo che colore mi piaceva quando ero piccola, vedevo tutto rosso. Rosso era il colore per eccellenza che ci portava verso il paradiso, era il colore degli ideali. ("L'Albania")

> Our ideals were red ... the revolution and our heroes' blood was red ... If I asked myself which had been my favourite colour as a child, everything I saw was red. Red was the colour *par excellence* which led us to heaven. It was the colour of our ideals.

Thus, in a photograph titled "Le ali di Chiara" ("Chiara's Wings"), we see a pair of red wings painted on the body of a woman turned towards a wall; this is used as the illustration on the cover of *La mano che non mordi*. In another photograph included in *Nothing Obvious*, a female body is lying on a wooden floor, her waist and face covered by a bright red drape (see *Figure 11.2*). The body, in an abandoned pose, occupies the right side of the image, and a dark shadow also partly covers it. It can be interpreted as a remaking of the past and of those ideals that enforced silence on women and feared their corporeality. At the same time, it is an act of repossession and a response to repressive experiences through a physicality that expresses both agency (that of the photographer and of the subject herself) and power.

Personal experiences need to be othered in order to be repossessed. Photography facilitates such a transfer into otherness through a process of re-envisioning and remaking. Through a performative relationship with photography, the artist can retake possession of her own female and exiled body and redefine her own identity as a woman, an Albanian, and a migrant.

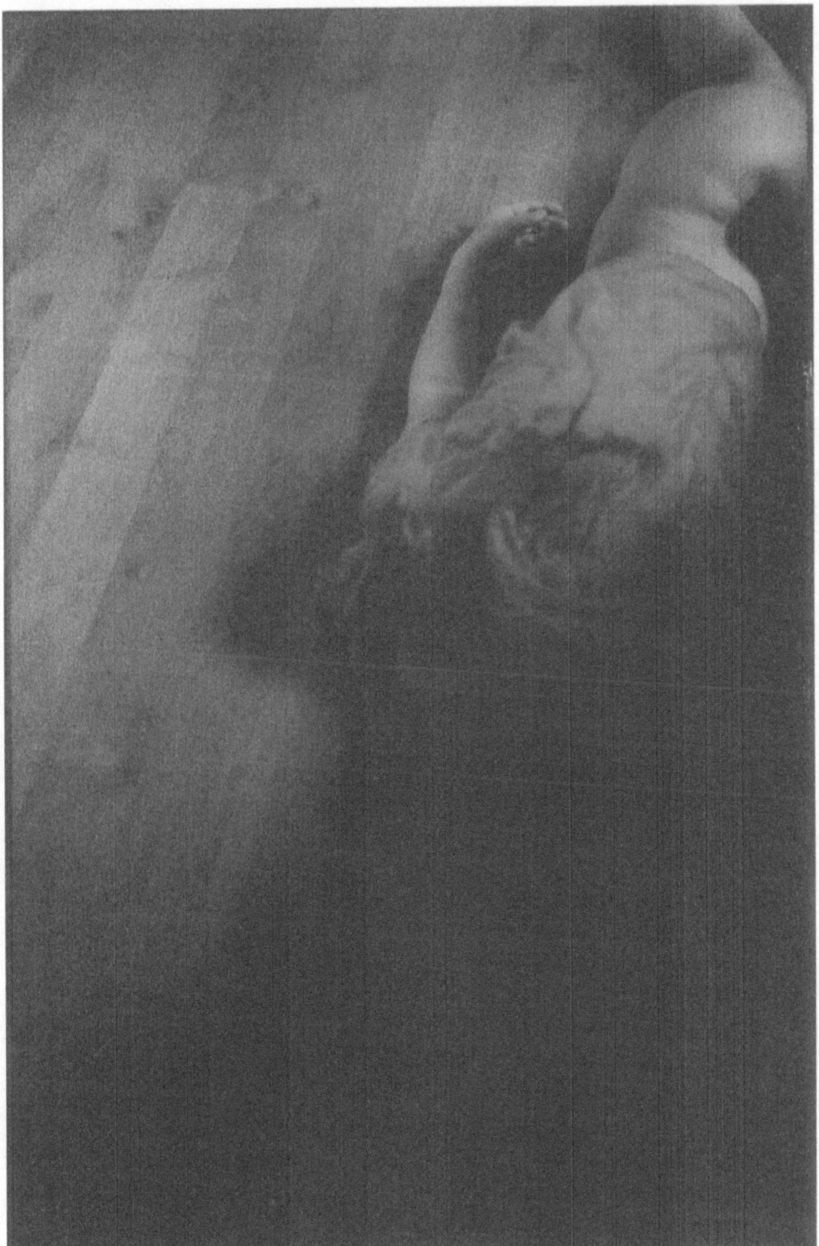

Figure 11.2 Ornela Vorpsi. In *Nothing Obvious.* © Ornela Vorpsi.

Such a remaking, however, implies a new appearance. According to Baudrillard in his controversial reflection on photography: "Whatever one brings into being in the domain of production will never be more than the image of oneself, an extension of the Same" (*Art and Artefact* 28). Baudrillard continues by explaining that "only that which comes from the domain of disappearance (from one's disappearance), is truly Other" (28). Thus, every photograph is a trace that marks the absence or "death" of a living body. Barthes wrote that "every photograph is this catastrophe" (*Camera Lucida* 96). Photographs outlive their subjects and present us with an absence. Every photograph points to its absent double and becomes "the advent of [one]self as other: a cunning dissociation of consciousness from identity" (12). Yet it is this disappearance or death that allows Vorpsi photographer-viewer, as in her written stories, to accomplish an act of reconquest and empowerment. Absence or loss implies a new appearance; this is a new body that, as Other – with all the experiences, foreignness, and trauma it embodies – is made distant and thus desirable. Vorpsi can reconcile her Albanian identity with her foreignness.

In these photographs, corporeality is emphasized so that the body can reacquire authority in opposition to its social and political suffocation. Bodies are presented in their beauty, as both flexible and fragile; they are not fixed in time and space. Their partial or multiplied appearance points to their resistance. Agency thus also rests with the subject. Decentred or out of focus, like the hazy, fragmented characters in Vorpsi's stories, these bodies compel the viewer's involvement in a process of remaking and repositioning. In this way, Vorpsi's visual images are part of a private performance whose intent is to respond to the surveillance of the socialist dictatorship as well as to the host country's scrutiny over her female foreign body. As noted earlier, in Vorpsi's books words are signs of exile, female oppression, and body fragmentation. Her spatial and physical way of writing references the fragmented Self of the female migrant. In her photographs, by contrast, fragmentation is not emphasized; instead, the body and its parts are multiplied and only partly displayed (see, for instance, *Figure 11.3* and *Figure 11.4*). This should be seen as an attempt to reiterate the body's acquired authority. The direct control of the photographic process and its product allows the photographer-viewer to regain power over spaces and forms:

> Today, my body belongs to me … I accept my veins and my heart and their caprices. For a fraction of a second, I am convinced that I cannot live

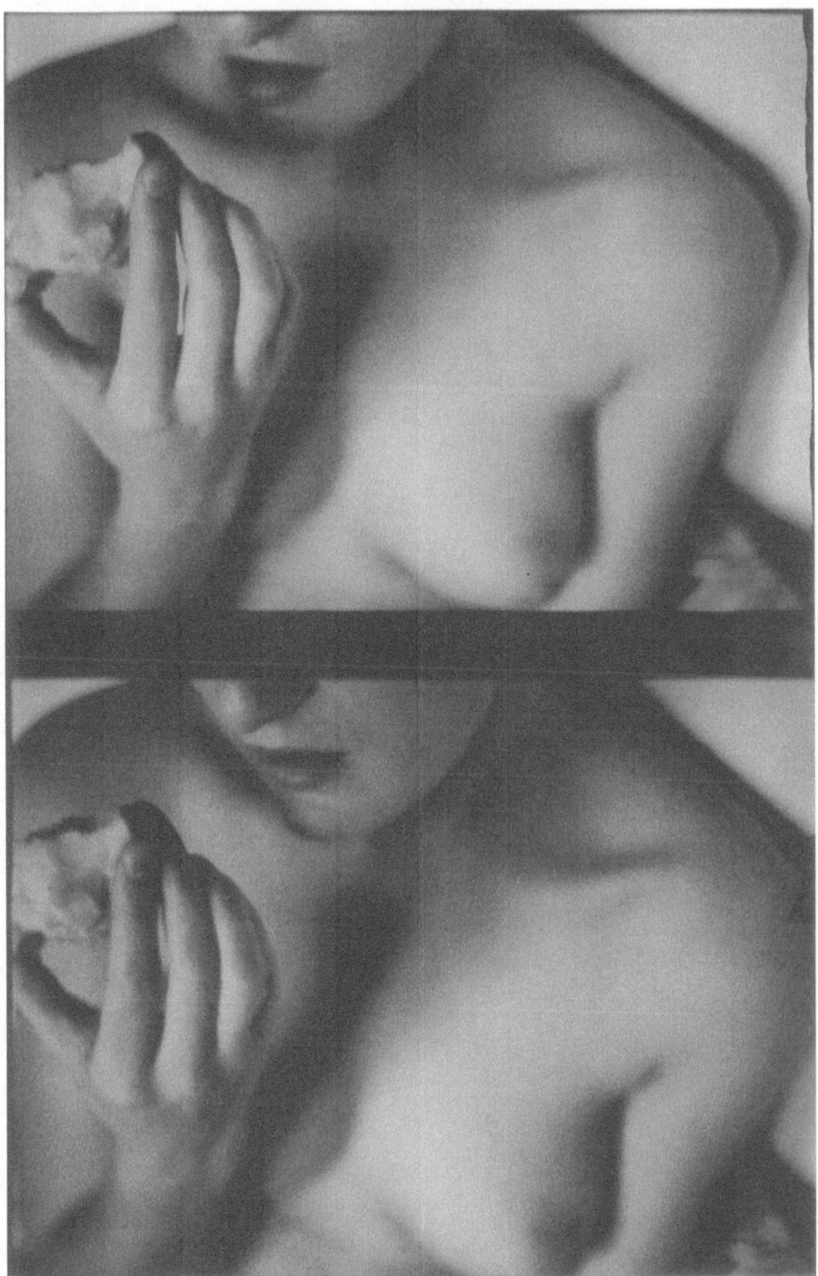

Figure 11.3 Ornela Vorpsi. In *Nothing Obvious.* © Ornela Vorpsi.

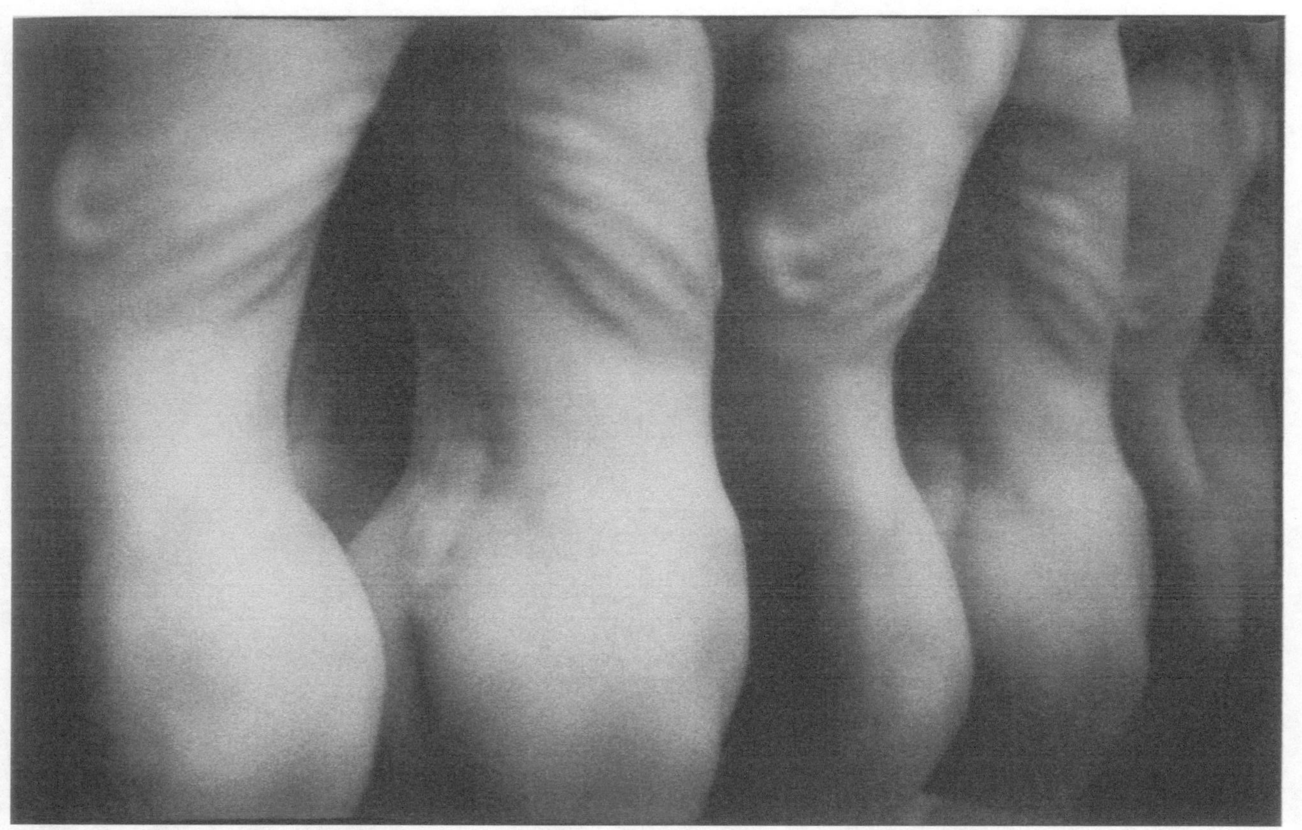

Figure 11.4 Ornela Vorpsi. In *Nothing Obvious*. © Ornela Vorpsi.

> without this vice, this useless thing that is pure egoism. [Art] is like obsessively coddling yourself, like being able to understand that you exist, like knowing you can move endlessly through open spaces and closures in a kind of madness that liberates you from the tiresome slavery of thinking. (*Nothing Obvious*, n. pag.)

Vorpsi is reclaiming her individuality, her space, and her right to define her personal identity. Consequently, in her photographs, faces rarely appear and models never meet the viewer's eye. In some of the pictures she has used as cover images for her books, the model also turns her back to the viewer. Facelessness is crucial, for if the face appears, the photograph becomes a portrait and invites viewers to capture the represented subject. Hiding the face not only accentuates a sense of intangibility and suspension but also facilitates the artist's alternative self-views (as does her characters' name changing in her books).[20]

It can be argued that through her photographic images, the author-artist enacts a repossession of her own Other; this is the otherness she brings with her as a foreigner both in a guest country and to her own culture. As Sayad has observed, emigrants are accused of "having lost their souls," of having been "deculturized" and "depersonalized" and, consequently, of "making their communities, their society or their nation lose their souls" (126). For instance, in *La mano che non mordi* the protagonist is accused by her own people of having become "verde di migrazione" (green by migration). This is "il verde della denutrizione, quello tipico di chi ha le radici in aria" (the green colour of malnutrition, typical of one whose roots are in the air; 51).

Vorpsi's photographs, then, are also a response to such accusations, in that they produce spaces where, through embodiment, memories and personal experiences are reassembled and empowered. Moreover, through photographs, the artist re-presents and re-writes (with light) her Self. In this way, she repositions herself as reading and viewing subject: she can recognize, accept, and empower herself both in the other and *as* the Other.

Conclusion: Dissolving Borders

For Kristeva, moving from one country to another, like femininity, implies both dealing with estrangement and renegotiating borders (A.-M. Smith 78–9).[21] The female expatriate subject is an "in-betweener," positioned simultaneously outside and inside things and facts. Vorpsi's artistic production can be understood as an attempt to deal with this condition by blending experiences. She achieves this by dissolving the borders between writing and photography. Indeed, her blurred photographs seem to refer to the blurring of boundaries between words and images, between the inside and outside position of an observer of familiar things, between the presence and the absence of the exiled, between the Other and the Self.

We need to perceive Vorpsi's language and photographic images as correlative to and communicating with one another. Both her words and her images challenge modes of spectatorship. Her books and photographs are built around a challenge to release corporeality from political and social restrictions and to retake control over others' visual appropriations.

Vorpsi's words and photographs are not, however, ambivalent means of representation, for the signifying potential of the photographs appears to be different from that of the words in her stories. In Vorpsi's writing, words and language present the author's transgressive subject position as well as her photographic perception of the world: a way of seeing and writing the Other and the Self. Through her written texts, the author can stand apart from the others and her fragmented female, migrant Self; Albania and the past are envisioned, recorded, and read from a distant perspective. Only in this way can life be repossessed.

The task of reconstructing and locating such a fragmented Self is, concurrently, carried out through silent photographic means. Vorpsi's photographs need to be culturally and epistemologically understood through her own words. It is through their non-verbality, indexicality, and mimetic potential that the artist can perform and reappropriate her own individuality far from any linguistic, cultural, and social constraints.

Text and photographs, therefore, become loci where the artist can simultaneously and repeatedly observe, reorganize, and reassess her identity as a woman, an Albanian, and an expatriate. All are characterized by movements between past and present, presence and absence, inside and outside, belonging and dislocation, distance and closeness, movements that stem both from her female identity and from her status of social, political, and cultural displacement.

NOTES

1 Non-Italian authors who have recently been examined for their use of and reflections on visual images in their writing about migration and exile

include W.G. Sebald (*Immigrants;* 1993); Oscar Hijuelos (*The Fourteen Sisters of Emilio Montez O'Brien;* 1994); and Yvonne Vera for her descriptions of (street and studio) photographs of Bulawayo in *Butterfly Burning* (1998) and *The Stone Virgins* (2002). In the Italian context, it is worth mentioning Younis Tawfik and his *Il profugo* (2006) as well as Ribka Sibhatu with her *Aulò: Canto poesia dell'Eritrea* (1998), which is illustrated by drawings attributed to the author and Marco Petrella.

2 For instance, see Ganguly and Saldívar-Hull. Examples of feminist work on nostalgia, memory, trauma, and practices of oral history, which are often linked to issues of exile (and the Holocaust), are Probyn, Kuhn, Hirsch, Kahane, and Caruth. See also Hirsch and Smith.

3 For one study on women's artistic production of the autobiographical occurring at the interface of visuality and textuality, see Smith and Watson. In the field of Italian Studies, recent attention has been paid to representations of women's immigration in contemporary Italian women's cinema by Luciano and Scarparo as well as Laviosa.

4 See Berger and Mohr; Price; and Scott.

5 It was translated into English in 2009. Apart from *The Country Where No One Ever Dies,* here all other translations from Italian into English are mine.

6 In 2010 this was published in Italy by Einaudi with the title *Bevete Cacao Van Houten!*

7 Among Vorpsi's distinctions are the renowned Italian literature prize Grinzane Cavour, the Premio Viareggio, the Premio Elio Vittorini, the Premio città di Vigevano and the Prix méditerranéen des Lycéens. The artist has shown her visual work at numerous exhibitions in France, Italy, Montenegro, Albania, and Belgium. In 2007–8, she lived in Berlin as a guest of the Artists-in-Berlin program of the German Academic Exchange Service.

8 Vesna Stanic left her country at the end of the 1970s. See Mauceri.

9 Consider also the term "intercultural literature" coined by Chiellino 389–90. There is no space here to expand on the different definitions and interpretations of these terms. For discussion on this phenomenon, see in particular Biasin and Gnisci, as well as Parati, *Mediterranean Crossroads.*

10 For further discussion of Vorpsi's visual narrative of estrangement and repression, see Alù.

11 For further analysis of Vorpsi's use of language, see Comberiati 215–55.

12 For Italophone writers living in Italy, the use of a language that is not their own has been explained as an effort to challenge, answer back, and resist the dominant European or Western culture by manipulating the Italian language. See Parati, "Strangers in Paradise." The acquisition and use of Italian has also been interpreted as the "precursor to the acquisition of material and cultural benefits associated with Italian and, by extension,

Europe: not so much a case of 'talking back' but talking 'up'"; Burns 127–48. Vorpsi has maintained her faithfulness to Italian although she has moved to France. Learning Italian, in her case, should be initially understood as a personal experience related to childhood dreams and hopes; later, speaking and writing in Italian became an act of self-exploration, outcry, and creativity.

13 See also A.-M. Smith 5–13.

14 See Van Gelder and Westgeest 54–63.

15 Cattani's essay may well be one of the few attempts to discuss the relationship between words and images in Vorpsi's artistic production. He too analyses Vorpsi's work through some of Kristeva's reflections on language and exile. His analysis, however, fails to highlight the further potential of photography and the way it may exceed language, in particular in relation to issues of performativity and subjectivity.

16 See Bazin, who presents a similar argument in another context (243).

17 According to Bazin, "seeing" an object is an act of collaboration between the mechanical objectivity of the photographic medium and the subjectivity of the viewer's response to the photograph. For Bazin, the surrealists managed to understand the unique potential of photography to enable an encounter between camera and viewer where the image of an object emerges in both its rationality and its irrationality. In the context of Vorpsi's books, her writing, similar to the photographic medium, stages the encounter between language and viewer-writer where the images produced stand between dream and reality.

18 See also Merrin 140.

19 As A.-M. Smith clarifies, non-verbal signifying systems can also depend on the symbolic. This happens whenever they are inscribed in a cultural framework or when language is used to talk about them (19).

20 Photographs of fragmented and multiplied bodies, functioning as a Lacanian mirror, supply a visual metaphor for the artist's fragmented and multiple Self. Haverty Rugg 1.

21 See also Kristeva, "Un nouveau" 7.

Writing with Light: Concluding Remarks

GIORGIA ALÙ AND NANCY PEDRI

Daguerre's success in fixing camera obscura images reached Italy between February and June 1839 through popular journals such as *Il Messaggiere Torinese*, *La Fama*, and *Il Politecnico*. The announcement of the new technology that came to be known as photography triggered a new literary trend: photography began supplementing and supporting literary narratives, especially through its claims to objectivity and reality. Scientific writing and then literary forms made sense of, complemented, and extended the cultural significance of this new means of visual recording. Although at times, as with any other word–image relation, photography and literature have been characterized by a "struggle for territory, a contest of rival ideologies" (Mitchell 43), from photography's inception up to today these two means of representation have been in constant dialogue within Italian literary production. With the invention of photography, which made claims to scientific truth even while exposing its own astonishing capacity to unveil new, previously unimagined worlds, literature would never again be the same.

In Italy, the attention paid to photography coincided with a new socio-economic context (a new unified nation with its contradictions and fragmentation) that encouraged writers to distance themselves from traditional literary models and from the constraints of national institutions (Dombroski 460). In this climate of change, photography entered a literary world that, although still strongly influenced by classicism, was in search of new materials and forms. Imbriani's, Valera's, De Amicis's, and Verga's fascination with photography can be seen, then, as reflecting a literature emerging from the pressures and innovations of modernity.

It should come as no surprise that photography has found one of its favourite loci in novels and short stories, two literary genres that often aim to reflect daily life. Indeed, this book has presented a variety of examples of photography intersecting with narrative prose. Since the second half of the nineteenth century, Italian writers have shared a concern with (re)presenting the real world, and photography, especially because of its indexicality (the Barthian that-has-been), seems to guarantee – at least superficially – fidelity to some sort of reality, both visual and verbal.

At the same time, however, Barthes's differentiation between *studium* and *punctum* – two different ways of being affected by a photograph, as our contributors have repeatedly reminded us – and the frequent prevailing of the latter demonstrate how difficult it is to fully control the meaning and the language of the photographic image. If the *studium* is a very general cultural element in a photograph, then the *punctum*, by contrast, is an acute effect, something that "pricks" the viewer and pierces our consciousness so that it can disturb and exceed the power of any written message. Photography, then, both in the real world and in works of literature, extends well beyond a purely documentary function to give rise to unpredictable meanings, emotions, and effects, even those related to the unreal.

As the contributors to this book have attested, the dialogue between photography and literature gives rise to worlds that are as real as they are fictional, as factual as they are fantastic. Photographic images and language long ago established their ability to influence literary writing in Italy by suggesting further imaginary, emotional, linguistic, and stylistic possibilities. As our authors have demonstrated, writing with light challenges literary realism even while often collapsing photographic authenticity and objectivity. The encounter between photography and literary writing opens the door to new representations of life. Each of the texts, literary or visual, analysed in this volume is enriched or completed by a further point of view (i.e., by means of words in a photograph or a photograph in a book) that multiplies or expands objects, events, places, and people. Spectral, visionary, ambiguous, fragmentary, unreliable, distorted, and temporally and spatially displacing are some of the adjectives the contributors have adopted to define photography and the act of seeing. Counter-intuitively, these adjectives suggest that in Italian literature, photography often makes reality appear more immaterial, dreamy, hallucinatory, unexpected, unreachable, and exceptional than is commonly supposed. As Michael North reminds us, "photography is a kind of modern writing … neither linguistic nor pictorial but hovering in a kind of utopian space between, where the informational utility of writing meets the immediacy of sight" (4). It is up to the individual to accept it or refuse it, as in the case of the protagonist in Del Giudice's novel, who eventually decides to rely solely on literature.

This suggests why issues of realism, objectivity, and indexicality have often arisen in this book, as they frequently do in other Western literatures, whose encounter with photography has long been a topic of analysis and passionate discussion among diverse critics. What has come into view here, however, is the particularity of the Italian case, a particularity that lies in the way such questions link up with the powerful Italian aesthetic and visual perspective (as also expressed by Verdicchio) within a narrative prose that reflects the diversity of Italian culture and the complexities of Italian literary history. Taken together, the essays have shown that the relationship between literature and photography in Italy has not simply been a response to social and cultural changes since the advent of photography. It has also been evolving in relation to specific and more personal literary and aesthetic expressions. Their coming together has created a narrative universe that crosses genres and disciplinary borders and that experiments with forms and formats. The union of photography and literature has given rise to changes in imaginative reproduction that are now challenging established categories. Our authors have detailed how their encounter has evolved from Imbriani's extravagant, hybrid fiction that breaks with literary canons in post-unification Italy to Verga's and Capuana's visual modality within *verismo*, from the photo-literary works of Crocenzi and Giacomelli and the imaginative vision of Vittorini in postwar Italy to De Carlo's, Tabucchi's, De Luca's, and Del Giudice's postmodern, minimalist responses to society and notions of the real, up to Vorpsi's writing, which is representative of the changing, transnational boundaries of Italy's culture.

This book does not claim to have discovered a new field of study, nor does it pretend to have reached a consensus on how the interaction between photography and Italian literature should be studied. Instead, it has begun to chart a field that has been neglected in Italian Studies despite the diversity and abundance of material being produced in Italy. In the hope of joining and complementing other studies that focus on photography's role in a given national literature, this collection has begun to trace out and accentuate what is unique to Italy's encounter between photography and literature.

We hope the essays in this book have challenged theories about the interaction between literary works and photography in Italy and stimulated new ones. We contend that further avenues of exploration in this field are necessary. There is, for instance, a strong need to conduct a more systematic and critical study of the interactions between these two representational modes within a specific period or within particular regions in the Italian cultural and literary panorama. Such an approach would elucidate the interrelations among photography, literature, and the sociohistorical context in which the two modes are perceived. It would also enrich our understanding of the histories of photography and literature and their strong intersection. This methodology would be of particular interest to those who wish to study the impact of digital photographic technology on contemporary Italian literature.

In terms of critical approaches, Martino's contribution on Moravia's *L'uomo che guarda* suggests it would be worthwhile to resort to translation theory to investigate the function of photography in literature – and the related issues of objectivity and realism, similarity and resemblance. This neglected methodology would shed light on the particular language of both modes; but most importantly, it may lead to a theoretically sound framework for something that many word-and-image experts suspect: that a new language requiring a new literacy comes into being where photography and literature meet.

With regard to genre, much work needs to be done exploring the role photography has played in particular literary genres, such as poetry, the short story, and theatre, and in intermedial genres such as opera, film, and comics. Although genre studies may seem outdated, given the postmodern penchant for border crossing, more and more studies are surfacing that approach genre not only as influencing composing and reading processes but also as impacting issues of narrative authority and persuasion, both of which are at the heart of many of the essays in this book. A different way of conceptualizing genre would be to study the use of photography in (for instance) Italian travel literature, migration literature, and colonial and post-colonial literature. Such studies would be welcome additions to work done in English, French, and German contexts.

Thematic studies would also contribute much. The contributors have shown that the meeting of writing and photography has responded to forms of desire and affect as well as to questions of identity, memory, and location. Further thematic studies focused, for example, on questions of displacement and nostalgia would also contribute much to this growing field of study, as would studies that examine ekphrasis or what has been referred to as "impossible photographs."

It is evident from this brief and incomplete list that the discussion is still very much open. We strongly encourage further research that will unravel the encounter between literature and photography in Italy.

Bibliography

Abbott, Berenice. "Photography at the Crossroads." 1951. Trachtenberg 179–84.

Abruzzese, Alberto. "Il letterato nell'era tecnologica." *Letteratura italiana: Produzione e consumo*. Ed. Alberto Asor Rosa. Vol. 2. Turin: Einaudi, 1983. 449–71.

Abruzzese, Alberto, and Carlo Grassi. "Il nuovo immaginario." *Letteratura italiana. Storia e geografia: L'età contemporanea*. Ed. Alberto Asor Rosa. Vol. 3. Turin: Einaudi, 1989. 1177–222.

Adams, Timothy Dow. "Light Writing and Life Writing: Autobiography and Photography." *Modern Fiction Studies* 40.3 (1994): 459–92.

–. *Light Writing & Life Writing: Photography in Autobiography*. Chapel Hill: U of North Carolina P, 2000.

Agamben, Giorgio. *Infanzia e storia: Distruzione dell'esperienza e origine della storia*. 1978. Turin: Einaudi, 2001.

Agosti, Stefano. "L'immagine, la scrittura." *Libri nuovi* VIII (June 1976): 3.

Ajello, Epifanio. "Guido Gozzano: La foto che non c'è." Dolfi, *Letteratura*. Vol. 2. 331–44.

–. *Il racconto delle immagini: La fotografia nella modernità letteraria italiana*. Pisa: ETS, 2009.

Albertazzi, Silvia, and Ferdinando Amigoni, eds. *Guardare oltre: Letteratura, fotografia e altri territori*. Rome: Meltemi, 2008.

Alighieri, Dante. *La divina commedia*. Milan: Mondadori, 1966–7. Electronic edition http://www.liberliber.it/mediateca/libri/a/alighieri/la_divina_commedia/pdf/la_div_p.pdf.

Alù, Giorgia. "Resistance Written and Imaged: The Distancing Visual Narrative of Ornela Vorpsi." *Journal of Romance Studies* 14.1 (Spring 2014): 1–18.

Ammirati, Maria Pia. *Il vizio di scrivere: Letture su Busi, De Carlo, Del Giudice, Pazzi, Tabucchi e Tondelli*. Soveria Mannelli: Rubbettino, 1991.

Amodeo, Fabio, Antonio Giusa, and Raffaella Turrin, eds. *Luigi Crocenzi: Un racconto per immagini*. Spilimbergo, Catalogue of the Exhibition. Spilimbergo: Centro di Ricerca e Archiviazione della Fotografia (C.R.A.F), 2003.

Andreoli, Annamaria. *D'Annunzio*. Rome: Il Mulino, 2004.

Antonelli, Sergio. "Il primo Vittorini." *Belfagor* 10.1 (31 Jan. 1955): 89–91.

Antonello, Pierpaolo. "Microfisica del racconto." *Nuova Corrente* 115 (1995): 129–46.

Arago, Dominique François. "Report on the Commission of the Chamber of Deputies." 1839. Trachtenberg 15–26.

Armstrong, Carol. *Scenes in a Library: Reading the Photograph in the Book*. Cambridge: MIT P, 1998.

Armstrong, Nancy. *Fiction in the Age of Photography: The Legacy of British Realism*. Cambridge: Harvard UP, 2002.

Arvigo, Tiziana. "Uno sguardo su Tabucchi." *Nuova Corrente* 115 (1995): 91–112.

Asor Rosa, Alberto. "Il neorealismo o il trionfo del narrativo." 1983. *Cinema e letteratura del neorealismo*. Ed. Giorgio Tinazzi and Marina Zancan. Venice: Marsilio, 1990. 79–102.

Attridge, Derek. "Roland Barthes's Obtuse, Sharp Meaning and the Responsibilities of Commentary." *Writing the Image after Roland Barthes*. Ed. Jean-Michel Rabaté. Philadelphia: U of Pennsylvania P, 1997. 77–89.

Austin, John Langshaw. *How to Do Things with Words*. Ed. J.O. Urmson and Marina Sbisà. Cambridge: Harvard UP, 1975.

Baer, Ulrich. *Spectral Evidence: The Photography of Trauma*. 2002. Cambridge: MIT P, 2005.

Baetens, Jan. "Conceptual Limitations of Our Reflection on Photography: The Question of 'Interdisciplinarity.'" Elkins, *Photography Theory* 53–73.

Baetens, Jan, Diarmuid Costello, et al. "The Art Seminar." 2005. Conversation. Elkins, *Photography Theory* 129-203

Baetens, Jan, and Mireille Ribière. *Time, Narrative and the Fixed Image*. Amsterdam: Rodopi, 2001.

Bakhtin, Mikhail. *Problems of Dostoevsky's Poetics*. 1984. Ed. and trans. Caryl Emerson. Minneapolis: U of Minnesota P, 2003.

Baldwin, Gordon. *Looking at Photographs: A Guide to Technical Terms*. Los Angeles: J. Paul Getty Museum, 1991.

Barbu, Zevedei. "'Chosisme': A Socio-Psychological Interpretation." *European Journal of Sociology* 4 (1963): 127–47.

Barone, Mario. "Piccole immagini di un uomo normale." *L'Ora* 26 June 1981: 3.

Barthes, Roland. *Camera Lucida: Reflections on Photography*. Trans. Richard Howard. New York: Hill and Wang, 1981.

–. *La chambre claire: Note sur la photographie*. Paris: Gallimard-Seuil, 1980.
–. "Le Message Photographique." 1961. *L'obvie et l'obtus: Essais critiques III*. Paris: Seuil, 1982. 5–21.
–. "The Photographic Message." *Image / Music / Text*. Trans. Stephen Heath. New York: Hill and Wang, 1977. 15–31.
–. "Rhetoric of the Image." 1964. Trachtenberg 269–85.
Batchen, Geoffrey. *Burning with Desire: The Conception of Photography*. Cambridge: MIT Press, 1999.
–. "*Camera Lucida*: Another Little History of Photography." Kelsey and Stimson 76–91.
Baudelaire, Charles. "The Modern Public and Photography." 1859. Trachtenberg 83–90.
Baudrillard, Jean. *Art and Artefact*. Ed. Nicholas Zurbrugg. Brisbane, Australia: Institute of Modern Art, 1997.
–. *The Intelligence of Evil or the Lucidity Pact*. London: Berg, 2005.
–. *Within the Horizon of the Object: Objects in This Mirror Are Closer Than They Appear. Photographs 1985–1998*. Ed. P. Weibel. Graz: Hatje Cantz, 1999.
Bazin, André. "The Ontology of the Photographic Image." 1945. Trachtenberg 237–44.
Belpoliti, Marco. "Belpoliti a Giorgio Messori, 13 gennaio 1995." Ed. Marco Belpoliti and Elio Grazioli. *Riga 8. Italia* (1995): 205–9.
Benjamin, Walter. *Gesammelte Schriften*. Ed. Rolf Tiedemann and Hermann Schweppenhäuser. Frankfurt am Main: Suhrkamp Verlag, 1982–9.
–. *Illuminations*. 1973. Ed. Hannah Arendt. London: Fontana, Collins, 1982.
–. *Opere di Walter Benjamin*. Ed. Giorgio Agamben. Turin: Einaudi, 1982–93.
–. "A Short History of Photography." 1931. Trachtenberg 199–216.
–. *Walter Benjamin: Selected Writings*. Ed. Howard Eiland and Michael Jennings. 4 vols. Cambridge: Belknap Press of Harvard UP, 1996–2003.
–. *The Work of Art in the Age of Its Technological Reproducibility, and Other Writings on Media*. Ed. Michael W. Jennings, Brigid Doherty, and Thomas Y. Levin. Cambridge: Belknap Press of Harvard UP, 2008.
–. "The Work of Art in the Age of Mechanical Reproduction." *Illuminations*. New York: Schocken, 1968. 217–52.
Berger, John. "Courbet and the Jura." 1980. Dyer 330–5.
–. "Understanding a Photograph." 1972. Dyer 216–18.
–. *Ways of Seeing*. London: Penguin, 1972.
Berger, John, and Jean Mohr. *Another Way of Telling*. New York: Vintage, 1982.
Bernard, Claude. *An Introduction to the Study of Experimental Medicine*. New York: Dover, 1957.

Bertelli, Carlo, and Giulio Bollati, eds. *Storia d'Italia. Annali 2. L'immagine fotografica, 1845–1945.* Vol. 2. Turin: Einaudi, 1979.

Bertone, Giorgio. *Lo sguardo escluso: L'idea di paesaggio nella letteratura occidentale.* Novara: Interlinea, 2000.

Biasin, Gian Paolo. *Le periferie della letteratura.* Ravenna: Longo, 1997.

Biasutti, Renato. *Il paesaggio terrestre.* Turin: UTET, 1962.

Biondi, Mario. "Non scendete da quel treno." *L'Unità* 21 May 1981: 9.

Bizzarri, Giorgio, and Eleonora Bronzoni, eds. *Esplorazioni sulla via Emilia: Vedute nel paesaggio.* Milan: Feltrinelli, 1986.

Blair, Sara. *Harlem Crossroads: Black Writers and the Photograph in the Twentieth Century.* Princeton: Princeton UP, 2007.

Bogardus, Ralph F. *Pictures and Texts: Henry James, A.L. Coburn and New Ways of Seeing in Literary Culture.* Ann Arbor: U of Michigan P, 1984.

Bollati, Giulio. "Note su fotografia e storia." Bertelli and Bollati 5–59.

Bonesio, Luisa. *Paesaggio, identità e comunità tra locale e globale.* Reggio Emilia: Diabasis, 2007.

Bordini, Carlo. "Perché abbiamo deciso di fare queste giornate." Io non sogno mai. Scrittura e sguardo in Giorgio Messori. Conference. Università La Sapienza, Roma. 23–4 Feb. 2010. Address.

Bovo, Luigi, et al. "Italia religiosa: L'oggi del prete." *Rocca. Quindicinale della pro civitate christiana* 1 (Oct. 1968): 28–33.

Brady, Emily. *The Aesthetics of Natural Environment.* Edinburgh: Edinburgh UP, 2003.

Brunet, François. *Photography and Literature.* London: Reaktion, 2009.

Brunetta, Gian Piero. *Spari nel buio. La letteratura contro il cinema italiano: Settant'anni di stroncature memorabili.* Venice: Marsilio, 1994.

Bryant, Marsha, ed. *Photo-Textualities: Reading Photographs and Literature.* Newark: U of Delaware P; London: Associated UP, 1996.

Burns, Jennifer. "Language and Its Alternatives in Italophone Migrant Writing." *National Belongings: Hybridity in Italian Colonial and Postcolonial Culture.* Ed. Jacqueline Andall and Derek Duncan. Oxford and New York: Peter Lang, 2010. 127–48.

Cacciari, Massimo. "Il 'fotografico' e il problema della rappresentazione." *Le idee della fotografia: La riflessione teorica dagli anni Sessanta a oggi.* Ed. Claudio Marra. Milan: Mondadori, 2001. 340–4.

Calvino, Italo. "L'avventura di un fotografo." *Gli amori difficili.* Milan: Mondadori, 1993. 49–64.

–. "Cinema and the Novel." *The Uses of Literature: Essays.* San Diego: Harcourt, 1986. 74–80.

–. "La follia del mirino." *Saggi: 1945–1985.* Ed. M. Barenghi. Vol. 2. Milan: Mondadori, 1995. 2218–21.
–. Introduzione. *Treno di panna.* By Andrea De Carlo. Turin: Einaudi, 1981. 3–4.
–. *Palomar.* 1983. Milan: Mondadori, 1994.
–. *The Path to the Nest of Spiders.* Trans. Archibald Colquhoun. New York: Ecco, 1985.
–. "Il rovescio del sublime." *Collezioni di sabbia. Saggi. 1945–1985.* Ed. Mario Barenghi. Vol. 1. Milan: Mondadori, 1995. 573–9.
–. "Visibilità." *Lezioni americane: Sei proposte per il prossimo millennio.* Milan: Mondadori, 2002. 91–110.
–. "Vittorini. Progettazione e letteratura." *Il menabò* 10. Turin: Einaudi, 1967. 73–95.
Capuana, Luigi. *Scritti critici.* Ed. Ermanno Scuderi. Naples: Giannotta, 1972.
–. *Semiritmi.* Ed. Enrico Ghidetti. Naples: Guida, 1972.
Caraion, Marta. *Pour fixer la trace: Photographie, littérature et voyage au milieu du XIXe siècle.* Genève: Librairie Droz, 2003.
Carli, Enzo, ed. *Giacomelli: La forma dentro. Fotografie 1952–1995.* Senigallia, Rocca Roveresca, Catalogue of the Exhibition. Milan: Charta, 1995.
Carpi, Leone. *L'Italia vivente: Studi sociali.* Milan: Vallardi, 1878.
Carteggio Verga-Capuana. Ed. Gino Raya. Palermo: Edizioni dell'Ateneo, 1984.
Caruth, Cathy. *Unclaimed Experience: Trauma, Narrative and History.* Baltimore: Johns Hopkins UP, 1996.
Cassanelli, Roberto. "Ritratto di borghese con 'camera': Roberto Romano fotografo (1870–1947)." *Ritorno a Ponte Stura.* By Lalla Romano. Turin: Einaudi, 2000. 129–52.
Cattani, Francesco. "Confini non ovvi: Ornela Vorpsi e Julia Kristeva." *Guardare oltre: Letteratura, fotografia e altri territori.* Ed. Silvia Albertazzi and Ferdinando Amigoni. Roma: Meltemi, 2007. 177–94.
Cavell, Stanley. *The World Viewed: Reflections on the Ontology of Film.* New York: Viking, 1971.
Celant, Germano, ed. *Mario Giacomelli.* Rome, Palazzo delle Esposizioni, Catalogue of the Exhibition. Milan–Modena: Photology-Logos, 2001.
Celati, Gianni. *Narratori delle pianure.* Milan: Feltrinelli, 2000.
–. *Passar la vita a Diol Kadd: Diari 2003–2006.* Milan: Feltrinelli, 2011.
Cenati, Giuliano. *"Torniamo a bomba"—I ghiribizzi narrativi di Vittorio Imbriani.* Milan: LED, 2004.
Centro di Ricerca e Archiviazione della Fotografia (C.R.A.F.). Crocenzi Fund. Spilimbergo.
Centro per la Cultura nella Fotografia (C.C.F.). "Discussione sul linguaggio fotografico." *Ferrania* (Feb. 1957): 43–4.

–. "Notizie del Centro per la Cultura nella Fotografia." *Fotografia* (Nov. 1958): 44.

Ceserani, Remo. "Il tema della fotografia nell'opera narrativa di Pirandello." Dolfi, *Letteratura*. Vol. 1. 245–64.

Cézanne, Paul. *Correspondance*. Paris: Grasset, 1937.

–. *Letters*. 1941. Ed. John Rewald. Trans. Marguerite Kay. Oxford: Cassirer, 1976.

Chambers, Ross. "An Address in the Country: Mallarmé and the Kinds of Literary Context." *French Forum* 11 (1986): 199–215.

Chiellino, Carmine, ed. *Interkul Literatur: Ein Handbuch*. Stuttgart: Metzler, 2000.

Chini, Renzo. *Il linguaggio fotografico*. Turin: SEI, 1968.

–. "Tutto nel fototesto e niente al di fuori." *Racconto e reportage fotografico*. Ed. Fotocineclub Fermo. Pollenza–Macerata: La Nuova Foglio, 1973. N. pag.

Clarke, Graham. *The Photograph*. New York: Oxford UP, 1997.

Colummi Camerino, Marinella. "Daniele del Giudice: Narrazione del luogo, percezione dello spazio." *Strumenti Critici* 89 (1999): 61–81.

Comberiati, Daniele. *Scrivere nella lingua dell'altro: La letteratura degli immigrati in Italia (1989–2007)*. Bruxelles: Peter Lang, 2010.

Contini, Gianfranco. "Elio Vittorini." *Letteratura dell'Italia unita: 1861–1968*. Florence: Sansoni, 1968. 876–7.

Correspondence Crocenzi–Giacomelli. 1956–1983. Archivio Mario Giacomelli, Senigallia.

Corsici, Arnaldo. "Storia delle origini della fotografía." *Bullettino della Società Fotografica Italiana* I (1889–90): 7–27.

Cottinelli, Vincenzo. *Sguardi: Novanta volti della cultura*. Brescia: La Quadra, 1995.

Craeybeckx, Herman. "Della utilità di uno studio sulla morfologia del linguaggio fotografico." *Ferrania* (Apr. 1957): 24–5.

Creekmur, Corey K. "Lost Objects: Photography, Fiction, and Mourning." Bryant 73–82.

Croce, Benedetto. *La letteratura della nuova Italia*. Bari: Laterza, 1922.

Crocenzi, Luigi. "Centro per la Cultura nella Fotografia. Nota n. 2." *Ferrania* (March 1956): 23.

–. "Il giornale dei peccati: *Un seminarista*." *Il caffè politico e letterario* (March 1955): 20–2.

–. Letter to the Editor. 3 Dec. 1954. MS. Archivio e Centro Studi Il Caffè di Giambattista Vicari. Montecalvo in Foglia, PU.

–. Letter to Giacomelli. 8 Nov. 1963. MS. Crocenzi Fund. Centro di Ricerca e Archiviazione della Fotografia (C.R.A.F). Spilimbergo.

–. Letter to Giacomelli. 13 Nov. 1963. MS. Crocenzi Fund. Centro di Ricerca e Archiviazione della Fotografia (C.R.A.F). Spilimbergo.
–. "Soggettivazione narrativa delle immagini fotografiche." *Ferrania* (May 1963): 16.
–. "Storie italiane: Cronache e racconti per immagini fotografiche." *Ferrania* (March 1957): 18–20.
–. *Storie di terra.* 1980. MS. Crocenzi Fund. Centro di Ricerca e Archiviazione della Fotografia (C.R.A.F). Spilimbergo.
Crovi, Raffaele. *Vittorini cavalca la tigre.* Rome: Avagliano, 2006.
Culler, Jonathan. *Literary Theory: A Very Short Introduction.* Oxford and New York: Oxford UP, 1997.
Cunningham, David, Andrew Fisher, and Sas Mays, eds. *Photography and Literature in the Twentieth Century.* Cambridge: Cambridge Scholars P, 2005.
Curreri, Luciano. "Il fascino della differenza nell'identità (in crisi) dello scrittore, del critico, dell'intellettuale: Bazlen, Debenedetti, Benjamin nella narrativa italiana 1983–(2001)–2004." *Cahiers d'études italiennes* 7 (2008): 159–69.
Damisch, Hubert. "Five Notes for a Phenomenology of the Photographic Image." *The Photography Reader.* Ed. Liz Wells. London: Routledge, 2003. 87–9.
D'Angelo, Paolo. "Estetica ambientale." *Dizionario dell'ambiente.* Ed. Giuseppe Gamba and Giuliano Martignetti. Milan: Isedi, 1995. 308–11.
–, ed. *Estetica e paesaggio.* Bologna: Il Mulino, 2009.
David, Micheal. *La psicoanalisi nella cultura italiana.* 1966. Turin: Bollati Boringhieri, 1990.
Davies, Judith. *The Realism of Luigi Capuana: The Theory and Practice in the Development of Late 19th-Century Italian Narrative.* Modern Humanities Research Association. Texts and Dissertations. Vol. 13. 1979.
De Amicis, Edmondo. *Ricordi del 1870–71.* Florence: Barbera, 1872.
De Benedetti, Giacomo. *Il personaggio-uomo.* Milan: Garzanti, 1970.
De Carlo, Andrea. "Alter Ego." Web. 13 Jan. 2004.
–. "Cinema." Web. 10 Jan. 2004.
–. "Fotografia." Web. 9 Jan. 2004.
–. *Treno di panna.* Turin: Einaudi, 1981.
De Luca, Erri. *Non ora, non qui.* Milan: Feltrinelli, 1989.
Del Giudice, Daniele. *Lo stadio di Wimbledon.* Turin: Einaudi, 1996.
De Zayas, Marius. "Photography *and* Photography and Artistic-Photography." 1913. Trachtenberg 125–32.
Derrida, Jacques. *Writing and Difference.* London: Routledge, 1978.
Di Bello, Patrizia, Colette Wilson, and Shamoon Zamir, eds. *The Photobook: From Talbot to Ruscha and Beyond.* London: Tauris, 2012.

–. "The Index of the Absent Wound (Monograph on a Stain)." *October* 29 (Summer 1984): 63–82.

Di Fazio, Margherita. "Scrittura e fotografia, fotografia e scrittura: Due percorsi a confronto." *Bianco e nero, nero su bianco: Tra fotografia e scrittura*. Ed. Bruna Donatelli. Napoli: Liguori, 2005. 93–108.

Di Monte, Michele, ed. *Paesaggio*. Spec. issue of *Rivista di estetica* 29.2 (2005).

Di Stefano, Paolo. "Preti gay, le vite lacerate." *Corriere della sera* 29 Nov. 1992: 13.

Di Tizio, Franco. *D'Annunzio e Michetti*. Pescara: Ianieri, 2002.

Diana, Carlo Giuseppe. "*Non ora, non qui* di Erri De Luca." Web. 10 Aug. 2012.

Didi-Huberman, Georges. *L'image survivante: Histoire de l'art et temps des fantômes selon Aby Warburg*. Paris: Minuit, 2002. Trans. it. *L'immagine insepolta. Aby Warburg, la memoria dei fantasmi e la storia dell'arte*. Trans. Alessandro Serra. Turin: Bollati Boringhieri, 2006.

Doane, Mary Ann. "Indexicality and the Concept of Medium Specificity." Kelsey and Stimson 3–14.

Dolfi, Anna, ed. *Letteratura & fotografia*. 2 vols. Rome: Bulzoni, 2005.

–. *Tabucchi: La specularità, il rimorso*. Rome: Bulzoni, 2006.

Dombroski, Robert S. "Writer and Society in the New Italy." *The Cambridge History of Italian Literature*. Ed. Peter Brand and Lino Pertile. Cambridge: Cambridge UP, 1996. 459–79.

Donati, Riccardo. "La meccanica del mancato possesso: Italo Calvino, Stefano D'Arrigo e la macchina celibe." Dolfi, *Letteratura*. Vol. 2. 147–82.

Dubois, Philippe. *L'Acte photographique*. Paris: Nathan, 1990.

–. *L'atto fotografico*. Trans. Bernardo Valli. Urbino: Quattro Venti, 1996.

–. "Photography *Mise-en-Film*: Autobiographical (Hi)stories and Psychic Apparatuses." Trans. Lynne Kirby. *Fugitive Images: From Photography to Video*. Ed. Patrice Petro. Bloomington: Indiana UP, 1995. 152–72.

Dusi, Nicola. *Il cinema come traduzione. Da un medium all'altro: Letteratura, cinema e pittura*. Turin: UTET, 2003.

Duttlinger, Carolin. "Imaginary Encounters: Walter Benjamin and the Aura of Photography." Horstkotte, Silke, and Pedri, *Photography* 79–101.

–. *Kafka and Photography*. Oxford: Oxford UP, 2007.

Dyer, Geoff, ed. *John Berger: Selected Essays*. London: Bloomsbury, 2001.

Eco, Umberto. *Opera aperta: Forma e indeterminazione nelle poetiche contemporane*. 2nd ed. Milan: Bompiani, 1967.

–. *The Role of the Reader: Explorations in the Semiotics of Texts*. Bloomington: Indiana UP, 1984.

Edwards, Steve. "Snapshooters of History: Passages on the Postmodern Argument." *The Photography Reader*. Ed. Liz Wells. London: Routledge, 2003. 180–95.

Eidelberg, Ludwig. *Encyclopaedia of Psychoanalysis*. London: Collier-MacMillan, 1968.
Elkins, James, ed. *Photography Theory*. New York: Routledge, 2007.
–. *What Photography Is*. New York: Routledge, 2011.
Entin, Joseph B. *Sensational Modernism: Experimental Fiction and Photography in Thirties America*. Chapel Hill: U of North Carolina P, 2007.
Falaschi, Giovanni. Introduzione e note. *Conversazione in Sicilia*. By Elio Vittorini. Milan: Rizzoli, 1986. 5–54.
Falqui, Enrico. "Conversazione in Sicilia: Illustrata." *Tempo* (26 Jan. 1954). Rpt. in *Il Novecento letterario*. Florence: Vallecchi, 1961. 170–75.
Fanon, Frantz. *Black Skin, White Masks*. London: Pluto, 1986.
Fava, Lia Guzzetta. *Verga fra Manzoni e Flaubert*. Rome: Edizioni Studium, 1997.
Ferrigni, Pietro. "Della fotografia nei suoi rapporti coll'arte e coi costumi." *Bullettino della Società Fotografica Italiana* I (1889–90): 36–47.
Ferris, David. S., ed. *The Cambridge Companion to Walter Benjamin*. Cambridge: Cambridge UP, 2004.
Flusser, Vilém. *Towards a Philosophy of Photography*. Minneapolis: U of Minnesota P, 1984.
Fofi, Goffredo, and Giovanni Giovannetti, eds. *Scrittori per un secolo*. Milan: Linea d'ombra, 1993.
Forti, Marco, and Sergio Pautasso, eds. *Il Politecnico*. Milan: Rizzoli, 1975.
Fossati, Vittore. *Appunti per una fotografia di paesaggio*. Ed. Roberta Valtorta. Caraglio, Cuneo: Marcovaldo, 2004.
–. Mostra at Castelnovo ne' Monti (Reggio Emilia). 31 Mar. 2008. Seminar.
–. "Re: esercizi per l'occhio sinistro." Message to the author. 30 Dec. 2008. E-mail.
–. "Re: mon Ventù." Message to the author. 17 Feb. 2009. E-mail.
–. "Vedi alla lettera 'C'." *Ereditare il paesaggio*. Ed. Giovanna Calvenzi and Maddalena d'Alfonso. Milan: Electa, 2008. 156–7.
Fossati, Vittore, and Giorgio Messori. *Viaggio in un paesaggio terrestre*. Reggio Emilia: Diabasis, 2007.
Foucault, Michel. "The Ethic of Care for the Self as a Practice of Freedom: An Interview with Michel Foucault on January 20, 1984." By Raul Fornet-Betancourt et al. Trans. J.D. Gauthier. *Philosophy and Social Criticism* 12.2–3 (Summer 1987): 112–31.
Freud, Sigmund. "Fetishism." *The Future of an Illusion, Civilization and Its Discontents, and Other Works*. London: Hogarth, 1962. 152–7.
–. *A General Introduction to Psychoanalysis*. 1915–17. Trans. Joan Riviere. New York: Pocket Books, 1970.

–. "Instincts and Their Vicissitudes." 1915. *The Freud Reader*. Ed. Peter Gay. London: Vintage, 1995. 562–8.

–. *The Interpretation of Dreams.* Ed. James Strachey. New York: Basic, 1965.

Ganguly, Keya. "Migrant Identities and the Constructions of Selfhood." *Cultural Studies* 6.1 (1992): 29–50.

Garra Agosta, Giovanni, and Walter Settimelli. *Giovanni Verga fotografo*. Milan: Centro Informazioni 3M, 1970.

Gersheim, Helmut, and Alison Gersheim. *L.J.M. Daguerre (1787–1851): The World's First Photographer*. Cleveland, New York: World Publishing, 1956.

Ghirri, Luigi. *Lezioni di fotografia*. Ed. Giulio Bizzarri and Paolo Barbaro. Compagnia Extra 17. Macerata: Quodlibet, 2010.

Ghirri, Luigi, Gianni Leone, and Enzo Velati, eds. *Niente di antico sotto il sole: Scritti e immagini per un'autobiografia.* Ed. Paolo Costantini and Giovanni Chiaramonte. Turin: Società Editrice Internazionale, 1997.

–, eds. *Viaggio in Italia*. Alessandria: Il Quadrante, 1984.

Giacomelli, Mario. "La buona terra." 1964–6. *Mario Giacomelli*. Ed. Arturo Carlo Quintavalle. Milan: Feltrinelli, 1980. 182–200.

–. "Caroline Branson." 1967–73. *Mario Giacomelli*. Ed. Arturo Carlo Quintavalle. Milan: Feltrinelli, 1980. 223–43.

–. "Fotografias de Mario Giacomelli. *Io non ho mani che mi accarezzino il volto.*" *Imagen y sonido* (March 1965): 2–9.

–. Interview with Giovanna Calvenzi. *Il fotografo* (Feb. 1984): 34–41.

–. *Io non ho mani che mi accarezzino il volto*. 1961–3. *Mario Giacomelli*. Ed. Arturo Carlo Quintavalle. Milan: Feltrinelli, 1980. 172–81.

–. Letter to Crocenzi. 22 Sept. 1965. MS. Crocenzi Fund. Centro di Ricerca e Archiviazione della Fotografia (C.R.A.F.). Spilimbergo.

–. "Le Prospettive dell'Uomo d'Oggi." *Reportage e racconti fotografici: Seconda mostra "Città di Fermo."* Fermo, catalogue of the exhibition. Ed. Fotocineclub Fermo. Fermo: 1963. 20–1.

–. "I Seminaristi." *Almanacco letterario Bompiani 1969. L'Inquietudine religiosa.* Ed. Giancarlo Bonacina and Paolo De Benedetti. Milan: Bompiani, 1968. 13–20.

–. "Surrealist Seminarians." *Jubilee* (Mar. 1965): 45–9.

–. "Un uomo una donna un amore." 1960–1. *Mario Giacomelli*. Ed. Arturo Carlo Quintavalle. Milan: Feltrinelli, 1980. 155–63.

Giacomelli, Mario, and Piero Racanicchi. "Io non ho mani." *Popular Photography Italiana* (Feb. 1964): 40–8.

Gidley, Mick, ed. *Writing with Light: Words and Photographs in American Texts.* New York: Peter Lang, 2009.

Gieri, Manuela. *Contemporary Italian Filmmaking: Strategies of Subversion*. Toronto: U of Toronto P, 1995.

Giovannetti, Giovanni. *Un archivio italiano: Scrittori di lingua italiana nelle fotografie*. Milan: Effigie, 2006.

Gnisci, Armando. *Letteratura italiana della migrazione*. Rome: Lilith, 1998.

Goldberg, Vicki. *Light Matters: Writings on Photography*. New York: Aperture, 2005.

Greenberg, Clement. *The Collected Essays and Criticism*. Ed. John O'Brian. Chicago: U of Chicago P, 1986.

____. "Four Photographers: Review of *A Vision of Paris* by Eugène-Auguste Atget; *A Life in Photography* by Edward Steichen; *The World Through My Eyes* by Adreas Feininger; and *Photographs* by Cartier-Bresson, Introduced by Lincoln Kirstein" (*New York Review of Books*, 23 January 1964), in *The Collected Essays and Criticism: Modernism with a Vengeance 1957–1969*, vol. 4, ed. John O'Brian. Chicago: U of Chicago P, 1993. 183–7.

Guerra, Simona. *Mario Giacomelli: La mia vita intera*. Milan: Mondadori, 2008.

Guerrieri, William. "Opere incongrue e fotografia: Note a margine di una ricerca." *Paesaggi dissonanti. Fotografia e opere incongrue: Una ricerca per la legge regionale 16 / 2002*. Ed. Piero Orlandi. Bologna: Compositori, 2003. 21–2.

Handke, Peter. *Die Lehre der Sainte-Victoire*. Frankfurt: Suhrkamp Verlag, 1980.

–. *The Lesson of Mount Sainte-Victoire: Slow Homecoming*. Trans. Ralph Manheim. London: Methuen, 1985.

Haverty Rugg, Linda. *Picturing Ourselves: Photography and Autobiography*. Chicago: U of Chicago P, 1997.

Henisch, Heinz K., and Bridget A. Henisch. *The Photographic Experience, 1839–1914: Images and Attitudes*. University Park: Pennsylvania State UP, 1994.

Henning, Michelle. "The Subject as Object: Photography and the Human Body." *Photography: A Critical Introduction*. Ed. Liz Wells. London: Routledge, 2004. 159–92.

Henninger, Katherine. *Ordering the Façade: Photography and Contemporary Southern Women's Writing*. Chapel Hill: U of North Carolina P, 2007.

Hill, Sarah Patricia. "Texts as Photographs, Photographs as Texts: Lalla Romano and the Photographic Image." *Italian Culture* 24–5 (2006–7): 45–62.

Hill, Sarah Patricia, and Giuliana Minghelli, eds. *Stillness in Motion: Italy, Photography, and the Meanings of Modernity*. Toronto: U of Toronto P, forthcoming.

Hirsch, Marianne. *Family Frames: Photography, Narrative, and Postmemory*. Cambridge: Harvard UP, 1997.

–. "The Generation of Postmemory." Horstkotte and Pedri, *Photography* 103–28.

Hirsch, Marianne, and Valerie Smith, eds. *Signs* 1.1 (2002).

hooks, bell. "The Oppositional Gaze." *The Feminism and Visual Culture Reader.* Ed. Amelia Jones. London: Routledge, 2003. 94–105.

Horstkotte, Silke. "Visual Memory and Ekphrasis in W. G. Sebald's *The Rings of Saturn.*" Jacobs 117–29.

Horstkotte, Silke, and Nancy Pedri. "Introduction: Photographic Interventions." Horstkotte and Pedri, *Photography* 1–29.

–, eds. *Photography in Fiction.* Spec. issue of *Poetics Today.* 29.1 (Spring 2008).

Hunter, Jefferson. *Image and Word: The Interaction of Twentieth Century Photographs and Texts.* Cambridge: Harvard UP, 1987.

Hutcheon, Linda. *The Politics of Postmodernism.* London: Routledge, 2002.

Imbriani, Vittorio. *Merope IV.* Biblioteca del minotauro, 53. Milan: Serra e Riva, 1984.

–. *I romanzi.* Ed. Fabio Pusterla. Milan: Garzanti, 2006.

Jacobs, Karen, ed. *Photography and Literature.* Spec. issue of *English Language Notes.* 44.2 (2006).

Jakob, Michael. *Il paesaggio.* Trans. Adriana Ghersi and Michael Jakob. Bologna: Il Mulino, 2009.

–. *Le paysage.* Paris: Infolio, 2008.

Jakobson, Roman. "On Linguistic Aspects of Translations." 1959. *The Translation Studies Reader.* Ed. Lawrence Venuti. London: Routledge, 2000. 138–42.

–. *Saggi di linguistica generale.* 1963. Trans. Luigi Heilmann and Letizia Grassi. Milan: Feltrinelli, 1966.

Kahane, Claire. "Dark Mirrors: A Feminist Reflection on Holocaust Narrative and the Maternal Metaphor." *Feminist Consequences: Theory for the New Century.* Ed. E. Bronfen and M. Kavka. New York: Columbia UP, 2001. 161–88.

Kelsey, Robin. "Photography, Chance and *The Pencil of Nature.*" Kelsey and Stimson 15–33.

Kelsey, Robin, and Blake Stimson, eds. *The Meaning of Photography.* New Haven: Yale UP, 2008.

Koppen, Erwin. *Literatur und Photographie: Über Geschichte und Thematick Einer Medienentdechung.* Stuttgart: Metzler, 1987.

Kozloff, Max. *Photography and Fascination.* Danbury, New Hampshire: Addison, 1979.

Kracauer, Siegfried. *The Mass Ornament: Weimar Essays.* Trans. Thomas Y. Levin. Cambridge: Harvard UP, 1995.

Kramer, Rita. *Maria Montessori: A Biography.* New York: Putnam, 1970.

Krauss, Rosalind. "Notes on the Index: Seventies Art in America." *October* 3–4 (1977): 58–81.

–. *The Originality of the Avant-Garde and Other Modern Myths.* Cambridge: MIT P, 1985.
–. "The Photographic Conditions of Surrealism." *October* 19 (Fall 1981): 3–34.
–. *Le photographique: Pour une théorie des écarts.* 1974–85. Paris: Macula, 1990.
Kriebel, Sabine T. "Theories of Photography: A Short History." Elkins, *Photography Theory* 3–49.
Kristeva, Julia. *Histoire d'amour.* Paris: Denoël, 1983. 16–17.
–. "Un nouveau type d'intellectuel: Le dissident." *Tel Quel* 74 (Winter 1977): 3–8.
–. *Revolution in Poetic Language.* Trans. Margaret Waller. New York: Columbia UP, 1984.
Kuhn, Annette. *Family Secrets: Acts of Memory and Imagination.* London: Verso, 1995.
La Porta, Filippo. "Io non sogno mai: Scrittura e sguardo in Giorgio Messori." Io non sogno mai. Scrittura e sguardo in Giorgio Messori. Conference. Università La Sapienza, Rome. 23–4 Feb. 2010. Address.
Lacan, Jacques. *The Four Fundamental Concepts of Psychoanalysis.* Ed. Jacques-Alain Miller. Trans. Alan Sheridan. New York: W.W. Norton, 1998.
Lanslots, Inge. "Il silenzio in Erri De Luca: Spazio e tempo differiti." *Narrativa* 10 (1996): 229–44.
Laura, Ernesto G., et al., eds. *Vivere il cinema: Sessant'anni del centro sperimentale di cinematografia 1935–1995.* Rome: Istituto Poligrafico e Zecca dello Stato, 1995.
Laviosa, Flavia, ed. *Visions of Struggle in Women's Filmmaking in the Mediterranean.* London: Palgrave, 2009.
Lefebvre, Martin. "The Art of Pointing: On Peirce, Indexicality, and Photographic Images." Elkins, *Photography Theory* 220–44.
Lemagny, Jean-Claude. "Presentazione." *Giacomelli: La forma dentro. Fotografie 1952–1995.* Senigallia, Rocca Roveresca, catalogue of the exhibition. Ed. Enzo Carli. Milan: Charta, 1995. 10–15.
Leslie, Esther. *Walter Benjamin: Overpowering Conformism.* London: Pluto, 2000.
Livorni, Ernesto. "Trompe-l'Oeil in *Notturno indiano* di Antonio Tabucchi." *I tempi del rinnovamento. Atti del convegno internazionale: Rinnovamento del codice narrativo in Italia dal 1945 al 1992.* Ed. Serge Vanvolsem, Franco Musarra, and Bart Van den Bossche. Vol. 1. Rome: Bulzoni-Leuven UP, 1995. 431–53.
Lolla, Maria Grazia. "As It Was or Could / Might / Should Have Been: Social Science and Novelistic Practice in Post-Unification Italy." Romance Studies Colloquium on Storytelling. Montclair State University. 1–3 Oct. 2009. Address.
Lombroso, Cesare. *Criminal Man.* Durham: Duke UP, 2006.

Louvel, Liliane. "Photography as Critical Idiom and Intermedial Criticism." Horstkotte and Pedri, *Photography* 31–48.

–. *Poetics of the Iconotext.* Ed. Karen Jacobs. Trans. Laurence Petit. Surrey: Ashgate, 2011.

Luciano, Bernadette, and Susanna Scarparo. "'Vite sospese': Representing Female Migration in Contemporary Italian Documentaries." *Italian Studies* 65.2 (2010): 192–203.

Lury, Celia. *Prosthetic Culture: Photography, Memory, and Identity.* London: Routledge, 1998.

Madrignani, Carlo A. *La domenica letteraria di F. Martini e di A. Sommaruga.* Rome: Bulzoni, 1979.

Maffioli, Monica, ed. *L'Italia d'argento: Storia del dagherrotipo in Italia, 1839–1859.* Florence: Alinari, 2003.

Mallarmé, Stéphane. *Selected Poems.* Trans. Carlyle Ferren MacIntyre. Berkeley: U of California P, 1957.

Manganelli, Giorgio. *Saloons.* Milan: Adelphi, 2000.

Mantegazza, Paolo. "Seduta di inaugurazione della Società Fotografica Italiana." *Bullettino della Società Fotografica Italiana* I (1889–90): 4–7.

Manzoni, Alessandro. *I promessi sposi.* Ed. Angelo Marchese. Milan: Mondadori, 1985. Electronic edition http://www.liberliber.it/mediateca/libri/m/manzoni/i_promessi_sposi/pdf/manzoni_i_promessi_sposi.pdf.

Marcus, Millicent. *Italian Film in the Light of Neorealism.* Princeton: Princeton UP, 1986.

Marra, Claudio, ed. *Le idee della fotografía: La riflessione teorica dagli anni Sessanta a oggi.* Milan: Mondadori, 2001.

Martino, Emanuele. *Cara Fotografia: Racconti.* Florence: Meridiana, 2008.

Marzocchini, Vincenzo. *Letteratura e fotografia: Scrittori, poeti, fotografi.* Bologna: CLUEB, 2005.

Mauceri, Maria Cristina. "L'Europa venuta dall'Europa." *Nuovo planetario italiano: Geografia e antologia della letteratura della migrazione in Italia e in Europa.* Ed. Armando Gnisci. Troina: Città Aperta Edizioni, 2006. 113–54.

Mauri, Paolo. *L'opera imminente.* Turin: Einaudi, 1998.

Mauro, Alessandra, ed. *Mario Giacomelli: La figura nera aspetta il bianco.* Rome: Contrasto, 2009.

McCance, Dawne, ed. *The Photograph.* Spec. issue of *Mosaic: A Journal for the Interdisciplinary Study of Literature* 37.4 (2004).

McLaughlin, Martin. "Andrea De Carlo: The Surface of Consciousness." *The New Italian Novel.* Ed. Zygmunt G. Baranski and Lino Pertile. Edinburgh: Edinburgh UP, 1993. 75–88.

Melis, Rosanna. *La bella stagione del Verga: Francesco Torracca e i primi critici verghiani (1875–1885).* Catania: Biblioteca della Fondazione Verga, 1990.

Mercenaro, Giuseppe. *Fotografia come letteratura*. Milan: Mondadori, 2008.

Merleau-Ponty, Maurice. "Eye and Mind." *The Primacy of Perception and Other Essays on Phenomenological Psychology, the Philosophy of Art, History, and Politics*. Ed. James M. Edie. Trans. Careton Dallery. Evanston: Northwestern UP, 1964. 159–90.

Merrin, William. *Baudrillard and the Media: A Critical Introduction*. Cambridge: Polity, 2005.

Messori, Giorgio. "Fin dove può arrivare l'infinito?" *Luigi Ghirri. Vista con camera: 200 fotografie in Emilia Romagna*. Ed. Paola Ghirri and Ennery Taramelli. Milan: Motta, 1992. 193–4.

–. "Forse l'esilio comincia nei sogni a occhi aperti." *Narratori delle riserve*. Ed. Gianni Celati. Milan: Feltrinelli, 1992. 179–84.

–. "Le mattine del mondo: L'incontro di Luigi Ghirri con l'opera di Giorgio Morandi." *Il senso delle cose: Luigi Ghirri, Giorgio Morandi*. Ed. Paola Borgonzoni Ghirri. Reggio Emilia: Diabasis, 2005. 61–71.

–. "Il mio incontro con Viaggio in Italia." *Racconti dal paesaggio, 1984–2004: A vent'anni da Viaggio in Italia*. Ed. Roberta Valtorta. Milan: Lupetti, 2004. 102–5.

–. *Nella città del pane e dei postini*. Reggio Emilia: Diabasis, 2005.

–. *Storie invisibili e altri racconti*. Ed. Gino Ruozzi. Reggio Emilia: Diabasis, 2008.

Messori, Giorgio, and Beppe Sebaste. *L'ultimo buco nell'acqua*. Reggio Emilia: Aelia Lelia, 1993.

Metz, Christian. "Photography and Fetish." *October* 34 (Autumn 1985): 81–90.

Minghelli, Giuliana. "L'occhio di Verga: La pratica fotografica nel Verismo italiano." *L'anello che non tiene* 20–1 (Spring-Fall 2008–9): 59–86.

Miraglia, Marina. "D'Annunzio e la fotografia." *D'Annunzio e la promozione delle arti*. Ed. Rossana Bossaglia and Mario Quesada. Milan: Mondadori, 1988. 55–9.

–. "'Genere' e 'Tableau vivant': Appunti veloci su due opposte tendenze delle età del collodio e della gelatina bromuro d'argento." *Segni di luce*. Ed. Italo Zannier. Vol. 2. Ravenna: Longo, 1991–3. 107–14.

–. "Note per una storia della fotografia italiana (1839–1911)." *Storia dell'arte italiana: Situazioni momenti indagini: Illustrazione, fotografia*. Ed. Federico Zeri. Vol. 2. Turin: Einaudi, 1981. 423–542.

Mitchell, W.J.T. *Picture Theory: Essays on Verbal and Visual Representation*. Chicago: U of Chicago P, 1994.

Montale, Eugenio. "L'arte e la vita." *Il secondo mestiere: Prose 1920–1979*. Ed. G. Zampa. Vol 1. Milan: Mondadori, 1966. 1615–20.

Montandon, Alain. *Iconotextes*. 1990. Paris, CRCD Clermont-Ferrand: Ophrys, 2002.

Montessori, Maria. *The Absorbent Mind.* New York: Holt, 1995.
–. *The Montessori Method.* New York: Schocken, 1964.
Montier, Jean-Pierre. "Avant-Propos." Montier, Louvel, Méaux, and Ortel 7–14.
Montier, Jean-Pierre, Liliane Louvel, Danièle Méaux, and Philippe Ortel, eds. *Littérature et photographie.* Rennes: Presses universitaires de Rennes, 2008.
Moravia, Alberto. *L'uomo che guarda.* Milan: Bompiani, 2006.
Morello, Paolo. "Verifiche intorno alla fotografia in Italia, 1943–1953." *Realismi: Arti figurative, letteratura e cinema in Italia dal 1943 al 1953.* Ed. Luciano Caramel. Milan: Elect, 2001. 55–64.
Mormorio, Diego, ed. *Gli scrittori e la fotografia.* Rome: Riuniti, 1988.
–. *Io, la fotografia ovvero l'attimo quotidiano: Monologo teatrale.* Villanova Monteleone: Soter, 2008.
Moses, Gavriel. *The Nickel Was for the Movies: Film in the Novel from Pirandello to Puig.* Berkeley: U of California P, 1995.
Mulvey, Laura. "Visual Pleasure and Narrative Cinema." *Film Theory and Criticism: Introductory Readings.* Ed. Leo Braudy and Marshall Cohen. 5th ed. New York: Oxford UP, 1998. 833–44.
Muzzarelli, Federica. *Il corpo e l'azione: Donne e fotografia tra Otto e Novecento.* Bologna: Atlante, 2007.
Napoli, Carlo. "Speciale rapporto sui seminari in Italia: Dove si fabbrica il prete." *L'Espresso* (15 Mar. 1970): 8–25.
Neera. *Fotografie matrimoniali.* 1883. Catania: Giannotta, 1900.
Nemiz, Andrea. *Capuana, Verga, De Roberto fotografi.* Palermo: Edikronos, 1982.
Nobile, Max, and Lalla Romano. *Terre di Lucchesia.* Lucca: Pacini, 1991.
North, Michael. *Camera Works: Photography and the Twentieth-Century Word.* Oxford: Oxford UP, 2005.
Novak, Daniel A. *Realism, Photography, and Nineteenth-Century Fiction.* Cambridge: Cambridge UP, 2008.
Ortel, Philippe. *La littérature à l'ère de la photographie.* Nîmes: Chambon, 2002.
Osborne, Peter D. *Travelling Light: Photography, Travel, and Visual Culture.* Manchester: Manchester UP, 2000.
Pandini, Giancarlo. "Treno di panna." *Il tempo* (24 July 1981): 3.
Panicali, Anna. *Elio Vittorini: La narrativa, la saggistica, le traduzioni, le riviste, l'attività editoriale.* Milan: Mursia, 1944.
Parati, Graziella. *Mediterranean Crossroads: Migration Literature in Italy.* London: Associated UP, 1999.
–. "Strangers in Paradise: Foreigners and Shadows in Italian Literature." *Re-visioning Italy: National Identity and Global Culture.* Ed. Beverly Allen and Mary J. Russo. Minneapolis: U of Minnesota P, 1997. 169–90.

Parr, Martin, and Gerry Badger. *The Photobook: A History*. 2 vols. London: Phaidon, 2004–6.

Pasolini, Pier Paolo. *Empirismo eretico*. Milan: Garzanti, 2000.

Patt, Lise, Christel Dillbohner, and Winfried Georg Sebald, eds. *Searching for Sebald: Photography after W.G. Sebald*. Ann Arbor: U of Michigan P. 2008.

Pavese, Cesare. *Il mestiere di vivere: Diario 1935–1950*. Turin: Einaudi, 1952

Pedri, Nancy. "Disenchanted with the Referent: Photography in Emanuele Martino's *Cara fotografia: Racconti*." *Italica* 91.2 (Summer 2014): 203–18.

–. "Documenting the Fictions of Reality." Horstkotte and Pedri, *Photography* 155–73.

–. "From Photographic Product to Photographic Text: Lalla Romano's Movement Away from Ekphrasis." *Rivista di studi italiani* 19.2 (Dec. 2001): 141–61.

–. "Reading the Photographic Text with Lalla Romano." *Literary Texts and the Arts: Interdisciplinary Perspectives*. Ed. Corrado Federici and Esther Raventós-Pons. Studies in Literary Criticism and Theory 18. New York: Peter Lang, 2003. 99–116.

Peirce, Charles Sanders. *Collected Papers of Charles Sanders Peirce*. Ed. Charles Hartshorne and Paul Weiss. 2 vols. Cambridge: Harvard UP, 1960.

–. *The Essential Peirce*. Vol 2. Bloomington: Indiana UP, 1998.

–. "Logic as Semiotic: The Theory of Signs." *Philosophical Writings of Peirce*. Ed. Justus Buchler. New York: Dover, 1955. 98–119.

–. "Semiotica: I fondamenti della semiotica cognitiva." Trans. Massimo A. Bonfantini et al. Turin: Einaudi, 1980.

Pelizzari, Maria Antonella. "Centers and Peripheries in Contemporary Italian Photography." *Afterimage* 25.1 (1997): 6.

–. *Photography and Italy*. London: Reaktion, 2011.

Perniola, Mario. *L'estetica del novecento*. Bologna: Il Mulino, 1997.

–. *Del sentire*. Turin: Einaudi, 1971.

Pintor, Giaime. "L'allegoria del sentimento: *Conversazione in Sicilia*." 1941. *Il sangue d'Europa*. Turin: Einaudi, 1977. 95–8.

Plécy, Albert. "Il Linguaggio dell'immagine." *Ferrania* (May 1958): 36.

Praz, Mario. "Pittura di ritratto e fotografie." *Perseo e la medusa: Dal romanticismo all'avanguardia*. Milan: Mondadori, 1979. 190–7.

Price, Mary. *The Photograph: A Strange Confined Space*. Stanford: Stanford UP, 1994.

Probyn, Elspeth. *Outside Belonging*. New York: Routledge, 1996.

Prodger, Phillip. *Time Stands Still: Muybridge and the Instantaneous Photography Movement*. Oxford: Oxford UP, 2003.

Prosser, Jay. *Light in the Dark Room: Photography and Loss*. Minneapolis: U of Minnesota P, 2004.

Proust, Marcel. *Remembrance of Things Past*. Trans. C.K. Scott Moncrieff and Terrence Kilmartin. 3 vols. New York: Random House, 1982.

Pudovkin, Vsevolod. *Film Technique and Film Acting*. 1926. Trans. Ivor Montagu. New York: Grove, 1970.

Pusterla, Fabio. Introduction. *I romanzi*. By Vittorio Imbriani. Parma: Fondazione Pietro Bembo, Guanda, 1992. ix–lviii.

Quintavalle, Arturo Carlo, ed. *Mario Giacomelli*. Milan: Feltrinelli, 1980.

Rabaté, Jean-Michel. *Writing the Image after Roland Barthes*. Philadelphia: U of Pennsylvania P, 1997.

Rabb, Jane M. "Introduction: Notes Toward a History of Literature and Photography." Rabb, *Literature* xxxv–lx.

–, ed. *Literature and Photography. Interactions, 1840–1990: A Critical Anthology*. Albuquerque: U of New Mexico P, 1995.

Ragusa, Olga. "Alberto Moravia: Voyeurism and Storytelling." *The Southern Review* 4 (1960): 127–41.

Rak, Michele. *La produzione dell'arte nella società industriale*. Palermo: Palumbo, 1981.

Ravazzoli, Flavia. "Viaggi tangenziali e storie ribattute: L'insonnia narrativa di Antonio Tabucchi." *Autografo* 4 (1985): 23–37.

Reff, Theodore. *Manet: Olympia*. London: Penguin, 1976.

Ria, Antonio, ed. *Lalla Romano: Natura morta e fiori*. Milan: Compagnia del Disegno, 2002.

–. *Lalla Romano, pittrice*. Turin: Einaudi, 1993.

–, ed. *Lalla Romano: Ritratti, figure e nudi 1921–1960*. Acqui Terme: Repetto & Massucco, 2001.

Ricci, Franco. *Painting with Words, Writing with Pictures: Word and Image in the Work of Italo Calvino*. Toronto: U of Toronto P, 2001. 43–9.

Rizzarelli, Maria. *Elio Vittorini: Conversazione illustrata: catalogo della mostra*. Acireale: Bonanno, 2007.

Roberts, John. *The Art of Interruption: Realism, Photography, and the Everyday*. Manchester: Manchester UP, 1998.

Romano, Lalla. *Dall'ombra*. Turin: Einaudi, 1999.

–. *L'eterno presente: Conversazione con Antonio Ria*. Turin: Einaudi, 1998.

–. "Il frutto del grano." Romano, *Opere*. Vol. 2. 1602.

–. Introduzione. *Sguardi: Novanta volti della cultura*. Brescia: La Quadra, 1995. 9–10.

–. *Le lune di Hvar*. Turin: Einaudi, 1991.

–. *Metamorfosi*. Turin: Einaudi, 1951.

–. "Il mio primo romanzo di immagini." Romano, *Opere*. Vol. 2. 1597–8.

–. *Nei mari estremi*. Turin: Einaudi, 1987.

–. *Nuovo romanzo di figure*. Turin: Einaudi, 1997.
–. *Opere*. Ed. Cesare Segre. 2 vols. Milan: Mandadori, 1992.
–. *La penombra che abbiamo attraversato*. Turin: Einaudi, 1964.
–. "Perché scrivo." Romano, *Opere*. Vol. 2. 1568–9.
–. "Poesia della pittura." Romano, *Opere*. Vol. 2. 1576–9.
–. *Ritorno a Ponte Stura*. Turin: Einaudi, 2000.
–. *La treccia di Tatiana*. Turin: Einaudi, 1986.
Ronchi, Rocco. "Immagine vita." *Diario Gerra* 1 (2008): 59–79.
–. *Il pensiero bastardo: Figurazione dell'invisibile e comunicazione indiretta*. Milan: Marinotti, 2001.
Rossellini, Roberto, dir. *Roma, città aperta*. 1945. *War Trilogy*. Criterion Collection, 2010. Film.
Rugg, Linda Haverty. *Picturing Ourselves: Photography and Autobiography*. Chicago: U of Chicago P, 1997.
Ruozzi, Gino. "Storie invisibili e altri racconti di Giorgio Messori." Emmestudio Community Marketing Agency. 8 November 2013. Web. 5 June 2014.
Ruthenberg, Myriam Swennen. "Prove di domanda: Intervista silenziosa con Erri De Luca." *Gradiva: International Journal of Italian Literature* 7.1 (1999): 51–62.
Ryan, James R. *Picturing Empire: Photography and the Visualization of the British Empire*. Chicago: U of Chicago P, 1997.
Saldívar-Hull, Sonia. *Feminism on the Border: Chicana Gender, Politics and Literature*. Berkeley: U of California P, 2000.
Sanguineti, Edoardo. Introduzione. *Conversazione in Sicilia*. By Elio Vittorini. Turin: Einaudi, 1966. vii–xv.
Sayad, Abdelmalek. *The Suffering of the Immigrant*. Cambridge: Polity, 2004.
Schaeffer, Jean-Marie. *L'image précaire: Du dispositif photographique*. Paris: Seuil, 1987.
Schloss, Carol. *In Visible Light: Photography and the American Writer, 1840–1940*. Oxford: Oxford UP, 1987.
Schmitz, Helmut. "Walter Benjamin." *Art: Key Contemporary Thinkers*. Ed. Diarmuid Costello and Jonathan Vickery. Oxford: Berg, 2007. 160–3.
Schwartz, Marcy E., and Mary Berth Tierney-Tello, eds. *Photography and Writing in Latin America: Double Exposures*. Albuquerque: U of New Mexico P, 2006.
Scott, Clive. *The Spoken Image: Photography and Language*. London: Reaktion, 1999.
Scruton, Roger. "Photography and Representation." *Critical Inquiry* 7.3 (Spring 1981): 577–603.

Segre, Cesare. "Fotografia come pittura." *Intorno a Lalla Romano: Saggi critici e testimonianze*. Ed. Antonio Ria. Milan: Mondadori, 1996. 43–8.

–. Introduzione. Romano, *Opere*. Vol. 2. xi–lviii.

–. "Lalla Romano fra pittura e scrittura." Ria, *Lalla Romano, pittrice* 207–9.

Sekula, Allan. "The Invention of Photographic Meaning." *Artforum* (Jan. 1975): 27–45.

–. *Photography Against the Grain: Essays and Photo Works 1973–1983*. Halifax: P of the Nova Scotia College of Art and Design, 1984.

Serao, Matilde. *The Conquest of Rome*. 1885. Trans. Ann Carsar. London: Pickering and Chatto, 1991.

–. *La conquista di Roma*. 1885. Ed. Wanda De Nunzio Schilardi. Rome: Bulzoni, 1997.

–. *Il ventre di Napoli*. Milan: Treves, 1884.

Settimelli, Walter, ed. *Giovanni Verga: Specchio e realtà*. Rome: Magma, 1976.

Sironi, Marco. *Geografie del narrare: Insistenze sui luoghi di Luigi Ghirri e Gianni Celati*. Il castello di Atlante, n. 18. Reggio Emilia: Diabasis, 2004.

Sliwinski, Sharon. "A Note on Punctum." Elkins, *Photography Theory* 248–53.

Smith, Anne-Marie. *Julia Kristeva: Speaking the Unspeakable*. London: Pluto, 1998.

Smith, Sidonie, and Julia Watson, eds. *Interfaces: Women / Autobiography / Image / Performance*. Ann Arbor: U of Michigan P, 2005.

Snyder, Joel, and Neil Walsh Allen. "Photography, Vision, and Representation." *Critical Inquiry* 2 (1975): 143–69.

Solomon-Godeau, Abigail. *Photography at the Dock: Essays on Photographic History, Institutions, and Practices*. Minneapolis: U of Minnesota P, 1991.

Sontag, Susan. *On Photography*. 1977. New York: Anchor, 1990.

Sonthonnax, Paul. "Henri Cartier-Bresson scrittore per immagini." *Ferrania* (July 1958): 31.

Sorge, Paola. "Santissimi gay." *La Repubblica* 24 Aug. 1993.

Spinazzola, Vittorio. "Conversazione in Sicilia." *Letteratura italiana. Le opere. Il Novecento II. La ricerca letteraria*. Vol 4. Turin: Einaudi, 1996. 407–27.

Spunta, Marina. "A Balanced Displacement: Images of Vision and Silence in Erri De Luca's *Non ora, non qui*." *Forum Italicum* 35.2 (2001): 383–402.

–. "Fossati's and Messori's *Viaggio in un paesaggio terrestre* – An Imaginative Journey through Writing, Photography, Landscape, and Painting." *Italian Studies* 66.1 (Mar. 2011): 104–22.

–. "The New Italian Landscape: Between Ghirri's Photography and Celati's Fiction." *Translation Practices: Through Language to Culture*. Ed. Ashley Chantler and Carla Dente. Amsterdam: Rodopi, 2009. 223–38.

–. "Sense of Home and 'Exile' in Giorgio Messori's Narrative Fiction." *Romance Studies* 29.4 (November 2011): 285–98.

Stahel, Urs. *Well, What Is Photography? A Lecture on the Occasion of the Tenth Anniversary of Fotomuseum Winterthur*. Zurich: Scalo, 2003.

Steimatsky, Noa. "Photographic *Verismo*, Cinematic Adaptation, and the Staging of a Neorealist Landscape." *A Companion to Literature and Film*. Ed. Robert Stam and Alessandra Raengo. Oxford: Wiley-Blackwell, 2004. 205–29.

Stoppani, Antonio. *Il Bel Paese: Conversazioni sulle bellezze naturali, la geologia e la geografia fisica d'Italia*. Milan: Agnelli, 1876.

Struk, Janina. *Photographing the Holocaust: Interpretations of the Evidence*. London and New York: Tauris, 2004.

Sturken, Marita, and Lisa Cartwright. *Practices of Looking: An Introduction to Visual Culture*. Oxford: Oxford UP, 2001.

Swinnen, Johann. "Recycling of Reality: Searching for a Historical Infrastructure from Paradox to Paroxysm." *Photography: Crisis of History*. Ed. Joan Fontcuberta. Trans. Graham Thomson. Barcelona: Actar, n.d. 176–88.

Szarkowski, John. *The Photographer's Eye*. New York: Museum of Modern Art, 1966.

Tabucchi, Antonio. *Notturno indiano*. 1984. Palermo: Sellerio, 2004.

–. *Indian Nocturne*. Trans. Tim Parks. Edinburgh: Canongate, 2013.

Taddei, S.J. Nazareno. "Appunti di teoria del racconto fotografico." *Racconto e reportage fotografico*. Ed. Fotocineclub Fermo. Pollenza-Macerata: La Nuova Foglio, 1973. N. pag.

Tagg, John. *The Burden of Representation: Essays on Photographies and Histories*. 1988. Minneapolis: U of Minnesota P, 2005.

–. *The Disciplinary Frame: Photographic Truths and the Capture of Meaning*. Minneapolis: U of Minnesota P, 2009.

Tani, Stefano. "La giovane narrativa: Emerging Italian Novelists in the Eighties." *Postmodern Fiction in Europe and the Americas*. Ed. Theo D'Haen and Hans Bertens. Amsterdam, Antwerp: Rodopi, Restant, 1988. 161–92.

Taramelli, Ennery. *Viaggio nell'Italia del neorealismo: La fotografia tra letteratura e cinema*. Turin: Società Editrice Internazionale, 1995.

Tellini, Gino. *L'invenzione della realtà: Studi verghiani*. Pisa: Nistri Lischi, 1993.

Termine, Liborio. *Paul Valéry e la mosca sul vetro: Fotografia e modernità*. Turin: Aleph, 1991.

Thompson, Jerry L. *Truth and Photography: Notes on Looking and Photographing*. Chicago: Dee, 2003.

Tisseron, Serge. *Le mystère de la chambre claire*. Paris: "Champs" Flammarion, 1996.

Tomasevskij, Boris. "Sjuzetnoe postroenie." *La costruzione dell'intreccio in formalisti russi.* 1928. Ed. Tzvetan Todorov. Turin: Einaudi, 1968. 307–50.

Trachtenberg, Alan, ed. *Classic Essays on Photography*. New Haven: Leete's Island, 1980.

Tucker, Jennifer. *Nature Exposed: Photography as Eyewitness in Victorian Science.* Baltimore: Johns Hopkins UP, 2005.

Turoldo, David Maria. *Io non ho mani*. Milan: Bompiani, 1948.

Turri, Eugenio. *Antropologia del paesaggio*. 1974. Venezia: Marsilio, 2008.

Turroni, Giuseppe. "I seminaristi di Mario Giacomelli." *Ferrania* (March 1964): 2–7.

Valentini, Alvaro. Introduction. *Mostra di fotografia: Premio Porto San Giorgio*. Porto S. Giorgio, Villa degli Oleandri, catalogue of the exhibition. 1959. N. pag.

–. Introduction. *Premio annuale internazionale di fotografia Porto San Giorgio*. Porto S. Giorgio, catalogue of the exhibition. 1960. N. pag.

Valera, Paolo. *Milano sconosciuta*. 1879. Milan: Ambrosoli, 1880.

–. *Le terribili giornate del maggio '98*. Ed. Enrico Ghidetti. Bari: De Donato, 1973.

Valéry, Paul. "The Centenary of Photography." 1939. Trachtenberg 191–8.

Valtorta, Roberta. "La fotografia di Vittore Fossati: Il mondo come enigma." *Vittore Fossati: Appunti per una fotografia di paesaggio*. Ed. Roberta Valtorta. Caraglio, Cuneo: Marcovaldo, 2004. 13–18.

Van Gelder, Hilde, and Helen Westgeest. *Photography Theory in Historical Perspective*. Chichester: Wiley, 2011.

Van Lier, Henri. *Philosophie de la photographie*. Paris: Les Cahiers de la Photographie, 1983. Trans.: *Philosophy of Photography*. Leuven: Leuven UP, 2007.

Vanon, Michela. "Mario Giacomelli: Sogni e incubi di un poeta." *Photo italiana* (Dec. 1984): 44.

Verdicchio, Pasquale. *Looters, Photographers, and Thieves: Aspects of Italian Photographic Culture in the Nineteenth and Twentieth Centuries*. Madison: Farleigh Dickinson UP, 2011.

Verga, Giovanni. *The House by the Medlar Tree*. Trans. Raymond Rosenthal. Berkeley: U of California P, 1983.

–. *I Malavoglia*. Milan: Rizzoli, 2002.

–. *Le novelle*. Ed. Nicola Merola. Vol. 1. Milan: Garzanti, 1980.

Vittorini, Elio. *Conversazione in Sicilia*. Milan: Bompiani, 1941.

–. *Conversazione in Sicilia*. Milan: Bompiani, 1953.

–. *Conversazione in Sicilia*. 1953. Milan: Rizzoli, 2007.

–. "Conversazione in Sicilia." *Nome e lagrime*. Florence: Parenti, 1941.

–. "La foto strizza l'occhio alla pagina." *Lettere 1952–1955*. Ed. Edoardo Esposito and Carlo Minoia. Turin: Einaudi, 2006. 365–74.

–. *Il garofono rosso*. 1947. Milan: Mondadori, 1967.

Vogl, Mary B. *Picturing the Maghreb: Literature, Photography, (Re)presentation*. Lanham: Rowman and Littlefield, 2003.

Vorpsi, Ornela. "L'Albania è una ferita che brucia ancora." Interview with Maria Cristina Mauceri. *Kúmá*. 11 Apr. 2006. Web. 15 June 2010.

–. *Buvez du Cacao Van Houten!* Paris: Actes Sud, 2005.

–. *The Country Where No One Ever Dies*. Trans. Robert Elsie and Janice Mathie-Heck. Champaign: Dalkey Archive, 2009.

–. "Fahrenheit." Radio interview. RAI, Radio 3. National Public Radio. 7 Sept. 2006. Web. 14 Feb. 2009.

–. *Fuorimondo*. Turin: Einaudi, 2012.

–. *La mano che non mordi*. Turin: Einaudi, 2007.

–. *Nothing Obvious*. London: Thames and Hudson, 2001.

–. *Il paese dove non si muore mai*. Turin: Einaudi, 2005.

–. *Vetri rosa*. Rome: Nottetempo, 2006.

Wagner, Peter, ed. *Icons – Texts – Iconotext: Essays on Ekphrasis and Intermediality*. Berlin: de Gruyter, 1996.

Walton, Kendall. "Transparent Pictures: On the Nature of Photographic Realism." *Critical Inquiry* 11.2 (Dec. 1984): 246–77.

Warner, Mary Marien. *Photography: A Cultural History*. 2nd ed. Upper Saddle River: Pearson Prentice Hall, 2006.

Watt, Stephen. "Photographs in Biographies: Joyce, Voyeurism, and the 'Real' Nora Barnacle." Bryant 57–72.

Weber, Thomas. "Erfahrung." *Benjamins Begriffe*. Ed. Michael Opitz and Erdmut Wizisla. Frankfurt: Suhrkamp Verlag, 2000. 230–59.

West, Rebecca. *The Craft of Everyday Storytelling*. Toronto: U of Toronto P, 2000.

Weston, Edward. "Seeing Photographically." 1943. Trachtenberg 169–75.

White, Jonathan. *Italian Cultural Lineages*. Toronto: U of Toronto P, 2007.

Wolin, Richard. *Walter Benjamin: An Aesthetic of Redemption*. Berkeley: U of California P, 1994.

Woodhouse, John. *Gabriele D'Annunzio*. Oxford: Oxford UP, 1998.

Zannier, Italo, ed. *Luigi Crocenzi: Cultura della fotografia*. Spilimbergo: Centro di Ricerca e Archiviazione della Fotografia (C.R.A.F.), 1996.

Zannier, Paolo, ed. *Segni di luce: La fotografia italiana dall'età del collodio al pittorialismo*. 3 vols. Ravenna: Longo Editore, 1993.

Zola, Emile. *The Naturalist Novel*. Montreal: Harvest, 1964.

Contributors

Epifanio Ajello is Associate Professor of Italian and Comparative Literature at the University of Salerno (Italy). He collaborates with various journals including *Allegoria, Lettere Italiane,* and *Sinestesie.* His publications include *Ad una certa distanza. Sui luoghi della letterarietà* (1999) and *Carlo Goldoni. L'esattezza e lo sguardo* (2001). Ajello has also edited volumes on Guido Gozzano, Francesco Linguiti, and Carlo Goldoni. His *Il racconto delle immagini. La fotografia nella modernità letteraria* was published in 2009.

Giorgia Alù is Senior Lecturer at the University of Sydney. She has published on women's travel writing, representations of Southern Italy, and the relationship between literature and photography in contemporary women's writing. She is the author of *Beyond the Traveller's Gaze: British Expatriate Women in Sicily (1848–1910)* (2008). She is now working on a project on women's narrative, mobility, and photography.

Marco Andreani has recently completed a PhD on Mario Giacomelli, Luigi Crocenzi, and Italian photography in the 1950s and 1960s at the University of Parma (Italy). In 2006, with Roberto Signorini, he edited and translated from French *L'immagine precaria. Sul dispositivo fotografico* by Jean-Marie Schaeffer.

Sarah A. Carey is Andrew W. Mellon Fellow at Stanford University. She has published in *Quaderni d'Italianistica* and *Carte Allineate.* Her current research interests include nineteenth-century Italian writers and photography, *poesia visiva* in 1960s Italy, and visual culture in Italian cinema.

Sarah Patricia Hill is Senior Lecturer at Victoria University of Wellington (NZ). Her research interests focus on twentieth-century Italian literature, cinema, and visual culture and the history and theory of interactions between the visual arts and literature, with a particular interest in photographic technologies. She also works on connections between Italy and New Zealand, especially in relation to Italian migrants and migrant writing. She has recently co-edited a volume titled *Stillness in Motion: Italy, Photography and the Meanings of Modernity* (forthcoming).

Maria Grazia Lolla teaches at Harvard University. She has published on the impact of antiquarianism on eighteenth- and nineteenth-century scholarship and aesthetics. She is now working on a research project titled "Rivers Unknown to Song," on antiquarian and archaeological explorations in transnational contexts, as well as on a book about photography, fiction, and sociological texts in fin-de-siècle Italy.

Mariarita Martino teaches at the University of Warwick (UK). She has recently completed a PhD on psychoanalytic approaches to intersemiotic translation from a written code (novel) to a visual code (film). She has contributed to *The Little Black Book of Books* (2007) and writes about the phenomenology of written and visual scopophilia. She has taught at the University of Birmingham, the University of Manchester, the University of Venice, and the University of Siena.

Donata Panizza is completing a postdoctoral research project at Rutgers University. She has worked at MNAF–Museo Nazionale Alinari della Fotografia and at the Perform Art Gallery in La Spezia. She contributes to the art magazine *Exibart*.

Nancy Pedri is Associate Professor of English at Memorial University of Newfoundland. Her major fields of research include word-and-image relations in contemporary literature, photography in fiction, and comics. She has edited *Travelling Concepts III: Memory, Narrative, Image* (2003), a special issue of *Poetics Today* (Spring 2008) on photography in fiction, and *Picturing the Language of Images* (2013). Her work on word and image relations has appeared in *International Journal for Canadian Studies*, *Texte*, *Journal of Literary Studies*, and *Rivista di studi italiani*.

Marina Spunta is Senior Lecturer at the University of Leicester (UK). Her research interests include postwar Italian fiction, photography, and cinema, particularly the debates about orality and about space, place, and landscape. She is the author of *Voicing the Word: Writing Orality in Contemporary Italian Fiction* (2004) and has co-edited *Orality and Literacy in Modern Italian Culture* (2006) and *Proteus, the Language of Metamorphosis* (2005). She has published in a number of journals on various contemporary writers and has completed a monograph on the writer Claudio Piersanti. Her current project investigates the representations of space and landscape in postwar Italian fiction, photography, and cinema, with a special focus on the Po Valley region.

Pasquale Verdicchio is Professor of Cultural Studies, Film, Creative Writing, and Literature at the University of California at San Diego. His essays on Italian and Italian North American cultures are collected in the volumes *Devils in Paradise: Writings of Post-Emigrant Cultures* (1997) and *Bound by Distance: Rethinking Nationalism through the Italian Diaspora* (1997). As a translator he has published the works of Pier Paolo Pasolini, Alda Merini, Antonio Porta, and Antonio Gramsci, among others. His own most recent poetry collection is *This Nothing's Place* (Guernica, 2008). He has recently published a monograph titled *Looters, Photographers, and Thieves: Aspects of Italian Photographic Culture in the Nineteenth and Twentieth Centuries* (2011).

Index

absence, 39, 46, 48, 134, 180
abstract, 30, 83, 147, 157, 179–80, 188
abstraction, 172, 262
Academie Française, 27
Adams, Timothy Dow, 5, 104, 285
adaptation, 103, 228
advertising, 48, 51, 234
aesthetics, 6–8, 71–4, 76, 78–9, 83–4, 88–90, 93–5, 162
affectivity, 71, 76, 79, 83, 87, 89
agency, 13, 50, 55, 256, 270, 272
aide-memoire, 122, 124
Alfieri, Vittorio, 103
Alighieri, Dante, 53, 57, 66, 285
allegory, 34, 36, 191, 195, 206–7, 209, 211
allusion, 113, 115, 199, 205
ambiguity, 18, 53, 63, 104, 129, 131–2, 134–6, 142, 161, 163, 181, 196, 198, 280
ambivalence, 158, 165, 256
Anceschi, Luciano, 72, 96, 277
angle, 23, 38, 58, 83, 88, 146, 235, 241, 256, 268
anonymity, 58
Antonioni, Michelangelo, 66, 245, 253
anxiety, 50, 95, 111, 113, 199, 239, 240
appearance, 7, 30, 33, 42, 49, 52, 56, 62–3, 73, 80, 86, 93, 101, 105–7, 109–10, 114–15, 119, 200, 243–4, 251, 258, 264, 272
Arago, François, 27, 135, 286, 288
architecture, 9, 87
Aristarco, Guido, 213; *Cinema nuovo*, 213
Armstrong, Nancy, 5, 22, 286
art historian, 51, 105
Artaria, 7
artefact, 46, 171, 272
artificial, 104, 181, 237, 239, 264
artwork essay, 72
atmosphere, 65, 164, 208, 267
Augenblick, 74
aura, 15–16, 71–5, 81, 84, 86, 94, 208, 238
auratic effect, 16, 74–5
authenticity, 61, 73, 123, 187, 280
authorship, 104
autobiography, 77, 101, 104, 109, 115; autobiographical fiction, 117
avant-garde, 10, 24, 164

background, 13, 30, 88, 144, 161, 163, 172, 174, 209, 239, 248, 259

Baetens, Jan, 5, 22, 286
Balázs, Béla, 143
Balzac, Honoré de, 42, 231
Baroque, 52
Barthes, Roland, 5, 13–14, 16–17, 22, 24, 31–2, 36, 46, 104–5, 119–20, 124, 137, 146–8, 166, 189, 194, 196, 246, 257, 267, 272, 280, 286, 302; *Camera Lucida*, 16–17, 22, 24, 32, 50, 119, 124, 148, 189, 194, 246, 272; *punctum*, 137, 148, 166, 196, 246, 280; *studium*, 148, 246, 280; that-has-been, 18, 280; what-has-been, 32
Baudelaire, Charles, 27, 287
Bayard, Hyppolite, 34
Bazin, André, 5, 16, 136, 213, 278, 287
beauty, 16, 71, 74–7, 89, 91, 93–4, 116, 120, 158, 257–8, 267–8, 272
Belli, Pozzi, 214
Benjamin, Walter, 14–16, 24, 52, 71–5, 78, 81, 84, 86, 89–90, 93–6, 119, 131, 137, 233, 245, 287, 292–3, 297, 303, 307
Berengo Gardin, Gianni, 11
Berger, John, 5, 80, 105–7, 120, 135, 243, 277, 287, 292
Bernard, Claude, 43–4, 48, 287
Bertone, Giorgio, 84, 288
Bevilacqua, Pietro, 72, 95
Bizzarri, Giorgio, 76, 288
black and white, 47, 157, 208–9, 232, 245, 270
blind, 89, 93, 181, 194
blurred images, 59–60; blurring, 23, 67, 103, 179, 181, 276
body, 20–1, 32–3, 40, 44, 46, 56, 68, 83, 108, 111, 120, 128, 161, 167, 171, 178, 229, 245–6, 255–8, 260–1, 266, 268, 270, 272, 276
Bollino, Fernando, 72
Bonesio, Luisa, 71, 288
border, 4, 12, 63, 65, 115, 200, 211, 275–6, 281–2
Bordini, Carlo, 77, 288
Bozidar, Stanisic, 255
Brady, Emily, 71, 96, 288
Bragaglia, Antonio, 10
Bronzoni, Eleonora, 76, 288
Brunet, François, 4–5
Bryant, Marsha, 4–5, 95, 288, 280, 307
Bufalino, Gesualdo, 23
Butor, Michel, 231

calotypes, 7, 22
Calvino, Italo, 6, 10, 15, 23, 51, 53, 56–64, 66, 68–9, 208, 212, 235–6, 244–5, 249, 253, 288, 292, 302
camera, 3, 5, 7–9, 13, 19–20, 36, 40, 41, 48, 54, 112, 119, 135–6, 145, 162, 186, 197, 218–19, 228–30, 233–7, 240–5, 247–8, 250, 252, 256–7, 259, 263–4, 278–9; gaze of, 16, 20, 48, 55, 74, 91, 106–7, 112, 116–17, 119, 125–6, 132, 176, 181–2, 186, 195, 208, 221, 226–8, 233, 235–6, 239, 241, 243, 247, 250, 256, 258–9, 266–7; lens, 7, 20, 41, 55, 148, 162, 197, 199, 215, 217, 219, 228–30, 236–7, 239–40, 243, 245–8, 250, 256, 259, 267; as monocular mode of vision, 247; power of, 9, 13, 15, 19, 28, 31–2, 35, 40–1, 44, 48–50, 52, 57, 74, 83, 120, 124, 127, 134, 136–7, 142, 163, 174, 176, 243, 256–7, 270, 272, 280; as predatory weapon, 244; and social control, 19
camera obscura, 48, 279
Capa, Robert, 147
capitalism, 93

caption, 4, 35, 38, 148, 150, 157–9, 162, 171–2, 205, 208–9, 214
Capuana, Luigi, 9, 15, 42, 101, 281, 289, 291, 300
Caraion, Marta, 5, 289
Carbone, Mario, 10
Cardarelli, Vincenzo, 165
Carducci, Giosuè, 9
Carpi, Leone, 8, 289
Carpi, Sebastiano, 189–90
Carrà, Carlo, 10
Carroll, Lewis, 119
Catholic Church, 158, 161
Celati, Gianni, 11, 15, 23, 51, 53, 56, 62–9, 72, 76, 289, 299, 304–5
celebrity, 233, 252
censorship, 7, 202, 213
Centro di ricerca e archiviazione della fotografia (CRAF), 149, 151–5, 165, 210
Cerati, Carla, 11
Cézanne, Paul, 74–5, 79, 81, 83–4, 86, 96–7, 232; *A Modern Olympia*, 232
character, 42, 47, 55, 57–9, 103, 105–7, 110, 113, 117, 143, 150, 162, 167, 170–1, 176–8, 182–4, 186, 189–90, 195, 197–8, 200, 205, 207–9, 214, 221, 226, 230, 231–2, 234, 245, 266
Chatwin, Bruce, 89
chosisme, 218, 229, 231
chronology, 259
cinema, 6, 10, 18, 22, 66–7, 107, 109, 143–4, 206, 237–40, 250, 253, 277
cinematography, 66, 143, 206–7
clarity, 141, 163, 172, 240, 243
class struggle, 257
classical literature, 7
classicism, 279
close-ups, 245, 262
cognition, 15, 21, 52, 219–20, 257
collaboration, 10–12, 78, 96, 120, 144, 147, 278
collage, 156
collective expression, 7
collective identity, 58
collective voice, 68
colour, 47–8, 68, 83, 86, 198, 208, 234, 239, 247, 249, 254, 266–7, 270, 275
Coman, Ingrid, 255
Comerio, Luca, 36
communication, 10, 142, 164, 220, 234
communism, 41
composition, 57, 83–4, 144, 218, 227
connotation, 13, 16, 29, 33–4, 36, 105, 146, 195–6
contamination, 58, 236
contemplation, 71, 73, 75, 77–8, 83, 94, 96, 200
content, 20, 59, 78, 96, 103, 113, 121, 129, 167, 173, 204–5, 220–1, 225, 227, 229–30, 232, 234, 246, 255–6
context, 4, 12, 20, 30, 46, 59, 62–3, 69, 76, 160, 163, 180, 194, 205, 219, 221, 223, 225, 228, 230–1, 234, 248, 255, 264, 277–9, 282
convention, 61–2, 107, 117, 123, 131, 147, 169, 173, 199
Corazzini, Sergio, 165
corporality, 20
Corsici, Arnaldo, 40, 290
Cottinelli, Vincenzo, 290
Courbet, 74–5, 79–81, 83, 96, 287
cover, 47, 113, 177, 204, 235, 255, 258, 270, 275
Craeybeckx, Herman, 144, 290
Croce, Benedetto, 101, 118–19, 290
Crocenzi, Luigi, 10, 18–19, 141–9, 151–2, 156–7, 162, 164–6, 203, 207, 210, 281, 286, 290–1, 294, 307, 309
cropping, 173–4

Crovi, Raffaele, 214, 291
Cubist, 248
cultural rootedness, 72
cultural value, 51

D'Angelo, Paolo, 71, 94, 96, 291
D'Annunzio, Gabriele, 3–4, 9, 23, 286, 292, 299, 307
D'Arrigo, Stefano, 23, 292
Daguerre, Louis, 7, 29–31, 33, 48, 50, 294; daguerrotype, 7, 22
Damisch, Hubert, 5, 137, 291
darkness, 80, 177, 208, 237–8, 251
De Amicis, Edmondo, 9, 15, 35–7, 39, 279, 291
De Carlo, Andrea, 12, 20, 23, 233–7, 241, 243, 245–6, 249, 252–3, 281, 285, 289, 291, 298
De Luca, Erri, 12, 17, 122–5, 128–35, 281, 291, 297, 303–4
De Martino, Ernesto, 10
De Roberto, Federico, 9, 300
de Saussure, Ferdinand, 147
de-eroticization, 115
death, 17, 63, 77–8, 91, 96, 123, 125, 128–31, 191, 200, 213, 257, 266, 272
decay, 74, 83
decolonization, 254
deficiency, 42
Del Giudice, Daniele, 12, 19, 169, 285, 290–1
Deledda, Grazia, 9
demonstration, 173
denotation, 16, 105, 146, 194–5
description, 15, 31, 37, 41, 44, 54–6, 59, 67, 74, 77, 101–3, 105, 107–10, 112–16, 137, 150, 156, 162, 174, 185, 195, 205, 209, 211–12, 218–19, 222, 226, 228–31, 233, 238–9, 246, 248, 255, 261, 264, 277
design, 27, 44, 52, 234
designers, 144
desire, 5, 20, 28, 42, 46, 49, 52, 57–8, 61, 76, 88, 90, 102, 107–8, 110, 112–13, 115, 117, 119–20, 158, 160–1, 163, 167, 170, 175, 196, 198, 222–4, 226, 228–30, 237, 242, 252, 254, 256–7, 270
Dessì, Giuseppe, 11
di Giovanni, Bertoldo, 167
Di San Secondo, Rosso, 9
Di Scalzo, Claudio, 124
dialogue, 4, 6, 8, 16, 34, 42, 70, 72, 74–7, 79, 81, 84, 86, 91, 94–5, 177, 186, 195, 199, 207–8, 279–80
diary, 67, 143, 164, 193
didactic, 22, 144, 192
diegesis, 142, 148, 164, 223–5, 228, 231
Dionysian, 161, 163
director, 10, 44, 145, 160, 166, 206, 234, 250, 252–3
discourse, 18, 52, 55, 96, 145, 148, 162, 164, 167, 170, 230, 247, 261
dislocation, 254, 264, 268, 276
disorientation, 238–9
displacement, 75, 77, 87, 93–4, 124–5, 129–31, 134, 254–5, 282
displacing, 280
display, 27, 44, 56, 113, 237, 240, 254–5, 258, 272
distance, 20, 30, 32, 36, 47, 52, 55, 64, 73–4, 81, 83, 86–8, 116, 120, 128, 132, 178, 180, 222–3, 238–9, 243–6, 249, 251, 253, 256, 259–60, 262–4, 267, 276, 279
distortion, 16, 59, 239, 245, 280
documentary, 15–16, 18, 20, 23, 33, 36, 80, 83, 122–3, 135–6, 162, 195, 206, 209, 211, 280
Domenica letteraria, 49

double, 132, 169, 171, 181, 185, 188, 194, 205, 272
doubling, 80, 250
drawing, 9, 13, 32–3, 71, 75, 80, 95, 156, 167, 214, 232, 248, 253, 255, 277
dream, 87, 93, 101, 103, 119, 141, 144, 162, 167, 177, 198, 213, 261, 268, 270, 278, 280
Dubois, Philippe, 24, 104, 147, 160, 189, 292
Dubuffet, Jean, 232
Dusi, Nicola, 220, 292

Eco, Umberto, 6, 69, 190, 292
Ecumenical Studies Center Giovanni XXIII, 166
editing, 144–5, 156, 166
effacement, 60
ego-documents, 256
Eisenstein, Sergei Mikhaïlovitch, 143
emblem, 36, 202, 208
embodiment, 268, 275
emotion, 3–4, 94, 106, 116, 142, 161, 234–5, 243, 263, 280
empathy, 77, 94
Emporium, 9
empowerment, 20, 255, 272
enunciation, 228, 231, 262
enunciator, 224
environment, 33, 44, 177, 203, 214, 237, 239, 263
ephemerality, 78, 93
epistemology, 233, 255, 276
equivalence, 145, 219, 221, 223, 228, 231
Erfahrung, 16, 72, 95, 307
erotic, 20, 111, 113, 232; eroticization, 114–15
escapism, 142
estrangement, 94, 164, 211, 255, 275, 277
ethology, 235
Evans, Walker, 10
evidence, 9, 33, 36, 51, 115, 123–4, 135, 170, 200, 255
exhibition, 67, 76, 144, 156, 166, 277
exhibitionism, 20, 217, 221–3, 226–7
exile, 77, 96, 254–5, 270, 272, 276–8
experimental novel, 9, 43
extradiegetic, 136, 224
eyes, 37, 40, 42, 53, 55, 57, 64, 83, 105–6, 111, 114, 116, 126, 132, 134, 163, 172, 179, 181, 188–9, 204, 209, 217, 228, 236, 245, 249–50, 259, 261

fabula, 194, 208
fact, 12, 16–17, 20, 31–2, 35, 40, 42, 49, 55, 61, 63, 66, 83, 102–3, 109, 114, 117–18, 124, 135–6, 146, 156, 160, 162, 172, 180–1, 187–9, 196–7, 205, 209, 212, 225, 230–1, 236, 243, 245, 263, 265, 267, 275
fairy tale, 205, 209
family, 11, 61–2, 105; album, 16, 122–3, 127, 192, 213
fantastic, 16, 101, 280
fantasy, 18, 57, 90, 101, 103, 110, 117
Fascism, 58, 62
fashion, 7, 30, 52, 194, 203, 240, 252
feeling, 44, 61, 88, 94, 195–6, 200, 235, 243, 260–1, 263
Fellini, Federico, 253
female, 20, 107–8, 114, 120–1, 218, 232, 254–5, 257–8, 262, 264–5, 268, 270, 272, 275–6; body, 20, 108, 120, 268, 270, 272; condition, 262; figure, 107, 114, 120; icons, 120; identity, 254–5, 264, 276; image, 121; nude,

218, 232, 255, 268; objectification, 19, 107–8, 114, 244, 268; subjectivity, 107
feminine, 162
Ferrania, 144, 166
Ferrigni, Pietro, 34, 41, 293
fetish, 111–13, 121; fetishism, 111–12, 119–20
fiction, 5, 12, 16–17, 19, 28, 30, 33, 50, 63, 70, 72, 77, 96, 101–6, 109, 115, 117–18, 137, 162, 170, 176, 187, 190–1, 206–8, 211, 267, 281
field, 4–7, 12–13, 47, 70, 79, 86, 144, 165, 172–3, 177, 194, 247, 254, 277, 281–2, 283
Filippi, Filippo, 47
film, 10, 66, 68, 73, 83, 107, 109, 120, 143, 145, 148, 162, 172–3, 204, 206–7, 209, 214, 242, 248, 250, 253, 282
filmic language, 209
filter, 249, 267
First World War, 9
fixity, 122–4, 132, 164
flâneur, 71
flash forward, 125
flashback, 109, 110, 125
Flaubert, Gustave, 102, 119, 231
Fogazzaro, Antonio, 9–10
Fortini, Franco, 165
Fossati, Vittore, 12, 15–16, 70–89, 91–7, 293, 304, 306
fragmentation, 21, 29, 73, 77–8, 90, 107, 111, 120, 125, 148, 178, 181, 187, 191, 200, 233–7, 240–1, 243, 246, 248, 251–2, 257, 259, 264, 267, 272, 276, 278–80
frame, 3, 7, 16, 20, 59, 61, 67, 81, 84, 87–8, 91, 105, 109, 111, 122, 125, 128, 131, 133, 136, 143, 145–6, 179–80, 184, 198, 207–8, 223, 237, 243, 254, 256, 259, 268
framework, 28, 160, 199, 251, 278, 282
freeze, 23, 124, 254, 263, 267
Freud, Sigmund, 111, 119–20, 121, 161, 167, 223, 231, 293–4; *Schaulust*, 223
Friedrich, Caspar David, 75, 79, 86–8
Futurism, 10

gender, 254
generic boundaries, 101
genre, 9, 21, 30, 59, 62, 66–7, 73, 103–4, 109, 120, 150, 192, 195, 231, 254, 280–2
German Romanticism, 71
Ghirri, Luigi, 11–12, 23, 62–3, 65–6, 72–3, 76–7, 79–80, 84, 91, 94, 96, 294, 299, 304–5, 307, 309
Giacomelli, Mario, 18–19, 66, 141–2, 144–8, 150, 153–61, 163–7, 281, 289–91, 294–5, 297–8, 302, 306, 309
Giacometti, Alberto, 75, 96
Giorgione, *Sleeping Venus*, 232
Giovannetti, Giovanni, 24, 293, 295
globalize, 72
Goldoni, Carlo, 309
Gor'kij, Maxim, 89
Gozzano, Guido, 8, 23, 309; L'Amica di nonna Speranza, 8
Gramsci, Antonio, 143, 311
graphics, 144
graphos, 13
Greenberg, Clement, 10, 51, 295
Griffith, D.W., 166
Guttuso, Renato, 213–14

Hajdari, Gezim, 255
Handke, Peter, 84, 96, 295

handmade, 33, 101
Haverty Rugg, Linda, 5, 278, 295, 303
Hawthorne, Nathaniel, 119
hermeneutics, 232, 242
Hijuelos, Oscar, 277
Hirsch, Marianne, 5, 136, 277, 295–6
historical novel, 30–1, 103, 113
history, 14, 19, 21–2, 24, 30–1, 40, 50–1, 58, 67, 69, 71, 73–5, 89, 91, 93, 96, 124, 131, 134, 189, 200, 209, 253, 277, 281
home, 68, 77, 96, 129, 244, 251
homosexuality, 161
Hoxha, Enver, 255, 257
Hugo, Victor, 36
humanism, 165; humanist photographers, 23
hybrid, 73, 77, 104, 187, 281
hyperrealists, 235
hyperreality, 185, 188

Ibrahimi, Anilda, 255
icon, 120, 124, 147–8, 169, 188–9, 212
iconoclast, 101
iconography, 208, 236
iconotext, 16, 22, 70
idealism, 165
identity, 58–9, 94, 103, 125, 127–8, 131, 143, 159, 199, 250–1, 254–5, 264, 268, 270, 272, 275–6, 282
Il Fotografo, 39
Il Secolo, 102
illusion, 18, 80, 93, 116, 198, 251, 267
illustrated novel, 19, 214
illustration, 8–9, 51, 60, 191–3, 200, 209, 212–13, 224, 231, 270
imaginary, 8, 28–9, 31, 36, 39–40, 57, 105, 132, 174, 176, 193, 200, 211, 213, 225, 230, 280; imagination, 4, 12, 17, 53, 56, 71, 74–5, 79–81, 83, 87–8, 94, 131, 136, 176, 191, 194, 199–200, 209, 211, 265
Imbriani, Vittorio, 8, 17, 37–9, 101–13, 115, 117–21, 279, 281, 289, 296, 302
imitation, 102
immediacy, 16, 97, 132, 144, 162, 236, 262, 281
immigrant, 258
immobility, 124–5, 164
immortality, 78, 94
imprint, 102, 104, 147–8, 169, 172, 180, 188
incest, 115
incommunicability, 241
incompleteness, 102, 264
indeterminacy, 129, 177, 185
index, 17–18, 24, 148, 160, 169, 172–4, 180, 187, 189, 212, 292; indices, 147–8, 172–4, 187
indexicality, 18, 24, 124, 147, 169, 276, 280–1
individuality, 268, 275–6
information, 47, 170–3, 177, 187, 189, 192–3, 236, 245, 267
Ingres, Jean-Auguste-Dominique, 232
instability, 65, 185
Instamatic, 244
insubstantiality, 34, 43, 49
intention, 11, 20, 59, 72, 93, 173–4, 180, 192–3, 195, 197–8, 206, 227
interdisciplinary study, 22
intermedial studies, 70
interpretation, 33, 68–9, 117, 119–21, 164, 169, 177, 196, 199, 203, 219–20, 231, 255
intersemiotic, 20, 70, 217–21, 230; studies, 70; translation, 20, 217–21
intersubjective, 220
intertext, 84; intertextuality, 76, 87
intradiegetic narrator, 228

investigation, 10, 13, 142, 223, 235, 252, 254
invisibility, 15, 28–9, 37, 40–1, 44–5, 47–50, 59, 198, 233, 248–9, 262
irony, 77, 87–8, 199–200
island, 86–9, 91, 213
isolation, 77, 88, 150, 241, 262
isomorphism, 172, 189
Italian: literature, 1, 3, 6, 12–13, 15, 21–2, 57, 101, 104, 142, 166, 277, 280–2; National Exposition, 27; photography, 21, 77, 96; Studies, 4, 6, 12, 254, 277, 281; Unification, 7
Italophone literature, 256

Jakobson, Roman, 166, 218, 296
Jadrejcic, Tamara, 255
journalism, 9, 51, 104
journey, 53, 80, 86–7, 89, 93, 170, 204–5, 207, 258
Joycean epiphany, 194
jpeg, 60
juxtaposition, 76, 170, 207, 212

kaleidoscope, 266–7
King, Clarence, 43–4, 48–9
knowledge, 5, 19–20, 28, 30–3, 41, 63–4, 72, 86, 110, 147, 164, 168, 176–7, 180, 197, 222–3, 234, 236, 244, 252, 257, 268, 275
Koppen, Erwin, 5, 296
Krauss, Rosalind, 24, 147, 164, 166, 189, 296
Kubati, Ron, 255

L'Illustrazione italiana, 9
L'Opinione, 42
La Lettura, 9, 203
La Patria, 102

landscape, 7, 11, 15–16, 23, 29, 54–5, 62–3, 67, 70–1, 73–81, 83–4, 86–7, 89, 91, 93–6, 177, 195, 197, 204, 208, 238–9, 251
language, 4, 13–15, 22, 30–1, 52, 60, 63–5, 69, 77, 103, 106, 111, 130, 142–5, 147, 162, 166–7, 177, 182, 186, 188, 208, 219–20, 225, 230, 234, 236, 239, 247, 259–64, 268, 276–8, 280, 282
latinismi, 103
Lenkovic, Kenka, 255
Leone, Gianni, 294
Leopardi, Giacomo, 145, 165
Levi, Carlo, 10
light, 12–13, 29, 42–3, 53, 56–7, 72, 87, 105, 113, 142, 164, 172–4, 177, 181, 198, 208–9, 228, 237–41, 248, 251, 261, 268, 275, 279–80, 282
lighting, 41, 84, 146
limelight effect, 252
linguistics, 147, 166
literary history, 30, 281
Lombroso, Cesare, 39, 141, 144, 165, 297, 301, 303, 304
look, 33, 83, 112, 121, 132, 175, 197–9, 223, 235, 256, 259

machismo, 267
magazine, 9, 32, 35, 39, 143, 150, 161, 234, 241
magic lanterns, 5
male, 20, 106–8, 116, 230, 266
Mallarmé, Stéphane, 20, 217–20, 224–7, 229–31, 290, 298; *Olympia*, 229
Manet, Edward, 20, 217–18, 220, 227, 232, 302; *Olympia*, 20, 217–18, 227, 232
Manganelli, Giorgio, 193, 298

manipulate, 62, 103, 259, 264, 277
Mantegazza, Paolo, 41, 298
Manzoni, Alessandro, 15, 53–4, 102, 112–13, 298
map, 133, 183–4, 241, 262; mapping, 241
Martino, Emanuele, 11, 298, 301
Marx, 41, 93
Master, Edgar Lee, 145
materiality, 32, 56, 79, 80
Maupassant, Guy de, 30
Maurensig, Paolo, 23
Mauri, Paolo, 190, 298
Mayer and Pierson, 120
Mazzucco, Melania, 12
memento, 110–11
memoir, 16
memory, 11, 19, 21, 24, 32–3, 60–1, 71, 74, 79, 83–4, 86–8, 93–4, 104, 106, 109–10, 117, 119, 122–4, 127, 130, 167, 214, 254, 257, 277, 282
Messori, Giorgio, 12, 15–16, 70–81, 83–4, 86–91, 93–7, 287–8, 293, 297, 299, 303–5
metafictional, 169, 185
metaliterary, 182
metaphor, 17, 39, 45, 55, 60, 78, 102, 113, 130, 183, 192, 213, 224–5, 233, 237, 241, 243, 246, 253, 262, 278
metatextual, 101
metonymy, 209
Michetti, Francesco Paolo, 9, 23, 292
Middle Ages, 30
migration, 4, 254, 256, 275–6, 282
mirror, 8, 38, 80, 88, 116, 175, 198, 212, 237, 267–8, 278
mise en scène, 208, 229
modernism, 30, 32
modernity, 55, 72–3, 89, 279
mondi nuovi, 5
monologic form, 253
montage, 143, 146, 150, 191, 193–4, 204, 207, 212
Montale, Eugenio, 145, 165, 170, 207, 299
Montessori, Maria, 43–4, 47–8, 296, 300
monument, 7–8, 36, 51
moral lesson, 47, 200
Morandi, Giorgio, 77, 299
Moravia, Alberto, 20, 23, 217–20, 222, 226, 228–31, 282, 300, 302
Mormorio, Diego, 11, 21, 300
mortality, 78, 90, 93
Mulas, Ugo, 145, 165
multimedial, 69
multisensorial experience, 83
myth, 87, 103, 116, 167, 205

name, 13, 28, 44–6, 63, 89, 103, 184, 192, 203, 209, 213, 231–2, 235, 261, 264–5, 275
narration, 10, 11, 17, 21, 58, 73, 76, 130, 141, 148, 176, 178, 191, 193, 204, 208–9, 211, 218, 221, 254, 256, 260; process, 130
narrative, 4, 6, 11, 13–14, 17–19, 22, 28, 39, 46–7, 50, 54–5, 59–60, 62–3, 66, 68–9, 78, 93, 96, 102–3, 110, 117, 120, 122–5, 128–32, 134–5, 146, 148, 150, 156, 162, 171, 176–7, 184, 188, 191, 193, 194–7, 202, 205, 207–9, 211, 217–19, 221–5, 228–30, 234, 236–7, 255, 259, 261, 265, 277, 279–82
narrator, 20, 47, 59, 107, 109, 110, 112–14, 116–17, 123, 125–33, 135–6, 150, 162, 170, 178, 184, 197, 199, 221, 223–4, 228, 233, 235, 237, 258–9, 267
nation, 254, 275, 279

naturalism, 8, 30, 43
nature, 5, 8, 17–18, 20, 22, 28, 31, 33, 44, 46, 48, 50, 71, 73–81, 83–4, 86, 88, 91, 93–4, 96, 104, 112, 117, 119–20, 158, 167, 173, 182, 189, 199–200, 205, 212, 222, 226, 234
Neera, 39, 43, 300
neorealism, 7, 52, 57–8, 142–3, 147, 162
neorealist aesthetics, 162
neutrality, 235
Niccolai, Giulia, 23
Nievo, Ippolito, 103
Nobile, Max, 300
normalcy, 36
nostalgia, 77, 88, 194, 200, 260, 277, 282
nouveau roman, 231, 235
novel, 8–10, 16–20, 23, 30–1, 37, 42–3, 45–8, 55, 57–8, 64, 101–4, 106, 108–10, 112–15, 117–21, 125, 130, 141, 144, 169–71, 174, 177–8, 182–5, 188–93, 195, 198, 200, 202–4, 207–9, 211–14, 217–24, 226, 228–31, 233–8, 251–3, 255, 257, 280–1
nude, 114, 218, 227, 232, 255, 268

objectification, 107
objectivity, 5, 8, 16–18, 136, 187, 233, 247, 262, 265, 278–82
observer, 14, 20, 34, 44, 47–9, 55, 63–4, 181, 195, 221, 224, 227, 237, 266–7, 276
Oldoini, Virginia (Countess of Castiglione), 120
oneiric, 101, 192, 262, 266
open work, 65, 69
Other, 256–7, 267, 272, 275–6

painting, 20, 27, 31, 33, 42, 51–2, 66, 73, 76–7, 81, 83–4, 86–8, 96, 101, 109, 116, 132, 141, 144, 147, 197, 212, 217–20, 222, 227, 230, 232, 235, 248
pamphlet, 266
panoramas, 5
paradigmatic, 104, 142, 146
paradox, 105, 121, 161, 167, 187
Pascoli, Giovanni, 9
pastiche, 10, 101
Patellani, Federico, 10
pedagogy, 43–4, 48
Peirce, Charles Sanders, 17–18, 147–8, 169, 188–9, 212, 297, 301
performativity, 268, 278
Permunian, Francesco, 165
Perniola, Mario, 96, 301
perspective, 8, 12, 20, 59, 66, 71, 79, 123, 148, 150, 163, 170, 192, 197–8, 199, 204, 211, 219, 221, 224, 226, 234, 238, 243, 252, 256–7, 266, 276, 281
Petrarca, Francesco, 53
Petrella, Marco, 277
phonetic, 225, 231
photo-: book, 10–11, 15, 70, 144; caption, 214; journalist, 144; literary, 6, 11, 15, 54, 56–7, 62, 66, 281; novel, 19, 141, 144, 212; realists, 236; reportage, 144–5, 150, 156; story, 141–6, 148, 150, 156–8, 166; text, 4, 11, 71–2, 78, 93
photograph: as absence, 16–17, 30, 34, 272, 276; as presence, 16, 39, 48, 51, 120, 132, 148; as resistance, 21, 164, 256–7, 260; fiction, 4, 8, 10, 11, 13, 17, 19–20, 23, 50, 68, 104–5, 136, 187, 190, 225, 280; fictive, 20, 217, 219, 223, 228, 230–1; imagined, 37, 39, 49, 89; non-existent, 37, 39
photographic: act, 11, 61; album, 16, 28, 110, 122, 127, 192, 196, 212;

duality, 12, 17, 18; effects, 10, 20, 31, 53, 56, 233–4, 239, 280; eye, 249; gaze, 16, 20, 106–7, 116; lens, 7, 41, 55, 148, 162, 197, 199, 217, 219, 228–30, 236–7, 239, 243–5, 246–8, 250, 259, 267; medium, 6, 19–20, 218, 278; negative, 248–9, 251; poetics, 21, 132, 246; point of view, 237, 247; practice, 20, 29–30, 35, 50, 101–2, 112, 119, 217–19, 256; seeing, 256
photography: abstract, 147; anniversary, 27, 34; blind-field, 194; digital, 51–2, 60, 189, 254, 282; etymology, 13; historical significance, 11; immaterial, 15, 29, 280; inception, 4, 13, 109, 279; invention, 4–6, 14, 27, 29–30, 34, 39, 48–9, 52, 57, 101, 119, 243, 279; light-writing, 13; literary, 65; neorealist, 10; pencil of nature, 31; political impact, 11; real, 9, 12, 16–17, 19, 32, 39, 45–6, 56, 75–6, 79–80, 102, 104–5, 111, 113–14, 123, 131, 136, 143, 145, 165, 169–70, 172, 175–6, 185, 189–90, 198, 207, 211–12, 250, 280–1; reception, 6, 181; scanning, 195–6; social impact, 11, 15, 49; socializing practice, 61; sociohistorical impact, 11; spectre, 17, 34, 40–2, 49; sun-drawing, 13; tangibility, 29, 33, 49, 60, 132, 158, 262; textuality, 8–9, 277; theory, 5, 12, 15, 21, 52, 147, 171–2, 174, 189, 218, 226; travel, 7, 28, 241; visible, 3, 20, 147, 250
photomontage, 34
phototext, 4, 70, 95, 166
phototropic, 57
Picasso, Pablo, *Parody of "Olympia,"* 232
picturesque, 9, 94
Pigliaru, Antonio, 11
Pinna, Franco, 10–11
Pirandello, Luigi, 6, 9, 23, 245, 300
place, 7, 20, 15–17, 23, 44, 47–8, 55, 59, 62–5, 67–8, 71, 73–7, 79, 80, 84, 86–91, 93–4, 96, 105, 107, 109, 124–5, 127, 130–1, 133, 156, 162–3, 173, 176–8, 183, 185, 189, 194, 200, 203–4, 208, 211–13, 218, 225, 227–8, 244, 250, 254, 256, 262, 268, 270, 280
pleasure, 106–7, 116, 120–1, 181, 221–3, 260, 264
Plécy, Albert, 144, 301
plot, 47, 59, 104, 108, 117, 164, 176, 193–6, 208, 231
Po River, 62
poem, 8, 20, 141–2, 145, 157–9, 165, 212, 217–1, 223–31
poetry, 10, 90–1, 103, 145, 166, 282
Polaroid, 217–8
polyphonic novel, 253
pop art, 227
portrait, 3, 8, 21, 23–4, 34, 39, 91, 105, 110, 18, 147, 150, 197–8, 200, 257, 268, 275
pose, 38, 43, 108, 129, 160, 163, 197–8, 218, 229, 240, 268, 270
positivism, 8, 15, 29, 43, 49, 102
post-colonial, 256, 282
postmodern, 12, 16, 71, 75, 93–5, 101, 187, 234, 245, 281–2; condition, 71, 75; age, 16, 75; sense of displacement, 93; sense of anxiety, 95; subject, 94
postmodernism, 72–3, 93–4, 187
pre-modern, 75
pre-verbal, 262
Primoli, Giuseppe, 9
Proust, Marcel, 194, 245, 302

psychoanalysis, 13, 50, 102, 120, 223–4
psychology, 144
Pudovkin, Vsevolod, 143, 145, 302
punctuation, 103, 193

Quintavalle, Arturo Carlo, 156, 159, 166–7, 294, 302
quotidian, 11, 211

RAI, 145, 307
reader, 6–7, 17, 33–6, 38–41, 47, 54, 59, 62, 69, 78, 102, 106, 109, 114, 117, 125, 134–6, 143, 162, 172, 177, 178, 185, 190, 192, 194, 196–7, 202, 204–5, 211–12, 224–5, 227, 235, 263, 267; reading, 15, 20, 28, 64, 67, 95, 108, 117, 123, 125–6, 129, 131–3, 135–6, 150, 157, 159, 164, 174–5, 192, 195, 197–8, 200, 203, 205, 213, 225, 275, 282
realism, 4, 7–8, 16, 18, 30, 57–8, 60, 80, 101–2, 117, 191, 211, 232, 234, 280–2; realistic representation, 119, 190
reality, 3, 8–10, 14–16, 18, 20, 32–3, 43, 45, 47, 52–3, 57, 59–61, 68, 75, 77, 80, 83, 86, 90, 94, 101–2, 105, 118–19, 124, 129, 131, 134, 136–7, 147–8, 158, 164–5, 169–72, 174, 176–9, 181, 183–8, 190–1, 200, 204, 211, 236, 240–3, 248, 256, 261, 267, 278–80
reciprocity, 247
redemption, 93
re-enchantment, 76
referent, 11, 16, 32, 53, 124, 130, 136–7, 147, 173, 189, 246
reflection, 7, 11–13, 24, 58, 72, 75, 77, 79–80, 83–4, 86–7, 89, 94, 106, 126, 128–9, 196, 211, 237–9, 251–2, 272, 276, 278
Renaissance, 5, 52, 164
replication, 111
reportage, 36, 144, 145, 150, 156
representation, 3, 8, 10–11, 14, 19, 21, 23–4, 31, 39, 49–50, 53, 55, 59–60, 71, 75–6, 79–80, 83, 91, 93–6, 101–2, 104, 109, 113, 119, 121, 135, 137, 169, 170–1, 180, 184–8, 190, 211, 225, 229, 232–3, 235–6, 241–2, 256, 261–4, 268, 276–7, 279–80
reproduction, 7, 16, 28, 36, 41, 48, 62, 73–4, 87–8, 109, 111, 165, 172, 184, 187, 281
resemblance, 18, 147, 189, 282
resistance, 21, 58, 68, 164, 166, 256–7, 259–60, 270, 272, 277
reverberation, 207
reversal, 79, 80, 186
revision, 33, 199, 202
Ria, Antonio, 201, 302, 304
Ribière, Mireille, 5, 286
Rilke, Rainer Maria, 89–90
Ritter, Joachim, 71
ritual, 157, 161, 245
Rivers, Larry, *I Like Olympia in Black Face*, 227, 232
Robbe-Grillet, Alain, 231
Romano, Lalla, 6, 11, 19, 124, 136, 191–3, 195–202, 208, 211–13, 289, 295, 300–4
Romano, Roberto, 198, 201, 289
Romantic: art, 87; literature, 103
Romanticism, 30, 71
Rossellini, Roberto, *Rome Open City*, 68, 303

Sanguineti, Edoardo, 6, 209, 303
Sapphic, 226
Sarraute, Nathalie, 231

Schaeffer, Jean-Marie, 18, 147, 169, 171, 180–2, 186–9, 303, 309
Scianna, Ferdinando, 145
Sciascia, Leonardo, 11
science, 8, 15, 27, 43, 48, 50, 52
scientist, 15, 27, 29, 33, 39, 43–4, 48–9
Scipione, Francesco Maffei, 103
scopophilia, 20, 119, 217–25, 228–31; literary, 217–18; object, 230; "peeping Tom" effect, 228; subject, 224–5, 228–30
screen, 126, 134, 184, 194, 225, 241, 267
Scuola italiana di paesaggio, 96
seascape, 91
Sebald, W.G., 21, 277, 296, 301
Second World War, 7, 58, 189
Sekula, Allan, 5, 22, 304
self-: awareness, 128, 183; objectification, 133; portrait, 34, 105, 268; reflexive, 77, 245
Sellerio, Enzo, 11, 213, 297, 305
semantic, 142, 181, 229
seminarian, 18, 142, 150, 153, 158–63, 166–7
semiotic, 52, 69, 144, 147, 163, 169, 171, 181, 185, 212, 218–20, 261–2, 266, 268
senses, 53, 83, 93–4, 159, 234, 262
sentimentality, 262
separation, 70, 116, 241–2, 261
sequence, 54, 67, 78, 141–6, 150, 156–7, 160, 162–5, 171, 194, 207, 240, 249
Serao, Matilde, 15, 23, 40, 304
Sereni, Vittorio, 165
setting, 129, 177, 213, 229, 268
sexuality, 266
short story, 11, 45–6, 67, 148, 236, 282
showing, 11, 45, 127, 150, 172, 211
Sibhatu, Ribka, 277
sign, 12, 14, 17, 52, 67, 146–7, 169, 172–3, 181–2, 188–9, 192, 198–9, 208, 218–20, 239, 272
silence, 77, 130, 202, 209, 211, 270
silent, 38, 88, 107, 130, 207, 211, 276; films, 207
simile, 220, 233, 248, 262–3
simulacra, 102, 187, 193, 245, 249, 250
snapshot, 31, 38, 58–9, 62, 105, 118, 143, 160, 164, 168, 200, 230
Snyder, Joel, 5, 304
Soavi, Giorgio, 213
social practice, 28
Società Fotografica Italiana, 34, 40–1
Soldati, Mario, 10
solitude, 83, 96, 157, 265–6
Sontag, Susan, 5, 19, 22, 24, 32, 110, 119, 136, 167, 174, 189, 244, 304
Sonthonnax, Paul, 144, 304
sound, 53, 89, 213, 225–6, 250, 265, 282
souvenir, 19, 36, 43, 49
space, 16, 31, 41, 63, 65, 71–3, 79, 83, 86–90, 94, 104, 107, 112, 122–36, 181, 189, 194, 196, 208, 227, 237–41, 248, 251, 254–5, 259, 263, 267–8, 272, 275, 277, 281
spectacle, 37, 47, 55, 114, 120, 158, 173–4, 189, 236, 266
spectatorship, 21, 257, 276
spectral, 42, 280
speech, 27–8, 33, 123, 130, 146, 168
Stanic, Vesna, 255, 277
Steichen, Edward, 104, 295
Stendhal (Marie-Henri Beyle), 231
still lifes, 147
stillness, 40, 126, 202
Stoppani, Antonio, 8, 305

story, 5, 10–11, 50, 55, 57–9, 62, 64, 67–8, 72, 127, 130, 135, 142–6, 160, 162, 166, 183, 191, 200, 211–12, 255, 257, 260–1, 263, 272, 276, 280, 292
storyboard, 117, 145, 150, 156, 160
storyline, 110, 145
storytelling, 17, 117
strangeness, 267
style, 7–8, 14–15, 20, 52, 58, 77–8, 81, 104, 157, 199, 218, 225, 229–31, 233–6, 245, 255
subconscious, 109
subjectivity, 20, 71, 74, 96, 106–7, 109, 187, 235, 256, 261, 265, 268, 278
subtraction, 77
superficial, 103, 234, 236; superficiality, 172, 235–7
surface, 3, 14, 17, 20, 130, 132–5, 163–4, 195–6, 200, 233–7, 241, 243–5, 248, 250–2
surreal, 40; Surrealist, 153, 166–7, 265, 278
surveillance, 259, 272
symbol, 83, 120, 147–8, 169, 192, 195–6, 209, 241; symbolic, 17, 90, 102, 107, 147, 167, 194–5, 207, 211, 261–2, 266, 268, 278
synchronism, 172, 189
syntactic, 146, 261
syntagmatic, 104, 146
syntax, 144, 211, 260

tableau vivant, 112, 120, 299
taboo, 115, 261
Tabucchi, Antonio, 12, 18, 143, 169, 187, 189, 281, 292, 297, 302, 305
Taddei, Nazareno, 146, 166, 305
Talbot, William Henry Fox, 7, 22, 136, 291
talking back, 278
Tawfik, Younis, 277
technical reproduction, 73
technology, 14, 31, 40, 48–53, 101, 144, 165, 236, 241, 243, 279, 282
telephoto lens, 236, 239, 243–4
television, 145, 241–2
Termine, Liborio, 28, 305
testimony, 31, 170, 209
thingness, 218
Tiberius, 89
time, 3–5, 7–12, 16–17, 19, 22–3, 27–9, 31–6, 38–9, 41, 44–5, 48–9, 51, 58, 60, 62, 66, 72–5, 77, 81, 86, 89–91, 94–6, 101–2, 104–5, 109–10, 112–13, 116, 118, 120–36, 143–7, 156–9, 161–4, 166, 169–70, 175–6, 179, 182, 184–6, 188–90, 193, 198–200, 202, 204–5, 207, 209, 212–13, 232, 234–7, 242–3, 248–9, 251–6, 259, 263, 267, 270, 272, 279–80
Titian (*Venus of Urbino*), 232
Torracca, Francesco, 46
Toscani, Oliviero, 234
tourist park, 83
trace, 6, 12, 15, 17, 45, 49, 62, 76, 81, 93, 96, 116, 127, 147, 172, 177, 180–2, 190, 195, 255, 267, 272, 281
tradition, 6, 53, 57, 63–4, 69, 71–3, 75–7, 83, 94, 101, 120, 144, 164, 232
transcription, 184
transgression, 161
translation, 13, 20, 68, 109, 189, 211, 217–21, 225, 228, 230–1, 282
trauma, 272, 277
travel writing, 4, 77, 170, 254, 282
trivial, 243
truth, 9, 16, 18, 102–4, 106, 109, 120, 123, 131, 136, 147, 162, 173, 176, 187, 226, 242, 279; truthfulness, 5, 188

Turoldo, David Maria, 142, 157–9, 161, 166, 306
Twain, Mark, 119

uncanny, 121, 256
uncertainty, 12, 31, 62, 80, 164, 184, 240, 268
Ungaretti, Giuseppe, 145, 306
unknowable, 129
unknowing, 62–3
unreliable, 280
unspeakable, 261
utopia, 91, 93

Valentini, Alvaro, 143–4, 166, 306
Valera, Paolo, 15, 23, 36–7, 39, 279, 306
Valéry, Paul, 14, 27–33, 49, 305–6
Van Lier, Henri, 18, 147, 169, 172–4, 180, 187, 189, 306
Velásquez, Diego, 232
Velati, Enzo, 294
Vera, Yvonne, 277
verbal, 4, 10, 14, 31, 53, 57, 146, 191–2, 195, 205, 207–8, 211, 218–19, 221, 225, 228–30, 233–4, 239, 255, 261–2, 280; text, 4, 14, 191, 205, 207–8, 211, 228, 230
Verga, Giovanni, 6, 9, 15, 24, 42, 45–7, 49–50, 53–4, 56, 58, 101, 279, 281, 295, 304, 306
Verismo, 7, 52, 55, 57, 101–2, 281, 299, 305
Vermeer, Johannes, 75, 86–7
viewer, 14, 16–17, 34, 46, 55, 59, 73, 75, 84, 91, 105, 109, 116, 122–3, 126, 130–2, 134–7, 164, 172, 195–6, 237, 259, 267–8, 272, 275, 278, 280; gaze, 16; eye, 84, 164, 275; perception, 109
viewpoint, 125–6, 256
violation, 161, 244, 259, 261
Visconti, Luchino, 214
visibility, 15, 20, 53–4, 64, 234, 248–9, 251–2
visible, 31, 52, 64, 88, 164
vision, 7, 15, 20, 54, 56, 64, 68, 70, 75–6, 79–80, 83, 86, 96, 105–6, 108, 114–15, 122, 130, 141, 163, 179, 181, 186, 191, 217–18, 223, 225, 228–30, 233, 242–3, 247, 250, 259, 265, 267, 281
visionary, 280
visual, 5–6, 8, 10, 15, 17, 20–3, 31, 33, 51–7, 60, 62, 64, 70–1, 78, 86, 95, 101–2, 104, 107, 109, 112, 116, 118, 125–6, 130–1, 134, 141, 144, 147–8, 156, 160, 162, 180–2, 186, 192–3, 197, 200, 205, 207–8, 211–12, 218, 222–3, 225, 228–30, 236–7, 239, 245, 247, 252–5, 257, 259, 262–5, 268, 272, 276–81; culture studies, 70, 95; language, 15, 52, 160; media, 10, 52, 107; metaphor, 17, 253, 278; text, 78, 147
visuality, 15, 54, 69, 71, 77–8, 277
Vittorini, Elio, 10, 19, 124, 143, 165, 191, 202–8, 211, 214, 277, 281
voice, 42, 47, 58, 62, 64, 67–8, 72, 90, 93–4, 127, 131, 150, 161, 177, 188, 209, 235
Voltaire, François-Marie Arouet, 103
Vorpsi, Ornela, 21, 254–78, 281, 285, 289, 307
voyeurism, 20, 120, 217, 222–3, 226, 228–30, 250, 253, 259

Walsh Allen, Neil, 5, 304
watching, 44, 105, 184

window, 40, 55, 114, 125, 128, 134, 178, 237–8, 240, 263, 270
witness, 33, 36, 38, 93, 129, 135, 194; witnessing, 10–12, 31, 55, 124, 127
Wolin, Richard, 73, 90, 93, 307
woman, 8, 20, 37–39, 44, 103–4, 106–8, 111–14, 116, 118, 121, 125, 142, 144, 157, 175–6, 199, 218, 220, 226–7, 229–30, 245, 248, 264, 268, 270, 276
working class, 142–3, 150, 158
writing, 3–10, 12–17, 19, 21–2, 27, 29, 32, 48, 52, 55, 58–9, 61–4, 67, 70, 73, 77–8, 81, 86, 91, 96, 102, 105, 147–8, 170–1, 174, 186, 188, 191–5, 197–200, 202, 207–8, 209, 211, 222, 231, 234, 236–7, 254–7, 259–62, 264–5, 272, 276, 278–82

Zavattini, Cesare, 144, 165
Zola, Émile, 30, 42–3, 119, 307
Zuhra Lukanic, Sarah, 255

www.ingramcontent.com/pod-product-compliance
Lightning Source LLC
LaVergne TN
LVHW090150080826
844660LV00013B/743/J

* 9 7 8 1 4 4 2 6 4 8 0 7 4 *